PENGUIN CLASSICS

CHRONICLES OF THE CRUSADES

JEAN DE JOINVILLE was born between 1224 and 1225, the second son of a nobleman of Champagne. Many of his family had gone on crusades and he grew up in their shadow. Because of a series of deaths he became Lord of Joinville in his early teens, although his mother administered the estates for him. Jean probably first saw Louis, the man who was to have so much effect on him, at Saumur in 1241, although he did not get to know him until he was on crusade. Following family tradition he took the cross in 1248 and went on the Seventh Crusade. He wrote his *Life of Saint Louis* in old age, as a tribute to a king and also a portrait of a loved friend.

•

GEOFFROY DE VILLEHARDOUIN was probably born between 1150 and 1154. His father was a nobleman of Champagne with estates in the southern part of the province. Geoffroy was not the eldest son but, because of his family and marriage connections, he became Marshal of Champagne in 1185 – an appointment which gave him experience in arbitration before he went abroad. He compiled his history of the Fourth Crusade a few years after the close of the expedition and wrote from first-hand knowledge. As Marshal of Romania he also had access to documents. Villehardouin probably remained in Romania till the end of his life: his chronicle ends abruptly at 1207 but there is evidence that he lived until about June 1218.

•

MARGARET SHAW was born in 1890 and took a B.A. degree by correspondence course from London University before going up to St Hugh's College, Oxford, to gain a 'first' in languages. She was at the Sorbonne when the First World War broke out, and returned to teach in Bradford, but she later went back to Paris and spent a long time there. She did research on Laurence Sterne, and published a book about his 'Letter to Eliza'. She became a tutor at St Hugh's, and taught in Repton in the Second World War. She translated two other books, Stendhal's *The Charterhouse of Parma* and *Scarlet and Black* for the Penguin Classics, and had begun on another when she died in 1963.

Linda Rickis 25/1/95

JOINVILLE
&
VILLEHARDOUIN

CHRONICLES OF THE
CRUSADES

TRANSLATED WITH AN INTRODUCTION

BY M. R. B. SHAW

PENGUIN BOOKS

PENGUIN BOOKS

Published by the Penguin Group
Penguin Books Ltd, 27 Wrights Lane, London W8 5TZ, England
Penguin Books USA Inc., 375 Hudson Street, New York, New York 10014, USA
Penguin Books Australia Ltd, Ringwood, Victoria, Australia
Penguin Books Canada Ltd, 10 Alcorn Avenue, Toronto, Ontario, Canada M4V 3B2
Penguin Books (NZ) Ltd, 182–190 Wairau Road, Auckland 10, New Zealand

Penguin Books Ltd, Registered Offices: Harmondsworth, Middlesex, England

This translation first published 1963
19 20

Copyright © The Estate of M. R. B. Shaw, 1963
All rights reserved

Printed in England by Clays Ltd, St Ives plc
Set in Monotype Bembo

Except in the United States of America, this book is sold subject
to the condition that it shall not, by way of trade or otherwise, be lent,
re-sold, hired out, or otherwise circulated without the publisher's
prior consent in any form of binding or cover other than that in
which it is published and without a similar condition including this
condition being imposed on the subsequent purchaser

Contents

Joinville: *The Life of Saint Louis*

Introduction

FEW events in history have been more coloured by romantic imagination than that series of expeditions to the Holy Land known as the Crusades. The very name conjures up a vision of gallant knights inspired by pure religious zeal, leaving home and country to embark on a just and holy war against the enemies of the Christian faith. The two chronicles here presented, each composed by a man who took part in such an expedition, give a truer picture of an enterprise in which the darker as well as the brighter side of human nature is shown in the actions of those who took the cross. However, since these chronicles deal with only two of the Crusades, it is well perhaps in this introduction to place them in their context as giving part of a struggle between Christians and Moslems for possession of the Holy Land that lasted for nearly two hundred years.

Jerusalem, the Holy City, had been a centre of pilgrimage from very early times. Its capture in 638 by the Moslem Caliph Omar had left the Christians free to practise their religion. Conditions remained the same until 1076, when Jerusalem passed into the hands of the Seljukian Turks, who desecrated the holy places, and brutally treated the Christians in the city, throwing some into prison and massacring others. Pilgrims who managed to make their way to the Holy Land brought back pitiful tales of the plight of their co-religionists in the East.

The idea of a Holy War to avenge these wrongs occurred to Pope Gregory VII, and to his successor Victor III; but the peoples of Western Christendom, preoccupied with their own affairs at home, paid small attention to their pleas. However, little by little, to the north of the Alps, the preaching of Peter the Hermit did much to influence popular opinion in favour of a war against the infidel, and when, at the Council of Clermont in November 1095, Pope Urban II, a Frenchman born, appealed to his countrymen to join an international expedition to recover Jerusalem, he met with an enthusiastic response. In 1096 two expeditions started for the East. One, led by

Peter the Hermit, consisted of an undisciplined mob, which was almost completely wiped out by the Turks in October of that year. The other, made up of properly organized troops in command of barons from Northern France and Flanders, Provence, and Southern Italy, arrived at Constantinople in December. Here they joined forces with the Byzantine Emperor. Passing through Asia Minor, where they helped the Greeks to capture Nicaea and defeated the Turks at Dorylaeum, they finally entered Syria. The people of the northern province of Edessa, in revolt against their Armenian ruler, invited Baudouin de Bouillon to take his place in March 1098. In June of that year the Crusaders captured Antioch; in July 1099 they took Jerusalem after a siege of only six weeks. This victory, one regrets to say, was followed by a merciless slaughter of Turks and Jews within the city. As a result of this first Crusade three Christian states were established in Syria: the principalities of Edessa and Antioch, and the kingdom of Jerusalem. The whole of this conquered territory was commonly known as Outremer (the land oversea).

For many years the barons of Outremer, by maintaining an offensive and defensive war against the surrounding enemy, managed to keep hold of the land they had gained without calling in aid from the West. In 1144, however, when the Turks overran the province of Edessa, the Queen-regent of Jerusalem, fearing lest, with Antioch now exposed on its northern border, the Turks might capture this province also, sent an urgent appeal to Pope Eugenius III to initiate a new Crusade. The Pope referred the matter to King Louis VII of France, a man of noted piety, who took the cross in 1146 at the Assembly of Vézelay, where Saint Bernard's eloquence moved many Frenchmen to follow their king's example. Travelling to Germany, the saint persuaded the Emperor Conrad to join the expedition. In 1147 an army led by the rulers of France and Germany set off on the Second Crusade, determined to do great things. In the end, however, instead of advancing on Edessa, the Crusaders made an unsuccessful attempt to capture Damascus, and returned home without accomplishing anything.

Meanwhile, in the East the Turks were increasing in strength, and the Christians growing weaker. Pilgrims who came to the Holy Land were often shocked by the luxury and license of life in Outremer. Internal disputes among the barons of the land wasted energy that might have been used in defending it. The death of King Amalric of Jerusalem in 1174, leaving the kingdom without a worthy successor, was shortly followed by Saladin's rise to power as head of a united Moslem Empire. In 1187 the Christians suffered their greatest disaster when, after Saladin had routed and destroyed their army at the Horns of Hattin on 3 July, he occupied Tiberias, Jaffa, Ascalon, and Gaza, and finally entered Jerusalem. The Moslem's humane treatment of its Christian population was in marked contrast to the conduct of those Crusaders who had captured the city in 1099.

Once again Western Christendom was roused to action. In 1189 a third Crusade, led by three sovereigns, Frederick Barbarossa of Germany, Philip Augustus of France, and Richard I of England, prepared to go oversea. Barbarossa, who started first, was drowned in a little river, on his way through Asia Minor, on 10 June 1190. His army, disheartened, dwindled away, till only a very small contingent was left. Early the next year Philip and Richard sailed from Messina to go to the help of the titular King of Jerusalem who, with a pitifully small army, was besieging Saladin in Acre. Theirs was an uneasy partnership from the first. Different in temperament – Richard hot-tempered, rash, and impetuous; Philip, cold and shrewd – their relations were still further complicated by the fact that the English king, as Duke of Normandy, was Philip's none too obedient vassal, while the French king, for his part, was jealous of Richard's power.

Philip arrived before Acre on 20 April 1191. Richard, delayed by a storm at sea, got there seven weeks later. When Acre surrendered on 12 July, the two kings raised their banners on the walls. Leopold of Austria, now in command of the German forces, had also placed his there, only to have it torn down and flung into the ditch, an insult for which a cruel vengeance was exacted later. Richard's slaughter of his Turkish prisoners after Acre surrendered casts a darker shadow on his name.

In August 1191, the French king, tired of crusading, and anxious about the state of things in his kingdom, returned to France. Richard took command of the remaining troops and continued the campaign. But although he defeated Saladin at Arsuf in September 1191, and successfully relieved Jaffa in August of the following year, he came within reach of Jerusalem only to veil his eyes from the sight of the city he dared not attempt to deliver. The sole achievement of this Crusade was a five years' truce with Saladin, which gave the

Christians possession of the main coastal towns as far south as Jaffa, and allowed pilgrims free right of entry into Jerusalem.

So we come to the Fourth Crusade, the story of which is told by Villehardouin in his *Conquest of Constantinople*, a work distinguished among other things by the fact that it is the first reliable record of these expeditions to be written in French. The earlier Crusades, it is true, had their historians, but these, among whom we may particularly note William, Archbishop of Tyre, gave their accounts in Latin. There were not wanting certain effusions in verse concerning the exploits of Crusaders oversea; but none of these has any historical value. Graindor de Douai, writing in the first half of the twelfth century, gives lively accounts in the *Chanson d'Antioche* and the *Chanson de Jérusalem* of the taking of these two cities in the First Crusade; but, on the other hand, he has little conception of the motive behind the expedition, and a very imperfect knowledge of the main events. Less reliable still are those imitations of the Old French epics, such as *Godefroi de Bouillon* or the *Chevalier du Cygne*, in which fantasy takes the place of fact. The Norman Jongleur produces, in his *Histoire de la Guerre Sainte*, a straightforward record of the Third Crusade, but from his position as a humble pilgrim in the ranks he has no more than an outside view of the events he chronicles. It remained for a leading actor in the Fourth Crusade to present the first trustworthy and fully-informed history of such an expedition, in his own native tongue and in prose.

The author of the *Conquest of Constantinople* was born some time between 1150 and 1154. His father, Vilain de Villehardouin, was a nobleman of Champagne with estates in the southern part of the province, not far from its chief town Troyes. Geoffroy was not the eldest of Vilain's sons, but thanks to his connexions by birth, and later by marriage, with many noble families in Champagne and the neighbouring provinces, and no doubt also to his power of commanding confidence and respect, he became in 1185 Marshal of Champagne. In those days, when fighting between neighbouring barons was no remote contingency, a marshal's duty was to see that everything was in order to resist or make an attack; if war broke out, he had to make all necessary arrangements for a campaign, and in his lord's absence take over command. In addition to this, he was his lord's deputy in everything that concerned the administration of the province. Villehardouin, so far as we know, had not been on active service before he went oversea, but there is evidence of the important part he had played as arbiter in disputes within the province and representative of his lord in negotiations with the king of France. In the course of his duties he became familiar with many of those noble personages whose names are cited in his chronicle, and gained, as marshal of a province, experience that prepared him for the tasks that lay before him in a wider field.

His work, while it follows a chronological order, is not a record of events set down from day to day, but rather a kind of official history of the Fourth Crusade, compiled a few years after the close of this abortive expedition, by one who could supplement his own memories of it by reference to existing documents – letters, treaties, army lists, and so on – to which, as Marshal of Romania, he had free access. A man of mature years and ripe experience, and in the confidence of those who had organized and taken a leading part in the various campaigns and other incidents he chronicles, Villehardouin speaks with authority. Even if – as with all histories written before time has set events in their full perspective – his interpretation is sometimes biased, he gives on the whole a very fair and honest account of an enterprise that began so well and ended so disastrously.

All the same, the accuracy and fairness of Villehardouin's presentation of his story have not escaped challenge from certain quarters. Some of his critics, for instance, assert that in laying the responsibility for the diversion of the crusade to Zara, and later to Constantinople, on the men who failed to report at Venice he takes no account of certain machinations going on behind the scenes; others allege that in so doing he deliberately arranges his story so as to free the leaders of the expedition from blame. Such criticism can be easily answered. No doubt the Venetians welcomed a situation that gave them a chance of increasing their influence in the Mediterranean; no doubt Philip of Swabia was eager to have his brother-in-law Alexius restored to power. While this may be so, it is difficult to imagine that French Crusaders would have consented to further the aims of Venice and Germany if, in their straitened circumstances, they had seen any other way of succeeding in their own enterprise. As for the idea that Villehardouin acted as an official apologist, this can quickly be discounted, in view of his honest account of actions on the part of these same leaders at a later date.

Villehardouin has also been accused of undue harshness in his judgement on the men who failed to join or deserted from the army. Certainly he is severe; but we must consider the circumstances. The barons had bound themselves in full council to abide by any agreement their envoys made in Venice, and, by feudal custom, all those who had pledged themselves to go on the expedition were equally bound. A man of honour himself, with a high conception of his military duties, Villehardouin found it unthinkable that any man worthy of the name of knight should break his promise, or fail to go where his leader should command. Why then, he wondered, had so many knights defaulted? In his indignation at the harm their defection had caused to the enterprise, it seemed to him that they must have thought it safer to go to Syria, where the Christians still held certain cities, than face the risks of campaigning in a country which was entirely in Moslem hands. None the less, with touching human inconsistency, in reporting the fate of those who went to Syria, it is not their want of courage but their lack of wisdom that Villehardouin blames. Speaking here in pity rather than in anger, he pays tribute to the memory of those good knights, regretting only that they made a bad choice, and paid the penalty for their sinful folly.

As for the allegation that Villehardouin, in his account of discord in the army and consequent desertions from it, makes no allowance for the religious scruples of those who protested against making war on Christians, it is difficult at this interval of time to determine how far such protestations were sincere, and how far they were put forward as a pretext for disbanding the army. In the case of the Abbot of Vaux there is some reason for suspicion; for this cleric, who was so active in stirring up dissension in the Crusaders' army, and who finally left it on the plea of religious scruples, showed no such squeamishness when in 1209 he played a leading part in the 'crusade' against the Albigenses, who were no less Christian than the Greeks.

All things considered, it is hardly to be wondered at that Villehardouin, convinced as he was that the only hope of delivering Jerusalem lay in keeping the army together, had little patience with those who wished to disband it and little sympathy with those who pleaded religious scruples. Had not the Pope himself, at first appalled by the attack on the Christian city of Zara, granted absolution to the Crusaders on the grounds that they had acted under constraint, and urged them to keep the army together? Moreover, at the very time that the Abbot of Vaux was making trouble, his Holiness, relying on the promise Alexius had given to bring the Greek Church under the authority of Rome, had finally, after some hesitation, let the Crusaders know that he would not oppose the expedition to Constantinople, provided it was managed in such a way as to bring about a reunion between the Roman and the Orthodox Church.

That hope was never to be fulfilled, nor did this army ever reach the Holy City. From the time that the Franks presented their ultimatum to the Emperor Alexius IV in February 1204 all thoughts of a Crusade were lost sight of in a series of contests between Franks and Greeks and the many troubles that followed the establishment of the Latin Empire of Romania by force of arms. In this latter part of the chronicle Villehardouin's bias must be taken into consideration. Recounting events from the French point of view, he interprets them, so far as he can, to the prejudice of the Greeks. What to them was the gallant attempt of a conquered nation to regain its lost independence was in his eyes a proof that they were by nature disloyal and treacherous. Apart from this bias, his chronicle gives a fair account of the long and tragic struggle between Christians of the East and West and one from which we can draw our own conclusions.

From the facts Villehardouin puts before us it is evident that, from their first assumption of power, the conquerors made the fatal mistake of underestimating the opposition they might have to meet. Confident, after the sudden collapse of resistance in Constantinople, that subduing the rest of the empire would be easy, and apparently unconscious of the bitter hatred aroused in a cultured race by insolent barbarians who had pillaged and wrecked their lovely city – one of the finest centres of civilization in the world – the Franks made no attempt to conciliate the Greeks.

At first it seemed as if their confidence was justified. Apart from a few isolated cities, still holding out against the conquerors, the whole of the land on the northern side of the straits submitted to foreign rule. The barons, however, as Villehardouin himself admits, instead of governing the lands allotted to them justly, thought only of what profit they could gain for themselves. This last provocation was too much for the Greeks. Rising in revolt, they drove the Franks out of Adrianople and Demotika, and took possession of these two important cities. In their eagerness to oust the conqueror by any possible means they entered into alliance with the powerful King of

Wallachia and Bulgaria. In the end Johanitza proved even more unwelcome than the Franks. But if the Greeks had cause to regret his
coming, so had their conquerors, as Johanitza's troops overran the
empire, capturing and destroying the fine cities of Romania, till only
two beside Constantinople remained in Frankish hands.

Meanwhile, on the other side of the straits, in Asia Minor, Theodore
Lascaris, husband of Alexius III's daughter Anna, was doing his best
to prevent the Franks from obtaining possession of the lands allotted
to them, and finally, as Villehardouin tells us, succeeded in accomplishing his aim. Acknowledged from the first by Greeks in Asia Minor
and those who rallied to his side from across the water as their
legitimate ruler, he was crowned emperor in 1206. The Empire of
Nicaea was to remain the headquarters of the Greek monarchy
until, with the fall of the Latin Empire in 1261, a descendant of the
Emperor Theodore returned to rule in Constantinople.

Villehardouin's chronicle ends somewhat abruptly with the death
of the Marquis de Montferrat in 1207. The fact that Henri de
Valenciennes, in his *Histoire de l'Empereur Henri*, continues the story
of Romania from the very point at which Villehardouin's account
breaks off suggests that the sudden ending of the *Conquest of Constantinople* was due to the author's death. The date of this is uncertain.
There is evidence that Villehardouin was still alive in 1212, and still
in Romania, where he probably remained for the rest of his life.
Documents relating to donations in memory of himself and his wife
afford proof that he died some time before June 1218. At all events,
he lived long enough to see the Emperor Henri, wiser and more far-
sighted than his ill-fated brother, conciliating the Greeks by giving
them a fair share of honours and offices, and establishing peace within
that part of the empire still remaining to him.

The *Conquest of Constantinople* is one of our main sources of information on the course of the Fourth Crusade,[1] but it is also a fitting
memorial of one whose constant practice of the knightly virtues of
loyalty and courage gives him a place among the noblest characters
of his day. A man of firm religious principles, Villehardouin's duty
to God, as he sees it, is to serve Him as faithfully and devotedly as a

---

[1] Nicetas Choniates, a Greek historian whose own palace was burnt and
plundered in the sack of Constantinople, gives a full account of the period up
to 1206 from the Greek point of view. His interpretation of events has been
taken into consideration in assessing Villehardouin's western bias.

good vassal serves his lord; and above and beyond all this to recognize that all events, whether as indications of God's pleasure or displeasure, are ordered by His will. Loyalty to God, moreover, entails complete integrity of conduct: all breaches of faith, all underhand dealings and acts of treachery, all covetousness and self-seeking, are not only contrary to the knightly code but violations of divine law. If the God Villehardouin serves is the 'God of Battles', if he accepts without question the legate's sanction of war against Greek Christians as just and holy, though we may regret the little place that love and mercy have in his religion, we cannot doubt the sincerity of his faith.

Equally loyal in his service of those to whom his earthly allegiance is due, Villehardouin interprets his duty as something more than blind obedience. A man of strong character and sound judgement, he does not fear to show his disapproval of the Emperor Baudouin's quarrel with the Marquis de Montferrat, but boldly intervenes to heal the breach. In this, as in other instances throughout the chronicle, his concern is to work for 'the common good of all'.

Courage, that other essential quality in a knight is, as he conceives it, a disciplined activity. It does not consist in shutting one's eyes to danger – there are many allusions in his work to the risks to which he and fellow-crusaders were exposed. Nor is it to be confused with rashness, which, as in the case of the disastrous fight at Adrianople, leads men to hazard not only their own lives but the enterprise to which they are committed. It is, in fact, an ability to make a cool and balanced appraisal of danger without giving way to fear. Such a courage is Villehardouin's; yet it comes to him so naturally that he takes it as nothing to boast about, relating each adventure that concerns himself as one in which his gallant companions have their full share.

A man of clear and balanced judgement, austere and reticent by nature, Villehardouin is distinguished for the simplicity and lucidity of his work. No obtrusion of his own personality, no flights of imagination, no long and picturesque descriptions such as his contemporary Robert de Clari[1] delights in, come in to break the clear

---

[1] Author of another eye-witness account of the Fourth Crusade, with the same title as Villehardouin's. His descriptions of what he saw for himself are not wanting in colour, but in his report of the expedition he relies too much on hearsay evidence – often incorrect – for his work to have any historical value.

line of a story that compels our interest by its masterly presentation
of the facts. Statesmanlike in his approach to the vicissitudes of an
expedition that began as a Crusade and ended as a war against
Christians, he shows, by his skilful choice and treatment of his
material, the political import of each turn of events as it leads on to
further action, and that with no more comment than will set it in
relief. He was a soldier as well as a statesman, and that sense of order
and discipline ingrained in men of his profession is plainly apparent
in his straightforward account of dissensions within the army, as
also of the many engagements in the long contest between Franks and
Greeks.

   Yet for all the general sobriety of his exposition of the uneven
course of the Fourth Crusade, his work is by no means lacking in
animation. Whenever, for instance, his story moves from conferences
and similar matters of routine to recollections of the army on campaign, the contrast between his lively, dramatic portrayal of its fortunes and his quieter presentation of other incidents in his work gives
light and shade to a chronicle that never varies in its simplicity, but
changes its tone and tempo as the occasion demands. Viewing this
chronicle as a whole, and remembering that Villehardouin, as a
pioneer among French historians, had no other guide save his own
native genius, we can only marvel at the skill of this soldier-statesman,
who marshals and deploys his facts as a good commander does his
forces to bring this story of high hopes defeated so vividly before our
eyes.

   After the failure of the Fourth Crusade to attain its first objective,
some time elapsed before a further attempt to break the power of the
Moslems was made. Then, in 1218, Jean de Brienne, titular King of
Jerusalem and actual ruler of the little kingdom of Acre, crossed the
sea to Egypt, and after a lengthy siege took Damietta in November of
the following year. Two years later, having accomplished little in the
meantime, his army, brought to bay when the Sultan of Egypt
flooded the low-lying lands of the Nile basin, was forced to surrender
and give Damietta back to the Turks.

   No Pope gave his blessing to the Sixth Crusade, nor was it undertaken from any religious motive. Its leader, the Emperor Frederick
of Germany, who was under sentence of excommunication at the
time, sailed for Acre in September 1228, to claim the kingdom of

Jerusalem for himself, by right of marriage with the daughter and heiress of Jean de Brienne. His army was small; he met with a very lukewarm reception from the barons of Outremer; but what he could not take by force of arms, he managed to secure by diplomacy. In February 1229, after somewhat lengthy negotiations with the Sultan, the Treaty of Jaffa was signed giving Frederick possession of the whole of Jerusalem with the exception of the mosque of Omar, and restoring to the Christians, Jaffa, Bethlehem, and Nazareth, together with the lordships of Toron and Sidon. This casual handing over of their cities shocked the Moslems; the Christians, for their part, were no less angered by terms which gave the infidels access to Jerusalem, and left it unfortified. Enmity between Franks and Turks persisted, and in 1244 the Holy City fell once more into Moslem hands.

Shortly after news of this disaster reached Europe, King Louis IX of France lay desperately ill in Paris. On his sickbed, he vowed that if, by God's help, he recovered his strength, he would go on crusade himself to recover Jerusalem. There were pressing affairs at home to be settled first, so that nearly four years passed before, on 12 August 1248, he left Paris on the first stage of his journey to the East. This Seventh Crusade, like most of the previous ones, did not reach Jerusalem. For all his personal courage, and his power of inspiring a like courage in others, the task of subduing the Turks in Egypt proved too much for one who was more of a saint than a military genius. Once again the hopes of the Crusaders were drowned in the Nile. The king's subsequent campaign in the Holy Land was brought to a sudden end by troubles in his own kingdom which necessitated his return to France. Nor, if he had stayed, was it likely that he would have accomplished anything. The barons of Outremer, proud and independent, had never taken kindly to intervention from the West. After availing themselves of the French king's help in recovering and re-fortifying some of their cities they were only too ready to assure him that they had no further need of his aid. The French nobles, moreover, tired of a war in which they saw no prospect of profit for themselves, had long been urging the king to return to France, and some of them, including the king's brothers, had already left the East.

Many years later, the fall of Antioch in 1268 set King Louis thinking of a new Crusade. His brother Charles, now King of Sicily, with ambitions of establishing himself as ruler of a Mediterranean empire, persuaded the all too unsuspicious king to begin with an attack on the Moslems in Northern Africa. It was, indeed, a wicked thing to encourage a man in such a weak state of health to undertake any expedition. In July 1270, ill as he was, King Louis landed near Carthage, but quickly fell a victim to the plague, and died at Tunis on 25 August. Charles lost heart and returned to Sicily. Prince Edward of England (later Edward I) who had promised to join King Louis at Tunis, arrived as the French were leaving. A little later he sailed for Acre, but found the state of things in Outremer too bad for him to do anything there but help in arranging a ten years' truce with the Turks. From that time onwards fighting between Moslems and Christians in the East continued, but attracted little attention in the West. The fall of Acre in 1291 marked the end of Christian rule oversea.

In the years that followed the death of King Louis, more than one record of his good reign and his saintly life appeared. Two of these – a chronicle by the king's confessor, Guillaume de Beaulieu, written in Latin, and an account in French compiled some few years later from various other records by a certain Guillaume de Nangis – remain half-forgotten on the shelves of learned libraries. A third, still widely known and read, and already translated several times into English, is the one presented here in a modern version as the *Life of Saint Louis*.

The author of this chronicle was, like Villehardouin, a native of Champagne. The second son of Simon, Lord of Joinville, a nobleman of high standing as Seneschal of the province, he was born some time between June 1224 and May 1225 in his father's lordly castle, above the little town of Joinville on the Marne. He was not the first of his family to go on crusade. His grandfather Geoffroy had been with the army besieging Acre in 1189, and had died there before the Crusaders took the town. Two of his uncles, Geoffroy and Robert, had taken the cross in the Fourth Crusade. Robert whom Villehardouin had met on his way back from Venice, had accompanied Gautier de Brienne to Apulia, and is said to have died there. Geoffroy had gone to Syria, and had been killed in 1203 in the Battle of Kalaat-el-Horn. A poem by Guy de Provins pays tribute to his outstanding courage. The boy who listened to tales of his kinsmen's exploits retained in later life a reverence for their memory. On his return from his own campaign oversea, he brought his uncle Geoffroy's shield to hang in the chapel of Saint Laurent at Joinville, and placed a tablet there on which he had inscribed, in his own words, a tribute to the good deeds of men of his family at home and on crusade.

Simon, our author's father, who succeeded his brother Geoffroy as Lord of Joinville, had taken part in the 'crusade' against the Albigenses. Later on he had fought with Jean de Brienne's army in Egypt, and been there when Damietta fell. His son would remember his father's tales of that difficult siege, and compare it with the easy capture of Damietta by King Louis. Among other memories of his childhood would be a certain night in 1230 when Simon left the castle and hurried to the relief of Troyes.

The boy was still in his early teens when his father died. Simon's eldest son was already dead, so Jean became Lord of Joinville. Simon's widow, who seems to have been a woman of strong character, administered the estates during her son's minority, and prepared him for the time when he would be old enough to assume the duties of Seneschal of Champagne, an office held by lords of Joinville for several generations. At that particular date such duties were not onerous. No longer called upon to administer justice within the province or take control of domestic arrangements in his lord's household, a seneschal's chief function was to attend his lord on occasions of special ceremony, and in addition to know how such affairs should be conducted, with due regard to questions of precedence, proper ways of behaviour, and suitable modes of dress. The youth, too young as yet to become a knight, who carved the Comte de Champagne's meat at the banquet in the great hall of Saumur in 1241, was already well acquainted with the duties of his office. In after years, the effect of his early training as seneschal would appear in his record of many strange things he saw and heard of during his stay in the East.

It was at Saumur apparently that Joinville had a first glimpse of the man who was to have such an influence on his life; but he did not, so far as we can gather, come into close personal contact with King Louis until they were together on crusade. When he decided to take the cross in 1248, there is little doubt that a desire to follow the example set by previous lords of Joinville was the determining factor in his choice. At the time he still regarded himself as the Comte de Champagne's vassal, and his refusal to go against feudal custom by taking an oath of loyalty to the sovereign over his lord's head, is a

clear indication of his relations with King Louis before they met in
Cyprus. His close attachment to the king was to come, and to inspire
his chronicle.

The *Life of Saint Louis* differs greatly in character, composition, and
content from Villehardouin's orderly and statesmanlike account of
the Fourth Crusade. Apart from a section dealing with early events
in the king's reign, a few details such as the king's ordinances for the
government of his realm, his last words to his son, and a handful of
anecdotes, all of which Joinville borrowed from earlier chronicles, it
is rather a collection of personal reminiscences than a history in the
proper sense of the word. Joinville's arrangement of his work, moreover, into a first part filled with illustrations of the king's piety and his
just administration, followed by a second covering, in more or less
detail, the story of King Louis's reign and his final canonization, is one
that inevitably leads to many repetitions.

Some of the difference between these two chronicles can doubtless
be ascribed to the fact that the earlier one is the work of a man in the
prime of life and the later that of a man well over eighty. Admittedly
Joinville is often garrulous, as old men are, and tends, as old men do,
to repeat himself. None the less as this veteran campaigner looks
back across half a century and more to the days when he fought and
suffered beside his beloved king, the freshness and vivacity of his
record of past experiences make us forget his age. He is still at
heart the same eager and impetuous young knight who so long ago
set out on the voyage oversea, and what in fact particularly dis-
tinguishes his work from Villehardouin's is rather a difference in the
temperament and outlook of these two authors than a difference in
their years.

Unlike the earlier chronicler, whose work, designed to bring out
the political significance of events, pays attention only to actions that
occupy the forefront of the stage, Joinville, more interested in the
impact of events on the people taking part in them, fills in a background that Villehardouin leaves vague. Thus, in depicting a battle,
instead of giving, as Villehardouin does, a general view of its progress,
Joinville takes us into the heart of the conflict, to show, in a series of
little incidents affecting individuals or groups of people, the various
reactions of the men who fought in this bitter Eastern campaign. If,
on occasion, he tells of a conference, he is not content to record the
final decision, but expands what Villehardouin would dismiss in a

brief sentence into a lively account of verbal exchanges between the people concerned. Throughout his chronicle, in fact, he stresses the human side of his story.

A curious observer of mankind in any shape or form, Joinville finds room in his work for such things as the weird habits and clothing of the Bedouins, the strange theology of the Old Man of the Mountain, the training of the Sultan's bodyguard, or the primitive burial customs of the Comans. Nor is his interest confined to human beings; if anything takes his fancy by the way, be it a fossilized fish, the legendary sources of the Nile, or a quaintly-fashioned crossbow, this man, who is part Crusader and part inquisitive traveller, never scruples to bring it in. The tangential course he pursues throughout his chronicle has its disadvantages, but these are largely compensated for by the vivid picture he gives of his own times and the ways of life in the East.

From chronicles that differ in so many ways one might reasonably expect a somewhat different image of each author to emerge. This is the case in so far as Villehardouin represents the ideal figure of a knight in armour, while Joinville reveals the natural man within. The frank and simple way in which he speaks of his grief at parting from his castle and his children, of the doubts and fears that beset him in the course of fighting and his shrinking from death at the hands of the Saracens, brings to light emotions common to but not always so honestly admitted by men of feeling subjected to the hard experience of war. His graphic, yet modest, account of his own part in various operations in the East and his praise of the courage shown by his companions are proof that he was by nature as brave and generous as he was sensitive and sincere. If we consider also Joinville's unfailing loyalty to the king he served, the force of character he displayed on more than one occasion, his solicitude, rare enough in a man of his rank, for the humbler Crusaders left in captivity, and his sense of responsibility for the welfare of people on his own estates, it is evident that this old chronicler, so unlike Villehardouin in his way of handling his material, is a man of equal integrity, and, though more warmly human, a no less gallant knight.

Viewed as a whole, the *Life of Saint Louis* contains much that has little or no connexion with what Joinville, in his preliminary dedication, put forward as its theme. None the less, for all its meanderings, the work achieves its purpose of doing full honour to the memory of this upright king. Indeed, so anxious is this friend and disciple of Saint Louis to pay a fitting tribute to his dead lord, that he pours into his chronicle illustration after illustration of his many virtues, when half of them would have more than sufficed. This excess of zeal is most apparent in parts of the work that deal with the king's life at home, and in which his constant devotion to God's service in public and private, his open-handed charity, his love for his people, and the large place he gives to justice in his conception of a ruler's duties are recorded at more than necessary length. In the portion dealing with events oversea the king's character emerges more dramatically from episodes which illustrate, among other things, his undaunted courage in battle, his patient endurance of sickness, and his fortitude in face of defeat and the harsh trials of captivity. Here, indeed, as Joinville depicts him, is a leader whose example puts courage into the faint-hearted and whose love for his men inspires in them a like devotion; here, too, is a monarch who does not stand on his dignity, but one a man can talk to, and even jest with, as a friend.

Such is the king whom Joinville loves and reveres, but not blindly. Always the loyal servant of his lord, he keeps his right to judge his master's actions. Thus, while in general approving of the king's independent character, as shown, for instance, in his refusal to let his conscience be ruled by clerics, Joinville is not so sure that it was wise of his lord to disregard advice from those who urged him to follow the 'good customs of the Holy Land' in distributing the spoil at Damietta. Full of admiration for the king's piety as he is, he none the less considers it out of place for him to remain praying in his chapel when kindness and courtesy demanded that he should go to meet his wife on her arrival at Sidon shortly after giving birth to a child. On occasion even he does not hesitate to speak frankly to his sovereign, as for instance when he agrees to stay for a further period in his service on condition that the king, for his part, will control his temper for the same length of time. So too, when the Abbot of Cluny, after making the king a present of two handsome palfreys, comes the very next day to lay a case before him, Joinville asks his lord whether his judgement had been influenced by this gift. On hearing that it had, Joinville drives his point home by advising the king to forbid all those concerned with administering justice in his realm to accept any gifts from persons who came to plead before them, lest they should be influenced in the same way.

Such instances, while they help us to recognize in Joinville's hero a human being rather than a sculptured saint, are not intended – nor should we so interpret them – as any slur on the memory of an honoured lord and friend. Joinville's *Life of Saint Louis* stands as a worthy tribute to a king who by his example set before the world of his day an ideal of how a Christian ought to live, a knight should bear himself, and a man in authority govern the people committed to his charge. All his love and reverence for this good king, no less than his grief at the loss of so dear a friend, find supreme expression in Joinville's dream of Saint Louis, which comes as a fitting conclusion to his book.

The works of Villehardouin and Joinville, to quote Sir Frank Marzials, 'take us back delightfully among "old forgotten far-off things".' Yet I would not go so far as to maintain, with this earlier translator, that their interest for us today lies almost entirely in their vivid evocation of the past. Nor do I agree with him in thinking that a version which 'follows the old French idiom as closely as possible, using turns of speech and a vocabulary that are either archaic, or suggest archaism', is best calculated to give a modern reader a full and true impression of their work.

To my mind, apart from their very real historical interest, these old chronicles have a perennial value as human documents, in which we find how little, in the passage of the centuries, the spirit of man and his pattern of behaviour in times of emergency have changed. True, they have certain features which differentiate them from works that are written today. But what in effect do these differences amount to? Little enough in Villehardouin's work, where his plain, straight-forward way of reporting old campaigns and obsolete modes of warfare is so closely akin to the manner adopted by an army commander writing his memoirs of the Second World War[1] that only a 'thin partition' seems to divide the knights of this distant century from the men of Alamein. The occasional quaintness of Joinville's outlook on the world around him, and his naïve acceptance of ideas no longer current in our more sophisticated and more scientifically-minded age, are admittedly echoes of a time long past. Set in relation to the rest of his chronicle, however, such interesting side-lights as his work provides on attitudes of mind in

[1] Lord Montgomery's account of his campaign in Northern Africa is one that I have particularly in mind.

the thirteenth century fall into place as background details. In the foreground we have a story that, like Villehardouin's, sets before us the ideal of knightly service on which our own conception of civilized man is based, and also, in its moving account of an army driven to defeat and imprisonment, depicts the hazards of war in clear, fresh colours that no lapse of time has dimmed.

So much for the content of these chronicles. What form will best convey their meaning to a modern reader? In my opinion, a version that attempts to imitate their archaic idiom – in which, among other things the vocabulary is so limited that the same words recur with monotonous frequency, and the sentences, often loosely constructed, are linked together by innumerable 'ands' – so far from giving an impression of their constant value, can only serve to emphasize unduly the accidental differences between their age and ours. Consequently, encouraged by the example set by such an expert translator as Mr Nevill Coghill in his modernized version of the *Canterbury Tales*, I have modelled my own translation on the language of today. Retaining only such few archaic terms as have no equivalent in current English,[1] varying the vocabulary by a free use of synonyms, and, where necessary, giving the sentences a more modern turn, I have endeavoured, with as little alteration of the original wording as possible, and with careful attention to preserve the proper tone and meaning, to render these two old chronicles in a colloquial style.

I say colloquial, because both these works were dictated,[2] and consequently bear the imprint of the spoken word. The authors were both men of breeding, but their speech differs in tone according to the temperament and situation of each speaker. Thus in Villehardouin's work we find the grave and measured, and, on occasion, formal mode of speech that befits a man of his austere character in high office, while Joinville, free of such cares as fall to the lot of a Marshal of Romania, gives expression to his own more genial nature in an easy, familiar style, resembling the friendly talk of men round a dinner-table, or beside the fire. How far I have succeeded in the

[1] These are explained in the glossary.
[2] It is not known whether Villehardouin could either read or write; such elementary skills were not then considered a necessary part of a knight's education. Three short documents in a large childish scrawl, with the statement 'this was written by me' or 'by my hand' appended, attest Joinville's pride in a rare achievement, but he, like Villehardouin, dictated his major work.

delicate task of harmonizing form and contents in this translation must be left to my readers to judge.

In conclusion I should like to say how much I am indebted to Dr E. V. Rieu, the Editor of the Penguin Classics, for his wise advice on the general principles of translation and the kind help he has given me in particular difficulties that have arisen in the course of my work.

M.R.B.S.

VILLEHARDOUIN

The Conquest of Constantinople

CHAPTER I

Muster-Roll of the Fourth Crusade
1199–1201

In the year of our Lord 1198, when Innocent was Pope in Rome, Philip was King of France and Richard King of England, there lived in France a man of saintly character called Foulques, who was in holy orders and priest of the parish of Neuilly, a small town lying between Paris and Lagny-sur-Marne. This same Foulques began to preach the Word of God throughout the Île de France and in other surrounding provinces; and God worked many miracles for his sake.

Reports of this good man's preaching were so widely circulated that news of it reached Pope Innocent, who thereupon sent a letter to France commanding the worthy priest to preach a Crusade in his name. A little later the Pope sent one of his cardinals, Monsignore Pietro da Capua, who had already taken the cross, to proclaim on his Holiness's behalf, an indulgence framed as follows: All those who take the Cross and remain for one year in the service of God in the army shall obtain remission of any sins they have committed, provided they have confessed them. The hearts of the people were greatly moved by the generous terms of this indulgence, and many, on that account, were moved to take the cross.

At the beginning of Advent in the year following that in which the worthy Foulques had delivered God's message, a tournament was held at the castle of Écry in Champagne. On that occasion it so happened, by God's grace, that Thibaut, Comte de Champagne et de Brie, took the cross, in company with the Comte Louis de Blois et de Chartrain. The Comte Thibaut was a young man of only twenty-two while the Comte Louis was just twenty-seven. Both these counts were nephews and cousins of the King of France, and nephews of the King of England as well. Their example was followed by Simon de Montfort and Renaud de Montmirail, two nobles of the highest rank. People throughout the country were greatly impressed when men of such high standing took the cross.

Those in the Comte Thibaut's domains who followed suit were Garnier, Bishop of Troyes, the Comte Gautier de Brienne, Geoffroy de Joinville, Seneschal of Champagne, and his brother Robert, Gautier de Vignory, Gautier de Montbéliard, Eustache de Conflans and his brother Guy de Plessier, Henri d'Arzillières, Ogier de Saint-Chéron, Geoffroy de Villehardouin, Marshal of Champagne, and his nephew Geoffroy, Guillaume de Nully, Gautier de Fuligny, Évrard de Montigny, Manassier de l'Isle, Macaire de Sainte-Mene-hould, Milon le Brébant, Guy de Chappes and his nephew Clarembaud, Renaud de Dampierre, Jean Foisnon, and many other brave and worthy men whose names are not recorded here.

Those who took the cross with the Comte Louis were Gervais du Chatel and his son Hervé, Jean de Virsin, Olivier de Rochefort, Henri de Montreuil, Païen d'Orléans, Pierre de Bracieux and his brother Hugues, Guillaume de Sains, Jean de Friaize, Gautier de Gaudonville, Hugues de Cormeray and his brother Geoffroy, Hervé de Beauvoir, Robert de Frouville and his brother Pierre, Orry de l'Isle, Robert du Quartier, and many others not mentioned here by name.

In the Île-de-France, Névelon, Bishop of Soissons, took the cross, in company with Mathieu de Montmorency and his nephew Guy, Châtelain de Coucy, Robert de Ronsoi, Ferry d'Yerres and his brother Jean, Gautier de Saint-Denis and his brother Henri, Guillaume d'Aunoi, Dreux de Cressonsacq, Bernard de Moreuil, Enguerrand de Boves and his brother Robert, and a number of other good and valiant men whose names are not given here.

On Ash Wednesday, at the very beginning of the following Lent, in the town of Bruges, the Comte Baudouin de Flandre et de Hainaut took the cross, together with his wife, the Comtesse Marie, who was the Comte de Champagne's sister. Their example was followed by the Comte Baudouin's brother Henri and his nephew Thierry, the son of the Comte Philippe de Flandre, as also by Guillaume, Advocate of Béthune and his brother Conon, Jean de Nesles, Governor of Bruges, Renier de Trit and his son Renier, Mathieu de Wallincourt, Jacques d'Avesnes, Baudouin de Beauvoir, Hugues de Beaumetz, Girard de Mancicourt, Eudes de Ham, Guillaume de Gommeignies, Dreuz de Beaurain, Roger de Marck, Eustache de Saubruic, François de Colemi, Gautier de Bousies, Renier de Mons, Gautier de Tombes, Bernard de Soubrenghien, and very many other worthy men not mentioned here by name.

A little later, the Comte Hugues de Saint-Pol, took the cross, and with him his nephew Pierre d'Amiens, Eustache de Canteleu, Nicolas de Mailly, Anseau de Cayeux, Guy de Houdain, Gautier de Nêle and his brother Pierre, and a number of other men whose names I do not know.

Later still the Comte Geoffroy du Perche took the cross, together with his brother Étienne, Rotrou de Montfort, Yves de la Jaille, Aimery de Villeroi, Geoffroy de Beaumont, and many others unknown to me by name.

Subsequently the barons held a conference at Soissons to decide when they would set off, and in what direction they would go. At the time, however, they were unable to reach a decision because it did not seem to them that as yet a sufficient number of people had taken the cross. Before two months of that same year had passed they gathered again for a conference at Compiègne. All the counts and barons who had taken the Cross were present at this meeting, during which many different points of view were put forward and considered. In the end it was agreed that they would send the best envoys they could find to make all arrangements for them, with full power to settle what should be done, exactly as if they were their lords in person.

Of the envoys chosen, two were appointed by Thibaut, Comte de Champagne et de Brie; two by the Comte Baudouin de Flandre et de Hainaut; two by the Comte Louis de Blois. The Comte Thibaut's envoys were Geoffroy de Villehardouin, Marshal of Champagne, and Milon le Brébant; the Comte Baudouin's Conon de Béthune and Alard Maquereau; those of the Comte Louis, Jean de Friaize and Gautier de Gaudonville.

The barons placed the management of the whole affair entirely in the hands of these six envoys. In confirmation of this they were given charters, duly drawn up and with seals appended, to the effect that all the barons would strictly abide by whatever agreements their envoys might enter into at any of the sea ports or other places to which they might happen to go.

So the six envoys set out on their mission. After discussing the matter among themselves they had unanimously agreed that they would find a greater number of ships at Venice than at any other port. They therefore mounted their horses and rode on day after day until, in the first week in Lent, they reached their destination.

CHAPTER 2

Treaty with the Venetians

THE Doge of Venice, a very wise and able man whose name was Enrico Dandolo, paid the French envoys great honour, and both he and the people of his household gave them a very cordial welcome. When, however, the letters they had with them had been duly delivered, the Venetians were very curious to know what business had brought these envoys to their country, since the documents they had presented were merely letters of credence, stating only that the bearers were to be accredited as if they were the counts in person, and that these would accept whatever arrangements their six emissaries saw fit to make.

The Doge accordingly said to the envoys: 'Sirs, I have read your letters, and we fully recognize that your lords are the highest in rank of all men, excepting only kings. They ask us to have confidence in whatever you say, and to believe that they will confirm any arrangements you make with us. So please speak freely and tell us what you want.'

'My lord,' replied the envoys, 'we beg you most humbly to summon your council, so that we may lay our lords' message before them. And let it be called tomorrow, if that be convenient to you.' The Doge replied that he would need four days to do this, and begged them to wait so long, until his council could meet. Then they could say what they required.

The envoys waited until the fourth day, as the Doge had appointed, and then returned to the palace, which was a most beautiful building and very richly furnished. There they found the Doge and his council assembled in a hall, and delivered their message to this effect: 'My lords,' said they, 'we have come to you on behalf of the great barons of France, who have taken the cross to avenge the outrage suffered by our Lord, and, if God so wills, to recapture Jerusalem. And since our lords know there is no people who can help them so well as yours, they entreat you, in God's name, to take pity on the land oversea, and the outrage suffered by our Lord, and graciously do your best to supply us with a fleet of warships and transports.'

'And how can this be done?' asked the Doge. 'In any way,' replied the envoys, 'that you care to advise or propose, so long as our lords can meet your conditions and bear the cost.' 'Indeed,' said the Doge, 'your lords are asking a great deal of us, and it seems to me that they have an extremely high enterprise in view. We will give you our answer in a week's time. And do not be surprised at so long a delay, since such an important matter demands our full consideration.'

At the end of the time fixed by the Doge the envoys returned once more to the palace. I cannot tell you here of all the many things said on that occasion, but the final outcome of the meeting was as follows: 'Sirs,' said the Doge, 'we will tell you what we have agreed to do, provided, of course, we can persuade our Grand Council and the commons of this state to give their assent. Meanwhile, you, on your part, must consult together to see whether you can accept our terms and bear the cost.

'We will build transports to carry 4,500 horses and 9,000 squires, and other ships to accommodate 4,500 knights and 20,000 foot sergeants. We will also include in our contract a nine months' supply of rations for all these men and fodder for all the horses. This is what we will do for you, and no less, on condition you pay us five marks per horse and two marks per man.

'We will, moreover, abide by the terms of the covenant we now place before you for the space of one year from the day on which we set sail from the port of Venice, to act in the service of God and of Christendom, wherever it may be. The total cost of all we have outlined here amounts to 85,000 marks.

'And we will do more than this. We will provide, for the love of God, fifty additional armed galleys, on condition that so long as our association lasts we shall have one half, and you the other half, of everything we win, either by land or sea. It now remains for you to consider if you, on your part, can accept and fulfil all our conditions.'

The envoys took their leave, saying they would consult together and give their answer on the following day. They discussed the matter at length that night and finally agreed to accept the Venetians' terms. So in the morning they appeared before the Doge and said: 'My lord, we are ready to conclude this agreement.' Thereupon the

Doge told them he would consult his people, and, according to their decision, he would let them know how matters stood.

The next day, that is to say three days after the Doge had outlined his proposals, this very wise and able statesman summoned his Grand Council, which was composed of forty men from amongst the wisest and most capable in the State of Venice. By exercise of his good sense and his keen intelligence, qualities he possessed in the highest degree, he brought them both to approve and agree to accept the proposed covenant. He did this gradually, persuading first a few, then more, then still more, till at last all the members of his council expressed their approval and consent. After this he assembled a good ten thousand of the common people in the church of San Marco – the most beautiful church in the world – where he invited them to hear a mass of the Holy Spirit, and pray to God for guidance concerning the request the envoys had made to them. All the people did this most willingly.

As soon as mass was ended the Doge summoned the envoys, and told them to ask the people most humbly for their assent to the drawing up of the agreement. The envoys came into the church, where they attracted the curious gaze of many people who had not previously seen them.

By wish and consent of his companions Geoffroy de Villehardouin explained their errand. 'Sirs,' he said, 'the noblest and most powerful barons of France have sent us to you. They earnestly appeal to you to take pity on Jerusalem, now in bondage to the Turks, and implore you, in God's name, to be so good as to join with them in avenging the insult offered to our Lord. They have chosen to come to you because they know that no other people have such great power on the sea as you yourselves. They have, moreover, commanded us to kneel at your feet, and not to rise till you consent to take pity on the Holy Land oversea.'

Thereupon the six envoys, in floods of tears, knelt at the feet of the assembled people. The Doge and all the other Venetians present also burst out weeping, and holding up their hands towards heaven, cried out with one accord: 'We consent! We consent!' There was such an uproar and such a tumult that you might have thought the whole world was crumbling to pieces.

As soon as this great tumult and this great surge of pity – greater than any man has ever witnessed – had finally subsided, the good

Doge of Venice, wise and worthy man as he was, mounted the steps of the lectern and spoke to the people. 'Sirs,' he said, 'behold the honour God has paid you in inspiring the finest nation in the world to turn aside from all other people and choose you to join with them in so high an enterprise as the deliverance of our Lord!'

I cannot tell you here of all the good and noble words the Doge uttered on this occasion. The upshot of it all was that the Venetian agreed to have the deeds of the covenant drawn up on the following day. This was accordingly done, and the documents duly engrossed. After this business was concluded, the fact that the expedition was going to Cairo, because from there the Turks could be more easily crushed than from any other part of their territory, was kept a *deceit?* closely guarded secret; to the public at large it was merely announced that we were going oversea. We were now in Lent; by Saint John's *TIME* Day in the following year – that is to say in 1202 – the barons and the rest of the Crusaders were to assemble at Venice, where the ships would be ready waiting to receive them when they arrived.

As soon as the charters had been drawn up, signed, and sealed, they were brought to the Doge in his great palace, where the Grand Council and the Privy Council were both assembled. As he handed these documents to the envoys the Doge fell on his knees, and with tears streaming down his face swore on the Holy Gospels to carry out faithfully all the conditions set down in them; and so did all the members of his council, forty-six in number. The envoys, in their turn, swore to honour their covenant and to keep, in all good faith, the oaths they had taken for themselves and on behalf of their lords. Many a tear of pity was shed at this meeting, immediately after *POPE* which both parties concerned sent messengers to Pope Innocent in *APPROVES* Rome, so that he might ratify this covenant. This he very willingly did.

The envoys borrowed 5,000 silver marks from people in the city, *?* and handed them over to the Doge so that the building of the fleet might begin. After this they took their leave before returning home, and then rode for several days till they reached Piacenza in Lombardy. Here Geoffroy, Marshal of Champagne, and Alard Maquereau left the others and went straight to France, while their companions made their way towards Genoa and Pisa to find out what help the people there might give them for the land oversea.

CHAPTER 3

The Army Seeks a Leader
MAY–SEPTEMBER 1201

As Geoffroy de Villehardouin was crossing over Mont Cenis, he happened to meet Gautier de Brienne, who was on his way to Apulia to recover some lands belonging to his wife, King Tancred's daughter, whom he had married since taking the cross. With him were a number of other Crusaders, including Gautier de Montbéliard, Eustache de Conflans, Robert de Joinville, and many people of good standing in Champagne.

On hearing from the Marshal what the envoys had done, the travellers were delighted, and expressed much appreciation of the way things had gone. 'We're already on our way,' they said, 'and when you come to Venice you'll find us quite prepared.' However, events turn out as God wills, and in the end they no longer found it possible to rejoin the army. That was a great pity, for they were all very good and valiant men.

So they parted, and went their several ways. Geoffroy de Ville-hardouin rode on for many days till at length he reached Troyes in Champagne, where he found his lord the Comte Thibaut ill and in very low spirits. All the same the count was highly delighted at his arrival. As soon as Geoffroy had told him what they had accomplished, he was so overcome with joy that he said he would go out riding, a thing he had not done for a very long time past. Alas! what a terrible pity! Except for that one occasion he never got astride a horse again.

He grew worse, and his illness became so grave that he made his last will and testament, in which he divided the money he would have taken with him on pilgrimage among his followers and companions. He had, indeed, many true friends among them – no man of his time had more. In his will he ordered that each of the beneficiaries, on receiving his share of the money, should swear on the Holy Gospels to join the army at Venice, as he himself had promised to do. There were, however, many who later failed to keep their oath, and incurred great blame for such defection. The count also left orders for a portion of his money to be set aside and sent to the army, to be spent there as might seem best.

So the Comte Thibaut died; few men in this world ever made a better end. He passed away surrounded by a great crowd of relations and vassals. As for the mourning over his death and at his funeral, I dare not venture to describe it, for never was more honour paid to any other man. That, indeed, was only right and fitting, since no man of his day was ever more deeply loved by his own people, or by others. He was buried beside his father in the church of Saint-Étienne at Troyes. He left behind him the Comtesse Blanche, his wife, a very good and beautiful lady who was the daughter of the King of Navarre. She had borne him a little daughter and was about to bear a son.

After the count was buried, Mathieu de Montmorency, Simon de Montfort, Geoffroy de Joinville, Seneschal of Champagne, and Geoffroy the Marshal approached the Duc Eudes de Bourgogne, and said to him: 'My lord, you can realize what a great loss the land oversea has suffered by the Comte Thibaut's death. We therefore beg you, in God's name, to take the cross and come to the aid of that land in his place. We will undertake to have all his money handed over to you, and will swear to you, on the Holy Gospels, while making others do the same, that we will serve you loyally, just as we should have served him.'

The duke, however, was unwilling to accept their offer. (In my opinion he might have shown more wisdom.) Geoffroy de Joinville was therefore instructed to make a similar offer to the Comte de Bar-le-Duc, who was the late Comte Thibaut's cousin. He also refused. *[margin handwriting: subjective]*

The pilgrims, and all those pledged to fight in God's service, were greatly disheartened by the Comte Thibaut's death. At the beginning of the month they met in conference at Soissons to determine what they should do. Among those present were the Comte Baudouin de Flandre et de Hainaut, the Comte Louis de Blois et de Chartrain, the Comte Geoffroy du Perche, the Comte Hugues de Saint-Pol, and many other men of high standing and repute.

Geoffroy de Villehardouin explained the situation. He told them of the offer they had made in turn to the Duc de Bourgogne and the Comte de Bar-le-Duc, and how they had both rejected it. 'My lords,' he added, 'just listen to me and I'll suggest a possible course of action, if only you'll agree to take it. The Marquis Boniface de ✱

[margin handwriting at bottom: ✱ omission of relation between G de V + Boniface - where did they meet prior to this suggestion?]

Montferrat is a very shrewd and able man, and one of the most highly regarded of any man alive. If you asked him to come here and take the cross, and put himself in the place of the late Comte de Champagne, with full control of the army granted him by you, I'm sure he would accept your offer at once.'

There was a great divergence of opinion regarding this proposal, but finally, after much discussion, every man present, from the highest to the lowest, agreed to it. The necessary letter was written, and envoys chosen to go and fetch the marquis. He arrived on the day they had appointed, by way of Champagne and the Île-de-France, where many people, and in particular the French king, his cousin, paid him much honour.

The marquis came to a conference summoned at Soissons, where a great concourse of counts, barons, and other Crusaders had gathered. As soon as they heard he was coming, they all went out to meet him and welcomed him with great honour. The following morning the conference was held in an orchard belonging to the abbey of Notre-Dame de Soissons. At this meeting everyone begged the marquis to comply with their request, and implored him, for God's sake, to take the cross and assume command of the army, so that he might take the place of the late Comte Thibaut de Champagne, and have control of his money and his men. They fell at his feet in tears; he in his turn knelt down before them and said he would gladly do as they asked.

Thus the marquis yielded to their prayers, and took over command of the army. Immediately afterwards the Bishop of Soissons, accompanied by the saintly Foulques and two Cistercian friars the marquis had brought with him from his own domains, conducted him to the church of Notre-Dame, where they fastened the cross to his shoulder. Thus the conference ended. The next day the marquis took leave of the barons before returning to his own domains to settle his affairs. He advised all of them to put their own affairs in order, and said he would meet them again in Venice.

The marquis went on from Soissons to attend a meeting of the Chapter at Cîteaux, which takes place every year on Holy Cross Day in September. There he found a very great number of abbots, barons, and other people of Burgundy, Foulques of Neuilly was also there to preach the crusade. On that occasion many took the cross, including Eudes le Champenois de Champlitte and his brother Guillaume,

Richard de Dampierre and his brother Eudes, Guy de Pesmes and his brother Aimon, Guy de Conflans, and a number of other Burgundians of good standing whose names are not given here. After them came the Bishop of Autun, the Comte Guignes du Forez, the two Hugues de Bergy, father and son, and Hugues de Coligny. Meanwhile, down south, in Provence, Pierre de Bromont, together with many others whose names I do not know, had also taken the cross.

Thus throughout the whole country people were getting ready to go on pilgrimage. Alas! what a great misfortune they suffered in the following Lent, before they were due to start. The Comte Geoffroy du Perche fell ill and took to his bed, leaving instructions in his will to the effect that his brother Étienne should have his money and take command of his men in the army. (The pilgrims would gladly have done without this exchange, had God so willed it.) Thus the count came to his end. This was indeed a very great loss; for he was a noble of very high rank and greatly esteemed, a truly good and valiant knight. He was deeply mourned by all the people on his lands.

CHAPTER 4

Delays and Disappointments
JUNE–SEPTEMBER 1202

AFTER Easter, and towards Whitsuntide, the Crusaders began to leave their different provinces. Many a tear, as you may well imagine, was shed for sorrow at parting from their lands, their own people, and their friends. On their journey southward they rode through Burgundy, over the Alps and Mont Cenis, then on through Lombardy, and gradually began to assemble at Venice, where they took up their quarters on the island of San Niccolo di Lido.

About the same time a fleet of ships, which carried a very large contingent of men-at-arms, had set sail from Flanders to travel round by the coast. The men in charge of this fleet were Jean de Nesles, Governor of Bruges, the Comte Philippe de Flandre's son Thierry, and Nicolas de Mailly. They had all promised the Comte Baudouin, and bound themselves by oath on the Holy Gospels, to sail through the Straits of Morocco,[1] and join the count and the army then assembling at Venice at whatever place to which they might hear he had gone. On this account the Comte Baudouin and his brother Henri had entrusted them with some of their own ships, loaded with clothing, food, and other supplies.

This fleet was very fine and well equipped; the Comte de Flandre and his fellow Crusaders had greatly relied on it, because it carried most of their best sergeants. But the men in charge, and all the people with them, broke the promise they had made to their lord, because, like so many others of their sort, they were afraid to face the great perils of the enterprise that the army in Venice had undertaken.

In much the same way the Bishop of Autun also failed to keep faith with us, as did the Comte Guignes de Forez, Pierre Bromont, and many others. These were severely blamed for their action, and achieved but little in the place to which they went. Among those from the Île-de-France who failed us were Bernard de Moreuil, Hugues de Chaumont, Henri d'Araines, Jean de Villers, Gautier de Saint-Denis and his brother Hugues, and with them many others, all of whom avoided coming to Venice because of the great risk involved,

[1] Straits of Gibraltar.

and sailed instead from the port of Marseilles. They were much despised and greatly blamed for this; and as a consequence of their bad conduct they met with much misfortune later on.

I will now leave speaking of these men to tell you something about the pilgrims, a great part of whom had already arrived in Venice. The Comte Baudouin de Flandre was there, and many others, when news reached them that a great number of their fellows were travelling by various routes to other ports. This seriously worried the barons, because it meant that they could not fulfil their promise to the Venetians, nor pay them the money that was due.

After conferring together, they decided to send reliable emissaries to meet the Comte Louis de Blois and the other Crusaders who had not yet arrived, in order to bid them pluck up their courage and beg them to take pity on the land oversea, while at the same time pointing out that no other route except by way of Venice could be of any advantage to them.

The men chosen for this mission were the Comte Hugues de Saint-Pol and Geoffroy de Villehardouin. They rode northwards till they reached Pavia in Lombardy, where they found the Comte Louis with a very great company of worthy knights and other men of good standing. By dint of encouragements and entreaties they persuaded a good number of those who would otherwise have taken a different road and gone to other parts to ride to Venice.

None the less, on coming to Piacenza, many good men had turned aside to travel on their own to Apulia. Among them were Vilain de Neuilly, one of the finest knights in the world, Henri d'Arzillières, Renaud de Dampierre, Henri de Longchamp, and Gilles de Trasignies. The last-named of these was sworn vassal of the Comte Baudouin, who had given him, out of his own pocket, five hundred *livres* to accompany him on this journey. Along with these men went a great company of knights and sergeants whose names are not recorded in this book. All this meant a serious decrease in the number of those who should have come to join the forces in Venice, and as a result the army was in a most unhappy predicament, as you will shortly hear.

The Comte Louis and the other barons with him made their way to Venice. Here they were received with much rejoicing and feasting as they took up their quarters on the island of San Niccolo alongside the other Crusaders. It was a truly magnificent army, made up of very fine men. No one has ever seen so great a fighting force, nor one so imposing either. The Venetians set up a market for them, as abundantly supplied as any one could desire with everything necessary for the use of horses and men. The fleet they had got ready was so fine and well equipped that no man in the whole of Christendom has ever seen one to surpass it. It comprised so great a number of warships, galleys, and transports that it could easily have accommodated three times as many men as were in the whole of the army.

But ah! what immeasurable harm was caused by those who had gone off to other ports when they should have come to Venice! Had they only done so, Christendom would have been exalted, and the land of the Turks brought low. The Venetians had faithfully fulfilled all their undertakings, over and above what was necessary, and since they were now ready to start they summoned the counts and barons to fulfil theirs, by paying the money due.

Every man in the army was called upon to pay the cost of his passage. A very considerable number said they could not pay the full amount, so the barons took from them what money they could get. Each man therefore paid what he could. However, after the barons had demanded the cost of each man's passage, and everyone had contributed something, the money collected did not amount to half – much less the whole – of the sum required.

The barons met to discuss the situation. 'The Venetians,' said they, 'have faithfully observed the terms of their agreement with us, and generously, too. But there aren't enough of us here to manage, by paying the cost of all our passages, to fulfil our contract with them. This is the fault of those who have gone to other ports. For God's sake therefore let each of us contribute some of his own money, so that we may honour the promise we made. It would indeed be better for each of us to give all he has than default, and so lose all the money we've already paid in, as well as failing to keep our agreement. For if our expedition does not take place, our plan for delivering the land oversea will come to nothing.'

This proposal was greeted with lively disagreement by the great majority of the barons and others present. 'We've paid for our passage,' they said, 'and if the Venetians are willing to take us, we're quite ready to go. If not, we'll make shift for ourselves, and go some other way.' (They said this, in actual fact, because they would have liked the army to be disbanded, and each man free to go home.) On the other hand a minority declared: 'We'd much rather give all we have and go as poor men with the army than see it broken up and our enterprise a failure. For God will doubtless repay us in His own good time.'

Immediately after this meeting the Comte de Flandre started to hand over all that he had himself, or had been able to borrow. The Comte Louis did the same, so did the Marquis de Montferrat, as also the Comte Hugues de Saint-Pol and those who were of their party. It was a marvel to see the many fine table-services of gold and silver plate borne to the Doge's palace to make up the payment due. However, when everyone had contributed his share, the amount was still 34,000 marks short of the sum required. Those who had retained their possessions were highly delighted and refused to add anything of their own, since they were now quite confident that the army would be broken up and the troops dispersed. But God, who gives hope to men in the depths of despair, was not willing for this to happen.

At this point the Doge spoke to his people. 'Sirs,' he said, 'these men cannot pay us anything more; and since they are unable to keep the agreement they made with us we can retain what they have already paid. Our right to do this, however, would not be recognized in every part of the world; and if we exercised it, we and our state would be greatly blamed. So let us offer them terms.

'The King of Hungary has taken from us our city of Zara in Sclavonia, one of the strongest places in the world; and we shall never recover it, even with all the forces at our disposal, except with the aid of the French. So let us ask them to help us reconquer it and we will allow them to postpone payment of the 34,000 silver marks they owe us until such time as God shall permit our combined forces to win this money by conquest.' This proposal was therefore put to the barons. Those who wished the army to be disbanded raised many objections. None the less the agreement was finally concluded and ratified.

Shortly after this a great concourse of people assembled one Sunday in the church of San Marco. Everyone in the state of Venice was present, and so were most of the barons and the other crusaders. Before the beginning of high mass, Enrico Dandolo, Doge of Venice, mounted the steps of the lectern and addressed the congregation. 'Sirs,' he said, 'you are associated with the best and bravest people in the world in the highest enterprise anyone has ever undertaken. Now I am an old man, weak and in need of rest, and my health is failing. All the same I realize that no one can control and direct you like myself, who am your lord. If you will consent to my taking the cross so that I can protect and guide you, and allow my son to remain here in my place to guard this state, then I shall go to live or die with you and with the pilgrims.'

On hearing the Doge's words, all the Venetians cried out with one accord: 'We beg you in God's name to take the cross and go with us.' At that moment the hearts of all those present, French and Venetians alike, were deeply moved, and many a tear was shed out of sympathy for this good and worthy man who would have had so much reason to remain behind. For he was very old, and although his eyes appeared bright and clear, he was none the less totally blind, having lost his sight through a wound in the head. He was a man of great heart. Ah! how little like him were those who had gone to other ports to escape danger!

The Doge stepped down from the lectern, and going towards the altar, knelt before it, weeping bitterly. They sewed the cross on to the front of his great cotton cap, because he wished everyone to see it. Numbers of Venetians now began to come up in crowds to take the cross. Up to that day very few had done so. As for our crusaders, they had watched the Doge's taking of the cross with joy and deep emotion, greatly moved by the courage and wisdom shown by this good old man.

As soon as possible after this the Venetians began to hand over the warships, galleys, and transports to the barons so that they might start on their way. But by now so much time had already passed that it was well on into September.

Here let me tell you of one of the most remarkable and extraordinary events you have ever heard of. In Constantinople, shortly before the time of which I have been speaking, there was an Emperor whose name was Isaac. He had a brother named Alexius, whom he had ransomed from captivity among the Turks. This Alexius had subsequently taken his brother prisoner and torn out his eyes, and by such treachery had made himself emperor in Isaac's place. He had kept his brother for a long time in close confinement, together with his son, who was also named Alexius. The young prince had escaped from prison and fled in a ship to a city on the coast called Ancona.

From there he had set off for Germany, to visit King Philip, who was his brother-in-law. On his journey through Italy he had stopped at Verona, where he had stayed for some time, and met a number of pilgrims and other people who were on their way to join the army.

Those who had helped him to escape, and were still with him, had said to him: 'My lord, there's an army quite near us in Venice, made up of people of the highest rank and the bravest knights in the world, who are about to go oversea. Why not appeal to them to take pity on you and your father, who have been so unjustly dispossessed? It's quite possible they'll be moved by your plight.' The young prince replied that he would gladly do as they said, since their advice was good.

So he had appointed envoys and sent them both to the Marquis de Montferrat, who was in command of the army, and to the other barons. After the French lords had interviewed these emissaries, they were filled with amazement at their story, and said to them: 'We quite understand the situation. Since the Prince Alexius is on his way to see King Philip we'll send our envoys with him. If your young lord will agree to help us to reconquer Jerusalem, we in our turn will help him to regain his empire which, as we know, has been wrongfully taken from him and his father.' So envoys had been sent to Germany, both to the Prince of Constantinople and to King Philip.

A little before the events I have just related, the barons and all the rest of the army had been deeply grieved by news of the death of the good and saintly Foulques, who had first preached the Crusade. But shortly after Alexius had sent his envoys to Venice their spirits were greatly cheered by the arrival of a company from Germany, including many men of high rank and standing such as the Bishop of Halberstadt, the Graf Berthold von Katzellenbogen, Garnier von Borlande, Dietrich von Los, Heinrich von Ulmen, Roger von Susteren, Alexander von Villers, and Orry von Daun.

CHAPTER 5

Siege of Zara

OCTOBER–NOVEMBER 1202

THE time had now come for the barons to assign the warships and transports to their various commanders. Heavens! what fine, strong war-horses were then put below deck! As soon as all the ships had been fully loaded with arms and provisions, and the knights and sergeants had come aboard, the shields were hung round the bulwarks and round the castles*¹ fore and aft, while banners, many and beautiful, were quickly hoisted aloft.

The warships, I can assure you, carried more than three hundred petraries* and mangonels,* as well as a plentiful supply of all such mechanical devices as are of use in taking a city. No finer fleet of ships ever set sail from any port. The time of their departure from Venice fell within the octave of Saint Remigius, in the year of our Lord 1202.

Our army arrived before Zara in Sclavonia on Saint Martin's Eve, and saw the city enclosed by high walls and lofty towers. You would have sought in vain for a more beautiful place, or one more strongly defended, or more prosperous. As soon as the pilgrims caught sight of it they were filled with amazement, and said to each other: 'How could such a city be taken by force, except by the help of God Himself?'

The first ships to reach Zara cast anchor and waited for the others. The next morning the day dawned very bright and clear. The galleys and the transports came up with the other ships that had been behind, and the whole fleet, advancing together, broke through the stout, well-made chain across the harbour, and took the port by storm. Then the army landed in such a way as to keep the harbour between themselves and the town. What followed was a most marvellous sight: knights and sergeants swarming out of the warships, numbers of sturdy war-horses taken out of the transports, countless fine tents and pavilions unloaded ready to pitch. Thus our forces encamped

¹ Asterisks in the text refer to the Glossary.

before Zara, which they started to besiege on Saint Martin's Day [11 November].

As yet, however, not all the barons had arrived. The Marquis de Montferrat, for one, was absent, having stayed behind to attend to some business of his own. Étienne du Perche and Mathieu de Montmorency had been left ill in Venice. As soon as they had recovered the latter came to rejoin the forces at Zara; Étienne du Perche did not behave so well, for he deserted from the army and went to stay for a time in Apulia. With him went Rotrou de Montfort and Yves de la Jaille, together with many others, who were all much blamed for their defection. These men sailed for Syria in the following spring.

The morning after Saint Martin's Day certain citizens of Zara came out of the town and went to speak with the Doge of Venice in his pavilion. They told him they were ready to place the city and all their possessions at his discretion, provided their lives were spared. The Doge replied that he could not agree to such terms, nor indeed to any others, without first consulting the barons, with whom he would talk the matter over at once.

While he was on his way to confer with the barons, that group of men I have already mentioned, who wished to have the army disbanded, came and spoke to the deputation from Zara. 'Why do you want to surrender your city?' they asked. 'The French at any rate won't attack you; you've nothing to fear from them. If only you can defend yourselves against the Venetians, you've no cause to worry.' These trouble-makers picked one of their own party, named Robert de Boves, who went up to the walls of the city and repeated their words. The deputation therefore went back to Zara, and the matter of making terms was left in abeyance.

Meanwhile the Doge had met the barons and spoken to them. 'My lords,' he said, 'the people of this city are ready to surrender it at my discretion, on condition that their lives are spared. However, I will not make peace with them on these terms, nor on any others, except with your consent.' 'My lord,' replied the barons, 'we advise, and even beg you, to accept the terms they offer.' The Doge said he would do as they advised. So they all returned together to the Doge's pavilion to conclude the agreement, only to find that the deputation had gone away on the advice of those who wished to break up the army.

At this point a certain Abbot of Vaux, of the Cistercian order, rose to his feet and said: 'My lords, in the name of the Pope of Rome I forbid you to attack this city; for the people in it are Christians, and you wear the sign of the cross.' Greatly disturbed and vexed by such a protest, the Doge turned to the counts and barons. 'My lords,' he said, 'I was given power to make what terms I liked with this city, and now your own people have taken it from me. However, you have given me your promise to assist me in conquering it, and I now summon you to keep your word.'

Thereupon the counts and barons, with those who supported them, withdrew to confer together. 'The men responsible for breaking off negotiations,' they said, 'have acted outrageously; they haven't let a day pass without trying to break up our army. Now we may consider ourselves disgraced if we don't help to take the city.' They therefore went to the Doge and said: 'My lord, we'll help you to take Zara, in spite of those who've tried to prevent our doing so.'

Such was their decision. The next morning the troops encamped in front of the gates of the city. They set up their petraries and mangonels and other machines of war, which they had in plentiful supply; meanwhile, on the seaward side, scaling ladders were raised from all the ships in the harbour. The petraries now began to shoot stones at the walls and towers of Zara. This assault went on for about five days; and then sappers were set to work on one of the towers, and began to undermine the wall. The people inside the town no sooner saw what was happening than they offered to surrender, on the very terms they had previously rejected by the advice of those who wished to break up our army.

Thus Zara was placed in the Doge's hands, on condition that all the lives of its citizens should be spared. After this the Doge approached the barons and said: 'My lords, by God's grace and with your support we've taken this city. It's already winter, and we can't stir from here till Easter; for we'd have no chance of getting supplies in any other place, while this city, on the other hand, is very rich, and well-supplied with everything we may need. We'll therefore divide in two, and we shall occupy one half, while you take the other.' Everything was done according to plan. The Venetians occupied the part of the city towards the harbour, where their ships were lying; the French took the other part. The fine houses in each half of Zara were allotted as seemed most suitable. The army struck camp, and took up quarters inside the city.

Three days later, when everyone had been duly housed, it happened round about vesper-time that our troops encountered very serious trouble. Certain of the French and the Venetians became involved in a grim and bitter hand-to-hand tussle, and from every part of the city men ran to arms. The brawl increased to such an extent that soon there were very few streets in which there was not a fierce clash of swords and lances, bolts, and arrows; and many people were either killed or wounded.

The Venetians, however, could not stand up to the fight, and began to suffer serious losses. When matters were at this height, the chief men in the army, who did not wish any harm to happen, came fully armed into the midst of the mêlée, and began to separate the combatants. But as soon as they stopped the fighting in one place, it broke out in another. The conflict continued thus for a good part of the night; but none the less, after tremendous efforts and a great deal of trouble, it was finally stopped. Such a contest, I may say, was the greatest misfortune that ever happened to an army; ours indeed had a narrow escape from being completely wiped out. But God would not permit such a disaster.

Both sides suffered heavy losses. Among those killed was Gilles de Landas, a Flemish noble of high rank, who was struck in the eye and died from his wound in the course of the brawl. There were many other casualties, but these attracted less attention. The Doge and the barons worked their hardest during the rest of the week to calm the bitter feelings aroused by the fight, and laboured so effectually that peace was finally restored. All thanks to God for this.

CHAPTER 6

Discord in the Army

DECEMBER 1202–MAY 1203

TWO weeks later the Marquis de Montferrat, who had not yet re-joined the army, arrived at Zara in company with Mathieu de Montmorency, Pierre de Bracieux, and many other good men. A fortnight after that envoys sent from Germany by King Philip and the Crown Prince of Constantinople arrived in their turn. The barons assembled in a palace where the Doge of Venice was then living, and here the envoys delivered their message.

'My lords,' they said, 'we have been sent to you by King Philip and his brother-in-law, the son of the Emperor of Constantinople. "My lords," so says his Majesty, "I will send you my wife's brother, whom I commit into the hands of God – may He preserve him from death! – as also into yours. Since you are on the march in the service of God, and for right and justice, it is your duty, in so far as you can, to restore their possessions to those who have been wrong-fully dispossessed. The Prince Alexius will make the best terms with you ever offered to any people, and give you the most powerful support in conquering the land oversea.

'"Firstly, if God permits you to restore his inheritance to him, he will place his whole empire under the authority of Rome, from which it has long been estranged. Secondly, since he is aware that you have spent all your money and now have nothing, he will give you 200,000 silver marks, and provisions for every man in your army, officers and men alike. Moreover, he himself will go in your company to Egypt with ten thousand men, or, if you prefer it, send the same number of men with you; and furthermore, so long as he lives, he will maintain, at his own expense, five hundred knights to keep guard in the land oversea."

'My lords,' the envoys added, 'we have full power to conclude this agreement, if you on your side are willing to accept its terms. We might point out that such favourable conditions have never before been offered to anyone, and the man who could refuse to accept them can have little wish to conquer anything at all.'

The barons replied that they would talk the matter over. A conference was therefore arranged for the following day. As soon as everyone had assembled the terms of the agreement were laid before them.

There was a great divergence of opinion in the assembly. The Cistercian Abbot of Vaux had something to say, in common with those who were eager to have the army disbanded. They all declared they would never give their consent, since it would mean marching against Christians. They had not left their homes to do any such thing, and for their part they wished to go to Syria.

The other party replied: 'My good lords, you can accomplish nothing in Syria, as you can easily see if you consider the fate of those who deserted us to sail from other ports. We must insist that only by way of Egypt and Greece can we hope to recover the land oversea, if that ever happens at all. If we reject this agreement, it will be to our everlasting disgrace.'

So there was discord in the army. Nor can you wonder if the laymen were at loggerheads, when the Cistercians accompanying the forces were equally at variance with each other. The Abbot of Loos, esteemed for his goodness and his wisdom, preached to the troops, as did other abbots of his party, all earnestly exhorting them, in God's name, to keep the army together, and accept the proposed agreement, because, so they urged, 'it offered the best chance of winning back the land oversea'. The Abbot of Vaux, on the other hand, with those clerics who supported him, addressed the army on many occasions, declaring that the other party's plan was no good at all, and that they ought rather to make for Syria, and there do what they could.

At this juncture the Marquis de Montferrat, the Comte Baudouin de Flandre et de Hainaut, the Comte Louis de Blois et de Chartrain, and the Comte Hugues de Saint-Pol, together with others who sided with them, intervened in the dispute to announce that they, for their part, intended to accept the agreement, since they would be shamed if they rejected it. So they went to the Doge's palace, and after the envoys had been summoned, the covenant was confirmed, in such terms as have already been mentioned, by charters duly signed and sealed.

I must tell you here that only twelve persons in all took the oaths on behalf of the French; no more could be persuaded to come forward. The first to swear was the Marquis de Montferrat, and after him the

Comte Baudouin de Flandre, the Comte Louis de Blois, the Comte de Saint-Pol, and then the eight others of their party. So the covenant was ratified, and the charters drawn up. A date was then fixed for the Prince of Constantinople's arrival; this was to be a fortnight after Easter in the following year.

The army spent the whole of that winter in Zara, on guard against the King of Hungary. I can assure you that the hearts of our people were not at peace, for one party was continually working to break up the army, and the other to keep it together.

During this time many men from the lower ranks deserted and escaped in merchant ships. About five hundred of them got away in one ship, but all of them lost their lives by drowning. Another group escaped by land, thinking to travel safely through Sclavonia; but the people of that country attacked them, killing a great number, and those who were left came flying back to the army. Thus our forces dwindled seriously from day to day. About the same time Garnier von Borland, who had come to us from Germany, and held a high rank in our army, contrived to get a passage aboard a merchant ship, and so deserted. He was greatly blamed for such conduct.

Not long afterwards, one of the great barons of France, named Renaud de Montmirail, pleaded so earnestly that, with the support of the Comte Louis, he was sent on a mission to Syria in one of the ships of the fleet. He and all the knights who went with him swore on the Holy Gospels that not more than a fortnight after they had arrived in Syria and delivered their message they would come back to rejoin the army. On that condition Renaud was given leave to go. He took with him his nephew Hervé du Châtel, Guillaume, the *vidame* of Chartres, Geoffroy de Beaumont, Jean de Frouville and his brother Pierre, and many others. But they did not keep their oaths at all well; for they never came back to the army.

A little later our troops were greatly pleased on hearing news that the fleet from Flanders, of which I have already spoken, had arrived at Marseilles. Jean de Nesles, Governor of Bruges, who was in command of that army, together with the Comte Philippe de Flandre's son Thierry, and Nicolas de Mailly, sent to inform their lord the Comte Baudouin de Flandre that they were wintering in that port. They asked him to say what orders he had for them, assuring him at the same time that they would do whatever he commanded. After consulting the Doge of Venice and the French barons the count told them to sail at the end of March, and come to meet him at the port of Methone in Romania. Alas! they acted very badly; for they broke their word, and sailed instead for Syria, where, as they must have known, they could do nothing worth while. I can assure you, gentlemen, that if God had not loved our army, it could never have held together when so many people wished it ill.

In the course of the winter the barons conferred together and decided to send a deputation to Rome to see the Pope, who was seriously displeased with them on account of their capture of Zara. They chose as envoys two knights and two men in holy orders whom they knew to be well fitted for such a mission. One of the two clerics was Névelon, Bishop of Soissons, the other Jean de Noyon, chancellor to the Comte Baudouin de Flandre. The two knights were Jean de Friaize and Robert de Boves. These four men swore on the Holy Gospels that they would carry out their mission faithfully and loyally, and then rejoin the army.

Three were scrupulously faithful to their oath; the fourth, Robert de Boves, proved untrustworthy. Indeed, he could not have carried out his mission any worse; for he broke his word, and went off to Syria, as others had done before him. The remaining three performed their duty conscientiously, and delivered their message to the Pope as the barons had directed. 'Your Holiness,' they said, 'our lords beg you to take a merciful view of their capture of Zara, seeing that they acted as people who had no better choice, both through the fault of those who had gone to other ports, and because they had no other way of keeping the army together. They therefore ask you, as their good Father, to tell them what you are pleased to command, and they will readily obey.'

The Pope told the envoys he was well aware that they had been driven to act in this way through other people's default, and that he felt great compassion for them. So he sent back a message of greeting to the barons and the other Crusaders, giving them his blessing and informing them he gave them absolution as his sons. He begged and commanded them to keep the army together, since he knew well that without such forces the service of God could not be accomplished. Meanwhile he gave full authority to the Bishop of Soissons and Jean de Noyon to bind and to unloose the pilgrims until such time as his cardinal came to visit the army.

By now so much time had passed that it was already Lent, and the

Crusaders were beginning to get their fleet in trim to sail at Easter. On Easter Monday, after the ships had been loaded, our troops encamped close to the harbour, while the Venetians razed the city to the ground, with all its walls and towers. At this point an event occurred which was of serious concern to the army. Simon de Montfort, one of the great barons in command of the forces, having made a private agreement with our enemy the King of Hungary, went over to his side, and deserted us. With him went his brother Guy de Montfort, Simon de Neauphle, Robert Mauvoisin, Dreux de Cressonsacq, the Cistercian Abbot of Vaux, and many others. Nor was it very long before another noble of high rank in the army, called Enguerrand de Boves, also left us, taking with him his brother Hugues, and as many men from their domains as they could persuade to accompany them. Such defections were a great misfortune for the army, and a great disgrace to those who left it.

The warships and the transports now got under way. It was agreed that they should take port at Corfu, an island within the empire of Constantinople, where the first to arrive would wait for the late-comers, until they had all collected. This happened according to plan.

Before the Doge and the Marquis de Montferrat set off from Zara with the galleys, Alexius, the son of the Emperor Isaac of Constantinople, who had been sent there by King Philip of Germany, had arrived at the town. He was received with great joy and honour, and the Doge gave him as many galleys and other vessels as he required. So they left the port of Zara, borne onwards by a favourable wind, until at length they sailed into harbour at Durazzo. As soon as the people of that place saw their young lord arriving, they willingly surrendered their town into his hands and swore allegiance to him.

On leaving Durazzo the Prince Alexius and his party sailed to Corfu, and on their arrival found the army encamped before the town. The tents and pavilions were already pitched, and the horses had been taken out of the transports to give them an airing. The moment our troops heard that the son of the Emperor of Constantinople had arrived in port a crowd of good knights and sergeants, leading many a fine war-horse forth, could be seen hastening to meet him. So the army welcomed him with great joy and paid him much honour. The prince gave orders for his tent to be pitched right in the midst of the troops, while the Marquis de Montferrat, in whose charge

King Philip, the young man's brother-in-law, had placed him, had his own tent pitched close by.

The army stayed for three weeks in Corfu, which was a very fertile island, and well supplied with food. During this time a most unfortunate and painful incident occurred. A great number of those who were seeking to break up the army, and who on previous occasions had acted against its interests, now met together and declared that the enterprise on which we had embarked seemed to them likely to be very long and very dangerous. They would therefore remain on the island, and let the rest of the troops go on without them. Then, as soon as the army had left, they would contrive, with the help of the people of Corfu, to get a message through to the Comte Gautier de Brienne, who at the time was occupying Brindisi, asking him to send them ships to take them back to his town.

I cannot tell you the names of all those who had a hand in this affair; but I will mention a number of those who took a chief part in it. These were Eudes de Champlitte, Jacques d'Avesnes, Pierre d'Amiens, Guy, Châtelain de Coucy, Ogier de Saint-Chéron, Guy de Chappes and his nephew Clarembaud, Guillaume d'Aunoi, Pierre Coiseau, Guy de Pesmes and his brother Aimon, Guy de Conflans, Richard de Dampierre, and his brother Eudes. Apart from these there were many others who had secretly promised to join their party, but dared not for very shame admit it openly. Indeed, it is only true to say that more than half the men in the army were of the same mind.

As soon as the Marquis de Montferrat, the Comte Baudouin de Flandre, the Comte Louis, the Comte de Saint-Pol and the barons who agreed with them realized the situation, they were seriously disturbed. 'My lords,' said they, 'we're in a pretty desperate position. If these men leave us, as so many have already done on different occasions, the army's doomed, and we'll never conquer anything. So why don't we go and beg them, for God's sake, to show some consideration for themselves and for us, and not disgrace themselves nor deprive us of the chance of delivering the land oversea.'

They decided to do this, and all went in a body to a valley where the other party had gathered in conference, taking with them the young Prince of Constantinople and all the bishops and abbots who were with the forces. As soon as they arrived there they dismounted, while the others, seeing them come, also got off their horses, and came to meet them. The marquis and those with him fell at the feet of the other party, weeping bitterly, and said they would not get up again until these men had promised not to go away and leave them.

At this the would-be deserters were deeply moved, and burst into tears at the sight of their lords, their relations, and their friends on their knees before them. So they said they would consult together, and withdrew to a short distance to talk the matter over. The upshot of their deliberations was that they agreed to remain with the army until Michaelmas, on condition the others would duly swear on the Holy Gospels that from that time onwards, at what ever moment they might be required to do so, they would, in all good faith and without any double-dealing, provide them with sufficient ships in which to go to Syria within a fortnight of their making such a demand.

The compact was accordingly made and ratified by oath. Immediately there was great joy throughout the army. Every man got aboard his ship, and the horses were put into the transports.

CHAPTER 7

Voyage to Scutari

MAY–JUNE 1203

THE army sailed from the port of Corfu on the eve of Pentecost, in the year of our Lord 1203. The whole of the fleet was assembled there: the warships, the transports and galleys of the army, as also a fairly large number of merchant ships that were accompanying the forces. The day was fine and sunny, the wind mild and favourable; the ships had unfurled their sails to the breeze.

Geoffroy de Villehardouin, Marshal of Champagne, and the author of this work – who has never, to his knowledge, put anything in it contrary to the truth, and who was present, moreover, at all the conferences recorded in its pages – here testifies that so fine a sight had never been seen before. It seemed, indeed, that here was a fleet that might well conquer lands, for as far as the eye could reach there was nothing to be seen but sails outspread on all that vast array of ships, so that every man's heart was filled with joy at the sight.

The ships sailed on, across a wide expanse of water, till they came to Cape Malia, at the far end of the straits in between two stretches of open sea. Here they happened to meet two ships on their way back from Syria, full of knights, sergeants, and pilgrims who were part of the company that had gone to that country by way of Marseilles. On seeing our fleet so fine and well equipped these men were so overcome with shame that they did not dare show their faces. The Comte Baudouin de Flandre sent out a boat from his ship to inquire their business, and was told who they were.

A sergeant in one of these ships slipped over the side, and dropping down into the count's boat, called out to those he had left on deck: 'You men can do what you like with anything I've left behind. I'm going with these people, for it certainly seems to me they'll win some land for themselves.' This man was given a most hearty welcome by the troops, all of whom thought him a very good fellow. And after all, as people are wont to say, no matter how often a man may have gone astray, he can still come round to the right way in the end.

Continuing its course, the fleet sailed on as far as Negropont, on which there is a very fine town of the same name. Here the barons held a conference, after which the Marquis Boniface de Montferrat and the Comte Baudouin de Flandre sailed away southwards, with a great part of the galleys and the transports, till they came to the island of Andros, where they landed. The knights armed themselves and overran the whole region, until at length the people of Andros appealed to the Emperor's son to take pity on them, and gave him so much of their money and their goods that they managed to make peace with him. The knights then rejoined their ships and sailed on their way. But during the voyage they suffered a great misfortune; for Guy, Châtelain de Coucy, a nobleman of very high standing in the army, died, and was buried at sea.

Meanwhile, the ships that had not taken a southerly course had entered the Channel of Abydos, where the Straits of St George meet the open sea. They sailed up the straits as far as Abydos, a very beautiful and well-situated town on the side of the water nearest Turkey. Here the troops left their ships in harbour and went on shore. The people of Abydos came out to meet them, and surrendered the town to them there and then, as men who have not sufficient courage to defend themselves. However, the army established such a good guard over the town that the people in it did not lose so much as the smallest coin in their currency.

The troops stayed there for a week while waiting for those warships, galleys, and transports that had not as yet come up to join them. During that time they took possession of the corn as it was reaped, for it was the harvest season; and they had great need of such supplies, having little of their own stores left. By the end of the week, since God had granted them fair weather, all the remaining ships and the rest of the barons had reached Abydos.

The whole fleet then set sail together from the port. At the moment of departure, the Straits of St George to eastward, with the full array of warships, galleys, and transports, seemed as it were in flower. It was, indeed, a marvellous experience to see so lovely a sight. The ships sailed onwards up the straits, until, on the eve of Saint John the Baptist's Day, they came alongside Saint Stephen's, an abbey some four or five miles distant from Constantinople, and from which point all those on board the ships had a full view of the city. Here the fleet came into port and the ships cast anchor.

I can assure you that all those who had never seen Constantinople before gazed very intently at the city, having never imagined there could be so fine a place in all the world. They noted the high walls and lofty towers encircling it, and its rich palaces and tall churches, of which there were so many that no one would have believed it to be true if he had not seen it with his own eyes, and viewed the length and breadth of that city which reigns supreme over all others. There was indeed no man so brave and daring that his flesh did not shudder at the sight. Nor was this to be wondered at, for never before had so grand an enterprise been carried out by any people since the creation of the world.

After the barons and the Doge of Venice had landed they held a conference in Saint Stephen's Abbey, in the course of which many differences of opinion emerged. I do not propose to tell you here of all the speeches made on that occasion, but I think it well to relate how towards the close of the proceedings the Doge rose to his feet and addressed the meeting. 'My lords,' he said, 'I know more about conditions in these parts than you do, since I have been here before. You are now engaged on the greatest and most dangerous enterprise that any people up to this day have ever undertaken; it is therefore most important for us to act wisely and prudently. Let me point out that if we go overland there is an enormous tract of country to cover, while our people are short of money and have very little to eat. Consequently they will scatter in all directions in search of food. Now the whole of this region is very thickly populated, and we cannot keep such a strict watch over our men that we do not lose some of them on the way. And that is just what we cannot afford to do, for we have but very few men for the scheme we have in hand.

'There are islands close by – you can see them from here – inhabited by people whose farms produce corn and meat and other such commodities. I suggest we take our ships into harbour there, to collect what corn and other provisions these islands can supply, and then, when we have laid in sufficient stores of food, take up our stand before the city, and acquit ourselves as our Lord and Saviour shall ordain. For the man who has something to eat fights with a better chance of winning than the one with nothing in his stomach.' The barons agreed to act as the Doge had advised; and then the whole company dispersed to return to their ships.

The army rested that night. In the morning, which was Saint

John the Baptist's Day, the banners and pennons were hoisted on the
castles of all the ships, and the shields, now stripped of their coverings,
hung round every bulwark. Each man took care to see that such
arms and equipment as he would use were in fit condition, for everyone was well aware these would be needed before very long.

The sailors weighed anchor and spread their canvas to the wind;
God gave them a good following breeze such as they needed. The
fleet passed in front of Constantinople, so close to its walls and towers
that our men were able to shoot at many of the Greek ships. So many
people had crowded on to the battlements that it seemed as if there
could be no more left in the rest of the world put together.

Thus it happened, by God's will, that the barons had to abandon
the plan agreed on the day before of sailing towards the islands, so that
in effect it was just as though no one had ever heard such a project
mentioned. And now they were heading towards the mainland, as
straight as their ships could steer. The fleet was brought to harbour in
front of a palace belonging to the Emperor Alexius, at a place called
Chalcedon, which is situated directly opposite Constantinople, on the
side of the straits nearest Turkey. This palace was one of the most
beautiful and most enchanting that ever eye could see, with every
delight in it that a man could wish for, or that ought to be in a prince's
house.

After landing, the barons took up their quarters in the palace, or
round about it in the town. The greater part of them had their
pavilions pitched. When all was ready, the horses were taken out of
the transports, while the knights and sergeants landed with their full
equipment of arms, so that no one was left in the ships except the
sailors. The country round Chalcedon was beautiful and fertile, and
plentifully supplied with good provisions of all sorts and kinds. The
corn, which had just been reaped, was piled up in stooks in the open
fields, so that anyone in desperate need of it could take as much as he
wanted.

The barons spent the following day in the precincts of the palace.
Two days later, when God had sent them a favourable wind, the
sailors weighed anchor, and with canvas spread to catch the breeze,
passed up the straits, a good league above Constantinople, as far as
another palace belonging to the Emperor Alexius, at a place called
Scutari. Here all the ships, including the galleys and the transports,
cast anchor, while in the meantime all the knights who had been

quartered in and about the palace of Chalcedon had made their way by land along the shore.

The French army was thus encamped on the Straits of St George, both at Scutari and farther up the coast. On learning of its movements the Emperor Alexius brought his own army out of Constantinople and took up his position on the other side of the straits, directly opposite to the French encampment. Here he pitched his tents, so as to be ready to resist any attempt on our part to affect a landing by storm. The French troops remained where they were for the next nine days. Those who had need of supplies obtained them for themselves – and that meant every man in the army.

CHAPTER 8

Preparations for an Assault
26 JUNE–4 JULY 1203

WHILE the troops were at Scutari a company of good and trust-worthy men, whose duty was to stay outside the camp to guard the army against a surprise attack and to protect the foragers, started out one day to explore the country round about. Among this company were Eudes de Champlitte and his brother Guillaume, Ogier de Saint-Chéron, Manassier de l'Isle, and the Comte Gérard, a nobleman of Lombardy who was a vassal of the Marquis de Montferrat. They had with them about eighty good, stout knights.

In the course of their reconnaissance they caught sight of some pavilions pitched at the foot of a mountain some three leagues away from the camp. These belonged to the Emperor of Constantinople's Lord Admiral, who had with him about five hundred Greek knights. As soon as our people spied this encampment, they formed their men into four companies with the intention of attacking it. At this the Greeks in their turn drew up their troops in battle formation, and ranged them in front of the pavilion, to await our onslaught. Our men advanced and attacked them vigorously.

By God's help, this fight did not last long, for the Greeks soon turned their backs and fled. They were routed at the first encounter, and our men pursued them for a full league and more. In this skirmish the victors gained a good number of war-horses, cobs, palfreys, and mules, and such other booty as is usual in such an affair. After this they came back to camp, and were warmly welcomed by their companions, with whom they shared their spoils in a fit and proper way.

The next day the Emperor sent a certain Nicolas Roux, who was a native of Lombardy, as an envoy to our camp, with a letter addressed to the counts and barons. He found them in conference at the fine palace of Scutari, and after greeting them on behalf of the Emperor Alexius of Constantinople delivered his letter to the Marquis de Montferrat. The marquis took it and read it aloud in the presence of all the barons. It contained many different things which this book will not record, noting only that they were followed by a statement attesting the reliability of the bearer, Nicolas Roux, and a request that credence should be given to what he said.

'My good sir,' said the marquis, 'we have noted the contents of your letter. It tells us to give credit to what you say, and that we certainly will. So speak freely and let us know what is in your mind.'

The envoy, standing before the barons, answered thus: 'My lords, the Emperor Alexius has sent me to say he is well aware that, next to kings, you are the noblest men alive, and come from the best country in the world. He therefore seriously wonders why, and for what purpose, you have entered this land over which he rules. For you are Christians just as he is, and he knows very well that you have left your own country to deliver the Holy Land oversea, and the Holy Cross and Sepulchre. If you are poor and in want of supplies, he will give you a share of his provisions and his money, provided you withdraw from his land. If you refuse to leave, he would be reluctant to do you harm, yet it is in his power to do so. For were you twenty times as many as you are, you would not, supposing he chose to harm you, be able to leave this country without losing many of your men and suffering defeat.'

By wish and consent of the other barons and the Doge of Venice, Conon de Béthune, a wise and worthy knight and an eloquent speaker,[1] rose to answer the envoy. 'My good sir,' said he, 'you have told us that your lord wonders very much why our lords and barons have entered his dominions. Our answer is that we have not entered *his* dominions, since he has wrongfully taken possession of this land, in defiance of God, and of right and justice. It belongs to his nephew, seated here on a throne amongst us, who is his brother the Emperor Isaac's son. However, if your lord will consent to place himself at the mercy of his nephew, and give him back his crown and his empire, we will beg the prince to allow him enough money to live in a wealthy style. But unless you return to give us such a message, pray do not venture to come here again.' So the envoy left and went back to Constantinople to see the Emperor Alexius.

On the following day the barons conferred together and decided to show the young Alexius, son of the rightful Emperor of Constantinople, to the people of the city. So they issued orders for all the

[1] Also of some repute as a poet.

galleys to be armed. The Doge of Venice and the Marquis de Mont-ferrat went aboard one, taking the Prince Alexius with them, while as many of the knights and barons as wished to accompany them entered the others.

They passed along quite close to the walls of Constantinople, and showed the young man to the Greeks. 'Here is your natural lord,' they said. 'We ask you to believe that we have not come to do you harm, but on the contrary to guard and defend you, provided you act as you ought. The man you now obey as your lord rules over you without just or fair claim to be your Emperor, in defiance of God and the right. You know very well how treacherously he has acted towards the man who is his lord and his brother, putting out his eyes and wickedly and wrongfully taking his empire from him. Here is your rightful lord and master. If you rally to his side you will be doing as you ought; but if you hold back, we will do to you the very worst that we can.' However, out of fear and terror of the Emperor Alexius, not a single man of that land or in the city dared show him-self on the young prince's side. So the barons returned to camp, and each man went to his quarters.

The next day, after attending mass, they gathered in council to-gether, all on horseback, in the open fields. Many a fine war-horse was to be seen there, and many a good knight in the saddle. The purpose of the conference was to arrange the ordering of the divisions, their number, and composition. There was much discussion on differ-ent matters of detail, but in the end it was settled that since the Comte Baudouin de Flandre had under him a greater number of experienced men and more archers and crossbowmen than any other lord in the army, he should be given charge of the advanced guard.

Next it was arranged that the count's brother Henri, with Mathieu de Wallincourt, Baudouin de Beauvoir, and many good knights who had come with them from their domains, should form the second division.

The third was placed in charge of the Comte Hugues de Saint-Pol, who had with him his nephew Pierre d'Amiens, Eustache de Canteleu, Anseau de Cayeux, and many other worthy knights from the same province.

The Comte Louis de Blois et de Chartrain was made responsible for the fourth. This was a very large, powerful, and imposing division, for it contained a very great number of brave knights and other men of good fighting calibre.

The men of Champagne, under Mathieu de Montmorency, made up the fifth division. Geoffroy, Marshal of Champagne, was in this one, together with Ogier de Saint-Chéron, Manassier de l'Isle, Milon le Brabant, Macaire de Sainte-Menehould, Jean Foisnon, Guy de Chappes and his nephew Clarembaud, and Robert de Ronsoi. It included, one may say, a considerable number of good knights.

The Burgundians formed the sixth division. Among these were Eudes de Champlitte and his brother Guillaume, Richard de Dampierre and his brother Eudes, Guy de Pesmes and his brother Aimon, Othon de la Roche and Guy de Conflans, together with men from the same province and from their several estates.

The seventh division, which was a very large one, was commanded by the Marquis de Montferrat. In it were the Lombards, the Tuscans, the Germans, and the men from all the lands extending from Mont Cenis to Lyons on the Rhône. It was arranged that this division should form the rearguard.

The day was now fixed on which the troops were to embark on their ships and go forward to take the land by force, and either live or die. It was, I can assure you, one of the most formidable enterprises ever to be undertaken. The bishops and the other clergy addressed the forces, pointing out the need for each man to make his confession and draw up his will, since no one knew what might be the purpose of God concerning him. These instructions were willingly and piously obeyed by every man in the army.

CHAPTER 9

First Siege of Constantinople
5–17 JULY 1203

THE appointed day arrived. All the knights and their war-horses were aboard the transports, every man fully armed, with his helmet laced and his mount duly saddled and caparisoned. Men of the lower ranks, as people of less consequence in battle, were stationed on the great warships. Every galley had been armed and made ready.

The morning shortly after sunrise was fine and clear. On the other side of the straits the Emperor Alexius stood waiting for the attack, with his army drawn up in numerous divisions and furnished with all the equipment needed for battle. The trumpets sounded. Each transport was attached by a tow-rope to a galley, so as to reach the other side more easily. No one asked which ship should go first, but whichever could start soonest reached land before the rest. The knights disembarked from the transports; they leapt into the sea up to their waists, fully armed, with helmets laced and lances in hand. In like manner our good archers, sergeants, and crossbowmen, each in his company, landed as soon as their ship touched ground.

The Greeks seemed prepared to put up a fair show of resistance; but no sooner were the knights' lances lowered than they all turned round and fled, abandoning the shore to our men. Never, I may say, was any port more proudly taken. The sailors now began to open the doors at the side of the transports and lead out the horses. The knights mounted quickly, while the divisions began to draw up in due order.

The Comte Baudouin de Flandre et de Hainaut, who commanded the advanced guard, rode forward at their head, with the other divisions following in their appointed order, till they all reached the place where the Emperor Alexius had been encamped. He, however, had retreated towards Constantinople, leaving his tents and pavilions standing. Our men gained a large amount of booty there.

Our barons decided to encamp alongside the harbour, in front of the tower of Galata, which was at one end of the chain that stretched from Constantinople across the harbour entrance. Now any ship that wished to enter the port could only do so by getting past that chain.

Our barons realized clearly that if they did not take that tower and break that chain they would be in a terrible situation, and as good as dead. So they spent that night in front of the tower, in a ghetto known as Estanor, which was in fact a very fine and wealthy little town.

The army kept good guard that night. In the morning, about nine o'clock, the Greeks in the tower of Galata, supported by others who had come up in barges from Constantinople, launched an attack on us. Our troops ran to arms; Jacques d'Avesnes and his men, all of them on foot, were the first to tackle the enemy. He, I may say, met with fierce resistance and was wounded in the face by a lance. He was perilously near to being killed outright when one of his knights, named Nicolas de Jenlain, leapt on a horse and successfully rescued his lord from danger. This same knight acquitted himself so well in the encounter that he won great praise for his gallant conduct.

A call to arms was raised in camp; our men rallied round from all sides, and drove the enemy back so vigorously that many of these were killed or taken prisoner. Certain of the Greeks, instead of retreating towards the tower, ran to get into the barges by which they had arrived. Many of these were drowned, but some got safely away. As for those who went back towards the tower, our troops followed so hard on their heels that they could not close the gate. There was more heavy fighting at the entrance, but our men captured the position by force and made prisoners of all those inside the tower. Many Greeks were killed or taken in the course of that affair.

Thus the fortress of Galata was captured, and entry to the port of Constantinople won by force of arms. Our troops were greatly cheered by this success, and praised our Lord with thankful hearts. The people of the city, on the other hand, were greatly depressed. The next day our whole fleet of warships, galleys, and transports was brought into the harbour.

At this point the leaders of the army met in conference to consider what plan of action they should follow – whether to attack by sea or by land. The Venetians were strongly of the opinion that the scaling ladders should be set up on the ships and the whole of the assault be made from the sea. The French, for their part, protested that they could not give such a good account of themselves on the sea as the Venetians; but once on land, with their horses and their proper equipment, they could do much better service. So in the end it was decided that the Venetians would launch their attack from the sea while the barons and their army would tackle the enemy by land.

The troops remained in camp for the next four days. On the fifth the whole army got ready, and the divisions advanced on horseback, each in its appointed order, along the north-east side of the harbour, until they were in front of the palace of Blachernae. At the same time the ships sailed up the harbour to its farthest end, exactly opposite the place where the French troops were stationed. Here a river runs into the sea, and can only be crossed by means of a stone bridge. The Greeks had broken down this bridge; so the barons set the army to work the whole of that day and the following night repairing it. The next morning, as soon as the bridge was in fit condition, the divisions were armed. They rode forward in due order, one behind the other, to take up their position before the city. Not a soul came out to attack them, and that was indeed surprising, since for every man we had in the army there were at least two hundred in Constantinople.

The barons decided to encamp between the palace of Blachernae and the castle of Bohémond, which was, in fact, an abbey enclosed behind high walls. Here they pitched their tents and pavilions. It was a sight to fill the heart with pride and apprehension, for the city of Constantinople had a frontage stretching inland for a good six or seven miles, and the whole of our army was only large enough to lay siege to one of its gates. Meanwhile the Venetians, in their ships on the water, had raised their ladders, set up their petraries and mangonels, and put all in excellent order for the assault. The barons, for their part, now got their own petraries and mangonels ready, and prepared for the attack by land.

During all this time, I may say, our army was by no means left in peace and quiet. There was, in fact, not a single hour of the day or night that one of our divisions did not have to stand fully armed before the gate of Blachernae, to keep guard over the machines and repel sorties from the city. In spite of all such precautions the Greeks did not fail to make frequent sallies from the city by this gate or others, and gave our troops so little respite that the whole camp had to be called to arms about six or seven times a day. No one, moreover, was able to stir in search of food any farther than four bowshots from the camp; and we were extremely short of supplies, except for flour and bacon, and very little indeed of these. The troops had no fresh meat at all, except what they got from the horses that were killed. There was, in fact, only sufficient food in the whole of the camp to last for the next three weeks. Our army was thus in an extremely desperate situation, for never, in any city, have so many been besieged by so few.

At this point the barons worked out an excellent plan of defence. They fortified the camp by enclosing it within a stout palisade of good, thick wooden planks and crossbeams, so making themselves far stronger and safer than before. The Greeks, however, continued to make such frequent sallies that they gave the troops no rest. None the less, whenever the enemy came out, our men in camp repulsed them vigorously, and on each occasion the Greeks suffered heavy losses.

One day, when the Burgundians were on guard, a company of the best troops in the Greek army made a sudden sally from the city and attacked them. Our men, for their part, flew at the enemy and attacked them so fiercely that they drove them back. In their pursuit of the Greeks they followed so close to the gate that men on the walls threw great heavy stones down on top of them. In this affair one of the best Greeks in the city, named Constantine Lascaris, was captured, while still on horseback, by Gautier de Neuilly. During the fight Guillaume de Champlitte's arm was broken by a stone. This was a great pity, for he was a very good and gallant knight.

I do not propose to tell you of all the blows given and received in this encounter, nor the number of dead and wounded. I will, however, mention that, before the fight was over, a knight in the service of the Comte Baudouin's brother Henri came to join the fray. He had nothing to protect him but a padded jerkin, a steel cap, and a shield hung from his neck. None the less he acquitted himself so well that he won great honour.

There were very few days on which no sorties were made; but I cannot record them all. Sufficient to say that the Greeks continued to press our men so hard that they could neither sleep, nor eat, nor rest, except fully armed. I might perhaps mention one sortie from a gate along the walls, in which the enemy once more lost heavily. One of our knights named Guillaume du Gi was killed in this encounter. On the same occasion Mathieu de Wallincourt distinguished himself, but lost his horse, which was killed on the drawbridge before the gate. Many other knights also did gallant service here. At the gate on the other side of the palace of Blachernae and from which the Greeks sallied out most frequently, Pierre de Bracieux won himself greater honour than anyone else, chiefly because his quarters were nearest to it so that he could more often take a hand in the fight.

Our army was subjected to these perils and trials of strength for close on ten days, until, one Thursday morning, everything, scaling ladders and all, had been prepared for the main assault. The Venetians, meanwhile, had made their own preparations on the water. The order of assault had been so arranged as to leave three divisions on guard outside the camp, while the other four advanced to attack the city. The Marquis de Montferrat's troops kept guard over the camp on the side towards the open country, supported by the Burgundian division and the men of Champagne under Mathieu de Montmorency. The Comte Baudouin de Flandre et de Hainaut led his division forward to the assault, in company with those in command of his brother Henri, the Comte Louis de Blois et de Chartrain and the Comte Hugues de Saint-Pol.

The French planted two scaling ladders against a barbican close to the sea. The wall here was strongly manned by Englishmen and Danes, and the struggle that ensued was stiff and hard and fierce. By dint of strenuous efforts two knights and two sergeants managed to scale the ladders and make themselves masters of the wall. A good fifteen of our men got up on top, and were quickly engaged in a hand-to-hand contest of battle-axes against swords. The Greeks inside the barbican plucked up courage and fought back so savagely that they drove our men out, while retaining two as prisoners. These captives were led before the Emperor Alexius, who was overjoyed to see them. Such was the outcome of the assault as far as the French were concerned. Many were wounded and many were left with broken limbs. The barons were greatly upset by such a state of affairs.

Meanwhile the Doge of Venice had not omitted to do his part, but had drawn up all his ships in battle formation, in a line extending some three cross-bow shots in length. Next the Venetians began to draw near to that part of the shore lying under the walls and towers. Then you could see their mangonels hurling stones from the decks of warships and transports, bolts from their crossbows flying across the water, archers loosing shower after shower of arrows, and the Greeks on their side fiercely defending the city from the top of its battlements, as the scaling ladders on the ships came so near that in many places swords and lances clashed one against the other. The din was so tremendous that it seemed as if both land and sea were crumbling in pieces. The galleys, however, did not dare to come to shore.

Let me tell you here of an outstanding deed of valour. The Doge of Venice, although an old man and completely blind, stood at the bow of his galley, with the banner of Saint Mark unfurled before him. He cried out to his men to put him on shore, or else he himself would deal with them as they deserved. They obeyed him promptly, for the galley touched ground and the men in it leapt ashore, bearing the banner of Saint Mark to land before the Doge.

As soon as the other Venetians saw this banner on land, and their lord's galley touching ground before them, every man of them felt deeply ashamed, and all made for the shore. The men in the transports leapt out and waded, while those in the bigger ships got into boats, and every one of them, each vying with the other to get there quickest, hastened to reach land. Then began a grand and marvellous assault on the city. Geoffroy de Villehardouin, author of this chronicle, here affirms that more than forty people solemnly assured him that they had seen the banner of Saint Mark flying from the top of one of the towers, but not one of them knew who had planted it there.

Now let me tell you of an event so marvellous that it might be called a miracle. The people within the city fled, abandoning the walls to the Venetians. These all rushed in through the gates, each trying to outstrip the others and took possession of twenty-five towers, which they manned with their own people. The Doge called for a boat to take messengers as quickly as possible to tell the barons that twenty-five towers had been seized, and to assure them that these could never be retaken. The barons, for their part, were so overjoyed that they could not believe the news to be true. Meanwhile the Venetians had begun to send boats to the French camp loaded with some of the horses and palfreys they had taken as booty in Constantinople.

When the Emperor Alexius saw that the Venetians had thus effected an entry into the city, he started to send his troops against them in such large numbers that they found it impossible to stand up against the enemy. They therefore set fire to the buildings between themselves and the Greeks. As the wind at that time was blowing from the Venetian side, the fire gradually became so great that the Greeks could not see their opponents, so these were able to withdraw in safety to the towers they had seized and conquered.

At this point the Emperor Alexius brought all his forces out of the city by some gates about a league away from our camp. So many men came streaming out that you would have thought the whole world was there assembled. After marshalling his divisions on the plain, the Emperor rode with them towards the French camp. That day the Comte Baudouin's brother, Henri de Flandre, was mounting guard over the machines, in company with Mathieu de Wallincourt, Baudouin de Beauvoir, and the men in their division. Over against them the Emperor Alexius had stationed a large contingent of his troops, with orders to issue by three gates and launch an attack on the camp from another side.

Our other six divisions now marched out of camp according to plan, and drew up in ranks in front of the palisade, the sergeants and squires on foot close behind their horses, the archers and crossbowmen in front. With them was also a company of knights on foot, for at least two hundred had lost their horses. They all stood quite still in front of the palisade, and very wisely too, for if they had advanced to attack the enemy on the plain, the Greeks were in such great numbers that they would, so to speak, have been drowned among them.

It looked as if the whole plain was covered with troops, advancing slowly and in good order. We were, it seemed, in a pretty desperate situation, since we had no more than six divisions, while the Greeks had close on sixty, and not one of them but was larger than any of ours. However, our troops were drawn up in such a way that they could not be attacked except from the front.

The Emperor Alexius now brought his men so far forward that either side could shoot at the other. On hearing of this the Doge of Venice sent orders to his men to come down from the towers they had taken, and declared he would live or die in the company of the pilgrims. So he came sailing towards the camp with as many men as he could bring with him, and was the first to set foot on shore.

For some considerable time the armies of the Crusaders and of the Greeks stood facing each other; for the Greeks did not dare to fling themselves on our ranks, and our men would not move away from their palisades. When the Emperor grasped the situation, he began to withdraw his troops, and as soon as he had rallied them he turned them round in the direction of the city. On seeing this the Crusaders' army started to march slowly towards him. The Greeks began to move away and finally retreated to the palace of Philopatrion.

I can assure you that God never delivered any people from greater peril than that from which He saved our troops that day. There was not a man in the army, however bold and courageous, whose heart was not filled with joy. Thus the battle was halted that day, and by God's will nothing further happened. The Emperor Alexius returned to the city, and our men went back to camp. Utterly weary and overwrought, they took off their armour and laid their weapons aside. They ate and drank little, since they were very short of supplies.

Let me now ask you to consider the miracles of our Lord – how wonderful they are whenever it pleases Him to perform them. That very night the Emperor Alexius collected as much of his money and his valuables as he could carry away, and taking with him those of his people who wished to go, fled and abandoned the city. The people of Constantinople were utterly astounded. They went to the prison in which the Emperor Isaac, whose eyes had been put out, was confined. They clothed him in his imperial robes, and carried him to the great palace of Blachernae, where they set him on a high throne, and swore allegiance to him as their lord. Then, with the Emperor Isaac's agreement, messengers were sent to tell the Prince Alexius and the barons that the usurper had fled, and the people of Constantinople had re-established his brother as their rightful Emperor.

As soon as the young prince heard the news he sent for the Marquis de Montferrat, who immediately summoned all the barons throughout the camp. As soon as they had all assembled in the pavilion of the Emperor Isaac's son, the prince told them the news. Their joy on hearing it was such as cannot well be described, for no greater joy was ever felt by anyone in this world. The whole company joined in the most devout and reverent praises of our Lord, for having within so short a time delivered them and exalted them so high from such a low estate. And therefore one may rightly say: 'The man whom God desires to help no other man can harm.'

CHAPTER 10

The Emperor's Covenant

As day was dawning, our men began to put on their armour and get their weapons ready to hand. Everyone throughout the camp did this, for none of them put much trust in the Greeks. Messengers started to come out of the city, all of them with the same tale to tell. The barons, in common with the Doge of Venice, decided to send their own envoys to Constantinople to find out how matters really stood. If what they had been told was true, they would request the father to ratify the covenants made by his son; otherwise they would not allow the young prince to enter the city. The envoys chosen for this mission were Mathieu de Montmorency and Geoffroy de Villehardouin, together with two Venetians appointed by the Doge.

These four men were conducted to the palace of Blachernae. As soon as the gate was opened they dismounted from their horses. The Greeks had posted Englishmen and Danes, equipped with battle-axes, at the gate and right up to the main door of the palace. On entering the building they found the Emperor Isaac, arrayed in such costly robes that one would have looked in vain to find a man anywhere more richly dressed. Beside him sat the Empress his wife, a very beautiful woman, who was the King of Hungary's sister. So many great lords and ladies were also there that there was hardly room to turn round. The ladies in particular were so richly attired that they could not have been any finer. All those who the day before had been against the Emperor were now only too willing to place themselves entirely at his disposal.

The envoys came and stood before the Emperor, while he and all the rest of the company paid them great honour. They told the Emperor that they wished to speak with him in private, on behalf of his son and the barons of the army. He got up and went into another room, taking with him no one except the Empress, his chancellor, his interpreter and the four envoys.

By common consent of his companions Geoffroy de Villehardouin, Marshal of Champagne, acted as spokesman. 'Your Imperial

Majesty,' he said, 'you know what service we have rendered your son, and you are aware that we have kept the terms of our agreement with him. We cannot, however, allow him to come here until he has given us a guarantee for the covenant he has made with us. He therefore, as your son, asks you to ratify this covenant in the same terms and the same manner as he has done himself.' 'What are the terms of this covenant?' asked the Emperor. 'I will tell you,' replied the envoy.

'The terms are as follows: First of all to place the whole of this empire under the jurisdiction of Rome, from which it has long since broken away; further, to give 200,000 silver marks to the army and a full year's supply of provisions to men of all ranks; to convey 10,000 men, in his own ships to Egypt, and keep them there at his own expense for a year; and, during his lifetime, to maintain, at his own expense, a company of 500 knights in the land oversea, to keep guard over it. Such is the covenant your son has made with us. It has been confirmed by oath and by sealed charters, and guaranteed, moreover, by your son-in-law, King Philip of Germany. We now desire you to confirm it yourself.'

'Indeed,' said the Emperor, 'these are very hard conditions, and I do not really see how we can put them into effect. All the same, you have rendered both my son and me such outstanding services, that if we were to give you the whole of our empire, it would be no more than you deserve.' Many various opinions were expressed on both sides in the course of the interview; but in the end the emperor ratified the covenant precisely as his son had made it, by oath and by charters with gold seals affixed. One of these documents was handed to the envoys, who after taking leave of the Emperor Isaac returned to camp to tell the barons they had accomplished their task.

The barons accordingly mounted their horses, and brought the young man back with great rejoicing to his father in Constantinople. On his arrival the Greeks flung open the gates of the city to him and celebrated his return with great jubilation and much feasting. The mutual delight of father and son was all the greater because they had not seen each other for such a long time, and also because by God's help and the support of the Crusaders, they had been rescued from such a state of poverty and distress and raised to such a height of power. Thus there was great joy inside Constantinople, and no less rejoicing in the Crusaders' camp outside, because of the honour and the victory God had granted to their forces.

The next day the Emperor and his son begged the barons in God's name to go and encamp on the further side of the harbour, in the direction of Estanor; since if they took up their quarters in Constantinople there was a risk of disputes arising between them and the Greeks, as a consequence of which the city might possibly be destroyed. The barons replied that they had already served the prince and his father in so many ways that they would not now refuse any request they might make. They therefore pitched their camp on the other side of the harbour, where they lived in peace and quiet, with a good and plentiful supply of food.

Many of our men, I may say, went to visit Constantinople, to gaze at its many splendid palaces and tall churches, and view all the marvellous wealth of a city richer than any other since the beginning of time. As for the relics, these were beyond all description; for there were at that time as many in Constantinople as in all the rest of the world. The Greeks and the French thus became on friendly terms with each other in all respects, including trade and other matters.

By common consent of French, Venetians, and Greeks it was settled that the new Emperor should be crowned on Saint Peter's Day, at the very beginning of August. So it was settled, and so it was done. The coronation of the Emperor Isaac's son was celebrated with the same dignity and honour as was the custom for Greek emperors of that day. Shortly afterwards, the new Emperor began to pay our army some of the money due. This was divided among the troops in such a way that each man was allotted the sum he had paid for his passage from Venice.

The new Emperor often came to visit the barons in their camp, and paid them great honour, as much indeed as he could. This, of course was only fitting, in view of the great service they had rendered him. One day he came to the camp to have a private interview with the barons in the quarters of the Comte Baudouin de Flandre. The Doge of Venice and the great barons were privately summoned to this meeting, at which the Emperor put forward a proposal. 'My lords,' he said, 'I am Emperor by God's grace and yours, and you have done me the greatest service that any people have ever yet rendered to any Christian man. I should like you to know that a number of my people do not love me, though they make a fair pretence of doing so. Moreover, the Greeks as a whole are full of resentment because it is by your help that I have regained my empire.

'Your association with the Venetians lasts only until Michaelmas, and you are soon due to leave. I cannot hope to carry out all I have promised to do for you within so short a time. The Greeks, I must tell you, hate me because of you; if you leave me, I shall lose my empire, and they will put me to death. So do this thing I ask of you: If you will remain here till March, I will retain your fleet in my service for a further year, dating from Michaelmas, and not only bear the cost of keeping the Venetians here, but also give you such things as you may stand in need of up till Easter. By that time I shall have established such a state of affairs in my empire that I cannot lose it again. Thus I shall be able to keep my covenant with you, since I shall have received the money which should come to me from all my lands. I shall also be provided with ships, so that I can either go with you myself or send them with your army, just as I promised. Then you will have the whole of the summer in which to make war against the Saracens.'

The barons replied that they would like to talk the matter over in private. They recognized quite clearly that the Emperor had given them a true picture of the situation, and were fully aware that such a course as he proposed was best, both for him and for themselves. They told him, however, that they could not consent to it except with the general agreement of the army. They would therefore find out the army's opinion on this matter and let him know what transpired. So the Emperor left and went back to Constantinople. The barons remained in camp, and the next day held a conference to which they summoned all the great lords and the leaders of the army, together with most of the knights. Here the Emperor's request was communicated to them exactly as he had made it.

This proposal gave rise to much discord in the assembly, as much indeed as had on many other occasions been provoked by those who wished the army to be disbanded, since the whole affair seemed to them to be lasting too long. The party that had stirred up dissension at Corfu now reminded the others of their oaths, and said: 'Give us the ships as you swore to do, for we wish to go off to Syria.'

Others begged them to be patient and said: 'My lords, for God's sake, don't let the honour He has paid us be of no avail. If we go to

Syria now, we shall get there at the beginning of winter, when it is impossible to make war; and so our Lord's work will remain un-done. But if we wait till March, we shall leave this Emperor safely established and go away well supplied with money and provisions. Then we can go to Syria, and from there make expeditions into Egypt. Our fleet will in any case remain here with us till Michaelmas, and indeed from Michaelmas till Easter, since the Venetians cannot leave us so long as winter lasts. That is the way in which we shall conquer the land oversea.'

Those who wished to break up the army did not care in the least whether there were good or bad reasons for doing so, provided it happened. But those who wished to keep it together worked so effectually that in the end, with God's help, the Venetians made a new agreement, confirmed by oath, to hold the fleet at our service for another year, reckoning from Michaelmas. The Emperor Alexius, I might add, paid them enough to make it worth their while. The Crusaders, on their side, solemnly swore to remain in association with the Venetians as before, and for the same time. Thus peace and concord were established in the army.

Shortly afterwards we suffered a great misfortune. Mathieu de Montmorency, one of the best knights in the whole kingdom of France, one of the most deeply loved and respected, was taken ill, and died. There was much mourning over his death, for it was a great loss to the army – one of the greatest they had as yet suffered through the death of any man. He was buried in the church of Saint John of the Hospital of Jerusalem.

A little later, on the advice of the Greeks and the French, the Emperor Alexius, with a very great following, left Constantinople with the object of establishing peace throughout his empire and bringing it under his authority. A good number of the barons went with him, while the rest stayed behind to guard the camp. Among those who accompanied the Emperor were the Marquis de Mont-ferrat, the Comte de Saint-Pol, the Comte Baudouin's brother, Henri de Flandre, Jacques d'Avesnes, Guillaume de Champlitte, Hugues de Coligny, and a fair number of others not mentioned here by name. The Comte Baudouin de Flandre et de Hainaut remained in camp with the Comte Louis de Blois et de Chartrain and the greater part of the Crusaders.

In the course of the Emperor's tour of his dominions, all the

Greeks, on either side of the straits, came to submit themselves to his authority, to swear allegiance to him and pay him homage as their lord – all, that is, except Johanitza, King of Wallachia and Hungary. This monarch was a native of Wallachia who had rebelled against his father and his uncle, and warred against them for twenty years. In the end he had won so much of their lands from them that he had become a very powerful king. He had, in fact, conquered so much of the territory on the north-west side of the straits that he now owned almost half. This Johanitza did not come to place himself at the Emperor's disposal, nor acknowledge his authority.

While the Emperor Alexius was away on his journey, an incident which had very disastrous consequences occurred in Constantinople. The Greeks and the Latins living in the city – and there were very many of the latter – became involved in a brawl. Certain people – I cannot say who they were – set fire to the city out of malice. The fire spread and became so terrible that no one could either put it out or get it under control. When the barons, from their camp on the further side of the harbour, saw the city blazing, they were overcome with grief and pity as they watched the great churches and the lordly palaces crumbling and falling in ruins, and the wide streets where the merchants had their shops being swallowed up in the flames. But there was nothing they could do about it.

The fire made headway above the harbour, penetrating into the most densely populated parts of the city and stretching right down to the sea on the other side, quite close to the basilica of Saint Sophia. It continued to rage for a whole week, and no one could put it out. Seen from the front, as it rolled onwards, blazing, it was well over half a league wide. What damage was done, or what riches and possessions were destroyed in the flames was beyond the power of man to calculate, nor could one tell the number of men, women, and children who perished at that time, for many were burnt to death.

After the disaster, none of the Latins living in Constantinople, no matter from what country they came, dared remain in the city any longer. But with their wives and children and such of their possessions as they had managed to save from the fire they came across the harbour to take refuge in the Crusaders' camp. Their number was by no means small; there were, in fact, some fifteen thousand of them, from all ranks of life. Later on, their arrival would prove to be of great advantage to us. At the time, however, it created a rift between the Greeks and the Franks, who were never again on such friendly terms as they had been before. Neither side knew which to blame for this coolness, and that weighed heavily on the minds of both parties.

About this time the barons and the rest of the army were deeply grieved by a sad event – the death of the Abbot of Loos, a wise and saintly monk of the Cistercian order, who had always had the interests of the army at heart.

CHAPTER II

Appeal to Arms

THE Emperor Alexius was away for a very long time on his tour of the empire; he did not in fact return to Constantinople until Saint Martin's Day. There was great joy at his arrival. Long cavalcades of Greek lords and ladies rode out of the city to greet their friends; our own people too came to meet their fellow Crusaders, and welcomed them with great delight. After entering Constantinople, the Emperor returned to the palace of Blachernae; the Marquis de Montferrat and the other barons went back to camp.

Very soon the young Emperor, who had managed all his affairs very well, and felt confident that he had now gained the upper hand, became filled with pride. He adopted a haughty attitude with the barons and those who had done him such great service, and no longer came to visit them in camp, as he had done before. They continually sent to him, begging him to pay them the rest of the money due. He for his part, kept on putting them off; from time to time he would send them certain paltry sums, but in the end he ceased to pay them anything at all.

The Marquis de Montferrat, who had done more for the Emperor and stood on better terms with him than any of the other barons, had often gone to see him. On such occasions he had reproached him for the wrong he was doing them, and had never failed to point out that they had done him greater service than had ever been rendered to any other man. But the Emperor had always asked for a fresh respite, and had never kept any of his promises; so that the barons were at last forced to recognize that, whatever his intentions towards them, they were anything but good.

At this point they held a conference with the Doge of Venice, at which they said they had now come to realize that the Emperor did not intend to honour any agreement he had made with them, and that he never told them the truth. They therefore decided to send reliable envoys to see him, to remind him of the services they had rendered him, and demand the fulfilment of his contract. If he would offer to do what they required, the envoys were to accept it; if not, they would have to defy him, and let him know that the barons would do everything in their power to recover the money due.

The envoys chosen for this mission were Conon de Béthune, Geoffroy de Villehardouin, Marshal of Champagne, and Milon le Brébant de Provins, together with three of the Doge of Venice's chief counsellors, whom he appointed to go in the party. They all mounted their horses, and with swords at their sides, rode together to the palace of Blachernae. Needless to say, in view of the treacherous character of the Greeks, they had embarked on a difficult and dangerous adventure.

They dismounted at the gate and entered the palace, where they found the Emperor Alexius and his father, the Emperor Isaac, seated on two thrones, side by side. Near them was seated the Empress, the father's wife and the son's stepmother, a good and beautiful lady who was the King of Hungary's sister. A great number of people of high rank were also present, giving to the assembly all the character of a powerful prince's court.

By common consent of the other envoys Conon de Béthune, a man of high intelligence and a ready tongue, acted as their spokesman. 'Your imperial Majesty,' he said, 'we have come to you on behalf of the barons of the army and the Doge of Venice. They wish us to remind you of the service they have done you – a service known to all and recognized by all. You and your father have both sworn to fulfil your covenant with them, and they have your charters to prove it. You have not, however, honoured this agreement as you ought.

'Our lords have frequently called on you to do so, and we now summon you, in their name and in the presence of all your nobles, to carry out the contract made between yourselves and them. If you do this, they will be extremely pleased; but if not, they will no longer regard you as their lord and their friend, but will use every means in their power to obtain their due. They ask us to tell you that they will not do anything to injure either yourself or any other person without fair warning of their intention to commence hostilities. For they have never acted treacherously – that is not the custom in their country. You have now heard what we have to say. It is for you to decide what action you wish to take.'

The Greeks were much amazed and deeply shocked by this openly defiant message, and declared that no one had ever yet been so bold as to dare issue such a challenge to an Emperor of Constantinople in his own hall. The Emperor Alexius himself, and all the other Greeks, who so often in the past had greeted them with smiling faces, now scowled fiercely at the envoys.

The noise of angry voices filled the hall. The envoys turned to go; they made their way to the gate and mounted their horses. There was not a man amongst them who was not extremely glad to find himself outside. And that was not at all surprising, since they had narrowly escaped the very grave danger of being either killed or taken prisoner. On their return to camp they told the barons how they had carried out their mission.

Thus the war began; and each side did its utmost to harm the other, both by sea and on land. The two armies fought against each other in many different places, but – God be praised – they never met in battle without heavier losses on the Greek side than on the French. The war went on for a very long time, right into the middle of the winter.

Finally, the Greeks thought of putting a very terrifying plan into operation. They took seventeen great ships, and filled them full of logs and shavings, pitch and tow, and wooden barrels. Then they waited until the wind was blowing from their side of the water. One night, at twelve o'clock, they set fire to the ships, and let them drift with all their sails unfurled to the wind. The flames from them rose so high that it seemed as if the whole world was on fire.

The ships came sailing on towards the Crusaders' fleet; the bugles sounded the alert, and from everywhere in the camp men sprang to arms. The Venetians and others who had ships hastened to get aboard them, and strove with all their might and main to take them out of range of danger. Geoffroy de Villehardouin, who composed this chronicle and was an eye-witness of the incident, affirms that no men ever defended themselves more gallantly on the sea than the Venetians did that night. They leapt into galleys and into longboats, and, in the face of the enemy, laid hold of the fire-ships, all ablaze as they were, with grappling irons, and forcibly pulling them out of the harbour into the main current of the straits, left them to drift burning out to sea.

So many Greeks had come down to the water's edge that there seemed to be no end to them; the noise they made was so great you would have thought both earth and sea were being swallowed up. They clambered into any boats they could find, and shot at our men as they were fighting the flames, so that many of them were wounded.

As soon as they had heard the call to arms the knights in camp had all got ready. Now our battalions poured out on to the plain in somewhat random order, according to the distance from their quarters. They were afraid the Greeks would advance from that direction to attack them.

Our men endured all this toil and anguish till it was light; but by God's help we lost nothing, except for a merchant ship laden with goods from Pisa, which caught fire and sank. We had all been in deadly peril that night, for if our fleet had been burned we should have lost everything, and could not have got away either by sea or by land. Such was the return the Emperor Alexius had wanted to make us for the services we had rendered him.

Now that the Greeks had managed to get on such bad terms with the Franks certain of them realized that there was no hope of making peace. So they secretly conspired together to betray their lord. Among them was one who was in greater favour with the Emperor and had done more to bring about his quarrel with the Franks than any other. This man's name was Murzuphlus.

Acting on the advice and with the consent of the others, one night towards twelve o'clock, when the Emperor Alexius was asleep in his room, Murzuphlus and others who ought to have been guarding him, snatched him from his bed and, leading him away prisoner, flung him into a dungeon. Then, with the help and approval of the other Greeks, Murzuphlus assumed the scarlet buskins, and so made himself emperor. Later he was crowned in Saint Sophia. Have you ever heard of any people guilty of such atrocious treachery!

On hearing that his son had been taken prisoner and Murzuphlus crowned in his stead, the Emperor Isaac was so overcome by fear that it made him ill, and within a very short space of time he died. As for Isaac's son, whom Murzuphlus held in prison, poison was ordered to be given him two or three times; but it was not God's will he should die that way. Later on Murzuphlus went and strangled the young man, and subsequently had it reported everywhere that his death was due to natural causes. Murzuphlus had him buried with such pomp and ceremony as is fitting for an emperor, and made a great show of mourning over his death.

But murder cannot be hid. Very soon both Greeks and French became aware that such a crime had been committed, and in the way I have told you. The barons of the army and the Doge of Venice held a conference at which the bishops and the clergy were also present. All the clergy, particularly those who had a special mandate from the Pope, agreed in pointing out to the barons and the other Crusaders that anyone guilty of such a murder had no right to hold lands, while those who consented to such a thing were accomplices in the crime; and over and above all this the Greeks as a people had seceded from the Church of Rome. 'We therefore tell you,' said the clergy, 'that this war is just and lawful; and if you fight to conquer this land with the right intention of bringing it under the authority of Rome, all those of you who die after making confession shall benefit from the indulgence granted by the Pope.' The barons and all the other Crusaders were greatly comforted and encouraged by this assurance.

The war between the Franks and the Greeks raged fiercely. It went on without respite, ever growing more and more violent, till hardly a day passed without some engagement either by land or sea. At one point, the Comte de Flandre's brother Henri rode out on a foray, taking with him a great part of the best men in camp. Among them were Jacques d'Avesnes, Baudouin de Beauvoir, Eudes de Champlitte and his brother Guillaume, and others from their part of the country. They left the camp about six o'clock one evening, and rode all night. Late the next morning, they reached the fine town of Philia, which they took. There they gained much booty in the way of cattle and clothing, as well as taking a good number of prisoners. These they put into boats and sent down the straits to the camp; for this town lay on the shores of the Euxine Sea.

They spent two days in Philia, enjoying an abundance of good things to eat, for the town was plentifully supplied with food. On the third day they left with the cattle and the other booty, and started to ride back towards the camp. Meanwhile the Emperor Murzuphlus had heard news of their movements. So he left Constantinople by night with a large body of troops, and went into ambush on the road by which our men would have to pass on their return journey. He watched them ride by with their beasts and their booty, one company after the other, until the rear-guard, which was under the command of Henri de Flandre, and made up of his own people, had arrived on the scene. Then Murzuphlus rushed out of ambush to attack them as they were entering a wood. The French immediately turned round to face them, and a fierce fight took place. With God's help, Murzuphlus was defeated, and barely escaped being taken prisoner. He lost his imperial standard and an icon which he had always had carried before him. It was one in which he and the other Greeks placed great faith, because it bore the picture of Our Lady. Besides this, about twenty of his knights were killed.

None the less, although Murzuphlus had suffered defeat, the war between his forces and the Franks continued to rage fiercely. By this time a great part of the winter was over. It was now close on Candlemas, and Lent was near at hand.

CHAPTER 12

Second Siege of Constantinople
FEBRUARY–APRIL 1204

FOR the moment I will turn from the army encamped before Constantinople to speak of the men who had gone to other ports, and of those in the Flemish fleet that had wintered at Marseilles. These had all sailed for Syria as soon as warmer weather arrived. Their number far exceeded the number of those engaged in fighting the Greeks. Let me say what a pity it was they had not come to join our army; had they only done so, the cause of Christianity would have gained a lasting advantage. But because of their sins God would not allow it; the unhealthy climate of Syria proved fatal to some; others went back to their own country. Not one of them did anything useful or worth while in the land to which they had gone.

One group of them, all very good men, had set off for Antioch to join Bohemond, Prince of Antioch and Count of Tripoli, who was at war with King Leon of Armenia. They intended to serve the prince as mercenaries. The Turks of that country, having heard of their coming, had lain in ambush at a spot by which they had to pass, and as soon as they came there had attacked them. In the fight the French had so much the worst of it that not one of them had got away; all were either killed or captured.

Vilain de Nully, one of the best knights in the world, together with Gilles de Trasignies and many others were among the dead in that encounter. Bernard de Moreuil, Renaud de Dampierre, Jean de Villers, and Guillaume de Nully, one of the most innocent souls alive, were among the prisoners. In fact, of the eighty knights that formed this company there was, as I have said, not one that got safely away. This book, indeed, gives ample proof that out of all those who failed to join the army in Venice there was not one who did not suffer harm or incur disgrace. That is why one can say that a man is wise when he chooses to follow the better course and keeps to it.

I will now leave this subject and return to the troops before Constantinople. These had put all their machines in working order, set up their petraries and mangonels and every other device of use in taking a city on their warships and transports, and raised scaling ladders so high on the lateen yards that it was a sight to wonder at.

The Greeks, for their part, seeing these preparations in hand, had begun to strengthen the defences of the city, which was already well entrenched behind high walls and towers. There was, however, no tower so high that they did not add two or three wooden storeys to it to heighten it still more. No city, in fact, had ever been so well fortified. In this way both Greeks and Franks had employed their time, working continuously during the greater part of Lent.

The barons now held a conference to discuss what plan of action to adopt. Plenty of different suggestions were put forward, but in the end the following decisions were taken: if, by God's grace, they effected an entry by force into the city, they would have all the booty collected in one place, and fairly and properly shared out among the troops; if in addition, they gained complete control of the city, they would choose six men from the French army, and six from among the Venetians, who would each be required to swear on the Holy Gospels that they would elect as Emperor the man whom they considered most fitted to rule in the best interests of the state. Whoever was thus elected Emperor would have as his share one quarter of all the booty, whether within the city or without, and would also be given possession of the palaces of Bucoleon and Blachernae. The remaining three-quarters of the booty would be divided into two equal parts, one to be allotted to the Venetians and the other to the French. After this they would select twelve of the wisest and most capable men in the French army, and twelve equally qualified Venetians, who would be responsible for allotting fiefs and offices and arranging what services were to be rendered to the Emperor for such honours.

This compact was confirmed by oath on the part of French and Venetians alike, with the provision that at the end of March in the following year anyone who wished to leave would be free to go where he pleased. Those who remained, however, would come under the jurisdiction of the Emperor to perform such service for him as he required. To complete the compact a final clause was added to the effect that anyone failing to observe its terms would do so on pain of excommunication.

The fleet was now well equipped and armed, and all the provisions the Crusaders would need had been put aboard. On the Thursday after mid-Lent Sunday all the troops embarked on the warships, and the horses were put into the transports. Each division had its own ships, ranged one beside the other, the warships alternating with galleys and transports. It was, I can assure you, a marvellous sight to see the fleet drawn up in battle-formation, in a line extending well over half a French league.

On the Friday morning the warships, galleys, and other vessels approached the city in due order, and began to deliver a fierce and determined assault. In many places the Crusaders landed and advanced right up to the walls; in many others the scaling ladders on the ships came so close to the battlements that those on the walls and the towers crossed lances hand to hand with their assailants. The assault continued, fast and fierce and furious, in more than a hundred places, till round about three o'clock in the afternoon.

But, for our sins, our troops were repulsed in that attack, and those that had landed from the galleys and transports were forcibly driven back aboard. I must admit that on that day our army lost more men than the Greeks, and the latter were greatly delighted. Some of our people withdrew from the assault, taking their ships right out of the battle; others let their vessels ride at anchor so near the walls of the city that each side was able to launch stones from petraries and mangonels at the other.

That evening, towards six o'clock, the barons and the Doge of Venice assembled for a conference in a church on the further side of the harbour, close to where they had been encamped. Many different points of view were exchanged at that meeting; the French, in particular, were greatly distressed by the reverse they had suffered that day. Many of those present advised an attack on the city from another side, at a place where the defences were weaker. The Venetians, who had more experience of the sea, pointed out that if they went to that side, the current would carry them down the straits, and they would be unable to stop their ships. There were, I might say, certain people in the company who would have been only too pleased if the current had borne them down the straits, or the wind had done so; they did not care where they went, so long as they left that land behind and went on their way. Nor was that to be wondered at, for we were in very grave danger at the time.

After much discussion, it was finally decided to spend the next day, which was a Saturday, and the whole of Sunday, repairing the damage done to the ships and the equipment, and to renew the assault on the Monday. This time they would have the ships that carried the scaling ladders bound together, two by two, so that each pair could make a combined attack on one tower. This plan was adopted because, in that day's engagement, they had noticed that when only one ship had attacked each tower, the greater number of men on a tower than on a ladder had made it too heavy a task for a ship to undertake alone. It was therefore reasonable to assume that two ships together would do more effective damage than one. This plan of binding the ships in pairs was carried out while the troops were standing by on the Saturday and the Sunday.

Meanwhile the Emperor Murzuphlus had come to encamp with all his forces on an open space directly opposite our lines, and had pitched his scarlet tents there. Thus matters remained till the Monday morning, when all the men on the various ships got their arms and equipment ready. The citizens of Constantinople were now much less afraid of our troops than at the time of our first assault. They were, in fact, in such a confident mood that all along the walls and towers there was nothing to be seen but people. Then began a fierce and magnificent assault, as each ship steered a straight course forward. The shouts that rose from the battle created such a din that it seemed as if the whole earth were crumbling to pieces.

The assault had been going on for a considerable time when our Lord raised for us a wind called Boreas, which drove the ships still further on to the shore. Two of the ships which were bound together – the one called the *Pilgrim* and the other the *Paradise* – approached so close to a tower, one of them on one side and one on the other, as God and the wind drove them onwards, that the ladder of the *Pilgrim* made contact with it. Immediately a Venetian, in company with a French knight named André Durboise, forced their way in. Other men began to follow them, and in the end the defenders were routed and driven out.

The moment the knights aboard the transports saw this happen, they landed, and raising their ladders against the wall, climbed to the top, and took four more towers. Then all the rest of the troops started to leap out of warships, galleys, and transports, helter-skelter, each as fast as he could. They broke down about three of the gates and entered the city. The horses were then taken out of the transports; the knights mounted and rode straight towards the place where the

Emperor Murzuphlus had his camp. He had his battalions drawn up in front of the tents; but as soon as his men saw the knights charging towards them on horseback, they retreated in disorder. The Emperor himself fled through the streets of the city to the castle of Bucoleon.

Then followed a scene of massacre and pillage: on every hand the Greeks were cut down, their horses, palfreys, mules, and other possessions snatched as booty. So great was the number of killed and wounded that no man could count them. A great part of the Greek nobles had fled towards the gate of Blachernae; but by this time it was past six o'clock, and our men had grown weary of fighting and slaughtering. The troops began to assemble in a great square inside Constantinople. Then, convinced that it would take them at least a month to subdue the whole city, with its great churches and palaces, and the people inside it, they decided to settle down near the walls and towers they had already captured.

All was done according to plan. The main part of the army encamped close to the ships, outside the battlements. The Comte Baudouin de Flandre quartered himself in the scarlet tents the Emperor Murzuphlus had left standing. His brother Henri settled down in front of the palace of Blachernae, while the Marquis de Montferrat and his men remained near the most densely populated parts of the city. Thus the whole of the army was stationed in and around Constantinople, which our troops had taken on the Monday before Palm Sunday.

The Comte Louis de Blois, I might add, had been suffering all the winter from a quartan fever, and had not been fit enough to arm himself like the rest. This was a great misfortune for the army, since he was a very good and gallant knight. He lay in bed in one of the transports.

Our troops, all utterly worn out and weary, rested quietly that night. But the Emperor Murzuphlus did not rest; instead, he assembled his forces and said he was going to attack the Franks. However he did not do as he had announced, but rode along certain streets as far away as possible from those occupied by our army, till he came to a gate called the Golden Gate through which he escaped, and so left the city. All the Greeks who could manage to do so followed him in his flight. But our army knew absolutely nothing of all this.

During that night, near the place where the Marquis de Montferrat had encamped, certain unknown persons, fearing the enemy might attack them, set fire to the buildings between themselves and the

Greeks. The fire began to take hold on the city, which was soon blazing fiercely, and went on burning the whole of that night and all the next day till evening. This was the third fire there had been in Constantinople since the French and Venetians arrived in the land, and more houses had been burnt in that city than there are in any three of the greatest cities in the kingdom of France.

That night passed, and the next day came; it was a Tuesday. Early that morning all the troops, knights and sergeants alike, armed themselves, and each man went to join his division. They left their quarters thinking to meet with stronger resistance than they had encountered the day before, since they did not know that the Emperor had fled during the night. But they found no one to oppose them.

The Marquis de Montferrat rode straight along the shore to the palace of Bucoleon. As soon as he arrived there the place was surrendered to him, on condition that the lives of all the people in it should be spared. Among these were very many ladies of the highest rank who had taken refuge there, including the Empress Agnes, sister of the King of France, the Empress Marie, sister of the King of Hungary, and a number of other noble ladies. Words fail me when it comes to describing the treasures found in that palace, for there was such a store of precious things that one could not possibly count them.

In the same way that the palace of Bucoleon was surrendered to the Marquis de Montferrat, so the palace of Blachernae was yielded to the Comte de Flandre's brother Henri, and on the same conditions. There too was found a great store of treasure, not less than there had been in the palace of Bucoleon. The Marquis de Montferrat and Henri de Flandre each garrisoned the castle surrendered to him, and set a guard over the treasure.

The rest of the army, scattered throughout the city, also gained much booty; so much, indeed, that no one could estimate its amount or its value. It included gold and silver, table-services and precious stones, satin and silk, mantles of squirrel fur, ermine and miniver, and every choicest thing to be found on this earth. Geoffroy de Villehardouin here declares that, to his knowledge, so much booty had never been gained in any city since the creation of the world.

Everyone took quarters where he pleased, and there was no lack of fine dwellings in that city. So the troops of the Crusaders and the

Venetians were duly housed. They all rejoiced and gave thanks to
our Lord for the honour and the victory He had granted them, so
that those who had been poor now lived in wealth and luxury. Thus
they celebrated Palm Sunday and the Easter Day following, with
hearts full of joy for the benefits our Lord and Saviour had bestowed
on them. And well might they praise Him; since the whole of their
army numbered no more than twenty thousand men, and with His
help they had conquered four hundred thousand, or more, and that
in the greatest, most powerful, and most strongly fortified city in
the world.

CHAPTER 13

Election of an Emperor

THE Marquis de Montferrat, commander-in-chief of the army, now issued, on behalf of the barons and the Doge of Venice, a general order to the troops to collect and hand over all the booty, as had been agreed on oath and under pain of excommunication. Three churches were set aside for the reception of the spoil, and certain of the most notably trustworthy men among the French and the Venetians were posted in each to act as guards.

Each man began to bring in such booty as he had taken. Some performed this duty conscientiously, others, prompted by covetousness, that never-failing source of all evil, proved less honest. From the very first, those who were prone to this vice began to keep some things back, and became, in consequence, less pleasing to our Lord. Ah God! how loyally they had behaved up to now! And up to now, in all their undertakings, our Lord had shown His gracious care for them, and had exalted them above all other people. But those who do right often have to suffer for the misdeeds of the unrighteous.

In this case, when the army's gains in money and kind had been collected it turned out that the whole amount had not been handed in. There were many, in fact, who had kept things back, undeterred by fear of excommunication by the Pope. Everything brought to the churches was put together, and divided in equal parts between the French and the Venetians, according to the sworn agreement. After the Crusaders had received their share, they first handed over 50,000 silver marks to the Venetians, and then divided another 100,000 among their own people. The money was allotted in this way: one mounted sergeant received as much as two sergeants on foot, one knight as much as two mounted sergeants. No man, whatever his rank or his personal merits, received a larger amount, except by special arrangement – or unless he happened to steal it.

In cases of theft stern justice was meted out to those proved guilty; many of these were hanged. The Comte de Saint-Pol hanged one of his own knights, with his shield at his neck, for keeping back certain booty. There were however many men, of all ranks, who kept things back without ever being found out. None the less, the total value of the spoil was very great; for apart from what was stolen and what was paid to the Venetians, what remained available for distribution amounted to about 400,000 silver marks, as well as ten thousand horses of different breeds. In this way the spoils of Constantinople were divided among the victors.

After this task was completed the whole army was summoned to a conference, at which the troops with one accord declared that an emperor must be elected, as had already been agreed. Discussion went on so long that the matter of choosing the twelve persons responsible for electing an emperor was adjourned to another day. Naturally, where such a high dignity as the imperial throne of Constantinople was concerned, there could be no lack of men who aspired to, or coveted, that honour; yet the greatest disagreement at the meeting was on the question of whether the Comte Baudouin de Flandre or the Marquis de Montferrat should be chosen; for everyone said it must be one or the other.

When the chief men in the army saw how people were divided on this point, some in support of the count, others upholding the marquis, they conferred together. 'If we elect one of these two great men,' they said, 'the other will leave the army and take his people with him. Then we may lose this land, just as Jerusalem was nearly lost, when, after it was conquered, Godefroy de Bouillon was elected king. At that time the Comte de Saint-Gilles was so filled with spite and envy that he incited the other barons, and anyone else he could persuade, to withdraw from the army. Many people left, and so few remained that, if God had not taken them under His protection, the land of Jerusalem would have been lost. We must therefore take care to see that such a misfortune doesn't happen to us.

'We ought rather to find some way of keeping both these lords in the army. So let whichever of them is by God's will elected emperor do all in his power to keep the other satisfied. Let him, for instance, gain the other's allegiance by granting him all the lands across the straits, towards Turkey, and also the Isle of Greece on this side. By such means we shall keep them both.' This proposal was favourably received by all, and both the men concerned gave their willing assent to it.

The day appointed for the final conference arrived, and everyone assembled. Twelve electors were chosen, six of them French and the other six Venetians. These all swore on the Holy Gospels to elect, conscientiously and loyally, the man who would best serve the interests of the state and govern the empire most worthily.

After the electors had been chosen a day was fixed for the election of an emperor. On that day the twelve men met in a very fine palace, one of the most beautiful in the world, where the Doge of Venice was then living. An amazing concourse of people had gathered there, for everyone wished to see who would be elected. The twelve electors were summoned and taken into a very richly furnished chapel inside the palace. The door was shut, so that they remained alone. Meanwhile, the barons and the knights waited in a great palace a little way from the chapel.

The council lasted until the electors were all agreed. Then, by common consent, they appointed one of their number, Névelon, Bishop of Soissons, to act as spokesman. They all came out of the chapel and went to the place where the barons and the Doge of Venice were assembled. Many eyes, as you can imagine, were turned towards the twelve, for everyone was anxious to hear the result of the election. The bishop delivered his message. 'My lords,' he said, 'by God's grace we have agreed on the choice of an emperor. You have all sworn that the man whom we elect shall be accepted by you, and that if anyone should dare to challenge his election you will come to his support. We name him now at the very hour in which our Lord was born: The Comte Baudouin de Flandre et de Hainaut.'

Shouts of joy resounded in the palace. The count was escorted out of the building and borne to the church. The Marquis de Montferrat, for his part, was the first to support him on one side, and to pay him all the honour he could. Thus the Comte Baudouin de Flandre et de Hainaut was elected Emperor, and a day fixed for his coronation, three weeks after Easter. Many a rich robe, I may say, was specially made for that occasion, and there was no lack of money to pay for the making.

Before the day appointed for the coronation the Marquis Boniface de Montferrat married the lady who had been the Emperor Isaac's wife, and was the King of Hungary's sister. About the same time, Eudes de Champlitte, one of the noblest barons in the army, fell ill and died. His brother Guillaume and his friends mourned him deeply and wept bitterly over his death. He was buried with great honour in the church of the Holy Apostles.

Coronation day arrived, and the Emperor Baudouin was crowned with much rejoicing and great dignity in the Church of Saint Sophia, in the year of our Lord 1204. There is no need to speak of the jubilation and the festivities attending that event, except to say that the barons and the knights did all they could to honour the occasion. The Marquis Boniface de Montferrat and the Comte Louis de Blois et de Chartrain did homage to the new Emperor as their lord. After his joyful coronation, the Emperor was escorted in great pomp, and with a great procession, to the lordly palace of Bucoleon, a more magnificent building than had ever been seen before. Here, as soon as the festivities were over, he settled down to attend to business.

The Marquis de Montferrat now called upon the Emperor to keep the promise he had made, and give him, as he had bound himself to do, possession of the land across the straits towards Turkey, and the Isle of Greece. The Emperor acknowledged his obligation and said he would gladly fulfil it. The marquis, seeing him so ready and willing to keep his word, asked him whether, in exchange for those lands, he would grant him the kingdom of Salonika, because it lay near the territory of the King of Hungary, whose sister he had married.

After much serious discussion of pros and cons the Emperor finally granted the land of Salonika to the marquis, who thereupon did him homage for it as his lord. At this there was great rejoicing in the army, for the marquis was one of the most highly esteemed knights in all the world, and one whom his fellow knights loved most, since no one was more open-handed and generous than he. Thus the marquis was persuaded to remain in the empire.

CHAPTER 14

A Case of Strained Relations
MAY–SEPTEMBER 1204

THE Emperor Murzuphlus had not as yet gone more than four days' journey from Constantinople. He had taken with him the wife and daughter of the Emperor Isaac's brother Alexius, who had fled from the city a long time before. He was now living at Mosynopolis with those who had fled with him, and still held a great part of the land.

About this time certain Greek nobles of the highest rank left Constantinople, and a great number of them crossed over the straits to that part of the empire on the borders of Turkey. Each of them appropriated as much land as he pleased, to use it to his own advantage. Much the same thing was happening in various other parts of the empire.

The Emperor Murzuphlus did not wait long before taking the town of Tchorlu, which had already surrendered to the Emperor Baudouin. He took it by storm and sacked it, seizing everything he found there. When news of this reached the Emperor Baudouin he consulted the barons and the Doge of Venice. They unanimously agreed in advising him to march out of Constantinople with all the forces he had, to subdue the land, leaving only a sufficient garrison in the city to ensure its safety, since it had been newly conquered and was largely peopled with Greeks.

This plan was adopted. After the troops had been assembled, those who were to guard Constantinople were given orders to remain. Among those who stayed behind were the Comte Louis de Blois, who had not yet recovered from an illness, and the aged Doge of Venice. Conon de Béthune was left in charge of the palaces of Blachernae and Bucoleon, to keep guard over the city, together with Geoffroy de Villehardouin, Milon le Brébant, Manassier de l'Isle, and all their men. The rest got ready to go in the Emperor's army.

Before the Emperor Baudouin set out from Constantinople, he gave his brother Henri orders to go on ahead with a hundred very good knights. He rode with his company from city to city, and in every place to which he came the citizens swore allegiance to the

Emperor. He went on till he came to Adrianople, a very fine and wealthy city, where the people gave him a very cordial welcome, and in their turn acknowledged the Emperor as their lord. He remained in that city until the Emperor Baudouin arrived.

On hearing that the army was advancing, the Emperor Murzuphlus did not dare to wait for it to arrive, but contrived to remain always two or three days' march ahead. He went on in this way till he came near Mosynopolis, where the Emperor Alexius was staying, and then sent messengers forward to tell Alexius he would give him help and do anything he required. Alexius replied that he would welcome Murzuphlus as if he were his own son, and give him his daughter in marriage, to make him his son in fact. So Murzuphlus encamped outside Mosynopolis, with all his tents and pavilions, while Alexius remained in the town. Then they met and conferred together, after which Alexius gave Murzuphlus his daughter in marriage, and they entered into alliance with each other, declaring they would be as one.

The two Emperors stayed where they were for an indefinite time, the one in his camp and the other in the city, till one day Alexius invited Murzuphlus to come and dine with him, and afterwards go with him to the baths. The invitation was accepted. Murzuphlus arrived without ceremony and with very few attendants, as he had been asked to do. As soon as he was in the house, Alexius drew him aside into a private room, where he had him flung to the ground, and had his eyes torn out of his head. Judge for yourselves, after hearing of this treachery, whether people who could treat each other with such savage cruelty would be fit to hold lands or would deserve to lose them? When the troops belonging to the Emperor Murzuphlus heard what had been done, most of them scattered and fled in all directions, some this way, some that. A certain number, however, went over to the Emperor Alexius and remained with him, obeying him as their lord.

Meanwhile the Emperor Baudouin had left Constantinople with his army, and had ridden as far as Adrianople, where he met his brother Henri and his company of knights. All the people in the places he had passed on his way had come out to meet him, to place themselves at his disposal and acknowledge his authority. While the troops were at Adrianople they had heard how the Emperor Alexius had torn out the other Emperor's eyes. There was much talk about the incident; everyone roundly declared that people who could betray each other so treacherously had no right to hold lands.

The Emperor Baudouin made up his mind to ride straight to Mosynopolis, where the Emperor Alexius was living. The Greeks in Adrianople begged him, as their lord, to leave a garrison in their city because Johanitza, King of Wallachia and Bulgaria, had subjected them to frequent attacks. The Emperor left with them Eustache de Saubruic, a very brave and worthy Flemish knight, together with forty very good knights and a hundred mounted sergeants.

The Emperor then left the city and rode towards Mosynopolis where he expected to find the Emperor Alexius. All the people of the regions through which he passed came to him to acknowledge his authority and place themselves under his rule. On hearing of this the Emperor Alexius withdrew all his troops from Mosynopolis and fled. The Emperor Baudouin rode on till he reached the city. The people of that place came out to meet him, and surrendered it to him as their lord.

The Emperor Baudouin now declared his intention of staying at Mosynopolis to wait for the Marquis de Montferrat, who had not yet arrived in camp. This was because he was bringing his wife with him, and had not therefore been able to travel at the same rate as the Emperor. However, he and his party rode steadily on till they reached Mosynopolis, which lies on a river, and pitched their tents and pavilions beside the stream. The next day the marquis went to see the Emperor, to talk with him and remind him of his promise.

'Your Majesty,' he said, 'I have had news from Salonika telling me that the people of my kingdom are ready and willing to receive me as their lord. As your vassal, I hold that land from you; so I beg you to give me leave to go there. As soon as I am in possession of my land I will bring you back all the supplies you need, and come ready prepared to do whatever you wish. But do not go and ruin my kingdom for me; but rather, if that meets with your approval, march with me against Johanitza, King of Wallachia and Bulgaria, who has wrongfully taken possession of part of my land.'

I do not know on whose advice the Emperor acted when he replied that he was determined in spite of everything to march to Salonika, and would afterwards attend to his other affairs. 'Your Majesty,' said the marquis, 'I earnestly beg you, since I am capable of getting possession of my land without your help, not to enter it.

If you do, I shall not feel you are acting for my good. I must tell you clearly that I shall not go with you, but break with you and your army.'

Alas! how ill-advised they both were, and how very wrong it was on the part of those who had caused this breach between them! For if God had not taken pity on them both, they would have lost all the conquests they had made, and Christendom itself would have been exposed to danger. Thus, by an unlucky chance and by unwise counsel, the Emperor and the marquis were driven to part company.

The Emperor Baudouin rode on towards Salonika as he had planned, with all his attendants and all his forces, while the Marquis de Montferrat turned back in another direction, taking away with him a great number of good men. Among those who went with him were Jacques d'Avesnes, Guillaume de Champlitte, Hugues de Coligny, and the Graf Berthold von Katzenellenbogen, together with the greater part of the men from the Empire of Germany, all of whom were on the marquis's side.

The marquis rode back till he came to the castle of Demotika, a very fine and imposing building, and very strongly fortified. After one of the Greeks in the adjoining town had surrendered the castle to him, he entered it and placed a garrison there. Then because his wife, the former Empress, was known to them, the Greeks began to rally to his side, and come in from all the country round, within a day or two's journey from Demotika, to acknowledge him as their lord.

Meanwhile, as the Emperor Baudouin rode on towards Salonika, he came to the castle of Christopolis, one of the strongest fortresses in the world. This was surrendered, and the people of the adjoining town all swore allegiance to him. Later on he came to another place called La Blanche, a very well fortified and prosperous town. This too surrendered, and the people did homage to him. From there he rode to Serrès, an equally prosperous and well fortified town; and here, too, the people acknowledged his authority and swore to obey him as their lord. Finally he reached the city of Salonika, and stayed for three days encamped outside. The people of that city, which at that time was one of the finest and wealthiest in the whole of Christendom, surrendered the place to him on condition that he would govern them in accordance with the usages and customs observed by all Greek emperors up to that day.

While the Emperor Baudouin was in the neighbourhood of Salonika, and people throughout the land were placing themselves at his
service and accepting him as their lord, the Marquis de Montferrat,
with all his men and a great number of Greeks who supported him,
had marched to Adrianople, pitched his tents and pavilions all round
about the city, and started to lay siege to it. Eustache de Saubruic,
who was inside, with the men whom the Emperor had left there, had
immediately manned the walls and towers, and made ready to defend
the city.

After that he had summoned two messengers and sent them off to
Constantinople, riding night and day. They went to see the Doge of
Venice, the Comte Louis and the other barons whom the Emperor
had ordered to remain in the city. They told these lords that Eustache
de Saubruic wished them to know that the Emperor and the marquis
had quarrelled, and the marquis had seized Demotika, which was one
of the finest and strongest castles in the empire, and had now started
to besiege the Emperor's men in Adrianople. When those in Constantinople heard this they were greatly troubled, thinking for
certain that all they had conquered would be lost.

So the Doge of Venice, the Comte Louis, and the rest of the barons
in Constantinople assembled in the palace of Blachernae. Greatly
perturbed and vexed by the news they had received, they inveighed
most bitterly against those who had stirred up ill-feeling between the
Emperor and the marquis. At the request of the Doge of Venice and
the Comte Louis, Geoffroy de Villehardouin, Marshal of Champagne,
who was on good terms with the marquis, and would, so they thought,
have more influence with him than anyone else, was implored to go
to the siege of Adrianople and, if possible, put an end to this strife.
He, for his part, moved by their entreaties and conscious of the
desperate need to settle the quarrel, replied that he was very willing
to go. He took with him Manassier de l'Isle, who was one of the best
and most highly esteemed knights in the army.

They set out from Constantinople and rode for several days till
they reached the beleaguered city. As soon as the marquis heard they
were approaching he came out of the camp and went to meet them,
accompanied by his chief advisers, Jacques d'Avesnes, Guillaume de
Champlitte, Hugues de Coligny, and Othon de la Roche. On seeing
the envoys, the marquis greeted them very kindly and courteously.

Marshal Geoffroy, speaking as a privileged friend, reproached the marquis very straightly for the way in which he had occupied the Emperor's lands and besieged his people in Adrianople, and that without explaining the situation to his friends in Constantinople, who would surely have helped him to obtain redress if the Emperor had done him any wrong. The marquis, however, did all he could to vindicate himself, and insisted that he had only acted in that way in return for the wrong the Emperor had done him.

None the less, the Marshal worked so hard to persuade him that, with God's help and the aid of those barons who were in their lord's confidence and devoted to him, he received the assurance that the marquis would place the matter in the hands of the Doge of Venice, the Comte Louis, Conon de Béthune, and the Marshal himself. As a result a truce was established between the army in camp and the men in the city.

On their departure Geoffroy de Villehardouin and Manassier de l'Isle were warmly thanked, both by the men in camp and those they had been besieging; for both groups were united in a desire for peace. But if the French were delighted, the Greeks were in like measure grieved and disappointed, because they would have been very glad to see our troops at variance and fighting against each other. Thus the siege of Adrianople was raised, and the marquis went back with all his men to the castle of Demotika, where he had left his wife.

The envoys returned to Constantinople to report what they had done. The Doge of Venice, the Comte Louis, and all the others were delighted to hear that the marquis had commissioned them to negotiate a peace. So they wrote a letter, and sent it by reliable messengers to the Emperor Baudouin, informing him that the marquis had referred the point at issue to them, with the assurance that he would abide by their decision. They added that, in their opinion, the Emperor was even more strongly bound to do the same, and since they, for their part, would not countenance a war of this kind on any pretext whatsoever, they begged him to do as they asked, and promise to accept their arbitration as the marquis had done.

While all this was happening the Emperor Baudouin had settled affairs to his liking in Salonika and had left the city, after placing a garrison there in charge of Renier de Mons, a very good and valiant knight. News had reached him that the marquis had taken Demotika and, in addition to establishing himself there, had conquered a great part of the surrounding territory and was besieging the Emperor's own people in Adrianople. On hearing this the Emperor had been beside himself with rage, and had instantly made up his mind to go to the relief of Adrianople and do the marquis all the harm he could. Ah! what mischief might have resulted from this discord! If God had not intervened to put things right, it would have meant the ruin of Christendom.

The Emperor Baudouin started to go towards Adrianople, riding day after day. While the army had been encamped before Salonika, a most unfortunate thing had happened: a sudden illness had attacked the ranks, and many had been obliged to take to bed. During the journey a good number, too ill to go any further, were left behind in castles along the Emperor's route; others, in great pain and discomfort, were brought along in litters. Many died at Serrès, among them the Emperor's chancellor, Jean de Noyon. He was a very learned and saintly priest, whose eloquent preaching of the word of God had greatly comforted and sustained our troops. The chief men in the army were full of sorrow at his death.

It was not very long before the army suffered still more misfortune, and first of all by the death of Pierre d'Amiens, a great and powerful noble, and a good and valiant knight. The Comte Hugues de Saint-Pol, who was his cousin, mourned him deeply, and every man in the army was truly sorry when he died. Shortly after this came the death of Gerard de Mancicourt. This was another great grief to the troops, for he was a knight whom everyone loved and esteemed. Gilles d'Aunoi and many other good men also died in the course of this journey. We lost, in fact, some forty knights in all, and the army was greatly weakened by their death.

The Emperor Baudouin, riding by daily stages, had by now covered such a distance that he encountered the messengers sent to him from Constantinople as they were coming to meet him. One of these, a knight named Bègue de Fransures, came from the lands belonging to the Comte Louis de Blois and was his vassal. A man with a shrewd mind and a ready tongue, he delivered the message from his lord and the other barons in a very spirited manner. 'Your Majesty,' he said, 'the Doge of Venice, my lord the Comte Louis, and the other barons now in Constantinople send greetings to you as their lord. They wish to complain to God and to you of those responsible for provoking this quarrel between yourself and the marquis which has nearly brought about the ruin of Christendom. They also ask me to say that

you have acted very unwisely in listening to such advice. Now they
would like you to know that the marquis has referred this dispute
between yourself and him to them, and they beg you, as their lord,
to do the same in your turn, and promise to abide by their ruling.
They wish you to understand that they will never consent to your
going to war with each other on any grounds whatsoever.'

The Emperor said he would give the envoys his answer shortly,
and went to summon his council. Among this group there were
many who had helped to provoke the quarrel, and who now regarded
the message sent from Constantinople as a shocking piece of imper-
tinence. 'Your Majesty,' they said, 'you have heard what these
people declare: that they will not, in fact, permit you to punish an
enemy who has wronged you. It seems that if you refuse to do as they
tell you, they will turn against you.'

Many arrogant opinions were expressed in the course of the conference, but in the end, since the Emperor did not wish to lose the
friendship of the Doge of Venice, the Comte Louis and other important people in Constantinople, the council agreed that he should
give the following reply to the envoys: 'I will not guarantee to refer
the dispute to those who sent you; but I will go to Constantinople
without doing anything to injure the marquis.' So the Emperor went
to Constantinople. The barons and all the other people came out to
meet him, and welcomed him with great honour as their lord.

Within four days of his arrival the Emperor had come to understand quite clearly that he had been ill-advised to quarrel with the
marquis. At this point the Doge of Venice and the Comte Louis
came to see him and said: 'Your Majesty, we beg you to refer this
matter to us, as the marquis has done.' The Emperor replied that he
would be very glad to do so. Envoys were therefore chosen to fetch
the marquis and bring him to Constantinople. One of these envoys
was Gervais du Châtel, another Renier de Trit, and the third Geoffroy
de Villehardouin; the Doge of Venice sent two of his own people
with them.

The envoys rode on day after day till they finally arrived at Demotika. Here they found the marquis with his wife and a great number
of people of good standing. After they had told him that they had
come to fetch him Geoffroy de Villehardouin begged him to come
to Constantinople, as he had promised, and settle his quarrel with
the Emperor in the way that those to whom he had referred it might

decide. The envoys would guarantee him safe conduct for himself, as also for all those who might go with him.

The marquis asked his people what they would advise. Some of them agreed that he ought to go, others advised him not to. However, after some discussion, he went to Constantinople with the envoys, accompanied by about a hundred of his knights. They rode for several days till they reached the city, where they were very warmly welcomed. The Comte Louis de Blois and the Doge of Venice came out to meet the marquis, together with a very large number of other people of high rank in the army who were all his devoted friends.

After this a conference was held at which the agreement formerly made between the Emperor and the marquis was discussed. As a result the city and kingdom of Salonika were given back to the marquis on condition that he handed over Demotika, which he had seized, to Geoffroy de Villehardouin, who promised to keep it till he heard, either by an accredited messenger or by letters patent, that the marquis was actually in possession of his kingdom. Then the Marshal would give Demotika back to the Emperor and place it under his jurisdiction. Thus peace was made between the Emperor and the marquis. There was great rejoicing throughout the army over this happy settlement, for very great harm might have resulted from such a quarrel.

The marquis took leave of his friends, and accompanied by the Emperor's envoys rode towards Salonika with his wife and his people. As they went from castle to castle, each in its turn, with all its domains, was handed over to the marquis in the name of the Emperor. When he came to the city of Salonika, those who were holding the place for the Emperor surrendered it in the same way. The governor of the place, whose name was Renier de Mons, had recently died. He was a very good man, and his death was a sad loss.

Gradually, throughout the kingdom of Salonika, men began to submit their lands and themselves to the marquis's authority, till at length a very great number of people had acknowledged him as their lord. One exception was a certain Greek of very high rank, whose name was Leon Sgure. This man, having gained possession of Corinth and Nauplia, two cities on the coast that are among the strongest under heaven, refused to swear allegiance to the marquis. On the contrary, he began to make war against him, and a very great number of Greeks ranged themselves on his side. There was another

Greek, named Michaelis, who had come from Constantinople with the marquis, and whom the latter believed to be his friend. But he suddenly went off, without saying a word, to the town of Arta, where he married the daughter of a wealthy Greek who held his land from the Emperor, and after seizing that land for himself, began to make war on the marquis.

By now the whole of the land from Constantinople to Salonika was at peace. The road from one city to the other was so safe that although it took twelve full days to cover the distance between them people were able to come and go as they pleased. So much time had now passed that we were at the end of September. The Emperor reigned in Constantinople, and the land was quiet under his rule. Nothing of any importance occurred in the city except the death of two good knights, Eustache de Canteleu and Aimery de Villeroi. This was a great grief to their friends.

CHAPTER 15

War against the Greeks
OCTOBER 1204–MARCH 1205

DIVISION of the lands within the empire now began. The Venetians were given their due share, the French received theirs. But no sooner was each man in possession of his land than covetousness, which has been the cause of so much evil in the world, prevented him from living in peace. All began, in a greater or less degree, to administer their estates with so little concern for the rights of others that the Greeks began to hate them and cherish resentment against them in their hearts.

The Emperor Baudouin gave the Comte Louis the duchy of Nicaea which was situated on the side of the straits towards Turkey, and was one of the most important fiefs in the empire. The land, however, on that side of the straits had not yet been brought under the Emperor's control, but stood out against him. A little later, the Emperor gave the duchy of Philippopolis to Renier de Trit.

The Comte Louis sent some hundred and twenty of his knights to conquer his land for him, with Pierre de Bracieux and Payïen d'Orléans in command. They left Constantinople on All Saints' Day, sailed across the Straits of St George to Abydos, and then went on to Spiga, a city on the coast inhabited by Latins. From there they began to make war against the Greeks.

Round about this time the Emperor Murzuphlus whose eyes had been put out – the same who had murdered the Emperor Isaac's son Alexius, whom the crusaders had brought with them to Constantinople – fled secretly across the straits with only a very small company of men. But Dietrich von Los, having heard of his flight from someone who informed against him, had him arrested and brought him back to the Emperor Baudouin at Constantinople. The Emperor was delighted at his capture, and asked his people what he should do with a man who had so treacherously murdered his lord.

It was agreed to inflict the following punishment: Towards the centre of Constantinople there stood a marble column, one of the highest and most finely carved that ever man's eye has seen. Murzuphlus was to be taken to the top of that column, and made to leap down in the sight of all the people, because it was fitting that such a signal act of justice should be seen by everyone. Murzuphlus was led to the column, and taken to the top, while all the people in the city flocked to the place to see that amazing sight. Then he was cast down, and he fell from such a height that every bone in his body was broken as soon as he reached the ground.

Now let me tell you of a marvellous coincidence. On that column from which Murzuphlus fell were figures of various kinds, carved in the marble, and among them was one representing an emperor falling headlong. Now a very long time before it had been prophesied that an emperor would be cast down from that very column. Thus the prophecy, as portrayed in the marble figure, came true.

It happened about the same time that the Marquis de Montferrat, while in the neighbourhood of Salonika, pounced on the Emperor Alexius – the same who had put out his brother's eyes – and took him prisoner, together with the Empress his wife. The marquis sent the scarlet buskins and the imperial robes belonging to Alexius to his lord the Emperor Baudouin at Constantinople, a courtesy which earned him the latter's gratitude. Subsequently the marquis dispatched the Emperor Alexius to Montferrat, to be held in prison there.

Not long after, on Saint Martin's day, the Emperor's brother Henri left Constantinople with about a hundred and twenty good knights, and marched down by the straits to the Channel of Abydos. There he sailed across the water to the city of Abydos, which he found well supplied with an abundance of good things, such as corn and meat, and everything else a man might need. After taking the city, he quartered his men there, and then he too began to make war on the Greeks round about. The Armenians of that region, and these were very many, began to rally to his side, for they detested the Greeks.

About the same time Renier de Trit left Constantinople with another band of a hundred and twenty knights, and went towards Philippopolis, which the Emperor had given him. He rode for several days, until, some way beyond Adrianople, he reached his destination. The people of Philippopolis welcomed him as their lord, and were very glad to see him. They were at that time in great need of help, for King Johanitza of Wallachia had been making many savage attacks on them. Renier de Trit came to their aid so effectively that he made himself master of a great part of the land, and many of those who had formerly sided with Johanitza now turned to him. In that part of the empire also fighting was very fierce.

Meanwhile the Emperor had sent about a hundred knights across the straits of St George to that part of the empire opposite Constantinople. Macaire de Sainte-Menehould was in command, assisted by Mathieu de Wallincourt and Robert de Ronsoi. After landing, they rode towards Nicomedia, which lies on the shores of a gulf and is a two days' journey by sea from Constantinople. As soon as the Greeks heard they were advancing, they evacuated Nicomedia and fled. So our men took up their quarters in the city, garrisoned it, and repaired the fortifications. From this region they began to make war on the Greeks, as others were doing elsewhere.

The land across the straits had a Greek named Theodore Lascaris as its lord. He had married the daughter of that Emperor Alexius who had put out his brother's eyes, and whom the Franks had subsequently driven out of Constantinople. Lascaris laid claim to the land in his wife's right, and carried on the war against the French on the far side of the straits, wherever they happened to be.

The Emperor Baudouin himself remained in Constantinople, together with the Comte Louis and a very small band of his men, as also the Comte Hugues de Saint-Pol, who was suffering from a severe attack of gout which affected his knees and feet, and the Doge of Venice, who was completely blind.

It was not long, however, before a very large body of men, including those who had left the army and sailed from other ports than Venice, arrived by sea from Syria. Among them were Étienne du Perche and Renaud de Montmirail, both of them cousins of the Comte Louis, who welcomed them very courteously and expressed his delight at their arrival. The Emperor Baudouin and the rest of the people in Constantinople also welcomed their coming, for both of them were men of high rank and great influence; and they had brought very many other good people with them. These included Hugues de Tabarie and Thierry de Tenremonde, together with a considerable number of Syrian troops, knights, light horsemen, and sergeants. Shortly after their arrival the Emperor granted the duchy of Philadelphia to Étienne du Perche.

One item among the news received at this time caused the Emperor Baudouin great distress. His wife, the Comtesse Marie, had been unable to go with him on crusade because she was pregnant, and had stayed behind in Flanders, where she had given birth to a daughter. As soon as she had recovered from her confinement, she had set off to join her husband oversea. She had sailed from the port of Marseilles, and had only just landed at Acre when messengers from Constantinople brought her news that the city had been taken and her lord elected Emperor, to the great joy of all Christian people. On hearing this the lady had made up her mind to join her husband immediately; but she was taken ill and had died. The whole of Christendom was plunged in grief by her death, for she was a truly good and gracious lady, and highly esteemed by all. News of this sad event was brought to Constantinople by people who had just arrived by sea. It was a great sorrow for the Emperor Baudouin, as for all the barons in the empire, for they had been eagerly looking forward to having her as their Empress.

Meanwhile the men who had gone to Spiga under the command of Pierre de Bracieux and Païen d'Orléans had fortified the castle of Panormos, and leaving a garrison to guard it, had ridden out to conquer the land. Theodore Lascaris, for his part, had got together as large a force as he could. On Saint Nicholas' Day, which precedes the Feast of the Conception of the Blessed Virgin, the two armies met on a plain below the castle of Poemanenos. A battle began in which our people were at a great disadvantage, for the Greeks had a really amazing number of men, while on our side, apart from a number of mounted sergeants, we had no more than a hundred and forty knights.

But our Lord orders all events as it pleases Him. By His gracious will the French overcame the Greeks, putting their troops to rout and inflicting heavy losses on them. Within the week, they surrendered a great part of the land to our army. They handed over the strongly fortified castle of Poemanenos, the city of Lopadium, which was one of the finest in the land, and Apollonia, which stood on the shore of a freshwater lake and was one of the strongest and most imposing castles anywhere to be found. Everything, in short, turned out to the advantage of our people, and with God's help they succeeded in subduing the land to their will.

Shortly after, on the advice of the Armenians, the Emperor Baudouin's brother Henri set out from Abydos, and leaving a garrison in the city, rode towards Adramyttium, a city on the coast about two days' journey away. This place was surrendered to him and so was much of the region round about. He quartered his troops in Adramyttium, because it was well supplied with corn and meat and other provisions, and from that base he made war on the Greeks in the surrounding country.

After his defeat at Poemanenos Theodore Lascaris gathered together as many people as he could, until he had assembled a great army. He placed this under the command of his brother Constantine, one of the ablest Greeks in the empire, who thereupon rode straight towards Adramyttium. The Emperor's brother Henri, hearing from the Armenians that a great force was marching against him, got ready to meet the enemy and marshalled his troops in battle order. He had with him some very good men, as for instance Baudouin de Beauvoir, Nicolas de Mailly, Anseau de Cayeux, Dietrich von Los, and Thierry de Termonde.

On the eve of mid-Lent Sunday, Constantine Lascaris and his great army arrived before Adramyttium. As soon as Henri heard he had come, he called the leaders of his army together and told them that he would not on any account let himself be shut up in the city, but would go out to meet the enemy. The Greeks advanced in full force, in great companies of horse and foot; our men marched out and began to attack them. There was much fierce fighting, with many a hand-to-hand encounter; but by God's help the French defeated the Greeks and drove them back in disorder. Many were killed or captured, and much booty was taken. After this the French lived in peace and comfort and with plentiful supplies of food, for the people of the land turned to their side, and began to bring them some of the produce from their estates.

Let us for the moment leave speaking of the men from Constantinople and return to the Marquis de Montferrat. He had, as you know, gone to Salonika, and had then marched against Leon Sgure, who held Nauplia and Corinth, two of the strongest cities in the world. His men started to lay siege to both these places at one and the same time. Jacques d'Avesnes, with many other good men, remained before Corinth; the rest encamped before Nauplia and besieged it.

Let me now tell you of something that happened in that region, round about the same time. Young Geoffroy de Villehardouin, the nephew of that other Geoffroy, who was now Marshal of Romania and of Champagne, had left Syria in the company of those who had recently arrived at Constantinople. It happened by chance that the wind carried his ship to the port of Methone, where it was so badly damaged that he was obliged to spend the winter in those parts. A certain Greek, who was a great noble of that country, having heard of his arrival, came to see him and greeted him very courteously. 'Sir,' he said, 'the Franks have conquered Constantinople and elected an emperor. If you will join with me, I will promise to be a loyal friend to you, and we shall conquer much of this land together.' So they made an alliance, confirmed by oath, and together conquered a great part of the country. Geoffroy de Villehardouin always found this Greek a very loyal ally.

But events turn out as God wills. The Greek was taken ill and died. His son rebelled against Geoffroy de Villehardouin and broke faith with him, and most of the castles in which Geoffroy had placed a garrison turned against him. News reached the young man that the Marquis de Montferrat was besieging Nauplia, so he went there to join him with as many men as he could collect together. After riding through the land for six days in very great peril he reached the marquis's camp, where he was very warmly welcomed and treated with the greatest courtesy by the marquis and all those who were with him. This was only right and fitting, since he was a very brave and honourable knight.

The marquis would have made him a generous grant of lands and money to keep him in his service; but he would accept nothing. Instead he went to Guillaume de Champlitte, who was a very good friend of his and said to him: 'I've just come, sir, from a very prosperous land, which is called Morea. Get together as many men as you can and leave this army, and with God's help we'll go and conquer it. When we've won it, I'll hold from you whatever part of it you're pleased to give me, and serve you as your vassal.' Guillaume de Champlitte, who had great confidence in Geoffroy and was very fond of him, went to the marquis to tell him what had been suggested, and the marquis gave both of them leave to go to Morea.

So Guillaume de Champlitte and his young friend left the marquis's camp, taking with them about a hundred knights, as well as a good number of mounted sergeants. They entered the land of Morea and rode onwards till they came to Methone. Michaelis heard that they had arrived in Morea with only a very small company of men, so he got together an astonishing number of his own people and rode after them, believing they were as good as captured already, and in his hands.

When our men heard he was coming they hastily repaired the walls of Methone, which had been in ruins for a long time past, and left their baggage in the town, with the servants to guard it. Then they rode out a day's march from the town and drew up ready for battle with as many men as they had. It looked as if the odds were against them, for they had no more than five hundred mounted men, while their opponents had well over five thousand. However since the outcome of events is ordered by God's will, when our men fought the Greeks they drove them back and defeated them. The enemy lost heavily in that encounter, while we on our side won a great number of horses, weapons, and armour, as well as a considerable amount of other booty. So our people went back to Methone very jubilant and well content.

Later they rode to Coron, a town on the coast, and laid siege to it. They had not been besieging it very long before the place surrendered. Guillaume gave it to Geoffroy de Villehardouin, who thus became his vassal, and Geoffroy placed a garrison there. Next they went to the castle of Kalamata, which was very fine and well fortified. Taking it was a long and arduous task, but they remained before it until it yielded to them. Afterwards the Greeks in Morea began to surrender in greater numbers than ever before.

The Marquis de Montferrat was still besieging Nauplia, but without the least success, for the place was too strongly fortified and in the effort to take it many of his men got quite worn out. Jacques d'Avesnes, for his part, continued to besiege Corinth, where he had been left by the marquis. Leon Sgure, who had remained in the city, and was a very shrewd and wily man, noticed that Jacques had only a small body of men with him, and did not keep good watch. So one morning at daybreak he came out of the city in full force, and got as far as the tents and killed many of our men before they could lay hold of their arms.

Among those killed was Dreux d'Estruen, a very good and valiant knight whose death was greatly lamented. Jacques d'Avesnes, who was in command, was very badly wounded in the leg; but those who were with him on that occasion later averred that they all owed their safety to his gallant behaviour. They had, indeed, all come very near to losing their lives, but by God's help they forced the enemy back into the castle.

Now the Greeks, who were by nature very perfidious, still harboured thoughts of treachery in their hearts. Perceiving at that time that the French were too widely scattered over the land and too busily occupied to attend to anything outside their own particular affairs, they thought they could the more easily get the better of them by underhand means. So they secretly chose envoys from all the cities in the empire and sent them to King Johanitza, regardless of the fact that he had long been their enemy and was still at war with them. These envoys told Johanitza that the Greeks proposed to make him Emperor; they would place themselves entirely in his hands, and kill all the French and Venetians in the empire. They swore, on behalf of all the Greeks, to obey him as their lord, provided he on his side would bind himself to defend and protect them as he would his own subjects. This pact was ratified by both parties.

About this time our people in Constantinople suffered a great loss. The Comte Hugues de Saint-Pol, who was badly afflicted with gout, and had long been confined to bed, became at last so ill that he died. This sad event caused great sorrow and was, indeed, a serious calamity. His men and his friends wept bitterly over his death. He was buried in the church of Saint George of Mangana.

During his lifetime the count had been lord of the very fine and well-fortified stronghold of Demotika, in which he had placed as garrison some of his knights and sergeants. Shortly after his death, the Greeks, in pursuance of their oath to the King of Wallachia, made a treacherous attack on the men in that castle, killing many and taking many captive. Very few escaped, and those who did fled for their lives to Adrianople, which the Venetians held at that time.

Not long after this the Greeks in Adrianople rose in armed revolt, and the men who had been stationed there to guard the city escaped from it in great peril of their lives. News of this reached the Emperor Baudouin, who was in Constantinople with the Comte Louis and a small handful of men, and it left them all troubled and dismayed. From that time onwards, equally unwelcome news began to come in daily; for everywhere the Greeks were rising, and wherever they found the French or the Venetians occupying the land they killed them.

The men who had fled from Adrianople, both the Venetians and others who were with them, had gone to Tchorlu, a city which the

Emperor Baudouin still held. There they found Guillaume de Blanvel, who was guarding the place for his lord. Thanks to the help and encouragement he gave them, and also because he consented to accompany them with as many men as he could spare, they turned back to a city some twelve leagues distant, called Arcadiopolis, which belonged to the Venetians. Finding it empty, they entered and occupied it.

Within three days the Greeks of that region gathered together, and from everywhere within the compass of a day's journey from Arcadiopolis, flocked to besiege the city. Then, from all sides, they began a fierce and terrifying assault. Our men defended themselves magnificently. They opened the gates and came rushing out in full force to attack the enemy. By God's will, the Greeks were routed, and our men began to cut them down and kill them. Then, as the enemy fled, they pursued them for a full league, killing many more, and capturing a great number of horses and much other spoil.

So they returned full of joy to Arcadiopolis, and sent news of their victory to the Emperor Baudouin in Constantinople, who greatly rejoiced to hear of it. None the less our men did not dare hold the city, but marched out the next day leaving it deserted, and went back to Tchorlu. Here they remained in a great state of apprehension, fearing the Greeks in the city as much as those outside, since these people had taken part in the oath sworn to the King of Wallachia, and bound themselves to betray all the Franks. Not a few of our people, in fact, did not dare remain in Tchorlu, but made their way back to Constantinople.

At this point the Emperor Baudouin, the Comte Louis, and the Doge of Venice, aware that they were gradually losing the whole of the empire, met to talk things over. As a result they agreed that the Emperor should order his brother Henri, who was then at Adramyttium, to leave whatever he had conquered and come to their assistance.

The Comte Louis, for his part, sent a message to Païen d'Orléans and Pierre de Bracieux, and all the men who were with them at Lopadium, telling them in their turn to abandon whatever they had conquered, except the coastal town of Spiga. Here they were to leave a garrison of as few men as possible, while the rest came to reinforce the troops on the other side of the straits.

Next, the Emperor instructed Macaire de Sainte-Menehould,

Mathieu de Wallincourt, and Robert de Ronsoi, who were in Nico-media with about a hundred knights, to leave and come to their aid.

On the Emperor's orders, Geoffroy de Villehardouin, Marshal of Romania and Champagne, left Constantinople with Manassier de l'Isle and as many men as they could get together – which was few enough considering that the whole of the empire was in a fair way to be lost. They rode to Tchorlu, which is about three days' journey from Constantinople, and there they found Guillaume de Blanvel and all the people with him in a great state of fear, though much re-assured by the arrival of the Marshal and his company. The visitors spent four days in Tchorlu. While they were there the Emperor Baudouin sent the Marshal such reinforcements as he could from the troops now coming in to Constantinople, so that by the fourth day there were eighty knights in the town.

Then Geoffroy de Villehardouin set off again with Manassier de l'Isle and their men. They rode on till they reached Arcadiopolis, where they stopped for the night. They spent a day there before moving on to Burgarophygon. The Greeks had evacuated this town, so they spent the night there. The next day they rode on to Nikitza, a very beautiful and well-fortified city, amply supplied with every-thing one could need. They found that all the Greeks had left the place and gone to Adrianople, but as Nikitza was only nine leagues distant from that city, in which a great multitude of the enemy had gathered, they decided to wait where they were till the Emperor Baudouin arrived.

Let me now tell you of an extraordinary incident. Renier de Trit, who was at Philippopolis, a good nine days' journey from Con-stantinople, with about a hundred knights, was deserted by his own son Renier, his brother Gilles, his nephew Jacques de Bondies, and his son-in-law Achard de Verdun. They took away with them some thirty of his knights, leaving him, as you can imagine, in very great peril. These men had thought to get safely to Constantinople, but they found the people of the country in revolt against them, and were defeated in a fight. The Greeks took them prisoner, and afterwards handed them over to the King of Wallachia, who had their heads cut off. Our people, I can assure you, felt little pity for these men, who had behaved so disgracefully to one whom they were in duty bound to treat in quite another way.

When some of Renier's other knights saw him thus deserted by those who were bound to him by closer ties than themselves, they felt less fear of shame on their own account, and some eighty of them deserted in a body, and went off by another route. So Renier de Trit was left surrounded by Greeks and with very few men of his own, for he had, in fact, no more than fifteen knights in all in Philippopolis and at Stenimaka – which is a very strong castle that he held, and where, later on, he was for a very long time besieged.

CHAPTER 16

Siege of Adrianople
MARCH–APRIL 1205

WE will now turn from Renier de Trit to speak once more of the Emperor Baudouin, whom we left in Constantinople extremely troubled and anxious, with his all too little band of men. He was waiting there for his brother Henri and all the troops from the other side of the straits. The first to arrive were the men from Nicomedia: Macaire de Sainte-Menehould, Mathieu de Wallincourt, and Robert de Ronsoi with their people, amounting in all to about a hundred knights.

The Emperor was extremely glad to see them. In consultation with the Comte Louis de Blois, he settled that they should leave Constantinople, with as many men as they had available, to follow Geoffroy de Villehardouin, who had left some time before. Alas! what a pity they did not wait till all the men from across the straits had joined them, seeing how small a force they had to cope with the dangers of such an expedition.

They left Constantinople with about a hundred and forty knights, and rode on day after day till they reached the castle of Nikitza, where Marshal Geoffroy had taken up his quarters. That night they met in conference and settled to go and encamp before Adrianople on the following day and besiege it. So they arranged the formation of their battalions, doing as best as they could with such people as they had.

The next morning, as soon as the sun was fully up, they rode, as had been arranged, to Adrianople, and took up their stand before the city. They found it very well defended, and saw the banners of Johanitza, King of Wallachia and Bulgaria, flying above its walls and towers. It was indeed a very strong and prosperous city, and very full of people. Our men began to make an assault with their little army on two of its gates. This was on the Tuesday before Palm Sunday. They remained three days before the city, in great anxiety and at a great disadvantage on account of their lack of men.

At this juncture Enrico Dandolo, Doge of Venice, undeterred by age and blindness, came to join them. He brought with him as many men as he had, and these were quite as many as had come with the Emperor Baudouin and the Comte Louis. The Venetians encamped in front of one of the gates. The next day they were joined by a troop of mounted sergeants. (If only these had been better men than they later proved to be!) Our troops were very short of supplies, because those who usually sold them provisions had not been able to come with them; nor could they go foraging for themselves because there were so many Greeks in the country round about that no one dared leave the camp. Meanwhile King Johanitza was advancing to the relief of Adrianople with a very great army; for he was bringing with him not only Wallachians and Bulgarians, but also some fourteen thousand mounted Comans, who had never been baptized.

In the end, because of the great shortage of food, the Comte Louis went out foraging on Palm Sunday. He took with him the Comte du Perche's brother Étienne, Renaud de Montmirail, who was the brother of the Comte Henri de Nevers, Gervais du Châtel, and more than half the men in camp. They went to the castle of Peutza, which they found well garrisoned with Greeks, and made a desperate effort to take it by storm. But they met with no success and had to return from their expedition empty-handed. During Holy Week the troops remained stationary, constructing machines of various kinds out of wooden planks, and setting such sappers as they had to dig below ground and undermine the walls. In such conditions they celebrated Easter day, encamped before Adrianople, with very few men for the work in hand and not enough to feed them.

Then came news that King Johanitza was marching against them to relieve the city. So they made all necessary preparations to meet him, and arranged that Geoffroy de Villehardouin and Manassier de l'Isle should stay to guard the camp, while the Emperor Baudouin and the rest of the troops would go out to confront Johanitza if he threatened to attack them.

The army waited on the alert till the Wednesday of Easter Week, by which time Johanitza had approached so near that his camp was a bare five leagues away. Then he sent his Comans charging right up to our camp. A call to arms was raised; our men rushed out in disorder and pursued the Comans for a full league and more. This was a very foolish action on their part, for when they wished to turn back the Comans let fly a veritable storm of arrows at them, and wounded many of their horses.

When at length they returned to camp the Emperor Baudouin summoned the barons to his quarters. They discussed the incident and all concerned in it admitted that they had acted very unwisely in pursuing for such a distance a body of troops so lightly armed. In the end it was settled that if Johanitza attacked again they would come out and draw up in their ranks in front of the camp to await his coming, and not stir from that position. Then a general proclamation was issued to the troops forbidding anyone to be so rash as to disregard this order, no matter what call to arms or what clamour of any kind he might happen to hear.

That night passed. In the morning, which was a Thursday in Easter Week, all the troops attended mass and then had their midday meal. The Comans came charging up to their tents; a cry was raised and everyone ran to arms, and came out of camp with all the battalions in proper order, according to plan.

The Comte Louis came out first with his battalion. He sent back a message to the Emperor urging him to follow and immediately started off in pursuit of the Comans. Alas! how little our army kept to the course of action agreed on the night before! Instead of remaining by the camp, our men pursued the Comans for nearly two leagues, attacking them at close quarters and keeping up the chase for a very long time. At length the Comans turned round and charged them, uttering piercing yells as they let their arrows fly.

There happened to be in our army certain companies of men below the rank of knights, who had little experience of fighting, and who now began to panic and give way. The Comte Louis, who had been the first to attack, was very badly wounded in two places. The Comans and Wallachians were beginning to press our forces hard. The Comte Louis had fallen from his horse; but one of his knights dismounted and helped him up into the saddle. Many of the count's men said to him: 'My lord, do get back to camp; you're too badly wounded.' But he always replied: 'God forbid I should ever be reproached with flying from the field and abandoning my Emperor.'

The Emperor, who was hard put to it on his side, gathered his men round him and told them that he, for his part, would never consent to fly, and that they were to remain with him. Those who were present at the time can testify that no knight ever defended himself more valiantly than he.

This combat went on for a very long time. There were some who bore themselves bravely in the encounter, others who took to flight. In the end, since God permits such disasters to occur, the French were defeated. The Emperor Baudouin, who would never consent to flee, remained on the field, as did the Comte Louis. The one was taken alive, the other was among the dead.

Alas! what a loss we suffered on that day! Among those who fell were Pierre, Bishop of Bethlehem, Étienne du Perche, Renaud de Montmirail, brother of the Comte de Nevers, Mathieu de Wallincourt, Robert de Ronsoi, Jean de Friaize, Gautier de Neuilly, Ferry d'Yerres, and his brother Jean, Eustache de Heumont and his brother Jean, Baudouin de Neuville, and many others whose names are not recorded here. Those who managed to escape went flying back to the camp.

As soon as Geoffroy de Villehardouin, who was keeping guard at one of the gates of the city, heard of this disaster, he left the camp as quickly as he could with all the men he had with him, and sent word to Manassier de l'Isle, who was on guard at another gate, telling him to follow. The Marshal rode forward at full speed at the head of his battalion to meet the fugitives, who on seeing him rallied round him. Manassier de l'Isle came up as quickly as he could to join him, so that together they formed a much stronger body. All those who came fleeing from the field and whom they were able to stop were taken into the ranks.

In between three o'clock and six the rout was stayed. But most of the fugitives were in such a panic that they fled past Villehardouin's troops to take refuge among the tents and pavilions. Such was the end of the retreat. The Comans, Wallachians, and Greeks came to a halt in front of our battalion, which they harassed unremittingly as they made full play with their bows and arrows. Our men, however, stood motionless with their faces towards the enemy. Both sides remained thus till nightfall, when the Comans and Wallachians began to retire.

Geoffroy de Villehardouin, Marshal of Champagne and Romania, now sent a message back to the camp requesting the Doge, who in spite of his age and blindness was very wise and brave and full of energy, to come to the plain where he himself stood with his battalion. The Doge did as he was asked. As soon as the Marshal saw him he called him aside to consult with him in private. 'My lord,' he said, 'you see what a disaster we have suffered. We've lost the Emperor Baudouin and the Comte Louis as well as most of our men, and some of the best ones too. We must now think how to save those that are left; for if God does not take pity on them, we're as good as lost.'

In the end they settled that the Doge would return to camp to put fresh heart into the troops, and give each man orders to put on his armour and stay quietly in his tent or pavilion. Meanwhile the Marshal would remain outside the camp with all his troops in battle order till it began to get dark, so that the enemy would not see them leave. Then, when it was completely dark, the whole army would move from its position before the city. The Doge of Venice would go first, and the Marshal with his men would form the rear-guard.

The army waited till it was night. Then the Doge of Venice left the camp as had been arranged, while Geoffroy de Villehardouin brought up the rear. They set off at a walking pace with all the troops, both horse and foot, the wounded as well as those who were uninjured – not one was left behind. They were making for Rodosto, a city on the coast, at a distance of three days' journey from Adrianople. Thus they left that city behind them and went on their way. All this occurred in the year of our Lord 1205.

During the night on which the army left Adrianople it so happened that one company had separated from the rest in the hope of reaching Constantinople earlier by taking a more direct route. Such conduct, I may say, met with general disapproval. In this company was a certain count of Lombardy who came from the Marquis de Montferrat's own domains. With him went Eudes de Ham, who was lord of a castle of that name in Vermandois, and some twenty-five knights whose names are not given here.

They travelled so fast, and went away so soon after the defeat of our troops, which had taken place on the Thursday evening, that by the following Saturday night they reached Constantinople, although, in ordinary circumstances, it was a good five days' journey. They told their news to the Cardinal Pietro da Capua, who was there as legate from the Pope of Rome, as also to Conon de Béthune, who was guarding the city, to Milon le Brébant, and other leading men. Everyone was greatly dismayed to hear of the disaster and thought for sure that all the others whom these men had left before Adrianople were lost, since they had received no news of them.

For the time being we will say no more about the people in Constantinople, who were now in great distress, but go back to the Doge of Venice and Marshal Geoffroy. These had ridden on through the night on which they had left Adrianople till at daybreak on the following day they reached the city of Pamphile. Now listen and you shall hear how all events are ordered by God's will. In that very city, Pierre de Bracieux and Païen d'Orléans had spent the night, with all the men from the Comte Louis' domains, about a hundred good stout knights and a hundred and forty mounted sergeants. They had just arrived from the other side of the straits and were on their way to join the army at Adrianople.

The moment they saw our troops advancing they hastened to arm, for they thought we were the Greeks. As soon as the newcomers were armed, they sent scouts to find out who we were, and these discovered that we were their own people retreating after a defeat. So the scouts went back to tell our friends that the Emperor Baudouin was missing, and that their lord the Comte Louis, from whose lands they came and who had been their leader, had been killed in the fight.

Sadder news could never have been told them. Many a tear was shed, and many hands were wrung in grief and anguish. The whole company rode forward, all armed as they were, till they came to where Marshal Geoffroy was keeping guard in the rear. He was overcome with anxiety because king Johanitza had arrived at daybreak before Adrianople with all his army, and finding we had left had ridden after us. Very fortunately he had not discovered where we were, since if he had caught up with us we should all have been irretrievably lost.

'Sir,' said Pierre de Bracieux and Païen d'Orléans to the Marshal, 'say what you want us to do, and we'll do it.' 'You can see what a state we're in,' said the Marshal. 'You're fresh, and so are your horses. So you can guard the rear while I go on ahead to keep our men in hand. They're frightened out of their wits, and badly need a word of encouragement.' The two men readily agreed to do as he asked. So they went to the rear, and being good and honourable knights, performed their duties very ably and conscientiously, as men who well knew how such things ought to be done.

Marshal Geoffroy rode on in front and led the army as far as a city called Cariopolis. Then seeing the horses were weary after marching all night, he entered the city and stabled the beasts till noon. The men saw to the feeding of their horses and then made a meal for themselves of such food as they could find, which was very little.

They stayed at Cariopolis the whole of that day until nightfall. Then, since Johanitza had been following them all day along the road they had taken, and was now encamped about two leagues away, all the troops in the city armed themselves and left as soon as it was dark. Marshal Geoffroy led the van, while those who had acted as rear-guard during the day formed up behind the army. They rode throughout the night and the whole of the following day, harassed by fear and exhausted by the efforts they were making, until at length they reached Rodosto, a very prosperous and strongly fortified city inhabited by Greeks. However, these people did not attempt to defend themselves, so our troops entered and took quarters there. At last they were in safety.

Having thus escaped after their defeat at Adrianople, the leaders of the army met in conference at Rodosto. The general opinion of the meeting was that they had more reason to fear for their friends in Constantinople than for themselves. So they chose reliable messengers and sent them by sea, with orders to travel night and day without stopping to tell their people in the city not to be anxious about them, since they had escaped, and to assure them that the troops now in Rodosto would come back to join them in Constantinople as soon as they possibly could.

At the time when these messengers arrived in Constantinople five fine great ships of the Venetian fleet were in harbour there, with a crowd of pilgrims, knights, and sergeants on board who were leaving that land to return to their own country. At least seven thousand men-at-arms were in these ships. Guillaume, Advocate of Béthune, was there, with Baudouin d'Aubigny and also Jean de Versin, who came from the Comte Louis' own estates and was his vassal; there were besides well over a hundred knights whom I will not mention by name.

His Eminence Pietro da Capua, cardinal-legate of Pope Innocent, Conon de Béthune, who had charge of Constantinople, and Milon de Brébant, with a number of other men of good standing, went in a body to the five ships, and with tears in their eyes implored the men aboard to have pity on their fellow-Christians, as also on their lords who had died in battle, and remain there for the love of God. However, the men on all the ships turned a deaf ear to their entreaties, and left the harbour. The ships spread their sails, and these men went their way, to arrive, as God ordained and the wind bore them onwards, at the port of Rodosto. This happened on the day following that on which the men who had escaped from their defeat at Adrianople had reached that place.

The same entreaties, accompanied by tears, as had been addressed to these men at Constantinople, now greeted them at Rodosto. Marshal Geoffroy and those who were with him earnestly pleaded with them to take pity on the empire and remain there; for they would never be able to give their help to any land that needed it more urgently. The men replied that they would think it over and give the others an answer on the following day.

Here let me tell you of an incident that occurred at Rodosto during the night. There was in our company a knight from the Comte Louis' domains, named Pierre de Frouville, who was held in honour as a man of good character and reputation. However, he stole away by night, leaving all his baggage behind him, and got aboard the ship in command of Jean de Versin, who was also the Comte Louis' vassal. Those on board the ships, who were to have given their answer to Geoffroy de Villehardouin and the Doge of Venice in the morning, spread their sails as soon as they saw day beginning to dawn and went off without a word to anyone. They were severely criticized for acting thus, both in the land to which they went and in the land they had left – Pierre de Frouville most of all. For, as wise men say, a man does a very foolish thing when through fear of death he commits an act that will be a reproach to him for ever.

CHAPTER 17

A Regency Established

AT this point I will turn my attention elsewhere, and leaving the army at Rodosto, tell you something more about the Emperor Baudouin's brother Henri. He had by this time left Adramyttium and was hastening towards Adrianople to come to the aid of the Emperor his brother. He had crossed the straits with a large company of those Armenians who had helped him against the Greeks. They were in all about twenty thousand, counting their wives and children, who had not dared to remain behind.

On his way to Adrianople he had learnt from certain Greeks who had fled from the battle in which our army was defeated that his brother, the Emperor Baudouin, was missing and that the Comte Louis and many other barons had been killed. Later on, he had received news from those who had escaped and were at Rodosto, together with a request that he would make haste to join them as quickly as he could. Since he was anxious to get to them as soon as possible he left the Armenians, who were travelling on foot with their baggage waggons, their wives, and their children, to follow on behind. As they could not keep up with his men, and because he thought they would travel safely and without fear of any risk, he went on ahead and encamped in a village called Cortocopolis.

That same day he was joined by Anseau de Courcelles, one of Geoffroy de Villehardouin's nephews, whom the Marshal had summoned from that part of the empire in which Makri, Trajanopolis, and the monastery of Bera are situated, and which had been given to Anseau as his own possession. With him came a number of the men from Philippopolis who had deserted Renier de Trit. The whole company included about a hundred good knights and five hundred mounted sergeants, all of whom had been on their way to Adrianople to help the Emperor Baudouin. But news having reached them, as it had reached others, of the Emperor's defeat, they had turned in the direction of Rodosto, and so had come to encamp at

Cortocopolis, the very village where the Emperor's brother Henri had pitched his own tents.

When Henri and his men saw them coming they ran to arms, thinking they were Greeks. The others, on their side, thought the same of them. Both parties advanced till they were near enough to recognize each other, and then they exchanged delighted greetings, and everyone felt more at ease. So they encamped together in the village for the night.

The next day they all set off again and rode straight towards Rodosto, which they reached that evening. There they found the Doge of Venice with Marshal Geoffroy and all the others who had escaped in the recent disaster. These greeted the newcomers very warmly; but many tears were shed for sorrow over the death of their friends. Alas! what a pity it was that this reunion of the forces had not taken place at Adrianople when the Emperor Baudouin was there; for in that case nothing would have been lost. But such was not God's pleasure.

The whole company spent the next two days together at Rodosto and during this time they viewed the situation and decided what action they should take. Among other things they accepted the Emperor Baudouin's brother Henri as their lord, and made him Regent of the Empire, to take over command of affairs in his brother's place. In the meantime, the Armenians, who had been following after Henri de Flandre had met with disaster. The people of those parts had gathered together and overcome them, so that all of them were either taken prisoner or killed outright.

Meanwhile King Johanitza, who was in the land with all his forces, had by this time occupied it almost entirely. The people everywhere, in the countryside, the cities, and the castles, had come over to him, and his Comans had overrun the whole territory right up to the gates of Constantinople. The Regent, the Doge of Venice, and the Marshal, who were still at Rodosto, which is three days' journey from the capital, met in conference. As a result, the Doge of Venice set a garrison of his men in Rodosto, which belonged to the Venetians. The next day all the troops assembled in their battalions and rode by gradual stages to Constantinople.

When they reached Selymbria, a city which was two days' journey from the capital, and belonged to the Emperor Baudouin, Henri de Flandre garrisoned it with his own troops, and then rode with the rest of the men to Constantinople. Here they were very warmly welcomed, for the people in the city were paralysed with fear. Nor is that to be wondered at, seeing we had lost so much of the empire, that outside Constantinople only Rodosto and Selymbria remained in our possession; all the rest of the land was in the hands of King Johanitza. Across the straits, moreover, only the castle of Spiga was under our control; apart from this the whole of the territory was held by Theodore Lascaris.

The barons now decided to send and ask for help from Pope Innocent of Rome, from France and Flanders, and from other countries. The envoys chosen for this mission were Névelon, Bishop of Soissons, Nicolas de Mailly, and Jean Bliaut. The rest remained in Constantinople, in great distress of mind, as men who feared they were about to lose their land. They remained in this unhappy state till Whitsuntide. During that period they suffered a great loss in the death, through illness, of Enrico Dandolo. He was buried with great honour in the Church of Saint Sophia.

By Whitsuntide King Johanitza had pretty well done all he wished to do in the land. But he could no longer keep his Comans together; they found it impossible to go on fighting during the hot weather, so they all went back to their own country. Johanitza, with an army made up of Bulgarians and Greeks, marched to attack the Marquis de Montferrat in Salonika. The marquis, who by this time had heard the news of the Emperor Baudouin's defeat at Adrianople, raised the siege of Nauplia, and taking with him as many men as he could get together hastened to Salonika and manned it with his troops.

Henri de Flandre, for his part, assembling as large a force as he could manage, marched to attack the Greeks in Tchorlu, which was a three days' journey from Constantinople. The town surrendered and the Greeks swore allegiance to Henri the regent – but in those days such an oath was often badly kept. Next he marched on Arcadiopolis, which he found deserted, for the Greeks had not dared to wait for his arrival. He continued on his way till he reached Bizoë, a very strong city, well garrisoned with Greeks. This place also surrendered. After that he rode to Apros, which had an equally strong garrison to defend it.

As our troops were preparing for an assault the Greeks in the city sent to ask for terms of surrender. But while negotiations were in progress, our men effected an entry into the city on another side. This was done without the knowledge of the regent and others concerned in the negotiations, and made them extremely annoyed. The French began to massacre the Greeks and seize everything of value in the city, snatching up anything that came to hand. Many of the Greeks were killed, and many captured. Thus Apros was taken; afterwards the army spent three days in the city. The Greeks as a whole were so terrified by this slaughter of their compatriots that they abandoned all the cities and castles in the land and fled for refuge to Adrianople and Demotika, both very fine cities, and strongly fortified.

About the same time, the King of Wallachia and Bulgaria, who was marching to attack the Marquis de Montferrat with all his forces, arrived before the city of Serrès. The marquis had set a strong garrison in that city, for Hugues de Coligny, a very brave and able knight of high rank was there in command, supported by Guillaume d'Arles, the marquis's own marshal, and a great number of his best men. King Johanitza besieged them in that city, and had not been there very long before he took the place by storm. During the taking of it the defenders were so unfortunate as to lose Hugues de Coligny, who met his death through a wound in the eye.

When this man, who was the best of them all, was killed, the rest of the garrison lost heart, and took refuge in the castle, which was strongly fortified. Johanitza drew up his petraries ready to attack this stronghold and besieged them there. He had not been doing this very long before the men inside began to ask for terms, an action which would cast a slur on their reputation later on. They agreed to surrender the castle to Johanitza, and he on his side made twenty-five men of the highest rank in his army swear to them that they would be given safe escort, with their horses and all their equipment, to Salonika, Constantinople, or Hungary – whichever of the three they preferred.

On these terms Serrès was surrendered. Johanitza ordered all its defenders to come out and encamp beside his army in the fields. At first he made a show of friendliness towards them, and even sent them presents. But after treating them in this way for three days, he behaved most deceitfully, and broke all his promises. He had them seized, stripped of all their possessions, and led away to Wallachia, naked, unshod, and on foot. Those who were poor, or of meaner birth, and therefore of little importance, he sent away to Hungary; as for the rest, he had their heads cut off. Such was the infamous treachery King Johanitza could commit. The army suffered on that occasion one of the greatest disasters that had ever befallen it. Johanitza had both city and castle razed to the ground, after which he went on his way to deal with the marquis.

Henri, Regent of the empire, rode with all his forces to Adrianople and besieged it. In doing so he placed himself and his army in great peril, for so many people, both within the city and without, hemmed him in on all sides that his men could rarely leave the camp to buy provisions or do more than a very little foraging. To make themselves more secure they enclosed their camp with palisades and stoutly barred gates, and told off part of their men to keep guard inside while the rest went out to attack the city. They also constructed machines of various kinds, prepared their scaling ladders and other things of use in an assault, and, in short, put themselves to a great deal of trouble in order to take the city. But they could not take it, for the place was too strong, and amply garrisoned with troops to defend it. On the contrary everything went against them, and many of their men were wounded. One of their best knights, Pierre de Bracieux, was struck on the forehead by a stone from a mangonel and nearly killed outright. However, by God's will, he recovered and was taken away in a litter.

When at length he saw that all their efforts to take the city would be fruitless, the regent withdrew his troops and left. During their retreat they were constantly harassed by the Greeks and the people of the land through which they passed. They rode on, day after day, till they came to Pamphile, where they found quarters and stayed for a couple of months. From there they made many forays in the direction of Demotika and other places round about, acquiring by this means a great number of cattle and a good store of other spoil. They remained in those parts until the beginning of winter, while supplies were sent to them from Rodosto and other places on the coast.

CHAPTER 18

King Johanitza Ravages the Empire
JUNE 1205–JUNE 1206

I WILL for the moment turn from Henri, Regent of the empire, to speak more particularly of Johanitza, King of Wallachia and Bulgaria, who had, as you know, captured Serrès and treacherously killed those who had surrendered to him. Afterwards, he had marched to Salonika and had spent a long time in that neighbourhood, laying waste a great part of the land. Meanwhile the Marquis de Montferrat had remained in his capital city, full of grief for the loss of his lord the Emperor Baudouin and the barons who had died at Adrianople, and bitterly distressed by the capture of his castle of Serrès and his men.

When Johanitza saw that he had done all he could in Salonika he turned back towards his own country, taking his army with him. The Greeks in Philippopolis – which the Emperor had given to Renier de Trit – had heard how the Emperor Baudouin had been lost, with many of his barons, and how Serrès had been taken from the marquis by Johanitza. They also knew that Renier de Trit's own relatives, including his son and his nephew, had abandoned him, and that he had very few people left. Believing, therefore, that the French would never again have the upper hand, a great number of the citizens who belonged to the Paulician sect went to Johanitza to surrender themselves to him and said: 'Your Majesty, ride to Philippopolis or send your army there, and we will deliver the whole city into your hands.'

When Renier de Trit, who was in Philippopolis, heard of this offer, he was very much afraid that these men would do as they said. So one morning at daybreak he left his house, and with as many of his own people as he had available went to a suburb of the city inhabited by the Paulicians[1] who had surrendered to Johanitza and set fire to it, so that much of that quarter was burned. Then he left Philippopolis and went to the castle of Stenimaka, which was about

---

[1] A sect that originated in Armenia in the seventh century. Its members inclined to the manichean heresy that good and evil are of equal power in the world, and the Devil is co-eternal with God.

three leagues away from the city, and was garrisoned by his own men. He and his people remained there for a very long time, some thirteen months in all, in close confinement, under miserable conditions and in great distress of mind, and so desperately short of food that they had to eat their horses. They were, moreover, a good nine leagues distant from Constantinople, so that any exchange of news between the castle and the city was out of the question.

While Renier and his men were at Stenimaka, King Johanitza came with his army to besiege Philippopolis. He had not been there very long before the people in the city surrendered it to him after he had promised to spare their lives. But in spite of this guarantee he first had the archbishop of the city put to death, and then gave orders for certain of the men of rank to be flayed alive and others to have their heads cut off; the rest of the citizens were led away in chains. Next, he had all the walls and towers of the city razed to the ground, its great palaces and fine houses burned to ashes. Thus the noble city of Philippopolis, one of the three finest cities in the whole empire of Constantinople, was utterly destroyed.

With this I end the story of Philippopolis, and leaving Renier de Trit shut up in Stenimaka, return to the Emperor Baudouin's brother Henri, who had remained at Pamphile till the beginning of winter. As soon as the cold weather set in he consulted his men and his barons, who advised him to set a garrison in the city of Rousion, which lay in a very fertile district and occupied a central position in the land. The men placed in charge of this garrison were Dietrich von Los, who acted as governor of the city, and Thierry de Termonde, who was given command of the troops. The regent gave them about a hundred and forty knights and a great many mounted sergeants; he ordered them to carry on the war against the Greeks, and keep guard over the outlying districts.

He himself went with the rest of his men to Bizoë, and left a garrison of about a hundred and twenty knights and a good number of mounted sergeants in that city, with Anseau de Cayeux in command. Another city, Arcadiopolis, was garrisoned by the Venetians. At the same time the regent restored Apros to Theodore Branas, a Greek who was married to the King of France's sister, and was, in fact, the only one of his compatriots who had remained on our side. The troops in all these cities continued to wage war against the Greeks, and made many raids into their territory. The Greeks, for their part, made as many surprise attacks on them. Henri himself had by this time gone back to Constantinople with the remainder of his men.

Meanwhile King Johanitza, although now very powerful and master of great possessions, had not remained idle, but had raised a great army of Comans and Wallachians. Three weeks after Christmas he sent these men into the empire of Constantinople to help the Greeks in Adrianople and Demotika. After the arrival of these reinforcements our enemies grew bolder and made raids on our troops with more assurance.

Four days before the feast of Candlemas, Thierry de Termonde, commander of the troops in Rousion, went out on a foray. He rode all night, taking some hundred and twenty knights with him and leaving very few men to guard the city. By daybreak they arrived at a village where a party of Comans and Wallachians were encamped, and took them so completely by surprise that none of the troops in that place had any idea they were coming. The French killed a great number of Johanitza's men and seized about forty of their horses. After doing the enemy such damage, they turned back towards Rousion.

On the very night our people had set out on this expedition a large body of Comans and Wallachians, some seven thousand strong, had ridden out with the object of doing us some harm. In the morning they came before Rousion, and stayed there for some considerable time. The very small band of men left to guard the city closed the gates and mounted the walls. At this the Comans and Wallachians turned round and began to withdraw. They had not gone more than a league and a half from the city when they met the French troops in command of Thierry de Termonde. As soon as these saw the enemy advancing, they formed themselves into four companies, and decided to withdraw towards Rousion, but at the slowest possible pace. If by God's grace they could reach the city, they knew they would be safe.

The Comans and Wallachians, together with the Greeks of that region, came charging towards them in full force. They fell upon the rear-guard and began to attack them very savagely. This company was made up of men belonging to the governor, Dietrich von Los; but he had gone back to Constantinople, so his brother Vilain[1] was now in command. The enemy pressed them very hard and wounded many of their horses. Loud shouts rang out and the tumult grew more

---

[1] Wilhelm?

violent, till at last the rear-guard, exhausted and overcome by numbers, were forcibly driven back on to the company led by André
d'Urboise and Jean de Choisy. So the French retreated, while keeping
up a sustained resistance against the enemy for a considerable time.

Then the enemy renewed their onslaught so fiercely that they
drove the companies already engaged back on the one led by Thierry
de Termonde. Nor was it long before they drove these back still
further on to the company under Charles du Frêne. The French, still
fighting stoutly, had by now retreated so far that they could see the
walls of Rousion only half a league away. Their opponents pressed
them harder and harder, so that the odds were too great against them;
many men were wounded, as were their horses. In the end, since it is
God's will that such disasters should happen, they could resist no longer
and were defeated, mainly because they were heavily armed and
their opponents lightly. Then the enemy began to slaughter them.

Alas! what a sad day for Christendom! Out of all the hundred and
twenty knights in that fight no more than ten escaped being either
killed or taken prisoner. Those few who got away came flying back
to rejoin their friends in Rousion. Among those killed were Thierry de
Termonde and that good knight Orry de l'Isle, whom everyone
esteemed, as also Jean de Pomponne, André d'Urboise, Jean de
Choisy, Guy de Conflans, Charles du Frêne, and Vilain, the brother of
Dietrich von Los, governor of the city. There is no room in this book
to give you the names of all those who were killed or captured. On
that most sorrowful day we met with the heaviest losses, and suffered
one of the worst disasters the Christian people of the empire had ever
experienced – and one of the most pitiful too.

The Comans, Greeks, and Wallachians, having done as much harm
in our land as they wished to do, now withdrew, each man to his own
country. This catastrophe happened to our army on the day before
the eve of Candlemas. Those of our men who had escaped after their
defeat, together with those who had been in Rousion, slipped out of
the city as soon as it was dark, and fled on through the night, to arrive
the next morning at Rodosto.

The sad news of this defeat reached Henri, Regent of the Empire, as
he was going in procession to the shrine of our Lady of Blachernae on
Candlemas Day. It caused great alarm to many people in the city,
who were now convinced that the Empire of Constantinople was
lost. The regent thought it advisable to place a garrison in Selymbria,

which is a two days' journey from Constantinople; so he sent Macaire de Sainte-Menehould with a company of fifty knights to keep guard over that city.

King Johanitza, for his part, was delighted when he heard news of how his people had fared, and all the more because they had killed or taken a very great part of the best men in the French army. So he sent out a summons throughout his land calling in as many men as he could get together, and after raising a great army of Comans, Greeks, and Wallachians, invaded the empire. The people in most of the cities and the castles rallied to his side, so that in the end he had such a mighty army that it exceeded all belief.

When the Venetians heard he was coming with so great a force they abandoned Arcadiopolis. Johanitza advanced with all his troops till he reached Apros, which was garrisoned with Greeks and Latins and belonged to Branas, who, as you know, had married the King of France's sister. The chief man among the Latins was Bègue de Fransures, a French knight from the county of Beauvaisis.

The King of Wallachia delivered an assault on the city and took it by storm. The number of citizens massacred was so great that it beggars all description. Bègue de Fransures was brought before Johanitza, who immediately had him put to death, together with all the Greeks and Latins who were of any consequence. All people of no importance or of humble birth, together with all the women and the children, were by his orders taken away to Wallachia. After this he had the whole city – a very fine and prosperous place and in a very fertile part of the country – destroyed and razed to the ground. Thus the ruin of Apros was accomplished.

Twelve leagues away, on the coast, lay Rodosto, a very large and wealthy city, strongly fortified and well garrisoned by Venetians. Besides all this, a body of mounted sergeants, some two thousand strong, had recently arrived to help guard the city. When these men heard that Apros had been taken by force and that Johanitza had had all the people in the city put to death they were so overcome by fear that they gave up the fight before it had begun. As God permits such misadventures, to happen to men, the Venetians rushed helter-skelter aboard their ships, each trying to outstrip the rest, and in such disorder that they almost drowned one another. The mounted sergeants, who came from Flanders, France and other countries, fled away by land.

What a disaster indeed, and one that need never have happened!

The city was so strong and so well enclosed by stout walls and towers that no one would ever have ventured to assault it, and Johanitza would never have thought of turning his army that way. But as soon as this king, who was then about half a day's journey from Rodosto, heard that its garrison had fled, he advanced on the city. The Greeks who had remained there surrendered the place to him, and he immediately had them taken, no matter what their rank, and led away captive to Wallachia – except for a few who escaped. Then he had the city destroyed and razed to the ground. Ah! what a terrible pity! for Rodosto was one of the finest and best-constructed cities in the empire.

Not far from Rodosto was another city called Panedor. This too surrendered to Johanitza, and he had it utterly destroyed, and its citizens led away captive to Wallachia, like the people of Rodosto. From there he rode to Heraclea, a city on the coast which belonged to the Venetians, and had a very good harbour. However, the Venetians had left it with only a very weak garrison, so Johanitza assaulted it and took it by force. There again a general massacre of the citizens followed. Those who escaped with their lives were taken away to Wallachia, while the city was destroyed, as had happened with the others.

From there Johanitza marched to Daonium. This was a very fine well-fortified city, but its people did not dare to defend it, so after it had been surrendered he had it razed to the ground. Then he went on to Tchorlu, which had already surrendered to him; he ordered his men to reduce the whole city to ruins, and take its people away captive. As castles or cities surrendered to him he dealt with them in the same way; even though he had promised their people safety, he had every one of these places destroyed and all the men and women led into captivity. He never, in short, kept any covenant he had made.

Before long the Comans and Wallachians had overrun the land as far as the gates of Constantinople, where the regent, with as many men as he had at his command, was then residing. He was feeling very sad and extremely worried at not being able to get enough men to defend his land. Because of this the Comans were seizing all the cattle in the countryside, carrying off men, women, and children wherever they found them, destroying castles and cities as they passed, everywhere causing such ruin and desolation that no one has ever heard tell of anything to surpass it.

On one occasion they assembled before Athyra, a city some twelve leagues from Constantinople, which Henri had given to Païen d'Orléans. This place contained a very great number of people, for the countryfolk from round about had taken refuge there. The Comans attacked it and took it by force. There the slaughter was so great that there had been nothing to exceed it in the cities where they had already been. During this time, as I have said before, every castle or city that surrendered to Johanitza under promise of safety was destroyed and razed to the ground, and its people led away captive to Wallachia.

At length, within a radius of five days' journey from Constantinople, nothing remained to be destroyed except the cities of Bizoë and Selymbria, which were garrisoned by the French. Anseau de Cayeux was in Bizoë with a hundred and twenty knights; Macaire de Sainte-Menehould, with fifty knights, was in Selymbria; the Emperor Baudouin's brother Henri was in Constantinople with the remainder of the troops. With only two cities outside Constantinople still in their possession, the fortunes of the French, I need hardly tell you, were at their lowest ebb.

When the Greeks who were in Johanitza's army – that is to say those who had surrendered to him and rebelled against the Franks – saw how he had destroyed their cities and their castles, and had broken every promise he had made to them, they felt they had been betrayed and gave themselves up for lost. After talking things over among themselves, they came to the conclusion that as soon as Johanitza came back to Adrianople and Demotika he would deal with them as he had dealt with other places, and if these two cities were demolished the empire would be lost to them for ever.

So they chose messengers in secret, and sent them to their compatriot Branas in Constantinople, imploring him to plead their cause with the Emperor's brother Henri and with the Venetians, so that they might make peace with them. They themselves, in their turn, would restore Adrianople and Demotika to the Franks, and give their undivided support to the regent, so that Greeks and Franks might live together as friends.

A conference was accordingly held in Constantinople. Many arguments were put forward, both for and against the proposal, but in the end it was settled that Adrianople and Demotika, with all the territory belonging to them, should be granted to Branas and his wife, and that Branas should do service for them to the Emperor and the empire. An agreement to this effect was drafted, and signed by both parties. Thus peace was re-established between the Greeks and the Franks.

King Johanitza, who had spent a long time in the empire, laying waste the country during the whole of Lent and for a good while after Easter, now turned towards Adrianople and Demotika, intending to deal with these cities as he had dealt with others in the land. As soon as the Greeks who were with him saw that he was moving in the direction of Adrianople, they began to steal away, both by day and by night, some twenty, thirty, forty, or a hundred at a time.

When Johanitza arrived before Adrianople he called upon the people to let him enter, as he had done elsewhere. They told him they would not allow him to do so, and addressed him in the following terms: 'Sir, when we placed ourselves in your hands and rebelled against the Franks, you swore to protect us faithfully and keep us safe. However, you have not done so, but have ruined our empire, and we know very well that you will deal with us as you have dealt with our fellow-countrymen.' When Johanitza heard this reply he went off and laid siege to Demotika. He erected sixteen large petraries round the city, and began to construct machines of every kind for use in the assault. Then he started to lay waste all the country round about.

The people of Adrianople and Demotika sent messengers to Constantinople, with instructions to beg the regent and Branas in God's name to come and relieve Demotika, which was being besieged. On receiving this message, our people in Constantinople held a conference to decide what action they should take concerning the relief of that city. Many of those present did not dare to advise our sending any troops out of Constantinople, and so endangering the lives of the few Christians that remained. All the same, it was finally decided that the army should march out of Constantinople and go as far as Selymbria.

The Cardinal whom the Pope had appointed as his legate in Constantinople preached to the troops and promised a full indulgence to all those who went on this expedition and met their death in battle. So Henri marched out of the city with all the men at his disposal and rode with them to Selymbria, where he encamped outside the city and stayed there for a week. Every day messengers came to him from Adrianople imploring him to take pity on its people and come to their relief; for if he failed to do so, they and their city would be lost.

After consulting his barons Henri decided, on their advice, to move to Bizoë, which was a very fine and well-fortified town. In accordance with this plan the army marched there and pitched their tents outside the walls on the eve of Saint John the Baptist's Day in June. On the very day they encamped messengers arrived from Adrianople to speak with the regent. 'My lord,' they said, 'we have come, to tell you that, if you do not relieve Demotika, it cannot hold out more than a week longer, for Johanitza's petratries have broken through our defences in four places and his men have twice got up on to the walls.'

Henri asked his barons what he should do. There was a good deal of argument about the matter, but in the end they said: 'Since we've come so far, sir, it will be an everlasting disgrace to us if we don't go and relieve Demotika. So we advise every one to make his confession and take communion, and then we'll get the troops in marching order.' They reckoned that they had in all some four hundred knights, and no more. So they sent for the messengers from Adrianople and asked them how many men Johanitza had in his army. The messengers replied that he had with him about forty thousand men-at-arms, without counting those on foot, whose numbers were unknown. It was indeed a perilous battle to undertake – so few against so many.

In the morning of Saint John the Baptist's Day everyone made his confession and received communion; the following day they marched forward. Geoffroy de Villehardouin, Marshal of Romania and Champagne, led the van with Macaire de Sainte-Menehould. Conon de Béthune and Milon le Brébant were in command of the second corps; the third was under Païen d'Orléans and Pierre de Bracieux; the fourth under Anseau de Cayeux; the fifth under Baudouin de Beauvoir; the sixth under Hugues de Beaumetz; Henri, Regent of the Empire, was in command of the seventh corps; the eighth, composed of Flemish troops, was under Gautier d'Escornai; the seneschal Dietrich von Los brought up the rear-guard.

So they rode for three days, in due marching order. No army ever advanced to seek battle in more perilous circumstances. They were in danger on two accounts: first because they were so few, and those they were about to attack so many; and secondly, because they did not believe that the Greeks, with whom they had so recently made peace, would give them whole-hearted support. On the contrary, they feared that if the army got into difficulties the Greeks would go over to Johanitza, who was now so near to taking Demotika.

However, when Johanitza heard that the French were coming, he did not dare wait for their arrival, but set fire to his machines, and struck camp. Thus he withdrew from Demotika, and everyone thought it a great miracle. On the fourth day after setting out Henri, Regent of the Empire, reached Adrianople, and pitched his camp beside the river in some of the most beautiful meadows in the world. As soon as the people in the city saw the French arriving, they came out in procession, bearing all their crosses, and showed such joy as has never been seen before. And well might they rejoice, for up till then they had been in a far from comfortable position.

CHAPTER 19

Offensive and Counter-Offensive

THE day after the relief of Adrianople the French heard that King Johanitza had taken up his quarters at a nearby castle, called Rodestuic. So in the morning the troops set off, and rode there to confront him. However, Johanitza broke up his camp and started to march back to his own country. The French followed on his track for the best part of five days, but he always managed to keep ahead of them. On the fifth day they encamped in a very beautiful spot beside a castle by the name of Fraïm, and spent the next three days there.

While they were there, a number of men who had done good service in the army broke away from the rest because of some disagreement between themselves and the regent. The leader of this group was Baudouin de Beauvoir; Hugues de Beaumetz went away with him, and so did Guillaume de Gommegnies and Dreux de Beaurain. All in all, about fifty knights left in this company. They never thought the rest would dare to stay on in that part of the country and defy the enemy.

However, Henri consulted the barons still remaining with him, and they advised him to march forward. So they rode on for a couple of days, and then pitched their camp in a very beautiful valley near a castle called Moniac, which was surrendered to them. After they had been there about five days they decided to go and relieve Renier de Trit, who was still under siege in Stenimaka, where he had been shut up for thirteen months. The regent remained in the camp, with a great part of the troops, while the rest went off to Stenimaka to rescue Renier de Trit.

I need hardly say that the men who went on this expedition did so at very great risk to themselves. Indeed, since they had to ride for three whole days across enemy-occupied country, few rescues can ever have been attended by such perils. Those who took part in this undertaking were Conon de Béthune, Geoffroy de Villehardouin, Milon le Brébant, Pierre de Bracieux, Païen d'Orléans, Anseau de

Cayeux, Dietrich von Los, Guillaume du Perchoi, and a body of Venetians commanded by Andreâ Valera. They all rode steadily onwards towards the castle of Stenimaka, and did not slacken rein till they came within sight of it.

Renier de Trit, who was on the outer wall of the castle, caught sight of the advanced guard, led by Marshal Geoffroy, with the other companies following after in very good order; but at first he could not tell what people they might be. And, indeed, since he had had no news of us for a very long time, it was hardly surprising that he felt some doubt about us, and wondered whether we might be Greeks advancing to besiege him.

Geoffroy de Villehardouin called certain Turcoples* and mounted crossbowmen out of the ranks, and sent them on ahead to find out the state of things in the castle; for since the army had had no news of its occupants for a long time past, none of us knew whether they were alive or dead. The moment these troops drew up in front of the castle, Renier and his men recognized that they were ours. You can well imagine how delighted they were. They ran out of the gate and hurried to meet their friends; then heartfelt greetings were exchanged between the parties.

The barons quartered themselves in a very fine town that lay below the castle and had been used as a base for attacking it. In the course of conversation they said they had frequently heard a report that the Emperor Baudouin had died in one of Johanitza's prisons, but had dismissed it as a mere rumour. Renier de Trit told them that the report of his death was true, and then they believed it. Many of them were deeply grieved, and wished with all their hearts that this loss had not been past repair.

The troops slept that night in the town. In the morning the whole company set out, leaving the castle of Stenimaka deserted. They rode on for two whole days, and on the third arrived at the camp below the castle of Moniac, that lies on the river Arta, where the Emperor's brother Henri was waiting for them. Everyone in camp rejoiced to know that Renier de Trit had been freed from his enforced confinement, and great credit was given to those who, at very grave risk to themselves, had brought him back in safety.

The barons now resolved to go to Constantinople and make arrangements for the coronation of Henri de Flandre as Emperor in his brother's place. Meanwhile they left Branas to guard the land with the help of the Greeks in that part of the empire and forty knights supplied by the regent. So accompanied by the other barons Henri, Regent of the Empire, left for Constantinople. They rode for several days till they reached the capital, where everyone welcomed them with delight. In August, on the Sunday after the feast of the Assumption the late Emperor's brother was crowned as Emperor with great honour and amid great rejoicing in the church of Saint Sophia. This was in the year of our Lord 1206.

When King Johanitza heard that a new Emperor had been crowned in Constantinople, and that Branas had been left in that part of the empire round Adrianople and Demotika, he assembled as large a force as he could get together. Branas, as it happened, had not rebuilt the walls of Demotika in those places where they had been breached by Johanitza's petraries and mangonels, and he had left a very inadequate garrison there. So Johanitza marched on Demotika, took it, and destroyed it, razing its walls to the ground. After that he overran the whole region, taking men, women, and children from their homes and cattle from the fields, and, in short, indulging in wholesale destruction wherever he went. So the people of Adrianople, seeing the way in which Demotika had been ruined, appealed to the Emperor Henri to come and save them.

The Emperor, after calling up as many men as were at his disposal, left the capital and rode steadily on towards Adrianople with all his troops in battle order. When King Johanitza, who was still in the neighbourhood of Adrianople, heard that the Emperor was advancing, he turned back towards his own country. The Emperor Henri rode on till he reached Adrianople, where he pitched his camp in a meadow outside the city.

The Greeks in that district came and told him how Johanitza was carrying off men, women, and children, and that he had destroyed Demotika and laid waste all the country round about. He was, they added, still only a day's march away. The Emperor decided to follow after him, and, if he found him waiting, engage him in battle and rescue the men and women he had captured and was taking away. So he rode after Johanitza, who retreated as fast as the Emperor advanced. After four days spent pursuing him, our troops arrived at a city called Beroë.

When the people of that city saw the Emperor Henri's army approaching, they all fled into the mountains, leaving the place deserted. The Emperor came and encamped with all his troops outside the city, which they found well supplied with corn and meat and other welcome provisions. They stayed there for a couple of days while the Emperor sent his men out to scour the surrounding country. They managed to secure a very large number of oxen, cows, and buffaloes, and other livestock. Then the Emperor left Beroë with all the spoil his men had collected and rode to another city, called Blisme, which was only a day's march away. Just as the other Greeks of Beroë had abandoned their city, so the people of Blisme abandoned theirs. The Emperor, finding the place well provided with everything his men could need, encamped outside it.

While they were there news came to them that the men and women whom Johanitza was carrying off were all in a valley some three leagues from the camp, together with their cattle and their carts. So the Emperor arranged that the Greeks from Adrianople and Demotika, with two companies of knights whom he himself would provide, should go after the captives and bring them back. This plan was carried out the next day. The Emperor's brother, Eustache, was placed in command of one company of knights, Macaire de Sainte-Menehould had charge of the other.

They all set out, French and Greeks together, and rode till they came to the valley of which they had been told; there they found the captives. Johanitza's troops engaged the Emperor's, and a fierce contest followed, in which men and horses were killed or wounded on either side. But by God's almighty power our men gained the upper hand and rescued the people Johanitza had taken. Then they turned round towards the camp, bringing back the men and women they had delivered in a long line in front of them.

In effecting this rescue, I can assure you, our people accomplished no mean feat. The captives numbered a good twenty thousand, men, women, and children together; there were, besides, about three thousand carts, loaded with clothes and other belongings, to say nothing of a vast number of cattle. As they passed along from the valley to the camp the line of people, carts, and cattle covered about a couple of leagues. It was night by the time they arrived in camp. The Emperor Henri was delighted to see them, and so were all the barons. These people were given quarters apart from the troops, and a strict guard was kept over them and their belongings, so that they did not lose a single pennyworth of what they possessed. The next day the

Emperor stayed quietly in camp for the sake of those he had delivered. On the following day he left the district, and continued on the march for several days till at length he reached Adrianople.

On his arrival there he gave the people he had delivered leave to go where they would. So they all went their several ways, either back to the place where they were born or to any other. The booty, of which there was an abundant store, was duly divided among the troops. After spending five days at Adrianople the Emperor Henri rode to Demotika to see the extent of damage done and find out whether its fortifications could be restored. He encamped outside the city, and both he and his barons realized that its walls were in so bad a state that it was no use trying to re-fortify it.

While the Emperor was there, one of the Marquis de Montferrat's barons, named Othon de la Roche, arrived to see him with a message from his lord. He had come to speak about a marriage, which had already been in question, between the marquis's daughter and the Emperor Henri. He brought news that the lady had come from Lombardy, after her father had sent there for her, and was now at Salonika. It was agreed that the marriage should be ratified by both parties. Thereupon the marquis's envoy returned to Salonika.

The Emperor, whose men had been busy storing the booty they had taken at Beroë safely away in camp, now re-assembled his army. He left Adrianople, and after marching for several days entered Johanitza's dominions with his troops. They arrived at a city called Thermae, which they took. They entered the place and collected a great amount of booty. They spent three days at Thermae, during which time they overran the surrounding country, and in addition to getting a great deal of spoil destroyed another city called Akilo.

Four days later, they left Thermae. It was a very beautiful city in a very good position, with the finest hot springs for bathing to be found anywhere in the world. After his men had collected a great amount of booty in the way of cattle and other things of value to carry away with them, the Emperor ordered them to set fire to the city and destroy it. Then the army left, and after several days' march arrived back at Adrianople. Our troops remained in the district till All Saints' Day, when the approach of winter made it impossible to carry on the war. So the Emperor Henri and all his barons, who were utterly tired of campaigning, turned back towards the capital, leaving one of his own men, named Pierre de Radinghem, among the Greeks in Adrianople, together with ten knights.

There was at that time a truce between the Emperor Henri and Theodore Lascaris, who held all the land on the southern side of the straits. But this Greek, instead of observing the terms of the truce, broke his word and violated it. So the Emperor, after consulting his barons, sent a contingent of troops across the straits to Spiga. Pierre de Bracieux, to whom part of the land over there had been assigned, was in command of the expedition. With him went Païen d'Orléans, Anseau de Cayeux, and the Emperor's brother Eustache, accompanied by a great part of the best men in the Emperor's army to the number of one hundred and forty knights. These began to make war in grim earnest on Theodore Lascaris, and did great damage in his land.

They rode to Cyzicus, a place which was surrounded by sea on all sides but one. A long time ago, access to it had been safeguarded by a series of fortifications, consisting of walls, towers, and moats, but these had more or less fallen into decay. The French troops occupied it, and Pierre de Bracieux, to whom that part of the land had been given, started to restore the defences, and built two castles, each with a stoutly barred gate. From there the troops overran the territory held by Lascaris, collecting much spoil and many head of cattle, which they brought back with them to their island retreat. Lascaris, for his part, made frequent raids on Cyzicus, so that the two armies often met and fought against each other, and there were losses on one side and the other. The war in those parts was fierce and full of perils.

Here I will leave the men of Cyzicus, to speak for a moment of the seneschal Dietrich von Los, to whom Nicomedia should have belonged. This city was only a day's march away from Nicaea, the capital city of the land of Theodore Lascaris. Dietrich made an expedition to the place with a great number of the Emperor's men, and found that the castle had been pulled down. So he enclosed and fortified the church of Saint Sophia, which was a very fine, tall building, and used it as a base for carrying on the war in the vicinity of Nicomedia.

About the same time, the Marquis de Montferrat left Salonika and went to Serrès, which Johanitza had destroyed. He rebuilt the defences and then went and fortified the castle of Drama in the Vale of Philippi. All the country round about was surrendered to him, and the people accepted him as their lord.

Meanwhile so much time had passed that Christmas was over and gone. Messengers from the marquis now came to the Emperor to tell him, on behalf of their lord, that he had sent his daughter in a galley to Enos. So the Emperor Henri deputed Geoffroy de Villehardouin and Milon le Brébant to go and fetch the lady. The two men rode out of the city and within a few days arrived at Enos. Here they went to see the marquis's daughter, who was a very good and beautiful lady, and greeted her on behalf of their lord the Emperor Henri. Afterwards they brought her back, with great honour to Constantinople. Her marriage to the Emperor Henri was celebrated with great pomp and great rejoicing in the Church of Saint Sophia, on the Sunday after Candlemas Day. Both bride and bridegroom wore a crown. The ceremony was followed by magnificent wedding festivities in the palace of Bucoleon, at which all the nobles of the land were present. In this manner Constantinople celebrated the marriage of the Emperor Henri and the marquis's daughter, who was now the Empress Agnès.

CHAPTER 20

War on Two Fronts

THEODORE LASCARIS, in the course of his war with the Emperor Henri, sent messengers to King Johanitza to tell him that all the Emperor's men were engaged in fighting the Greeks on the side of the straits towards Turkey, and the Emperor himself was left in Constantinople with very few people. In these circumstances, said Lascaris, Johanitza would have a good opportunity of taking his revenge. He himself, he added, would be attacking the French on one side of the straits, and if Johanitza, would attack them on the other, the Emperor would not be able to defend himself against them both. King Johanitza, as it happened, had already engaged a great army of Comans, who were on their way to join him; he now assembled as large a force of Wallachians and Bulgarians as he could. So much time had now gone by that we were at the beginning of Lent.

Macaire de Sainte-Menehould had begun to fortify a castle at Charax, which lies on the shore of a gulf, some six leagues from Nicomedia, and faces towards Constantinople. Guillaume de Sains began to fortify another castle at Kibotos, on the further side of the Gulf of Nicomedia, in the direction of Nicaea. The Emperor Henri had as much as he could do in the country round Constantinople, and so had all the barons on that side of the straits. Geoffroy de Villehardouin, Marshal of Romania and Champagne, and author of this chronicle, has no hesitation in affirming that no people, at any moment in their history, had to bear such a heavy burden of war, and that because their troops were scattered about in so many different places.

Johanitza now left Wallachia with all his forces, including the great army of Comans that had come to join him, and started to invade the empire. The Comans overran the country right up to the gates of Constantinople, while the king himself laid siege to Adrianople and set up thirty great petraries around the city which hurled stones at its walls and towers. Inside Adrianople there were only Greeks and Pierre de Radinghem, who had remained there on the Emperor's orders, with ten knights. So both Greeks and French together sent to the Emperor Henri to tell him how Johanitza had besieged them, and implored him to come to their aid.

On receiving this message the Emperor was quite distracted. His forces on the other side were so widely scattered, and everywhere so heavily engaged that they could do no more than they were already doing, while he himself had only a very small body of troops in Constantinople. None the less he undertook to march out of the city with as many men as he could get together during the fortnight after Easter. With this in view he sent to Cyzicus, where most of his people were, telling the men over there to come and join him. His brother Eustache, with Anseau de Cayeux and the main part of their men, set off at once across the water, so that only Pierre de Bracieux, and Païen d'Orléans with very few troops, remained in Cyzicus.

When Theodore Lascaris heard that Adrianople was being besieged, and that the Emperor Henri, out of sheer necessity, was recalling his men, and was, moreover, so heavily burdened with war on all sides that he did not know which way to turn, this Greek called up as many of his own people as he could to reinforce his army. Then he came and pitched his tents and pavilions before the gates of Cyzicus, and French and Greeks engaged in many skirmishes outside the city, with gains and losses for both parties. As soon as Lascaris saw that there were very few men left in Cyzicus, he put a great part of his army into as many ships as he had available on the sea, and sent them to the castle of Kibotos, which Guillaume de Sains was fortifying. These troops besieged the castle by sea and land, on the Saturday before mid-Lent Sunday.

Inside the castle were forty knights, all very good men, with Macaire de Sainte-Menehould as their leader. The place itself, however, was not as yet very strongly fortified, so the enemy could get at the defenders and attack them with swords and lances. The Greeks assailed the castle very fiercely both by land and by sea, and this onslaught lasted during the whole of Saturday. Our men defended themselves magnificently. Indeed, the author of this book affirms that no other company of forty knights ever resisted an attack more stoutly in the face of similar odds. That this was the case is evident from the fact that out of the forty knights that were there, all but five were wounded. One was killed, and that was Milon le Brébant's nephew, whose name was Gilles.

On the Saturday morning before this assault began, a messenger had come flying post-haste to Constantinople, and had found the Emperor Henri at dinner in the palace of Blachernae. 'Your Majesty,' he said, 'your men at Kibotos are being besieged by land and sea. Unless you send them help at once, they will all be taken and killed.'

With the Emperor were Conon de Béthune, Geoffroy de Ville-hardouin, Milon le Brébant, and a few others. They conferred to-gether very briefly; then the Emperor went down to the quayside and boarded a large galley, while each of the others took the first ship he could find. Next it was proclaimed throughout the city that every man there was to follow the Emperor in his urgent need, and go with him to rescue his men, who would otherwise be lost. Immediately the whole city of Constantinople was, as it were, aswarm with Venetians, Pisans, and other experienced seamen, all tumbling over one another in their haste to get to their ships. The knights, all fully armed, got aboard with them; whoever was ready first was soonest out of port in the Emperor's wake.

The oarsmen rowed their hardest all the evening as long as the light lasted, and on through the night till dawn on the following day. The Emperor Henri himself had so encouraged their efforts that a little after sunrise they came within sight of Kibotos, and saw the enemy surrounding it by land and sea. The men inside the castle had not slept that night, but had kept guard all the time however sick or wounded they might be, hopeless as men who expected nothing but death.

The Emperor saw that the Greeks had come up close to the walls and were about to renew their assault, while as yet he had only a few of his people with him. Among them were Marshal Geoffroy, who was in another ship, Milon le Brébant, some Pisans, and a number of knights. All in all, we had about seventeen ships of varying sizes, and some of them small, while the enemy had about sixty.

None the less our men realized that if they waited for the rest to arrive and let the Greeks assault Kibotos, their friends inside would all be killed or taken prisoner. So they decided to tackle the enemy on the water.

They sailed towards the Greek ships with all their own abreast, every man on board was fully armed, with helmet laced. As soon as the Greeks, who were on the point of attacking the castle, saw us coming they quickly recognized that we were a rescue party, and drew their ships away from the castle to come and meet us. At the same time the great army, both horse and foot, which they had arrayed on land, formed up in line along the shore. When those on board the enemy ships saw that the Emperor and his people were all the same determined to attack them they drew back towards their troops on shore, so that these might give them support with their bows and their mangonels.

The Emperor held them thus at bay with his seventeen ships, till the shouts of those coming from Constantinople began to reach him. Before night fell so many of these ships had arrived that everywhere the Franks were in greater force than the enemy on the sea. After casting anchor, the men aboard lay fully armed all night. They had decided that as soon as it was light they would draw up to the shore to engage the enemy and also seize their ships. However, round about midnight, the Greeks dragged all their ships to land, set fire to them, and burned them every one. Then they broke up their camp and fled.

The Emperor Henri and his men were very glad that God had granted them this victory, and very happy to feel they had rescued their friends. When morning came they all went to the castle of Kibotos, where they found its occupants very ill, and for the most part severely wounded. They examined the state of the castle and saw that it was so weak as not to be worth the holding. So they got all their people aboard the ships, leaving the place deserted.

King Johanitza, meanwhile, was still besieging Adrianople, and giving neither its citizens nor himself any rest. Night and day, his petraries – and he had plenty – kept up a constant hail of stones against the walls and towers of the city and damaged them considerably. He set his sappers to undermine the walls, and harassed the defenders with frequent assaults. The men inside Adrianople, both Greeks and Latins, resisted bravely, but all the same they sent frequent messages to the Emperor Henri, begging him to come to their relief and warning him that unless he did so they would all be utterly lost. These messages worried the Emperor extremely; for whenever he was on the point of going to help his men on one side of the straits, Theodore Lascaris kept most of his people so heavily engaged on the other that of necessity he was forced to draw back.

During the whole of April Johanitza remained before Adrianople. He came so near to taking it that in two places he breached the fortifications right down to the ground, so that his men were able to fight hand to hand with swords and lances against those inside the city.

Time and again he subjected Adrianople to assault, but the defenders fought back bravely. There were heavy casualties on both sides.

However, since all events are ordered by God's will, it so happened that the Comans, whom Johanitza had sent out to overrun the land, declared, on their return to camp with all their spoils, that they did not intend to remain any longer in his army, but would go back to their own country. So they parted from Johanitza, and since, without their help, he did not dare remain before Adrianople he withdrew his forces and left.

That so powerful a king should abandon a city so near to being taken seemed nothing short of a miracle to the besieged. But what God wills is bound to happen. None the less the people of Adrianople lost no time in begging the Emperor, for the love of God, to come to them as soon as ever he could, because, as they pointed out to him, if Johanitza happened to return, they would all be killed or taken prisoner.

The Emperor was preparing to go to Adrianople with as many men as he had available, when he received the very disturbing news that John Stirion, who was chief admiral of Lascaris's fleet, had entered the Channel of Abydos in the Straits of Saint George with seventeen galleys and had arrived before Cyzicus, which Pierre de Bracieux and Païen d'Orléans were holding, and was now besieging the place from the sea while Lascaris was attacking it by land. Moreover, the people of that region had risen against Pierre de Bracieux as had the people of Marmora, which also belonged to him. They had done him much harm and had killed many of his men.

When this news reached Constantinople it caused much dismay. The Emperor Henri consulted his chief men and his barons, and also the Venetians. They all agreed that if they did not go to the aid of Pierre de Bracieux and Païen d'Orléans, they would both be killed, and the land they were holding would be lost. So fourteen galleys were promptly armed and the men of highest standing among the Venetians went aboard, together with the Emperor's barons.

Conon de Béthune and his men were in one galley; Geoffroy de Villehardouin and his men in another; Macaire de Sainte-Menehould and his men in the third; Milon le Brébant in the fourth; Anseau de Cayeux in the fifth; the seneschal Dietrich von Los in the sixth; Guillaume du Perchoi in the seventh; the Emperor's brother Eustache in the eighth; and so on. Thus the Emperor Henri distributed among these galleys all the best men he had. When they sailed out of harbour at Constantinople everyone said that they had never seen galleys better armed, nor manned with finer men. So once again the march on Adrianople was put off.

The galleys, with all their men aboard, sailed down the straits, heading for Cyzicus. How Stirion, admiral of Lascaris's galleys, came to hear of it, I do not know; but he withdrew his own ships from before Cyzicus, and fled with them further down the straits. For two days and two nights our ships followed after him, through the Channel of Abydos and forty miles beyond. When they saw they could not come up with him, our men turned back and went to Cyzicus, where they found Pierre de Bracieux and Païen d'Orléans. Theodore Lascaris had already withdrawn his troops from before the city and gone back to his own land. Thus Cyzicus was relieved. The Emperor's men returned to Constantinople in their galleys, and prepared once more to march on Adrianople.

Theodore Lascaris now sent the main part of his forces into the land of Nicomedia. Dietrich von Los's men, who had fortified the Church of Saint Sophia and were at the moment occupying it, sent to their lord the Emperor imploring him to help them, since if no one came to their relief they could not hold out, especially as they had no provisions.

Out of sheer necessity the Emperor and his men were once again forced to abandon their plan of going to Adrianople, and cross over to the southern side of the Straits of Saint George to relieve their friends in Nicomedia.

When Lascaris's troops heard that the Emperor was coming they withdrew from that part of the country and retreated towards Nicaea. On hearing of this, the Emperor called his barons together to consult them. They decided to leave Dietrich von Los in Nicomedia with all his knights and sergeants, to guard the city and the country round about, while Macaire de Sainte-Menehould would be stationed at Charax, and Guillaume du Perchoi at Cyzicus, each of them to guard the land in his immediate neighbourhood.

After this the Emperor Henri and the remainder of his army returned to Constantinople, to prepare once again for the march on Adrianople. While he was thus engaged, Dietrich von Los left Nicomedia and together with Guillaume du Perchoi and all their men went out one day on a foraging expedition. Theodore Lascaris's men got wind of this and made a surprise attack on them. Now the Greeks were very many, and our people very few. A fight began, and both sides became involved in a hand-to-hand struggle. But before very long the few were not able to stand up against the many.

Dietrich von Los fought very bravely, and so did all his men. He was twice struck off his horse, and each time his men had great difficulty in getting him up again. Guillaume du Perchoi was also struck down, but he too was helped up and rescued by his men. In the end the pressure of superior numbers proved too strong for the French and they were defeated. Dietrich von Los, so severely wounded in the face that he was near to death, was taken in that encounter, together with the greater part of his men; very few escaped. Guillaume du Perchoi, wounded in the hand, fled from the field on a cob. Those who got away after their defeat took refuge in the Church of Saint Sophia.

The author of this chronicle has heard blame for this disaster attached – whether rightly or wrongly, he cannot say – to a certain knight named Anseau de Remi who, though one of Dietrich von Los's own vassals, and in command of his men, abandoned his lord in the fight.

Those who had managed to get back to the Church of Saint Sophia in Nicomedia – that is to say, Guillaume du Perchoi and Anseau de Remi – sent a messenger post haste to the Emperor Henri in Constantinople, with full details of the fight. They told him how the seneschal, Dietrich von Los, had been taken with his men; and how they themselves were being besieged in the Church of Saint Sophia in Nicomedia. They added that they had only enough food to last them five days, and that if he did not come to their relief they would all without doubt be killed or taken prisoner. In reply to this cry of distress, the Emperor and his men crossed the Straits of Saint George in a desperate hurry, everyone trying to get over there as fast as he could to rescue the men in Nicomedia. So the expedition to Adrianople was once again postponed.

As soon as the Emperor had crossed the straits, he set his troops in order and moved forward till after several days' march he reached Nicomedia. Theodore Lascaris and his brothers, who were conducting the siege, no sooner heard of his arrival than they withdrew to the further side of the mountain outside Nicomedia, in the direction of Nicaea. The Emperor encamped by the city in a very pleasant meadow beside a river, at the foot of the nearer slopes of that mountain. After his tents and pavilions were pitched he sent his troops out to scour the country round Nicomedia, because the people of that region had risen against the French as soon as they heard that Dietrich von Los had been taken. The Emperor's men seized a good number of cattle and took many prisoners.

The Emperor stayed for five days in the meadow beside Nicomedia. While he was there Theodore Lascaris sent envoys to see him with an offer to make a truce with him for two years, on condition that the Greeks were allowed to demolish Cyzicus and the fortified Church of Saint Sophia in Nicomedia. Lascaris, on his side, would undertake to hand over all the prisoners he had taken in the recent defeat of the Emperor's men, or on other occasions – and he had a great number of these in his land.

The Emperor consulted his people, who told him that they could not maintain war on two fronts at one and the same time, and that it was better to accept the loss of these two places than risk losing Adrianople and the main part of the empire. Besides, by agreeing to this truce they would break up the alliance between their two enemies, King Johanitza and Theodore Lascaris, who at the moment were friends and supported each other in the war.

Thus the matter was settled and the truce confirmed. After this the Emperor Henri summoned Pierre de Bracieux from Cyzicus. On his arrival, the Emperor managed, though not without some trouble, to persuade him to place Cyzicus in his hands. The Emperor himself surrendered this city, as also the Church of Saint Sophia in Nicomedia, to Theodore Lascaris, for him to demolish. Thus the truce was confirmed, and the two strongholds razed to the ground. Dietrich von Los and all the other prisoners were freed.

CHAPTER 21

Excursions Outside the Empire
JULY–SEPTEMBER 1207

AFTER the truce was concluded the Emperor Henri returned to Constantinople, and immediately announced his project of going to Adrianople with as large a force as he had at his command. He assembled his army at Selymbria; but so much time had already passed that this did not take place till the beginning of July, a week or so after Saint John the Baptist's Day. The Emperor set off and after several days' march arrived at Adrianople, where he pitched his camp in the meadows outside the city. The people of Adrianople, who had greatly longed for his coming, came out to meet him in procession, and welcomed him with great enthusiasm. The Greeks from all the country round about had also gathered there to greet him.

The Emperor remained only one day encamped outside Adrianople, just long enough time to see what damage Johanitza's petraries and his sappers had done to walls and towers of the city. This proved to be pretty extensive. The next day he started off again and marched towards Johanitza's country, taking four days on the way. On the fifth day he came to the foot of the Wallachian mountains, where there was a town called Eului, which Johanitza had newly re peopled. As soon as the inhabitants saw the French army coming they fled from the town, and took refuge in the mountains.

The Emperor and his army encamped before the town. Foraging parties set out to scour the land, and secured a great number of oxen, cows, and buffaloes, as well as other beasts. Some of the people from Adrianople had brought their carts along with them, and since they were poor and in need of food, they loaded these vehicles with wheat and other grain. The army stayed there three days; and every day foraging parties scoured the countryside in search of booty. But the land in those parts was very mountainous and there were many deep defiles, so that the army lost a number of its foragers because they were too venturesome and did not look where they were going.

In the end, the Emperor Henri placed his brother Eustache, his nephew Thierry de Flandre, Gautier d'Escornai, and Jean Bliaud each in charge of a company, and sent them, under the command of Anseau de Cayeux, to keep guard over the foragers. One day these four companies, in the course of their duty, got into very rough and mountainous country; and when the foragers had finished scouring the land and wished to return to camp they found the defiles very strongly guarded by the Wallachians of that region who had gathered there. These attacked the French doing much damage both to men and horses. Our men were hard put to it to escape defeat; so much so indeed that the knights were driven to dismount and fight on foot. None the less, by God's grace, they managed to return to camp, though not without suffering heavy losses.

The next day the Emperor Henri and his army left Eului, and went back by the way they had come, till after several days' march they arrived at Adrianople, where they stored the corn and other provisions they had brought back with them. The Emperor spent the next fortnight in the meadow outside the city.

About that time, the Marquis de Montferrat, who was at Serrès which he had rebuilt and fortified, made raids on all the country round as far as Mosynopolis, and gradually brought the whole of the land under his rule. When this was done he sent messengers to the Emperor Henri to say he would like to have a talk with him, and would meet him beside the river that runs below Ipsala. The two men had had no chance of speaking face to face since the French conquest of the empire; for so many enemies lay between them that it had been impossible for them to meet. So when the Emperor and his council heard that the marquis was at Mosynopolis they were delighted; and the Emperor sent back word by the messengers that he would come to meet the marquis on the day he had fixed.

The Emperor Henri started on his way, leaving Conon de Béthune with a hundred knights at Adrianople to guard the surrounding country. On the appointed day he and his men arrived at the place of meeting, which was in a pleasant meadow near the city of Ipsala. The Emperor approached the place from one side, the marquis from the other, and both expressed the greatest joy at meeting. Nor was this surprising, since they had not seen each other for such a long time. The marquis asked for news of his daughter the Empress Agnès, and was delighted when the Emperor told him she was expecting a baby. Then the marquis did homage to the Emperor Henri and became his man, to hold his lands from him, as he had held them from the late Emperor his brother. The marquis subsequently offered Geoffroy de Villehardouin, Marshal of Romania and Champagne, the choice of two cities: Mosynopolis, with all its dependencies, or Serrès – whichever he preferred – to hold as his own. So the Marshal became the marquis's vassal, but without prejudice to the allegiance he owed to the Emperor of Constantinople.

The marquis and the Emperor spent two very happy days together in the field below Ipsala. They said to each other that, as God had permitted them to meet again, so they might together face their enemies and harass them once more. They made an agreement to meet at the end of the summer, in the month of October, with all their forces, in the meadow outside Adrianople, and make war on the King of Wallachia. So they parted from each other, both very happy and in the best of spirits. The marquis went back to Mosynopolis, and the Emperor Henri returned to Constantinople.

The marquis had not been five days in his city before he rode out, on the advice of Greeks in the district, to make an expedition to the mountain of Mosynopolis, which was a long day's journey away. After he had ridden through the land and was turning homewards, the Bulgarians gathered together, and observing that he had only a small force with him, came in from all the country round and attacked his rear-guard. The moment the marquis heard his men raise a cry of alarm, he leapt on his horse, all unarmed as he was, with only a lance in his hand. When he reached the place where the Bulgarians were at grips with the rear-guard, he charged right in amongst them, and drove them back a good way.

As he flew after them, the marquis was fatally wounded in the thick of the arm, below the shoulder, and began to lose blood. When his men saw what had happened, their courage began to ebb, they lost heart and started to give way. Those who were nearest to the marquis held him up; he was losing so much blood that he began to faint. Realizing that they could expect no further help from their leader, his men gave way to panic and began to desert him. So, by an unlucky chance, they were defeated. Those who remained with the marquis – and they were very few – were killed. The Bulgarians cut off the marquis's head and sent it to Johanitza. That was one of the greatest joys the King of Wallachia had ever experienced.

Alas! what a tragic disaster, for the Emperor Henri, and for all the

men in the Empire, French and Venetians alike, to lose such a man
by such an unfortunate accident – a man who was one of the noblest
and most large-hearted of all the barons, and one of the finest knights
in all the world! This sad event occurred in the year of our Lord
1207.

JOINVILLE

The Life of Saint Louis

Dedication

To his good lord Louis, son of the King of France, and by the grace of God, King of Navarre and Count Palatine of Champagne and Brie, Jean, Lord of Joinville, his faithful vassal and his seneschal in Champagne, sends loyal and loving greetings.

My dear lord, I take the opportunity of telling you that our lady, the Queen your mother – may God grant her grace – begged me most earnestly to have a book written for her containing the pious sayings and the good deeds of our King, Saint Louis. I promised her I would do so, and I have now completed the book, which I have divided into two parts. The first part tells how, on all occasions, King Louis governed his life according to the will of God and the laws of Holy Church, as also for the good of his realm. The second part speaks of his outstanding valour and his great feats of arms.

My lord, since it is written: 'Do first those things relating to God's service, and He shall direct thee in all thy other doings,' I have devoted the first part of my book to those three matters I have mentioned above – that is to say to things concerning the good of the soul and the health of the body, and the right government of the people.

I have, moreover, dealt with these matters in such a way as to pay due honour to this true saint, because in this way I shall enable men to realize that no layman in our time ever lived in such a state of holiness as he did all his life, from the very beginning of his reign right up to the time of his death. I myself did not happen to be present when he died, but his son, the Comte Pierre d'Alençon – who loved me well – was there, and he told me what a good end his father made, as you will find described towards the close of this book.

In that connexion, it seems to me that those who omitted to place King Louis among the martyrs have paid him insufficient honour, in view of the great sufferings he endured in the six years I was with him on crusade, and more particularly because he followed the example of our Lord in taking the cross. For if Christ died on the cross, why, so to speak did he, for it was as a crusader wearing that holy sign that he passed away in Tunis.

The second part of my book will tell of his great deeds of chivalry and his marvellous acts of courage, which were such that on four occasions – which I shall later tell you about more fully – he voluntarily put his own life in danger in order to keep his people from suffering harm.

The first time he thus risked his life was when we arrived before Damietta. All his councillors, so I have been told, advised him to remain on board his ship till he saw how his knights, who were then about to land, were faring. The reason why they gave him this advice was that if he landed with his knights, and both he and they were killed, it would mean the failure of the whole enterprise; if, on the other hand, he remained in his ship, he would still be there to lead a fresh expedition to conquer Egypt. However, he would not listen to anyone, but leapt into the sea fully armed, with his shield at his neck and lance in hand, and was one of the first to reach the shore.

The next occasion was when the king was about to leave Mansourah and go to Damietta. His councillors, as I have been given to understand, advised him to travel there in a galley. This advice, so I have been told, was given him partly because, in the event of any diasaster happening to his men, he might be in a better position to rescue them from captivity; but it was given more particularly on account of the state of his health, undermined as it was by several diseases – that is to say a double tertian fever, severe dysentery, and the sickness then prevalent in the army, that affected his mouth and legs. Once again, he would not listen to anyone, but said he would never desert his people, and meet the same end as they did. It so happened that, on account of prolonged attacks of dysentery, it became necessary to cut away the lower part of his drawers, while the pain he suffered from army fever was so great that he fainted several times in the course of the evening.

The third occasion was during the four years he stayed on in the Holy Land after his brothers had returned to France. Our lives were in very great danger at that time, for during the whole of the period the king spent in Acre he had no more than one man in his army for every thirty the people in that city had at a later date when it was taken by the Saracens. I cannot myself think of any reason why the Turks did not come at that time and take us in Acre, unless it may be that the love God had for the king put such fear in the hearts of our enemies that they did not dare to attack us. For is it not written: 'Fear God and all men will fear thee'? So the king remained in the Holy Land against the advice of his councillors, putting his own life in danger to protect the people of that land, who would have been lost if he had not stayed to help them.

The fourth time King Louis accepted a similar risk was when we came alongside the island of Cyprus on our return from oversea. Our ship was driven so dangerously against the rocks that three yards of the keel on which she was built were carried away. The king sent for fourteen master mariners, from his own ship and from others in her company, and asked them what he should do. They all advised him to go aboard another ship, for they could not see how the one he was in would be able to stand up to the battering of the waves, since the nails which should have held her timbers together had all been loosened. They gave the king an instance of the danger to which the ship was exposed by telling him how, when we were sailing to the land oversea, one of our ships had been lost in a similar way. (I myself had met, at the Comte de Joigny's, a woman and child who were the sole survivors from this ship.)

To this the king replied: 'My good sirs, I know that if I leave this ship it will be considered derelict. Now there are, to my knowledge, eight hundred souls and more aboard. Since every man here values his life as much as I do mine, if I abandon ship no one will dare to stay, but all will remain in Cyprus. That is why, please God, I will not place so many of my people as are here in peril of death, but shall stay where I am, to save them.' So the king remained aboard his ship, and God, in whom he trusted, preserved us all from perils on the sea, till at length we came safely into harbour.

I may add that a certain Olivier de Termes, who had behaved well and given good proof of his valour while we were oversea, did, in fact, desert the king and stay behind in Cyprus. We did not catch sight of him again for about a year and a half. None the less, the king, by staying on his ship, saved all the eight hundred of his people aboard her from suffering any harm.

In the second part of this book I shall tell you of King Louis' death, and the saintly way in which he died.

Now as I have told you, my lord the King of Navarre, I promised my lady the Queen, your mother – may God show her mercy – that I would compose this book, and now, to fulfil my promise, I have had it written down. Moreover, since I can think of no one who has so much right to it as you, who are her heir, I send it to you, so that you and your brothers – and whoever else may hear it read – may take some good examples from it, and put them into practice, thus winning yourselves favour in the sight of God.

PART ONE

The Servant of God

IN the name of God Almighty, I, Jean, Lord of Joinville, Seneschal of Champagne, dictate the life of our good King, Saint Louis, in which I shall record what I saw and heard both in the course of the six years in which I was on pilgrimage in his company oversea, and after we returned to France. But before I speak to you of his great deeds and his outstanding valour, I will tell you what I myself observed of his good teaching and his saintly conversation, so that it may be set down in due order for the edification of those to whom this book is read.

This saintly man loved our Lord with all his heart, and in all his actions followed His example. This is apparent from the fact that as our Lord died for the love he bore His people, even so King Louis put his own life in danger, and that several times, for the very same reason. It was danger too that he might well have avoided, as I shall show you later.

The great love King Louis bore his people is shown by what he said, as he lay dangerously ill at Fontainebleau, to his eldest son, my Lord Louis. 'My dear son,' he said, 'I earnestly beg you to make yourself loved by all your people. For I would rather have a Scot come from Scotland to govern the people of this kingdom well and justly than that you should govern them ill in the sight of all the world.' This upright king, moreover, loved truth so well that, as I shall show you later, he would never consent to lie to the Saracens with regard to any covenant he made with them.

He was so temperate in his appetite that I never heard him, on any day of my life, order a special dish for himself, as many men of wealth and standing do. On the contrary, he would always eat with good grace whatever his cooks had prepared to set before him. He was equally temperate in his speech. I never, on any single occasion, heard him speak evil of any man; nor did I ever hear him utter the name of the Devil – a name in very common use throughout the kingdom – which practice, so I believe, is not pleasing to God.

He used to add water to his wine, but did so reasonably, according as the strength of the wine allowed it. While we were in Cyprus he asked me why I did not mix my wine with water. I replied that this was on the advice of my doctors, who had told me that I had a strong head and a cold stomach, so that I could not get drunk. He answered that they had deceived me; for if I did not learn to mix my wine with water while I was still young, and wished to do so in my old age, gout and stomach troubles would take hold on me, and I should never be in good health. Moreover, if I went on drinking un-diluted wine when I was old, I should get drunk every night, and it was too revolting a thing for any brave man to be in such a state.

The king once asked me if I wished to be honoured in this world, and to enter paradise when I died. I told him I did. 'If so,' said he, 'you should avoid deliberately saying or doing anything which, if it became generally known, you would be ashamed to acknowledge by saying "I did this," or "I said that."' He also told me not to contradict or call in question anything said in my presence – unless indeed silence would imply approval of something wrong, or damaging to myself, because harsh words often lead to quarrelling, which has ended in the death of countless numbers of men.

He often said that people ought to clothe and arm themselves in such a way that men of riper age would never say they had spent too much on dress, or young men say they had spent too little. I repeated this remark to our present king when speaking of the elaborately embroidered tabards that are in vogue today. I told him that, during the whole of our voyage oversea, I had never seen such embroidered tabards, either on the king or on any one else. He said to me that he had several such garments, with his own arms embroidered on them, and they had cost him eight hundred *livres parisis*. I told him that he would have put his money to better use if he had given it to God, and had his clothes made of good plain taffeta bearing his arms, as his father had done.

King Louis once sent for me and said: 'You have such a shrewd and subtle mind that I hardly dare speak to you of things concerning God. So I have summoned these two monks to come here, because I want to ask you a question.' Then he said: 'Tell me, seneschal, what is your idea of God?' 'Your Majesty,' I replied, 'He is something so good that there cannot be anything better.' 'Indeed,' said he, 'you've given me a very good answer; for it's precisely the same as the definition given in this book I have here in my hand.'

'Now I ask you,' he continued, 'which you would prefer: to be a leper or to have committed some mortal sin?' And I, who had never lied to him, replied that I would rather have committed thirty mortal sins than become a leper. The next day, when the monks were no longer there, he called me to him, and making me sit at his feet said to me: 'Why did you say that to me yesterday?' I told him I would still say it. 'You spoke without thinking, and like a fool,' he said. 'You ought to know there is no leprosy so foul as being in a state of mortal sin; for the soul in that condition is like the Devil; therefore no leprosy can be so vile. Besides, when a man dies his body is healed of its leprosy; but if he dies after committing a mortal sin, he can never be sure that, during his lifetime, he has repented of it sufficiently for God to forgive him. In consequence, he must be greatly afraid lest that leprosy of sin should last as long as God dwells in paradise. So I beg you,' he added, 'as earnestly as I can, for the love of God, and for love of me, to train your heart to prefer any evil that can happen to the body, whether it be leprosy or any other disease, rather than let mortal sin take possession of your soul.'

At another time King Louis asked me if I washed the feet of the poor on Maundy Thursday. 'Your Majesty,' I exclaimed, 'what a terrible idea! I will never wash the feet of such low fellows.' 'Really,' said he, 'that is a very wrong thing to say; for you should never scorn to do what our Lord Himself did as an example for us. So I beg you, first for the love of God and then for love of me, to accustom yourself to washing the feet of the poor.'

This good king so loved all manner of people who believed in God and loved Him that he appointed Gilles le Brun, who was not a native of his realm, as High Constable of France, because he was held in such high repute for his faith in God and devotion to His service. For my part, I believe he well deserved that reputation. Another man, Maître Robert de Sorbon, who was famed for his goodness and his learning, was invited, on that account, to dine at the royal table.

It happened one day that this worthy priest was sitting beside me at dinner, and we were talking to each other rather quietly. The king reproved us and said: 'Speak up, or your companions may think you are speaking ill of them. If at table you talk of things that may give us pleasure, say them aloud, or else be silent.'

When the king was feeling in a mood for fun, he would fire questions at me, as for instance: 'Seneschal, can you give me reasons why a wise and upright layman is better than a friar?' Thereupon a discussion would begin between Maître Robert and myself. When we had disputed for some length of time the king would pronounce judgement. 'Maître Robert,' he would say, 'I would willingly be known as a wise and upright man, provided I were so in reality – and you can have all the rest. For wisdom and goodness are such fine qualities that even to name them leaves a pleasant taste in the mouth.'

On the other hand, he always said that it was a wicked thing to take other people's property. 'To "restore",' he would say, 'is such a hard thing to do that even in speaking of it the word itself rasps one's throat because of the *r*'s that are in it. These *r*'s are, so to speak, like the rakes of the Devil, with which he would draw to himself all those who wish to 'restore' what they have taken from others. The Devil, moreover, does this very subtly; for he works on great usurers and great robbers in such a way that they give to God what they ought to *restore* to men.'

On one occasion the king gave me a message to take to King Thibaut, in which he warned his son-in-law to beware lest he should lay too heavy a burden on his soul by spending an excessive amount of money on the house he was building for the Predicants of Provins. 'Wise men,' said the king, 'deal with their possessions as executors ought to do. Now the first thing a good executor does is to settle all debts incurred by the deceased and restore any property belonging to others, and only then is he free to apply what money remains to charitable purposes.'

One Whitsunday the saintly king happened to be at Corbeil, where all the knights had assembled. He had come down after dinner into the court below the chapel, and was standing at the doorway talking to the Comte de Bretagne, the father of the present count – may God preserve him! – when Maître Robert de Sorbon came to look for me, and taking hold of the hem of my mantle led me towards the king. So I said to Maître Robert: 'My good sir, what do you want with me?' He replied: 'I wish to ask you whether, if the king were seated in this court and you went and sat down on his bench, at a higher place than he, you ought to be severely blamed for doing so?' I told him I ought to be. 'Then,' he said 'you certainly deserve a reprimand for being more richly dressed than the king, since you are wearing a fur-trimmed mantle of fine green cloth, and he wears no such thing.' 'Maître Robert,' I answered, 'I am, if you'll allow me to say so, doing nothing worthy of blame in wearing green cloth and fur, for I inherited the right to such dress from my father and mother. But you, on the other hand, are much to blame, for though both your parents were commoners, you have abandoned their style of dress, and are now wearing finer woollen cloth than the king himself.' Then I took hold of the skirt of his surcoat and of the surcoat worn by the king, and said to Maître Robert: 'See if I'm not speaking the truth.' At this the king began to take Maître Robert's part, and say all in his power to defend him.

A little later on the king beckoned to his son, the Prince Philippe – the father of our present king – and to King Thibaut. Then, seating himself at the entrance to his oratory, he patted the ground and said to the two young men: 'Sit down here, quite close to me, so that we shan't be overheard.' 'But, my lord,' they protested, 'we should not dare to sit so close to you.' Then the king said to me, 'Seneschal, you sit here.' I obeyed, and sat down so close to him that my clothes were touching his. He made the two others sit down next, and said to them: 'You have acted very wrongly, seeing you are my sons, in not doing as I commanded the moment I told you. I beg you to see this does not happen again.' They assured him it would not.

Then the king said to me that he had called us together to confess that he had wrongly defended Maître Robert against me. 'But,' said he, 'I saw he was so taken aback that he greatly needed my help. All the same you must not attach too great importance to anything I may have said in his defence. As the seneschal rightly says, you ought to dress well, and in a manner suited to your condition, so that your wives will love you all the more and your men have more respect for you. For, as a wise philosopher has said, our clothing and our armour ought to be of such a kind that men of mature experience will not say that we have spent too much on them, nor younger men say we have spent too little.'

I will tell you here of one of the lessons King Louis taught me on our voyage back from the land oversea. It so happened that our ship was driven on to the rocks off the island of Cyprus by a wind known as the *garbino*, which is not one of the four great winds. At the shock our ship received the sailors were so frantic with despair that they rent their clothes and tore their beards. The king sprang out of bed barefoot – for it was night – and with nothing on but his tunic went and lay with arms outstretched to form a cross before the body of Our Lord on the altar, as one who expected nothing but death.

The day after this alarming event, the king called me aside to talk with him alone, and said to me: 'Seneschal, God has just shown us a glimpse of His great power; for one of these little winds, so little indeed that it scarcely deserves a name, came near to drowning the King of France, his children, his wife, and his men. Now Saint Anselm says that such things are warnings from our Lord, as if God meant to say to us: "See how easily I could have brought about your death if that had been My will." "Lord God," says the saint, "why dost Thou thus threaten us? For when Thou dost, it is not for Thy own profit, nor for Thy advantage – seeing that if Thou hadst caused us all to be lost Thou wouldst be none the poorer, nor any the richer either if Thou hadst caused us to be saved. Therefore the warning Thou sendest us is not for Thy own benefit, but for ours, if so be we know how to profit by it."

'Let us therefore,' said the king, 'take this warning God has sent us in such a way that if we feel there is anything in our hearts or our bodies that is displeasing to Him, we shall get rid of it without delay. If, on the other hand, we can think of anything that will please Him, we ought to see about doing it with equal speed. If we act thus our Lord will give us blessings in this world, and in the next greater bliss than we can tell. But if we do not act as we ought, He will deal with us as a good lord deals with his unfaithful servant. For if the latter will not amend his ways after he has been given warning, then his lord punishes him with death, or with penalties even harder to bear.'

So I, Jean de Joinville, say: 'Let the king who now reigns over us beware; for he has escaped from perils as great as those to which we were then exposed, or even greater. Therefore, let him turn from doing wrong, and in such a way that God will not smite him cruelly, either in himself or in his possessions.'

In the conversations he had with me, this saintly king did every thing in his power to give me a firm belief in the principles of Christianity as given us by God. He used to say that we ought to have such an unshaken belief in all the articles of faith that neither fear of death nor of any harm that might happen to our bodies should make us willing to go against them in word or deed. 'The Enemy,' he would add, 'works so subtly that when people are at the point of death he tries all he can to make them die with some doubt in their minds on certain points of our religion. For this cunning adversary is well aware that he cannot take away the merit of any good works a man has done; and he also knows that a man's soul is lost to him if he dies in the true faith.

'Therefore,' the king would say, 'it is our duty so to defend and guard ourselves against this snare as to say to the Enemy, when he sends us such a temptation: "Go away! You shall not lure me from my steadfast belief in the articles of my faith. Even if you had all my limbs cut off, I would still live and die a true believer." Whoever acts thus overcomes the Devil with the very same weapons with which this enemy of mankind had proposed to destroy him.'

King Louis would also say that the Christian religion as defined in the creed was something in which we ought to believe implicitly, even though our belief in it might be founded on hearsay. On this point he asked me what was my father's name. I told him it was Simon. So he asked me how I knew it, and I replied that I thought I was certain of it, and believed it without question, because I had my mother's word for it. 'Then,' said he, 'you ought to have a sure belief in all the articles of our faith on the word of the Apostles, which you hear sung of a Sunday in the Creed.'

On one occasion the king repeated to me what Guillaume, Bishop of Paris, had told him about a certain eminent theologian who had come to see him. This man told the bishop that he wished to speak with him. 'Speak as freely as you like, sir,' said the bishop. However, when the theologian tried to speak to him he only burst into tears. So the bishop said: 'Say what you have to say, sir; don't be disheartened; no one can be such a sinner that God can no longer forgive him.' 'Indeed, my lord,' said the theologian, 'I cannot control my tears. For I fear I must be an apostate, since I cannot compel my heart to believe in the sacrament of the altar, in the way that Holy Church teaches. Yet I know very well that this is a temptation of the Enemy.'

'Pray tell me, sir,' said the bishop, 'do you feel any pleasure when the Enemy exposes you to this temptation?' 'On the contrary, my lord,' said the theologian, 'it worries me as much as anything can.' 'Now,' said the bishop, 'I will ask you whether you would accept any gold or silver if it were offered you on condition you allowed your mouth to utter anything derogatory to the sacrament of the altar, or the other sacraments of Holy Church?' 'My lord,' said the other, 'I can assure you that nothing in the world would induce me to do so. I would rather have one of my limbs torn from my body than consent to say such a thing.'

'I will now,' said the bishop, 'take a different approach. You know that the King of France is at war with the King of England; you also know that the castle nearest the boundary-line between their two domains is the castle of Rochelle in Poitou. So I will ask you a question: Suppose the king had set you to guard the castle of Rochelle, and had put me in charge of the castle of Montlhéri, which is in the very centre of France, where the land is at peace, to which of us do you think the king would feel most indebted at the end of the war – to you who had guarded La Rochelle without loss, or to me who had remained in safety at Montlhéri?' 'Why, in God's name, my lord,' cried the theologian, 'to me, who had guarded La Rochelle, and not lost it to the enemy.'

'Sir,' said the bishop, 'my heart is like the castle of Montlhéri; for I have neither temptation nor doubts concerning the sacrament of the altar. For this reason I tell you that if God owes me any grace because my faith is secure and untroubled, He owes four times as much to you, who have kept your heart from defeat when beset by tribulations, and have moreover such good-will towards Him that neither worldly advantage, nor fear of any harm that might be done to your body, could tempt you to renounce Him. So I tell you to be comforted; for your state is more pleasing to Our Lord than mine.' When the theologian heard this, he knelt before the bishop, at peace with himself, and well satisfied.

The king once told me how several men from among the Albigenses had gone to the Comte de Montfort, who at the time was guarding their land for his Majesty, and asked him to come and look at the body of our Lord, which had become flesh and blood in the hands of the priest. The count had answered: 'Go and see it for yourselves, you who do not believe it. As for me, I believe it firmly, in accordance with Holy Church's teaching on the sacrament of the altar. And do you know,' he added, 'what I shall gain for having, in this mortal life, believed what Holy Church teaches us? I shall have a crown in heaven, and a finer one than the angels, for they see God face to face and consequently cannot but believe.'

King Louis also spoke to me of a great assembly of clergy and Jews which had taken place at the monastery of Cluny. There was a poor knight there at the time to whom the abbot had often given bread for the love of God. This knight asked the abbot if he could speak first, and his request was granted, though somewhat grudgingly. So he rose to his feet, and leaning on his crutch, asked to have the most important and most learned rabbi among the Jews brought before him. As soon as the Jew had come, the knight asked him a question. 'May I know, sir,' he said, 'if you believe that the Virgin Mary, who bore our Lord in her body and cradled Him in her arms, was a virgin at the time of His birth, and is in truth the Mother of God?'

The Jew replied that he had no belief in any of those things. Thereupon the knight told the Jew that he had acted like a fool when – neither believing in the Virgin, nor loving her – he had set foot in that monastery which was her house. 'And by heaven,' exclaimed the knight, 'I'll make you pay for it!' So he lifted his crutch and struck the Jew such a blow with it near the ear that he knocked him down. Then all the Jews took to flight, and carried their sorely wounded rabbi away with them. Thus the conference ended.

The abbot went up to the knight and told him he had acted most unwisely. The knight retorted that the abbot had been guilty of even greater folly in calling people together for such a conference, because there were many good Christians there who, before the discussion ended, would have gone away with doubts about their own religion through not fully understanding the Jews. 'So I tell you,' said the king, 'that no one, unless he is an expert theologian, should venture to argue with these people. But a layman, whenever he hears the Christian religion abused, should not attempt to defend its tenets, except with his sword, and that he should thrust into the scoundrel's belly, and as far as it will enter.'

The Servant of his People

IN the midst of attending to the affairs of his realm King Louis so arranged his day that he had time to hear the Hours sung by a full choir and a Requiem mass without music. In addition, if it was convenient, he would hear low mass for the day, or high mass on Saints' days. Every day after dinner he rested on his bed, and when he had slept and was refreshed, he and one of his chaplains would say the Office for the Dead privately in his room. Later in the day he attended vespers, and compline at night.

A Franciscan friar once came to see him at the castle of Hyères, where we had disembarked on our return to France. In his sermon, intended for the king's instruction, he said that in his reading of the Bible and other books that speak of non-Christian princes he had never found, in the history of either heathen or Christian peoples, that a kingdom had been lost or had changed its ruler, except where justice had been ignored. 'Therefore,' said he, 'let the king who is now returning to France take good care to see that he administers justice well and promptly to his people, so that our Lord may allow him to rule his kingdom in peace to the end of his days.' I have been told that the worthy man who taught the king this lesson lies buried at Marseilles, where our Lord, for his sake, still performs many a a fine miracle. He would never consent to remain with the king for more than a single day, however strongly his Majesty pressed him to stay. All the same, the king never forgot the good friar's teaching, but governed his kingdom well and faithfully according to God's law.

In dealing with each day's business, the king's usual plan was to send for Jean de Nesles, the good Comte de Soissons, and the rest of us, as soon as we had heard mass, and tell us to go and hear the pleadings at the gate of the city which is now called the Gate of Requests.

After he had returned from church the king would send for us, and sitting at the foot of his bed would make us all sit round him, and ask us if there were any cases that could not be settled except by his

personal intervention. After we had told him which they were, he
would send for the interested parties and ask them: 'Why did you
not accept what our people offer?' 'Your Majesty,' they would reply,
'because they offer us too little.' Then he would say: 'You would do
well to accept whatever they are willing to give you.' Our saintly
king would thus do his utmost to bring them round to a right and
reasonable way of thinking.

In summer, after hearing mass, the king often went to the wood of
Vincennes, where he would sit down with his back against an oak,
and make us all sit round him. Those who had any suit to present
could come to speak to him without hindrance from an usher or any
other person. The king would address them directly, and ask: 'Is
there anyone here who has a case to be settled?' Those who had one
would stand up. Then he would say: 'Keep silent all of you, and you
shall be heard in turn, one after the other.' Then he would call Pierre
de Fontaines and Geoffroi de Villette, and say to one or other of them:
'Settle this case for me.' If he saw anything needing correction in
what was said by those who spoke on his behalf or on behalf of any
other person, he would himself intervene to make the necessary
adjustment.

I have sometimes seen him, in summer, go to administer justice to
his people in the public gardens in Paris, dressed in a plain woollen
tunic, a sleeveless surcoat of linsey-woolsey, and a black taffeta cape
round his shoulders, with his hair neatly combed, but no cap to cover
it, and only a hat of white peacock's feathers on his head. He would
have a carpet laid down so that we might sit round him, while all
those who had any case to bring before him stood round about. Then
he would pass judgement on each case, as I have told you he often
used to do in the wood of Vincennes.

I saw the king on another occasion, at a time when all the French
prelates had said they wished to speak with him, and he had gone to
his palace to hear what they had to say. Bishop Guy of Auxerre, the
son of Guillaume de Mello, was among those present, and he addressed
the king on behalf of all the prelates. 'Your Majesty,' he said, 'the
Lords Spiritual of this realm here present, have directed me to tell
you that the cause of Christianity, which it is your duty to guard and
defend, is being ruined in your hands.' On hearing these words the
king crossed himself and said: 'Pray tell me how that may be.'

'Your Majesty,' said the bishop, 'it is because at the present time excommunications are so lightly regarded that people think nothing of dying without seeking absolution, and refuse to make their peace with the Church. The Lords Spiritual require you therefore, for the love of God and because it is your duty, to command your provosts and your bailiffs to seek out all those who allow themselves to remain under the ban of the Church for a year and a day, and compel them, by seizure of their possessions, to get themselves absolved.'

The king replied that he would willingly give such orders provided he himself could be shown without any doubt that the persons concerned were in the wrong. The bishop told him that the prelates would not on any account accept this condition, since they questioned his right to adjudicate in their affairs. The king replied that he would not do anything other than he had said; for it would be against God and contrary to right and justice if he compelled any man to seek absolution when the clergy were doing him wrong.

'As an example of this,' he continued,' I will quote the case of the Comte de Bretagne, who for seven whole years, while under sentence of excommunication, pleaded his cause against the bishops of his province, and carried his case so far that in the end the Pope condemned all his adversaries. Now, if at the end of the first year I had forced the count to seek absolution, I should have sinned against God and against the man himself.' So the prelates resigned themselves to accepting things as they were; and I have never heard tell that any further demand was made in relation to this matter.

In making peace with the King of England, King Louis acted against the advice of his council, who had said to him: 'It seems to us that Your Majesty is needlessly throwing away the land you are giving to the King of England; for he has no right to it, since it was justly taken from his father.' To this the king replied that he was well aware that the King of England had no right to the land, but there was a reason why he felt bound to give it to him. 'You see,' said he, 'our wives are sisters and consequently our children are first cousins. That is why it is most important for us to be at peace with each other. Besides, I gain increased honour for myself through the peace I have made with the King of England, for he is now my vassal, which he has never been before.'

The king's love for fair and open dealing may be gathered from his behaviour in the case of a certain Renaud de Trit. This man had brought the king a charter stating that he had granted the county of

Dammartin in Gouelle to the heirs of the late Comtesse de Boulogne. However, the seal of the charter was broken, so that nothing remained of it except half the legs of the figure representing the king, and the stool on which his feet were resting. The king showed the seal to all of us who were members of his council, and asked us to help him come to a decision. We all unanimously expressed the opinion that he was not bound to put the charter into effect. Then he told Jean Sarrasin, his chamberlain, to hand him a charter he had asked him to get. As soon as this was in his hands the king said to us: 'My lords, here is the seal I used before I went oversea, and you can clearly tell from looking at it that the impression on the broken seal corresponds exactly with that of the one that is whole. Therefore I could not, with a clear conscience, keep back this land.' So the king sent for Renaud de Trit and said to him: 'I restore your county to you.'

PART TWO

CHAPTER I

Turbulence of Barons
1226–42

IN the name of God Almighty we have now put down in writing some part of the pious sayings and good teaching of our saintly King Louis, so that those who study this book may find such things introduced in their proper sequence, and may thus derive more profit from them than if they had been recorded amongst his deeds. From this point onwards we begin, in the name of God and in the name of King Louis, to speak of the things he did.

As I have heard him say, King Louis was born on Saint Mark the Evangelist's Day, shortly after Easter. On that day it is the custom, in many different places, to carry crosses in procession, and these are known in France as 'black crosses'. This may be taken in some way as a presage of the great number of people who were to die in the two Crusades – that is to say, the Crusade in Egypt, and the one during which the king himself died at Carthage – both of which caused great mourning in this world, and great rejoicing in paradise, for such as died as true Crusaders in the course of these two pilgrimages.

King Louis was crowned on the first Sunday in Advent (29 November 1226). Mass for that Sunday opens with the words: 'Unto thee, O Lord, do I lift up my soul. O my God, I trust in thee.' And indeed, the king always put great trust in God, even from his childhood up to the time of his death; for in the last words he spoke as he lay dying he called on God and his saints, and particularly on Saint James and our patroness Saint Genevieve.

God, in whom he put his trust, kept watch over him throughout the whole of his life, from his childhood up to the end; and especially in his early youth, when he had great need of protection, as you shall shortly hear. As for his soul, God kept it from harm through the

good instruction he received from his mother, who taught him both
to believe in God and to love Him, and brought her son up in the
company of religious-minded people. Child as he was, she made him
recite all the Hours, and listen to sermons on days of high festival.
He always remembered how she would sometimes tell him that she
would rather he were dead than guilty of committing a mortal sin.

King Louis had great need of God's help in his youth, for his
mother, who came from Spain, had neither relations nor friends in
the whole kingdom of France. Moreover, because the king was only
a child, and the queen, his mother, a foreigner, the barons made the
Comte de Boulogne, who was the king's uncle, their chief, and
behaved to him as if he was their lord. After the king was crowned,
certain of the barons presented the queen with a demand to be given
great estates, and because she refused they and the rest of the barons
assembled in a body at Corbeil.

The saintly king once told me that neither he nor his mother, who
were then at Montlhéri, dared to return to Paris until the people of
that city had come, fully armed, to fetch them. All the way, he said,
from Montlhéri to Paris, the roads had been thronged with people,
armed and unarmed, all calling on our Lord to grant their young
king a long and happy life, and defend and guard him from his
enemies. And God answered their prayers, as you shall later hear.

At the conference the barons held at Corbeil those present decided,
so it is said, that the good knight, the Comte de Bretagne, should
rise in revolt against the king; they agreed besides that the rest of
them, with no more than two knights apiece, would turn up to
accompany the count when he obeyed the summons the king would
send him. They arranged this because they wanted to see whether
the count would manage to get the better of that foreign woman, the
queen. Many people say that the count would have succeeded in
mastering the queen, and her son as well, if God had not helped the
king in his hour of need, as He never failed to do.

The help God gave him was such that the Comte Thibaut de
Champagne, who later became King of Navarre, arrived with a
company of three hundred knights, to place himself at his Majesty's
service. Because of this count's support of the king, the Comte de
Bretagne was forced to throw himself on his sovereign's mercy, and
make peace with him, so it is said, by surrendering the counties of
Anjou and Le Perche.

Since it is important for you to have a full understanding of certain things I shall be touching on later, I think it well at this point to make a slight digression. I will therefore tell you here that the good Comte de Champagne, known as Henri the Generous, had by his wife the Comtesse Marie – who was the sister of King Philip of France and sister-in-law of King Richard of England – two sons, the elder of whom was called Henri and the other Thibaut. The elder son went on pilgrimage to the Holy Land as a Crusader, at the time when King Philip and King Richard besieged Acre and took it.

As soon as Acre had been taken, King Philip returned to France, an action for which he was greatly blamed. King Richard remained in the Holy Land, performing such deeds of valour that the Saracens were terrified of him. So much so, indeed, as you will find recorded in the book on the Holy Land, that whenever a Saracen child began to cry, its mother, in order to keep it quiet, would call out: 'Stop that do, King Richard's here.' Whenever, too, any horses of the Saracens or the Bedouins shied at a bush, their masters would say to them: 'D'you think that's King Richard?'

This king, after long negotiations, arranged a marriage between the young Comte Henri de Champagne, who had remained with him, and the Queen of Jerusalem, who had inherited this kingdom from her father. By this queen the Comte Henri had two daughters, the elder of whom became Queen of Cyprus, while the younger was married to the Comte Érard de Brienne, from whom a noble line has sprung, as everyone in France or Champagne knows. For the moment I will say nothing about the Comte Érard's wife, but speak to you of the Queen of Cyprus, because she is concerned in the matter I have in hand.

Now to resume my story. After King Louis had, so to speak, checkmated the Comte de Bretagne, all the other French nobles were so angry with the Comte Thibaut that they decided to send for the Queen of Cyprus – who, as you know, was the daughter of the elder son of Henri the Generous – so as to dispossess the Comte Thibaut, whose father was the Comte Henri's younger son.

Certain of the barons, however, took steps to bring about a reconciliation between the Comte Pierre and the Comte Thibaut, and were so successful in their negotiations that the latter promised to take the Comte de Bretagne's daughter as his wife. A day was fixed on which the Comte de Champagne was to marry the young woman.

She was to be taken for the ceremony to a Praemonstratensian abbey
near Château-Thierry, called, so I believe, Val-Secret. The French
barons, nearly all of whom were related to the Comte Pierre, undertook to escort his daughter. After she had been conducted to Val-
Secret word of her arrival was sent to the Comte Thibaut, who was
then at Château-Thierry.

As the count was riding towards Val-Secret for the marriage
Geoffroy de Chapelle came to meet him, bearing a letter of credence
from the king. 'My lord,' he said, 'the king has heard that you have
made an agreement with the Comte de Bretagne to marry his daughter.
He therefore warns you that unless you wish to lose everything you
possess in the kingdom of France you must not do such a thing, for, as
you know, the count has done the king more harm than any man
alive.' So the Comte de Champagne, on the advice of those who were
with him, went back to Château-Thierry.

When the Comte Pierre and the French barons, who were expecting the Comte Thibaut to arrive at Val-Secret, heard what he had
done, they were almost beside themselves with rage at the affront he
had offered them, and immediately sent to fetch the Queen of Cyprus.[1]
As soon as she arrived they made a common agreement to send for
as many men-at-arms as they could, and enter Brie and Champagne
from the French side, while the Duc de Bourgogne, whose wife was
the daughter of the Comte Robert de Dreux, would enter Champagne
from Burgundy. They fixed a day for their forces to assemble
before Troyes, with the idea of taking that city if they could
accomplish it.

The Duc de Bourgogne called in all the men at his disposal; the
barons assembled theirs. The barons moved forward, burning and
destroying everything on one side; the Burgundians did equal damage
on the other. Meanwhile the King of France advanced from another
direction to attack them. The Comte de Champagne was so alarmed
that he set fire to all his towns himself before the barons could
reach them, so that his opponents might not find them full of supplies.
Among other towns the Comte Thibaut thus destroyed were Épernay,
Vertus, and Sézanne.

When the citizens of Troyes realized that they could not count on
support from their own lord, they sent to ask Simon, Lord of Join-

[1] Joinville reverses the order of events. The war took place in 1230. The
Queen of Cyprus arrived in France in 1233.

ville, the father of the present lord, to come to their aid. As soon as this message reached him, he got all his men-at-arms together, left Joinville that same night, and arrived at Troyes the next morning before daybreak. Thus the barons' plan to take the city was foiled. So they passed along in front of Troyes without attempting anything, and went to pitch their tents in a meadow known as the Field of Isle, where the Duc de Bourgogne was already encamped.

The King of France, hearing that they were there, advanced straight towards the place to attack them. Thereupon the barons sent and begged him to withdraw himself in person from the fight, and then they would go and confront the Comte de Champagne, the Duc de Lorraine, and the rest of the king's men, with three hundred knights less than the duke and the count had in their own army. The king sent back a message to say that he would not let them fight against his men unless he himself was there in person with them. The barons, in their turn, sent to tell the king that they, for their part, would willingly persuade the Queen of Cyprus to make peace. The king replied that he would not agree to any sort of peace, nor allow the Comte de Champagne to do so, till the barons had withdrawn their troops from the count's domains.

The barons acceded to his request, but only so far as to withdraw from Isle and go to encamp at a spot to the south of Jully. The king then encamped at the place from which he had driven them. As soon as they heard he was there, the barons struck camp and went to Chaource; but not daring to wait there for the king's arrival, they moved their camp to Laignes, which belonged to the Comte de Nevers, who was of their party. So the king persuaded the Comte de Champagne and the Queen of Cyprus to come to terms, and peace was concluded on the understanding that the count would give the queen estates bringing in about two thousand *livres* a year, together with a lump sum of forty thousand *livres*.

The king paid the latter sum on the Comte de Champagne's behalf, and in return the count sold the king some four of his fiefs – that is to say the counties of Blois, of Chartres, of Sancerre, and of Châteaudun. Certain people have said that the king only held these fiefs in pledge; but it is not the case, for I asked his Majesty about it when we were oversea. As for the estates which the Comte de Champagne gave to the Queen of Cyprus, these are now held in part by the present Comte de Brienne, and in part by the Comte de Joigny, because the great-grandmother of the Comte de Brienne, who was the Queen of Cyprus's daughter, married the great Comte Gautier de Briennne.

So that you may understand how the Comte de Champagne came to possess those fiefs he sold to the king I will tell you that his ancestor, the great Comte Thibaut, who now lies buried at Lagny, had three sons, the eldest of whom was Henri, the second Thibaut, and the youngest Étienne. Henri, who became Comte de Champagne et de Brie, was commonly known as Henri the Generous. He was well named, for he was generous both in his dealings with God and with the world: generous towards God, as is still evident from the Church of Saint Étienne at Troyes and the other beautiful churches which he built in Champagne, and generous in his conduct of worldly affairs, as appeared in the case of Artaud of Nogent, as well as on many other occasions of which I would willingly tell you if I did not fear to overload my book.

This man Artaud was a citizen of Nogent, and one whom the Comte Henri trusted more than anyone else in the world. He became so wealthy that he built the castle of Nogent l'Artaud at his own expense. Now it happened one Whitsunday, as the Comte Henri was coming down the steps of his great house at Troyes to go and hear mass at the Church of Saint Étienne, that a poor knight came to the foot of the steps and knelt down before him. 'My lord,' said he, 'I beg you to give me some of your money so that I may marry these two daughters of mine, who are standing here before you.' Artaud, who was behind the count, said to the suppliant: 'My good knight, it is not fitting on your part to ask my lord for money, for he has already given away so much that he has nothing left to give.' The large-hearted count turned towards Artaud and said to him: 'My good villein, you're not telling the truth when you say that I've nothing left to give, for, indeed, I have *you*. Take him, knight, for I give him to you, and what's more I'll stand guarantee for him.' The knight, in no way taken aback, seized hold of Artaud's cloak, and said he would not let him go till he had talked business with him. Before Artaud escaped, he had done business with the knight to the tune of five hundred *livres*.

The Comte Henri's second brother, Thibaut, was Comte de Blois; the third, Étienne, was Comte de Sancerre. These two brothers held from the Comte Henri everything they inherited, including their counties with all their dependent rights and privileges. Later they held these fiefs from any descendant of the Comte Henri who held the county of Champagne, until such time as the Comte Thibaut sold them to the king.

Now let me resume my story, and tell you how, after the events I have already recorded, King Louis held a plenary court at Saumur in Anjou. I was there and can assure you that it was the most well-ordered court I have ever seen. At the high table, next to the king, sat the Comte de Poitiers, whom his Majesty had knighted on Saint John's Day; next to him was the Comte de Dreux, another newly made knight; then came the Comte de la Marche and next to him the good Comte Pierre de Bretagne. In front of the king's table, facing the Comte de Dreux, sat my lord the King of Navarre,[1] in tunic and mantle of satin, well set off by a fine leather belt, a brooch, and a cap of gold tissue. I was set to carve his meat.

The king's brother, the Comte d'Artois, stood facing his Majesty, ready to serve his meat, while beside the count the good Comte Jean de Soissons wielded a carving knife. Imbert de Beaujeu, later High Constable of France, with Enguerrand de Coucy and Archimbaud de Bourbon, were on guard at the king's table, and behind them stood some thirty of their knights, in tunics of silk, to keep guard over their lords. Behind these knights stood a great company of sergeants, in suits of taffeta embroidered with the arms of the Comte de Poitiers. The king himself was wearing a tunic of blue satin and a bright red surcoat and mantle of the same material lined with ermine. On his head he wore a cotton cap, which was hardly becoming headgear for one who was still quite young.

The king held this banquet in the hall of Saumur, which was said to have been built by the great King Henry of England, so that he might hold his own banquets there. This hall is constructed on the model of a cloister in a Cistercian monastery; but I do not believe there is any other hall that even approaches it in size. I will tell you why I think so. It is because by the wall of the cloister where the king was dining, surrounded by his knights and sergeants who occupied a very great space, there was also room for a table at which twenty bishops and archbishops were sitting, and, in addition to all these prelates, Blanche the Queen Mother had a table near them at the far end of the cloister, facing the one occupied by the king.

In attendance on Queen Blanche were the Comte de Boulogne,

[1] At that time Comte de Champagne.

who later became King of Portugal, the good Comte Hugues de Saint-Pol, and a young German lad of eighteen, who was said to be the son of St Elizabeth of Thuringia. On account of this, so it was said, Queen Blanche kissed the boy on the forehead, as a pure act of devotion, because she thought his own mother must often have kissed him there.

At the end of the cloister, on the other side, were the kitchens, the wine cellars, the pantries, and the butteries, from which the king and the queen mother were served with meat, wine, and bread. To right and left of the main hall and in the central court so many knights were dining that it was more than I could do to count them. Many people declared that they had never, on any other festive occasion, seen such a number of surcoats and other garments of cloth of gold and of silk. It was said that no less than three thousand knights were present on that occasion.

After the festivities had come an an end the king went to Poitiers, taking the Comte de Poitiers with him, so that the latter's vassals might do homage to him for their fiefs. But his Majesty had no sooner arrived at Poitiers than he wished with all his heart that he were back in Paris, for he found that the Comte de la Marche, who had dined at his table on Saint John's day, had assembled as many men-at-arms as he could get together at the neighbouring town of Lusignan. The king remained at Poitiers for close on a fortnight, for he did not dare to leave the town till he had come to terms – I cannot say how – with the Comte de la Marche.

During that time I noticed that the count came several times from Lusignan to speak with the king at Poitiers, and each time he brought his wife with him. She had formerly been Queen of England,[1] and was the mother of its present king. There were many people who asserted that the king and the Comte de Poitiers had made peace with the Comte de la Marche on very unsatisfactory terms.

Shortly after the king's return from Poitiers the King of England came into Gascony to make war on his fellow monarch. Our saintly king rode out to fight against him with as large a force as he could get together. The King of England and the Comte de la Marche advanced to join battle with him before the castle of Taillebourg, which stands beside a wretched little stream called La Charente, at a point where one cannot cross except by a very narrow stone bridge.

[1] Isabelle, widow of King John, and mother of Henry III.

As soon as King Louis reached Taillebourg, and the two armies had come in sight of one another, our men, who were on the side of the stream where the castle stood, spared no efforts to get across to the other side. With great risk to themselves they passed over the stream in boats and on pontoon bridges, to fling themselves on the English. Then a fierce and furious fight began. The king, who saw the way things were turning, rushed headlong into danger with the others; but for every man he had with him when he had crossed the stream, the English had at least twenty. None the less, as God willed, the moment the English saw the king cross over, they lost heart and fled for refuge to Saintes. Some of our men followed them into the city but got entangled in their midst and were taken prisoner.

Those of our people who had been taken at Saintes reported later that they had heard talk of a serious quarrel between the King of England and the Comte de la Marche, in which the king had accused the count of sending for him on the pretext that he would find great support in France. At any rate, on the night of his reverse at Taillebourg the King of England left Saintes and went back to Gascony.

The Comte de la Marche, as one who saw there was no help for it, surrendered to King Louis, and took his wife and children with him to prison. Since he now had the count in his power, the king, in making peace with him, was able to obtain a great part of his land, but how much I cannot say, for I had nothing to do with the matter since at that time I was not as yet a knight.[1] I was told, however, that apart from the land the king thus gained, the Comte de la Marche paid ten thousand *livres parisis* into the royal treasury, and a similar sum every subsequent year.

While I was with the king at Poitiers, I had met a certain knight, called Geoffroy de Rançon, who, so I was told, had been greatly wronged by the Comte de la Marche. Because of this he had vowed on the Holy Gospels never to have his hair cut short, as is the custom with knights, but wear it long like a woman's until such time as he should be avenged on the count, either by his own hand or another's. As soon as this knight saw the Comte de la Marche, his wife, and his children kneeling before the king and crying for mercy, he immediately sent for a little stool, and had his hair trimmed there and then, in the presence of the king, the Comte de la Marche, and everyone else who was there.

[1] Joinville says 'I had never yet worn a hauberk.'

In the course of his recent campaign against the king of England and the barons King Louis had made many generous gifts of money, as I was told by those who returned from this expedition. But neither on account of such gifts nor on account of expenses incurred in that campaign, nor in any others, either oversea or at home, did he ever demand or accept any monetary aid from his barons, his knights, his men, or any of his fine cities in such a way as to cause complaint. Nor is this to be wondered at; for he acted thus on the advice of the good mother at his side, whose counsels he always followed, and also on the advice of certain wise and worthy men who had remained loyal servants of the crown since the time of his father and his grandfather.

Preparations for a Crusade
1244-8

A YEAR or two after the events I have just recorded it happened by God's will, that King Louis, who was then in Paris, was taken very seriously ill, and came at last so near to dying that one of the two ladies who were tending him wanted to draw the sheet over his face, maintaining that he was dead. But another lady, who was on the opposite side of his bed, would not allow it, and said she was sure his soul was still in his body.

As the king lay listening to the dispute between the two ladies our Lord worked within him, and quickly brought him back to such a state of health that although up till then he had not been able to utter a word he now recovered his speech. As soon as he was able to speak he asked for the cross to be given him; and this was promptly done. When the queen mother heard that the power of speech had come back to him she was as full of joy as it is possible to be. But on learning that he had taken the cross – which she heard from his own lips – she mourned as much as if she had seen him lying dead.

After the king had taken the cross his example was followed by his three brothers, Robert, Comte d'Artois, Alfonse, Comte de Poitiers, and Charles, Comte d'Anjou, who later became King of Sicily. To these we must add Hugues, Duc de Bourgogne, and Guillaume, Comte de Flandre, the brother of the lately deceased Comte Guy de Flandre, the good Comte Hugues de Saint-Pol and his nephew Gautier. The last-named bore himself gallantly oversea, and would have proved his worth still more if he had lived longer.

I must also include among those who took the cross the Comte de la Marche and his son Hugues le Brun, as well as two cousins of mine, the Comte de Sarrebruck and his brother Gobert d'Apremont. In virtue of our relationship, I, Jean, Lord of Joinville, later made the voyage oversea in their company, in a ship we hired together. At that time we made up a party of twenty knights, nine of whom were the Comte de Sarrebruck's men and nine belonged to me.

At Easter, in the year of our Lord 1248, I summoned my men, and all who held fiefs from me, to Joinville. On Easter Eve, when all the people I had summoned had arrived, my son, Jean, Lord of Ancerville, was born to me by my first wife, who was the Comte de Grandpré's sister. We feasted and danced the whole of that week. My brother, the Lord of Vaucouleurs, and other men of wealth and standing who were present, each provided a banquet one after the other, on Easter Monday and the three following days.

On the Friday I said to them: 'My friends, I'm soon going oversea, and I don't know whether I shall ever return. So will any of you who have a claim to make against me come forward. If I have done you any wrong I will make it good, to each of you in turn, as I have been used to do in the case of those who had any demand to make of me, or my people.' I dealt with each claim in the way the men on my lands considered right; and in order not to influence their decision I withdrew from the discussion, and afterwards agreed without demur to whatever they recommended.

Since I did not wish to take away with me a single penny to which I had no right, I went to Metz in Lorraine, and mortgaged the greater part of my land. I can assure you that, on the day I left our country to go to the Holy Land, I had in my possession, since my lady mother was still alive, an income of no more than a thousand *livres* from my estates. All the same I went, and took with me nine knights, and two knights-banneret besides myself. I bring these things to your notice so that you may understand that if God, who has never failed me, had not come to my help, I should scarcely have been able to hold out for so long a time as the six years that I remained in the Holy Land.

As I was getting ready to leave, Jean, Lord of Apremont, and Comte de Sarrebruck in his wife's right, sent to tell me he had made all preparations for his voyage oversea, and that he was taking with him nine knights besides himself. He proposed, if I was willing, that we should hire a ship between us. I agreed to this; so his people and mine went and hired a ship for us at Marseilles.

Just then the king summoned all his barons to Paris, and made them swear that if anything happened to him while he was away, they would remain loyal and faithful to his children. He asked me to do the same, but I refused to take the oath, since I was not then his vassal.

As I was on my way to Paris, I came across a cart in which three dead men, who had been killed by a clerk, were lying. They were, so I was told, being taken to the king. On hearing this, I sent one of my squires after them to find out what transpired. On his return, my squire told me that the king, as he came out of chapel, had waited on the steps to look at the dead men, and had asked the Provost of Paris how it had happened.

The provost had told him that the dead men were three of his sergeants from the Châtelet who had been going round unfrequented streets and robbing people. 'And,' said he to the king, 'they met this clerk whom you see here, and stripped him of all his clothes. The clerk, with nothing on but his shirt, went back to his lodgings, snatched up his crossbow, and got a child to carry his sword. As soon as he caught sight of the thieves, he shouted after them, saying he would kill them. He got his crossbow ready and shot at them, piercing one of them through the heart. The two others took to their heels; but the clerk seized hold of the sword the child was carrying and followed after them in the moonlight, which was very bright and clear.

'One of them,' added the provost, 'tried to get through a hedge into a garden, but the clerk struck at him with his sword, cutting right through his leg, so that it only holds to the boot, as you may see here. He then went after the other man, who tried to get into a strange house where the people were still awake; but the clerk struck him a blow with his sword right through the middle of his head and split it open down to the teeth, as your Majesty can also see. The clerk,' continued the provost, 'told what he had done to the neighbours in his street, and then came and gave himself up as your Majesty's prisoner. And now I have brought him to you, to do with him what you will. Here he is.'

'Young man,' said the king, 'your courage has lost you the chance of becoming a priest; but because of your courage I will take you into my service, and you shall go with me oversea. I am doing this not only for your sake, but also because I wish my people to understand that I will never uphold them in any of their misdeeds.' When the people who had gathered there heard this, they called on our Saviour, praying Him to intercede with God, so that He would grant the king a long and happy life and bring him back to them in joy and health.

Shortly after this incident I went back to my own county of Champagne, and settled with the Comte de Sarrebruck that we should both send our luggage in carts to Auxonne, from there to be taken by boat to Arles by way of the Saône and the Rhône.

CHAPTER 3

Voyage to Cyprus
1248

ON the day I left Joinville I sent for the Abbot of Cheminon, who was said to be the wisest and worthiest monk of the Cistercian Order. I myself, when I was at Clairvaux on Lady Day in the company of our saintly king, had heard much the same opinion expressed by a member of that community who had pointed him out to me, and asked me whether I knew him. So I had said to him: 'Why do you ask me that?' to which he had replied: 'Because I personally think him the most able and most saintly man in the whole of our Order. Let me tell you,' he had gone on to say, 'what I once heard from a certain pious monk who had slept in the same dormitory as the Abbot of Cheminon. One night – so this man declared – as they lay in bed in the dormitory, the abbot had uncovered his chest because he was feeling too hot, and he himself had seen the Mother of our Lord go up to the abbot's bed and draw his frock back over his chest, so that the night air might do him no harm.'

This same abbot of Cheminon gave me my pilgrim's staff and wallet. I left Joinville immediately after – never to enter my castle again until my return from oversea – on foot, with my legs bare, and in my shirt. Thus attired I went to Blécourt and Saint-Urbain, and to other places where there are holy relics. And all the way to Blécourt and Saint-Urbain I never once let my eyes turn back towards Joinville, for fear my heart might be filled with longing at the thought of my lovely castle and the two children I had left behind.

On our way to Marseilles I and my companions stopped for a meal at Fontaine-l'Archevêque, a little this side of Donjeux; and here the Abbot of Saint-Urbain presented a number of fine jewels to me and to the nine knights I had with me. From there we went to Auxonne, and then set off again with all our luggage, which had been loaded for us on to boats; and so travelled down the Saône to Lyons, while our great war-horses were led along the bank by the side of the boats.

At Lyons we embarked on the Rhône to go to Arles-le-Blanc. As we were going down the river we passed by the ruins of a castle called Roche-de-Glun, which the king had had pulled down because Roger, the lord of the castle, had been found guilty of robbing merchants and pilgrims.

We went aboard our ship at the port of Marseilles in the month of August (1248). On the day we embarked the door on the port side of the ship was opened, so that all the horses we wanted to take with us oversea could be put into the hold. As soon as they were inside, the door was closed and carefully caulked, as is done with a cask before plunging it into water, because, once the ship is on the high seas, that door is completely submerged.

When this operation was over, our captain called to his crew, who were standing in the bows. 'Are you ready?' he cried. 'Aye aye, sir,' they answered. 'You can let the priests and the clerks come forward.' As soon as these had assembled, our captain cried to them: 'In God's name, begin to sing!' Thereupon the whole company chanted the *Veni Creator Spiritus* in unison, at the end of which the captain called out to his crew: 'Unfurl the sails, in God's name!' This was promptly done.

Before very long the breeze had filled our sails and wafted us out of sight of land, so that we saw nothing but sea and sky around us, while each day the wind carried us farther and farther from the land where we were born. I give you these details so that you may appreciate the temerity of the man who dares, with other people's property in his possession, or in a state of mortal sin himself, to place himself in such a precarious position. For what voyager can tell, when he goes to sleep at night, whether or not he may be lying at the bottom of the sea the next morning?

We ourselves had a very strange experience while we were at sea. One evening, round about vesper time, as we were sailing along by the Barbary coast, we came to a mountain shaped exactly like a bowl. We sailed all night, and reckoned we had covered well over fifty miles; but when morning came we found ourselves back alongside that very same mountain.[1] Precisely the same thing happened another two or three times. Our sailors, utterly taken aback by this curious phenomenon, came and told us they feared our ship was in very great

[1] Very possibly the effects of adverse currents in the Mediterranean, and not so miraculous as Joinville imagines.

danger, now that we were thus held up so near the land of Barbary, which was in Saracen hands.

At this point a certain worthy priest, who was Dean of Maurupt, remarked that whenever he himself had suffered any serious inconvenience in his parish – whether from lack of water, excess of rain, or any other adverse circumstance – he had only to make three processions, on three successive Saturdays, round the district, for our Lord and His Mother to grant him quick relief. He told us this, as it happened, on a Saturday. We made our first procession round the two masts of our ship. I was feeling very ill at the time, so I got some men to carry me round in their arms. We never caught sight of that mountain again; and on the third Saturday we reached Cyprus.

By the time we got to the island the king was already there. We found abundant supplies laid in for his Majesty's use: as for instance, a good store of money in his treasury, and plentiful stocks of wine and grain. The king's men had made a sort of cellarage for him in the middle of the fields, close to the shore. Here they had stacked an enormous number of huge barrels of wine which they had begun to buy two years before the king's arrival, and which they had piled up so high one on top of the other that any one approaching them from the front might have taken them for barns. The wheat and the barley had been heaped in great mounds about the fields. The rain had been beating down so long on these heaps that it had caused them to sprout, and consequently appear to be covered with grass, so that, at a first glance, you might have imagined they were hillocks. However, when the time came to transport the grain to Egypt, it was found, on removing the first layer of green, that the wheat and barley underneath were in as good a condition as if they had only just been threshed.

The king himself, as I heard later on in Syria, would very willingly have gone straight to Egypt, without stopping in Cyprus, if his barons had not advised him to wait for those of his people who had not yet arrived.

While his Majesty was staying in the island, the great King of the Tartars sent envoys to him bearing many friendly and courteous messages, which indicated, among other things, that he was ready to help our king in conquering the Holy Land and delivering Jerusalem from the hands of the Saracens.

The king received these envoys in a gracious and friendly manner, and sent others of his own in return, who remained away for two years. By these men his Majesty sent the King of the Tartars a tent arranged for use as a Chapel – a very costly gift indeed, for it was made throughout of fine scarlet cloth. Moreover, in the hope of making our religion appear attractive to the Tartars, the king had ordered for this chapel a series of little figures carved in stone, representing the Annunciation of our Lady, and all other subjects relating to the Christian faith. The men to whom he entrusted these things were two members of the Order of Predicants, who knew the language of the Tartars, and would consequently be able to teach them the principles of our religion and show them what they ought to believe.

These two monks returned from Tartary at the time when the king's two brothers had just gone back to France. They found that the king had left Acre, where his brothers had parted from him, and had gone to Caesarea, which he was busy fortifying, for there was neither peace nor truce between him and the Saracens. I shall be telling you later how his Majesty's envoys were received in Tartary, just as they told it to him, and then you will hear of many strange and marvellous things. But I will not deal with the matter now, because, in order to do so, I should have to interrupt an account that I have already begun.

To go on with my story: Although I had less than a thousand *livres* a year from my land I had undertaken, when I went oversea, to bear, in addition to my own expenses, the cost of keeping nine knights and two knights-banneret. It so happened that by the time I arrived in Cyprus I had in hand, after my ship had been paid for, no more than two hundred and forty *livres tournois*. On that account some of my knights told me that unless I provided myself with funds they would leave me. But God, who has never failed me yet, came to my help in this emergency. For the king, who was then at Nicosia, sent for me to take me into his service, and gave me eight hundred *livres* to add to my funds, so that in the end I had more money than I actually required.

While we were staying in Cyprus, the Empress of Constantinople sent word to tell me she had arrived at Paphos, a town on that island, and asked me to go and visit her there, in the company of Érard de Brienne. When we got to Paphos we found that a violent gale of wind had severed the cables of the anchor that held her ship and driven it on to Acre. She had nothing left out of all her wardrobe except the mantle she was wearing and a surcoat for meals. We brought her back with us to Limassol, where the king and queen and all the barons in the French army received her with great honour.

The next day I sent her some cloth to make a dress, together with a piece of squirrel skin to trim it; to these I added a length of linsey-woolsey and some silk to serve as lining. Philippe de Nanteuil, a worthy knight of the king's household, happened to meet my squire as he was taking these things to the Empress. On learning his errand, this good man immediately went to the king and told him that I had put both himself and the other nobles to shame by sending a dress to the Empress, when they themselves, who ought to have thought of it already, had not done so.

The Empress had come to seek help from the king for her husband, who had stayed behind in Constantinople. She handled matters so well that she was able to take back with her a couple of hundred letters or more – from myself and other friends she had in Cyprus – in which we bound ourselves on oath to the effect that if, after the king had returned from oversea, either he or the legate wished to send a company of three hundred knights to Constantinople, we would hold ourselves ready to go in their party.

I may say that when the time came for our return to France, I myself, in order to carry out my sworn obligation, took the matter up with the king – in the presence of the Comte d'Eu, whose letter I have by me – and told him that if he wished to send three hundred knights to Constantinople, I would go in their company, as I had pledged myself to do. The king, however, replied that his funds did not allow it, for whatever great reserves of money he might once have had in his treasury, they were now completely exhausted.

After we had gone to Egypt, the Empress went to France, accompanied by her brother, my lord Jean d'Acre, for whom she subsequently arranged a marriage with the Comtesse de Montfort.

At the time of our arrival in Cyprus the Sultan of Iconium was the richest ruler in all the pagan world. He had, in one instance, done something quite sensational. He had melted down a great part of his gold, and poured it into large earthenware jars, of the kind that are used oversea to hold wine, and contain as much as three or four hogsheads. After this he had the jars broken, and left the huge ingots of gold uncovered in one of his castles, where everyone who entered there could see and handle them. There were at least six or seven of these enormous lumps.

Some idea of this potentate's great wealth may be gathered from a pavilion, worth at least five hundred *livres*, which the king of Armenia sent to the King of France, informing him at the same time that he himself had been given it by a *ferrais* of the Sultan of Iconium. Now a *ferrais*, I would have you know, is a servant who looks after a sultan's pavilions and keeps his houses clean.

In order to free himself from subjection to the Sultan of Iconium the King of Armenia went to the King of the Tartars, and to obtain help from him became his vassal. On his return to Armenia the king brought back with him so great a number of men-at-arms that he was in a strong enough position to make war on the Sultan of Iconium. The struggle between them lasted for a very long time, but in the end the Tartars killed so many of the sultan's men that their ruler ceased to be of any further consequence. In the meantime, so many exciting reports of the coming battle had been circulating in Cyprus that some of our sergeants, attracted by the chance of a fight and in the hope of gaining booty, had crossed over into Armenia; but not one of them ever came back.

The Sultan of Cairo, who was expecting our king to arrive in Egypt in the spring, thought that in the meantime he would go and overthrow his mortal enemy, the Sultan of Homs, and therefore went to besiege him in his city. The Sultan of Homs saw no way of getting the better of his enemy, for he realized that if the latter lived long enough he would certainly bring about his ruin. So he got in touch with the Sultan of Cairo's *ferrais*, and bribed him to poison his master.

This is the way in which it was done: The *ferrais*, who was aware that the sultan settled down every day after dinner to play chess on the mats at the foot of his bed, spread poison on the mat on which he knew his master used to sit each day. It so happened that, in shifting his position, the sultan, whose feet were bare, exposed a sore he had on his leg. The poison immediately entered the open wound and paralysed all that side of the sultan's body into which it had penetrated. Every time the venom attacked his heart, the sultan remained for two days unable to drink, or eat, or speak. So his people left the Sultan of Homs in peace, and brought their master back to Egypt.

CHAPTER 4

Landing in Egypt
1249

AT the very beginning of March, by royal command, orders were issued to all the ships belonging to the king, the barons, and the other Crusaders to take a fresh supply of wine and other provisions on board, so as to be ready to move when the king directed. As soon as his Majesty saw that everything was in due order, he and his queen went aboard their ships on the Friday before Whitsunday. On the Saturday, after telling his barons to follow in their ships straight to Egypt, King Louis set sail, with all the others in his wake. It was indeed a lovely sight to look at, for it seemed as if all the sea, as far as the eye could reach, was covered with the canvas of the ships' sails. The total number of vessels, both great and small, amounted to about eighteen hundred.

The king cast anchor at the head of a little hill which is known as Limassol Point; all the other ships anchored round about him. He went ashore on Whitsunday. After we had heard mass, a violent raging wind, coming across the sea from the direction of Egypt, began to blow so strongly that out of two thousand eight hundred knights whom the king was taking with him on this expedition, there remained no more than seven hundred whom the wind had not separated from his company and carried on to Acre and other foreign parts; nor did they manage to rejoin the king for a very long time after.

By Whitmonday the wind had fallen. The king and those of us who, by God's will, had remained with him, immediately set sail. On our way we were joined by the Prince of Morea and the Duc de Bourgogne, who had been staying in the prince's country. On the following Thursday the king arrived before Damietta, where we found the full array of the sultan's forces drawn up along the shore. It was a sight to enchant the eye, for the sultan's arms were all of gold, and where the sun caught them they shone resplendent. The din this army made with its kettledrums and Saracen horns was terrifying to hear.

The king summoned his barons to hear their views on what they thought he should do. Many of them advised him to wait till the rest of his people had rejoined him, since at the moment he had no more than a third of his forces remaining; but he would by no means agree to such a course. The reason he gave them was that such a delay would only serve to strengthen the morale of the enemy; and what was even more important, there was no harbour at Damietta in which he could wait for his men without fear of another wind arising to drive his remaining ships away to other lands, as had happened to the others on Whitsunday.

It was settled that the king should land on the Friday before Trinity Sunday and engage the Saracens in battle, unless they refused to fight. His Majesty ordered Jean de Beaumont to assign a galley to Érard de Brienne and myself, so that we and our knights might land, because the great ships could not get sufficiently close to the shore. As I was returning to my ship, it so happened, by God's will, that I came across a smaller one which had been given me by Madame de Beirut, first cousin to the Comte de Montbéliard and myself, and which carried eight of my horses.

When Friday came I and the Comte Érard both went, fully armed, to the king, and asked for the galley; thereupon Jean de Beaumont told us we were not to have one. When our people learnt that no galley was forthcoming they let themselves drop from our ship into the longboat, one on top of the other, as quickly as they could, so that the boat began to sink. Seeing it was sinking, little by little, the sailors fled back aboard the big ship and left my knights in the boat. I asked my skipper how many more people were in the boat than it could really hold; he told me twenty men-at-arms. I then inquired whether he could manage to land our men if I took a certain number off his hands. When he told me that he could, I kept back enough men for the rest to be taken in three journeys to the ship that carried my horses.

While I was seeing to the transport of my men, a certain knight called Plonquet, who was one of Érard de Brienne's men, tried to drop down from the great ship into the longboat; but it drew away, so that he fell into the sea and was drowned.

When I came back to my ship I put my little sloop in charge of one of my squires, named Hugues de Vaucouleurs, whom I knighted there and then, and gave him as companions two young knights-aspirant, Vilain de Versey and Guillaume de Dammartin. These, as it happened, were on very bad terms with each other. No one up to now had been able to make peace between them, and all because they had seized each other by the hair when they were together in Morea. However, I made them forget their grievances and embrace, for I swore to them on the Holy Gospels that we should not land so long as their spite against each other persisted.

Then we set our course towards the land, and came up alongside the boat attached to the king's great ship, with His Majesty aboard. Since we were going more quickly than they, the people on board began to hail us, and told me to land beside the standard of Saint Denis which was being borne on another ship in front of the king's. However, I paid no heed to them, but on the contrary landed my men in front of a great body of Turks, at a place where there were fully six thousand men on horseback.

No sooner had they seen us land than they charged towards us, spurring hotly. As for us, when we saw them coming, we stuck the sharp ends of our shields into the sand and fixed our lances firmly in the ground with the points towards the enemy. But the moment they saw the lances about to pierce their bellies, they wheeled round and fled.

Baudouin de Rheims, a very worthy knight who had just come on shore, sent me a message by his squire, asking me to wait for him. I let him know I should do so very willingly, for a man of his quality was well worth waiting for at such a critical moment. For this reply, I may say, he bore me good-will ever after. This good man brought along a thousand knights to join us. I can assure you that when I landed I had with me neither squire, nor knight, nor servant that I had brought with me from my own lands; yet God never left me unprovided with men.

To left of us, the Comte de Jaffa – my lord of Montbéliard's cousin, and of the house of Joinville – was just about to land; he made the finest show of any as he came towards the shore. His galley was covered, both under and above the water, with painted escutcheons bearing his arms, which are *or* with a cross of *gules patée*. He had at least three hundred rowers in his galley; beside each rower was a small shield with the count's arms upon it, and to each shield was attached a pennon with the same arms worked in gold.

As this galley approached, it seemed as if it flew, so quickly did the rowers urge it onwards with the powerful sweep of their oars; and what with the flapping of the pennons, the booming of the drums, and the screech of Saracen horns on board this vessel, you would have thought a thunderbolt was falling from the skies. As soon as this galley had been driven into the sand as far as it would go, the count and his knights leapt on shore, well armed, well equipped, and came to take their stand beside us.

I had forgotten to tell you that, immediately on landing, the Comte de Jaffa had his tents and pavilions pitched. The moment the Saracens saw them put up they all gathered in a body in front of us, and then came on again, spurring on their horses as if they meant to ride us down. But when they saw we did not intend to flee they soon turned round again and withdrew.

On our right hand, at about the distance of a long cross-bow shot from us, the galley that bore the standard of Saint Denis came to land. One of the Saracens, either because he could not hold in his horse, or because he thought the other Saracens would follow him, came charging in amongst the men who had just landed; but he was hacked in pieces.

When the king heard that the standard of Saint Denis was on shore he strode quickly across the deck of his ship, and in spite of all the legate, who was with him, could say, refused to be parted from the emblem of his sovereignty, and leapt into the sea, where the water came up to his armpits. He went on, with his shield hung from his neck, his helmet on his head, and lance in hand, till he had joined his people on the shore. When he had reached land and scanned the enemy, he asked who they were, and was told they were Saracens. He put his lance under his armpit, and holding his shield before him, would have charged right in among them if certain sagacious men who were standing round him had allowed it.

Three times the Saracens sent messages by carrier-pigeon to the sultan, to say that the king had landed; but they never received any message in return, because the sultan was incapacitated by the sickness which had taken hold on him. Assuming therefore that their lord was dead, the Saracens abandoned Damietta. The king sent a knight to find out if they had really left the city. He returned to inform the king that he had been into the sultan's palaces, and could affirm that the report was true. His Majesty immediately sent for the legate and all the bishops who were with the army, and they one and all joined in chanting *Te Deum laudamus*. Afterwards the king mounted his horse, the rest of us followed his example, and we all went and encamped before the city of Damietta.

The Turks had acted very unwisely in leaving Damietta without cutting down the bridge of boats, for had they done so it would have greatly hindered us. However, before they left, they did us much harm by setting fire to the bazaar, where all the merchandise and other goods that are sold by weight are collected. The consequences of this action were as serious for us as if – which God forbid! – some one were, tomorrow, to set fire to the Petit-Pont in Paris.

CHAPTER 5

Occupation of Damietta
1249

Now let us declare that God Almighty was very gracious to us when He preserved us from death and danger at the time of our disembarkation, seeing that we landed on foot and attacked an enemy on horseback. Our Lord also showed us great grace in delivering Damietta into our hands, for otherwise we could only have taken it by reducing the enemy to starvation. This we can regard as certain, for it was in that very way that King Jean (of Jerusalem) had taken this city a little more than a generation before.

Our Lord, however, can say of us, as He said of the children of Israel – *et pro nihilo habuerunt terram desiderabilem.*[1] And what does He say afterwards? He says that they forgot God their Saviour. And so did we forget Him, as I shall shortly tell you.

But first of all I will tell you how King Louis summoned his barons and asked them to help him decide how the booty taken in the city should be divided. The Patriarch was the first to speak. 'Your Majesty,' he said, 'I think it would be well for you to keep control of the wheat, the barley, and the rice, and whatever is needed to sustain life, so that you may keep the city supplied with food. I think too that you should have it proclaimed throughout the army that all other goods are to be brought to the legate's quarters, under pain of excommunication.' This proposal received general assent. It so happened, however, that the total value of the goods brought to the legate's quarters amounted to no more than six thousand *livres*.

After everything had been collected, the king and the barons sent for Jean de Valery, who was known as a wise and worthy man. 'My lord of Valery,' said the king, 'we are all agreed that the legate should hand over these six thousand *livres* to you for you to apportion them as you think best.' 'Your Majesty does me great honour,' replied the good man, 'and I thank you heartily. But, please God, I cannot

[1] 'They forgat God their saviour . . . they despised the pleasant land' (Ps. cvi, 21 and 24).

accept that honour, nor can I carry out your wishes. For if I did I should be acting contrary to the good custom of the Holy Land, by which, whenever a city belonging to the enemy is captured the king takes a third of all the goods found in it, and the other Crusaders two thirds. This custom was duly respected by King Jean when he took Damietta, and also, as old chroniclers tell us, by all the kings of Jerusalem before his day. If then it pleases you to hand over to me the two-thirds of the. wheat, the barley, the rice, and the other provisions, I shall gladly undertake to share them out among the Crusaders.' The king, however, did not decide to do this, and so matters remained where they were; but many people were displeased that his Majesty had chosen to ignore such a good old custom.

The king's men, who ought to have kept on good terms with the merchants by treating them generously, made them pay, so it was said, the highest rents they could exact from them for the shops in which they sold their goods. The report of this spread to other districts, and in consequence many merchants gave up the idea of bringing supplies to the camp. The barons, who should have kept their money so as to spend it to the best advantage at a proper time and place, took to giving great banquets at which an excessive amount of food was consumed. As for the main mass of the troops, they took to consorting with prostitutes, and because of this it happened that, after their return from captivity, the king discharged a great number of his people. When I asked him why he had done this, he told me that he had found out for certain that those he had discharged from his army had gathered for their débauches at a place no more than a short stone's throw from his own pavilion, and that at a time when the army as a whole was suffering the greatest distress and misery it had ever known.

I will now return to my main subject, and tell you how, shortly after we had taken Damietta all the sultan's horsemen assembled before the camp and attacked it from the landward side. The king and all his knights armed themselves. I, for my part, after putting on my armour, went to speak to the king, and found him fully armed and sitting on a chair, with the good knights of his own division, also in full panoply of war, around him. I asked him if he wished me and my men to go and stand outside the camp, so as to prevent the Saracens from damaging our tents. On hearing my question, Jean de Beaumont called out to me at the top of his voice and commanded me, in the king's name, not to leave my quarters till his Majesty ordered me to do so.

I have just spoken of the worthy knights who were with the king. They were eight in number, all good men who had won rewards for gallant conduct in the field, both in their own country and oversea. The names of those in special attendance on the king were as follows: Geoffroy de Sargines, Mathieu de Marly, Philippe de Nanteuil, and Imbert de Beaujeu, Constable of France. The last-named of these was not present on that occasion. He was at the moment outside the camp, with the captain of the king's crossbowmen, and most of the king's sergeants-at-arms, keeping guard so that the Turks should not do our tents and equipment any damage.

During this time Gautier d'Autrèche had got himself armed at all points in his pavilion. After mounting his horse, with his shield at his neck and his helmet on his head, he had the flaps of his pavilion lifted, and struck spurs into his horse to ride against the Turks. As he was going out of his pavilion, alone and unattended, all his men raised a loud cry and shouted 'Chatillon!' But it so happened that before he reached the Turks he fell; his horse leapt over his body and went careering forward, still covered with its master's arms, right into the midst of our enemies. This was because the Saracens, for the most part, were mounted on mares, and the stallion was consequently attracted to their side.

Those who watched the incident told us that four Turks came rushing towards my lord Gautier as he lay on the ground, and aimed great blows with their maces at his body as they went by. The Constable of France and several of the king's sergeants went and rescued him, and carried him back in their arms to his pavilion. When he arrived there he could not speak. Several of the army surgeons and physicians went to see him, and because he did not seem to them to be in danger of dying they bled him in both arms.

Very late that night Aubert de Narcy said to me that we ought to go and look in on him, for as yet we had not seen him, and besides he was a man of high repute and great valour. As we entered his pavilion his chamberlain came forward to meet us and asked us to move quietly, so as not to wake his master. We found him lying on a coverlet of miniver; we went up to him very softly, and saw that he was dead. When the king was told of this he remarked that he would not care to have a thousand men like Gautier, for they would want to go against his orders as this knight had done.

The Saracens came every night into our camp on foot, and killed our men where they found them sleeping. In this way they killed my lord of Courtenay's sentinel, and after cutting off his head and taking it away with them, left his body lying on a table. They acted thus because the sultan gave a gold bezant for every Christian man's head.

We had to endure this persecution because our battalions, as they took their turn at guarding the camp each night, made their rounds on horseback. When the Saracens wished to enter the camp they would wait until the mounted battalions had rattled past, and then creep into the camp behind the horses. So the king gave orders that, instead of keeping guard on horseback as they had been doing, the battalions should in future carry out this duty on foot. In consequence the whole camp was safely guarded by our men, who were spread out in such a way that each man was within arm's length of his neighbour.

After this arrangement had been made the king decided not to leave Damietta till his brother, the Comte de Poitiers, had arrived with the reserves of the French army. Meanwhile, to prevent the Saracens from charging on horseback into our camp, his Majesty had deep trenches dug all round it, and posted crossbowmen and sergeants on guard over them each night. A similar guard was stationed at the entrance to the camp.

When the feast of Saint Remigius had passed and no news had come of the Comte de Poitiers – a thing which greatly worried the king and all his army, for they feared he might have met with some disaster – I reminded the legate how the Dean of Maurupt, while we were at sea, had got us to go in procession on three successive Saturdays, and how before the third Saturday arrived we had landed in Cyprus. The legate paid attention to what I said, and had it proclaimed throughout the camp that there would be a procession on each of the three following Saturdays.

The first procession started from the legate's quarters and went to the church of our Lady in the city. This had formerly been a Saracen mosque, but the legate had now dedicated it in honour of the Mother of our Lord. On two successive Saturdays the legate preached the sermon, in the presence of the king and the chief men in the army, to all of whom he granted full indulgences.

Before the third Saturday came round the Comte de Poitiers

arrived. It would not in fact have been much use if he had tried to come any earlier, for in the interval between the three Saturdays such a violent tempest had raged at sea just outside Damietta that at least twelve score ships, both great and small, had gone to pieces and been lost, and all the people in them drowned. So if the Comte de Poitiers had come any sooner, he and his men would have perished in the sea.

As soon as the count arrived the king summoned all the barons of the army to decide in what direction he should go, whether to Alexandria or to Cairo. The good Comte Pierre de Bretagne, as well as the majority of the barons, agreed in advising him to go and besiege Alexandria, because that city had a good harbour, where the ships bringing food for the army could land their supplies. But the Comte d'Artois was of a contrary opinion, maintaining that he would never agree to their going anywhere except to Cairo, because it was the chief city in the kingdom of Egypt, and if you wished to kill the serpent, you must first of all crush its head. The king rejected the barons' advice in favour of his brother's.

CHAPTER 6

Operations on the Nile
NOVEMBER 1249–FEBRUARY 1250

AT the beginning of Advent the king set out with his army to go towards Cairo, as the Comte d'Artois had advised. Quite close to Damietta we came to a little stream that issued from the main river, and it was decided that the army should halt there for a day to dam it up, so that we might get by. This was done pretty easily, for we dammed this little arm close to its juncture with the river in such a way that its water flowed without much difficulty back into the main stream. During our passage over, the sultan sent five hundred of the best horsemen he could find in his army to harass the king's men and delay our march.

On Saint Nicholas's Day the king ordered us to make ready to ride forward, while at the same time forbidding anyone to be so bold as to attack the enemy around us. It happened, however, that when the army began to move forward, and the Turks realized that no attack on them was contemplated – for their spies had told them that the king had forbidden it – they grew bolder and flung themselves on the Templars, who formed the van. One of the Turks bore a Knight Templar to the ground, right in front of the hoofs of the horse on which Brother Renaud de Vichiers, at that time Marshal of the Temple, was mounted. On seeing this, the Marshal cried to his brother Templars: 'For God's sake, let's get at them! I can't stand it any longer!' He struck his spurs into his horse, and all the army followed. Now our men's horses were fresh, and those of the Turks already weary; and so, as I have heard, not one of the enemy escaped, but all perished. Some of them had fallen into the river and been drowned.

Before I go any further I must tell you about the river that flows through Egypt, and also about the earthly paradise. I do this so that you may understand certain things connected with my story.

This river then is different from all other rivers; for as these others flow down towards the sea more and more brooks and rivulets flow into them; but no other streams of any kind fall into this river which, as it happens, runs down one unbroken channel into Egypt, and then divides into seven branches that spread throughout the land.

After the time of year that comes within the octave of Saint Remigius (i.e. first week in October) these seven rivers spread themselves over the land and completely cover the plains. As soon as the floods recede the peasant farmers go out, each to till his own fields, with a plough that has no wheels, and with which they turn over the earth for the sowing of wheat, barley, cumin, and rice, all of which produce such fine crops that no one could wish for better. Nobody knows how these floods arise, unless it be by God's will; but if they did not happen no good thing would grow in the land, for the great heat of the sun would scorch it up, since it never rains in this country. The water of this river is always muddy; so when the natives wish to drink it, they draw some towards evening and add four crushed beans or almonds to it; the next morning it is so good to drink that no fault can be found with it.

Before this river enters Egypt, the people who usually do such work cast their nets of an evening into the water and let them lie outspread. When morning comes they find in their nets such things as are sold by weight and imported into Egypt, as for instance ginger, rhubarb, aloes, and cinnamon. It is said that these things come from the earthly paradise; for in that heavenly place the wind blows down trees just as it does the dry wood in the forests of our own land; and the dry wood from the trees in paradise that thus falls into the river is sold to us by merchants in this country. The water of this river is of such a nature that when we put some of it into those white earthenware pots that are made in Egypt, and hung them to the ropes of our pavilions, it became, even in the heat of the day, as cold as water drawn from a well.

The people of this country said that the Sultan of Cairo had often tried to discover the source of this river. With this object in view he had sent out people who took with them a kind of bread called biscuit, because it is twice baked, and lived on this until they came back again to the sultan. They reported that after they had gone a considerable distance up the river they had come to a great mass of rocks, so high and sheer that no one could get by. From these rocks the river fell streaming down, and up above, on the top of the mountain, there seemed to be a marvellous profusion of trees. They also said that they had seen a number of strange and savage creatures of different species, such as lions, serpents, and elephants, that came and looked at them from the banks of the river as they were going upstream.

Now I can take up my first point, and repeat that when the river enters Egypt it throws out its branches far and wide. One of these branches goes to Damietta, another to Alexandria, a third to Tanis, and a fourth to Rosetta.[1] It was to this last branch that the King of France came with his army. He pitched his camp between the stream that flows towards Damietta and the one that goes to Rosetta. On the further side of the latter stream the sultan's army had encamped in full force opposite our troops in order to prevent our passage – a thing which they could easily do, for no one could get across to approach the enemy, except by swimming over.

The king decided to build a causeway across the river so as to reach the Saracens. To protect those engaged in making it he ordered the construction of two movable towers. These were of the kind known as 'cat-houses',* for they stood in front of the 'cats' (or covered ways), with two 'houses' behind them, and served to shelter those on guard from stones from the Saracen machines, which were sixteen in number, all set up ready for action.

On our arrival at the river the king had given orders for the construction of eighteen ballistic machines, and put Jocelin de Cornaut in charge as chief engineer. Our machines let fly against the enemy's, and they, in their turn, pelted ours; but I never heard that ours had done much damage. The king's brothers kept guard at the covered ways by day, and we others kept guard by night. And thus we came to the week before Christmas.

As soon as the covered ways were finished, our men began to build the causeway – but not before, because the king did not want the Saracens, who were aiming at us all the time from across the river, to wound the men who were bringing up earth. All the same, in having this causeway built, the king and his barons acted without sufficient foresight in assuming that, because they had dammed up one of the arms of the river – an easy thing to do, since they had set themselves to dam it at the point where it left the main stream – they could dam up the Rosetta branch at a point where it was already half a league away from the main river.

To hinder the making of the king's causeway the Saracens dug holes

[1] See glossary under Nile.

in the earth at the side where their army lay, and as the stream came up to the holes, it rushed into them, making a great ditch full of water. Thus it happened that in one day they undid all that we had done with three weeks' labour; for as fast as we dammed up the stream on our side, they broadened its course by the holes they made on theirs.

In the place of the sultan who had died of the sickness he had contracted while besieging Homs, the Saracens had recently adopted as their chief a certain Scecedin,[1] who was the son of their sheikh. It was said that the Emperor Frederick had made him a knight. He ordered a company of his men to attack our camp near Damietta; they set out immediately and came to a town called Sharimshah, which is on the Rosetta branch of the river.

On Christmas Day I and my knights were dining with Pierre d'Avallon. While we were at table the Saracens came spurring hotly up to our camp and killed several poor fellows who had gone for a stroll in the fields. We all went off to arm ourselves but, quick as we were, we did not return in time to rejoin our host; for he was already outside the camp, and had gone to fight the Saracens. We spurred after him and rescued him from the enemy, who had thrown him to the ground. Then we brought him back to camp with his brother, the Lord du Val. The Templars, who had come upon hearing the alarm, covered our retreat well and valiantly. The Turks came after us, harassing us right up to the camp. In consequence of this the king gave orders for the camp to be enclosed on the Damietta side, from the stream of Damietta to the stream of Rosetta.

Scecedin, whom I have already referred to as the leader of the Turks, was the most highly esteemed of any in the pagan world. On his banner, which was barred, he bore on one bar the arms of the emperor[2] who had made him a knight, on another the arms of the Sultan of Aleppo, and on the third the arms of the Sultan of Cairo. He was known as Scecedin, son of the sheikh – which is as much as to say: 'the aged one, son of the aged one.' Such a name was a mark of singular prestige among the Saracens, for they are the people in the world who have most reverence for the old – always provided that God has preserved them from any taint of dishonour throughout their lives.

[1] Fakhr-ad-Din, the late sultan's vizier. Actually he had been appointed generalissimo by the widowed sultana.
[2] Frederick of Germany.

Scecedin, this valiant Turk, had boasted – so the king's spies reported – that he would dine in his Majesty's pavilion on Saint Sebastian's Day [20 January]. On hearing of this the king arranged his forces accordingly. His brother, the Comte d'Artois, was set to guard the covered ways and the engines; the king and the Comte d'Anjou – who later became King of Sicily – undertook to guard the camp on the side towards Cairo; the Comte de Poitiers and we, the men of Champagne, were told off to guard the side towards Damietta.

Meanwhile Scecedin had ordered his men to cross over to the island between the Damietta and Rosetta branches of the Nile* where our army was encamped, and had drawn up his forces in lines extending from one branch to the other. The Comte d'Anjou attacked these forces and routed them. Many were drowned in one river or the other. None the less a great number remained whom our people did not dare to attack, because the Saracen machines kept on casting stones on the land between the rivers.

During the Comte d'Anjou's attack the Comte Guy de Forez cut his way on horseback through the enemy's lines. He and his knights engaged a body of Saracen men-at-arms, who bore him to the ground. His leg was broken, and two of his knights had to carry him back in their arms. The Comte d'Anjou was with great difficulty extricated from the perilous position in which he had placed himself, but he won himself great honour on that day. On that same occasion the Turks came charging against the Comte de Poitiers and ourselves; we made a countercharge, and pursued them a long way. Some of their people were killed; but we returned without loss.

One night when we were keeping guard over the towers that protected the covered ways, the Saracens brought forward a machine called a petrary, which they had not done before, and put Greek fire into its sling. When the good knight, Gautier d'Écurey, who was with me, saw this he said to us: 'My friends, we're in the greatest peril we've ever been in, for if they set fire to our towers and we remain here we'll all be burnt alive. On the other hand, if we leave the posts we've been set to guard, we are dishonoured. Therefore no one can defend us in this peril but God alone. What I advise is for all of us to fling ourselves on our elbows and knees each time they hurl their fire at us, and pray to our Saviour to preserve us in this hour of peril.'

As soon as they launched their first missile we threw ourselves on our elbows and knees as the good knight had directed. That first mass of flame passed between our two towers and fell on the ground in front of us, just where our troops had been making the dam. The men sent to put out the fire were getting ready to extinguish it, when the Saracens, seeing they could not aim straight at them because of the two pavilion wings which the king had had put up, began to shoot their darts right up into the clouds, so that they fell on the firemen's heads.

This Greek fire was such that seen from the front as it darted towards us it appeared as large as a barrel of verjuice, and the tail of fire that streamed behind it was as long as the shaft of a great lance. The noise it made in coming was like that of a thunderbolt falling from the skies; it seemed like a dragon flying through the air. The light this huge, flaming mass shed all around it was so bright that you could see right through the camp as clearly as if it were day. Three times that night the enemy slung Greek fire at us from their petraries, and three times they shot it from their swivel crossbows.

Each time our saintly king heard the Saracens hurling Greek fire at us he sat up in his bed, raised his hands in prayer, and said, weeping: 'Gracious Lord, guard my people for me!' I truly believe his prayers did us good service in our need. All that night, every time the fire had fallen he sent one of his chamberlains to ask us how we were faring, and whether the flaming missiles had done us any harm.

Once when they hurled Greek fire at us it fell near the tower which Pierre de Courtenay's men were guarding, and struck the bank of the stream. Thereupon a knight called l'Aubigoiz came up to me and said: 'My lord, unless you come and help us we shall all be burnt; for the Saracens have shot so many of their fire-tipped bolts at us that it seems like a great hedge of flame advancing towards our tower.' We rushed to the place and found that he had spoken truly. We put out the fire, but before we had completely extinguished it, the Saracens had struck every one of us with the arrows they shot from across the stream.

The king's brothers kept guard over the towers by day, and went to the top of them to shoot bolts from their crossbows at the men in the Saracens' camp. The king now decided that when the Comte d'Anjou was on guard by day, we should take over at night. One day when the Comte d'Anjou was at his post and we were due to go on guard at nightfall, we all felt very sick at heart, because by now the Saracens had well-nigh shattered our towers. This time they brought their petraries out in full daylight, although so far they had only brought them out at night, and started bombarding our towers with Greek fire.

They had drawn up their machines so close to the causeway our men had built to dam the stream, and were hurling so many great stones on top of it that no one dared approach the towers. Consequently both of them were burnt up. The Comte d'Anjou was so beside himself that he tried to throw himself at the fire in order to put it out. But if he was mad with rage, I and my knights praised God for such an accident; for if we had had to be on guard that night, we should all have been burnt alive.

When the king heard of this disaster he sent for all the barons in his army and begged each of them to give him some wood from their ships to build a new covered way, and so help dam up the stream. He explained to them very clearly that there was no wood available for this except what could be got from the ships which had brought our goods and equipment up the river. Each man brought as much as he was willing to give, and when the tower was built, the value of the wood supplied amounted to over ten thousand *livres*.

The king also decided that the new covered way should not be pushed forward on to the causeway until the day came when it was the Comte d'Anjou's turn to mount guard, so that he might have a chance of making amends for the burning of the other towers when he was in charge of them. As it had been decided, so it was done. As soon as the Comte d'Anjou came on guard the king had the new covered way pushed forward along the causeway to the place where the two other towers had been burnt.

When the Saracens saw what was going on, they arranged for all their sixteen machines to cast their missiles on the causeway at the very spot to which the covered way had been brought. Then perceiving that our men were afraid to approach that place because of the stones that were falling on the causeway, they brought up a petrary which launched Greek fire at the new construction and burnt the whole thing. God showed Himself very gracious towards myself and my knights in this matter, for if we had mounted guard that night we should have been in as great danger as we were on that occasion of which I have already spoken.

In view of this new set-back the king called all his barons together and asked for their advice. They unanimously agreed that there was no use in trying to build a causeway on which to approach the Saracens, because our men could not possibly dam up as much of the stream on our side as the enemy could set free again on the other.

At this point the Constable Imbert de Beaujeu informed the king that a Bedouin had come to him and told him that he would show us a good ford, provided we gave him five hundred bezants. The king said he would agree to the money being given him, provided he really did as he promised. So the constable spoke to the Bedouin; but the man said he would not show us the ford unless we paid him the money in advance. It was consequently agreed that the bezants should be given him, and these were handed over to him without delay.

The king decided that the Duc de Bourgogne and the men of highest rank from oversea who were with the army should stay to guard the camp, so that no harm might happen to it, while he himself and his three brothers would cross by the ford at the place which the Bedouin was to show them. This plan was put into action, and everything made ready for the crossing by Shrove Tuesday, which was the day on which we reached the Bedouin's ford. There, at the first sign of dawn, we gathered round from all points, and as soon as we were ready we entered the water with our horses swimming under us. By the time we got to the middle of the stream we touched ground and our horses found safe footing. On the further bank, we saw a good three hundred Saracens drawn up, all mounted on their horses.

Then I called out to my knights and said: 'Now then, gentlemen, look only to the left, and make your way in that direction. The banks here are wet and muddy, and the horses are slipping down on top of their riders and drowning them.' And indeed some of our people were drowned in the crossing, among them Jean d'Orléans, who was carrying a banner *vivré*.[1] So we turned in a direction that brought us upstream, where we found a dry place to land, and so crossed over – God be praised! – without one of our number falling down. As soon as we had crossed the stream the Turks took to flight.

It had been arranged that the Templars were to form the vanguard, with the Comte d'Artois following them in command of the second division. But as it turned out, the count had no sooner got across the stream than he and all his men flung themselves on the Turks, who fled before them. The Templars let him know that he had gravely

[1] With wavy lines.

insulted them in assuming the lead when he should have followed after; they begged him to let them go on ahead, as had been arranged by the king. But the count, as it happened, did not venture to answer them, because of an error on the part of Foucaud de Merle, who was holding the bridle of his horse. This man was a very good knight, but being completely deaf, he heard nothing at all of what the Templars were saying to his lord, and kept on shouting: 'After them, men, after them!'

At this the Templars, thinking they would be shamed if they let the Comte d'Artois get in front of them, struck spurs into their horses and rushed headlong in pursuit of the Turks, who fled before them, right through the town of Mansourah and on into the fields beyond towards Cairo. When our men tried to return, the Turks in Mansourah threw great beams and blocks of wood down on them as they passed through the streets, which were very narrow. The Comte d'Artois was killed there, together with Raoul de Coucy and so many other knights that the number of dead was estimated at three hundred. The Templars, as their Grand Master told me later, lost on this occasion some two hundred and eighty men-at-arms, and all mounted.

CHAPTER 7

The Battle of Mansourah
8 FEBRUARY 1250

IN the meantime, I and my knights had decided to go and attack some Turks who were loading their baggage in their camp on our left; so we fell on them. As we were pursuing them through the camp I caught sight of a Saracen on the point of mounting his horse; one of his knights was holding the bridle. At the moment he had both his hands on the saddle to pull himself up, I gave him a thrust with my lance just under the arm-pits and struck him dead. On seeing this, his knight left his lord and the horse, and thrusting his lance at me as I passed, caught me between the shoulders, pinning me down to the neck of my horse in such a way that I could not draw the sword at my belt. I therefore had to draw the sword attached to my horse. When he saw me with my sword drawn he withdrew his lance and left me.

When I and my knights came out of the Saracens' camp we found what we reckoned to be about six thousand Turks, who had left their tents and retreated into the fields. As soon as they saw us they came charging towards us, and killed Hugues de Trichâtel, Lord of Conflans, who was with me bearing a banner. I and my knights spurred on our horses and went to the rescue of Raoul de Wanou, another of my company, whom they had struck to the ground.

As I was coming back, the Turks thrust at me with their lances. Under the weight of their attack my horse was brought to its knees, and I went flying forward over its ears. I got up as soon as ever I could, with my shield at my neck and sword in hand. One of my knights, named Érard de Siverey – may God grant him grace! – came to me and advised our drawing back towards a ruined house where we could wait for the king, who was on his way. As we were going there, some on foot and some on horseback, a great body of Turks came rushing at us, bearing me to the ground and riding over my body, so that my shield went flying from my neck.

As soon as they had passed, Érard de Siverey came back to me and took me with him to the walls of the tumble-down house. Here we were joined by Hugues d'Écot, Frédéric de Loupey, and Renaud de Menoncourt. While we were there the Turks attacked us from all sides. Some of them got into the house and pricked us with their lances from above. My knights asked me to hold on to their horses' bridles, which I did, for fear the beasts should run away. Then they put up a vigorous defence against the Turks, for which, I may say, they were afterwards highly praised by all men of good standing in the army, both those who witnessed their bravery and those who heard of it later.

During this incident, Hugues d'Écot received three wounds in the face from a lance, and so did Raoul de Wanou, while Frédéric de Loupey had a lance-thrust between his shoulders, which made so large a wound that the blood poured from his body as if from the bung-hole of a barrel. A blow from one of the enemy's swords landed in the middle of Érard de Siverey's face, cutting through his nose so that it was left dangling over his lips. At that moment the thought of Saint James came into my mind, and I prayed to him: 'Good Saint James, come to my help, and save us in our great need.'

Just as I had uttered this prayer Érard de Siverey said to me: 'My lord, if you think that neither I nor my heirs will incur reproach for it, I will go and fetch you help from the Comte d'Anjou, whom I see in the fields over there.' I said to him: 'My dear man, it seems to me you would win great honour for yourself if you went for help to save our lives; your own, by the way, is also in great danger.' (I spoke truly, for he died of his wound.) He consulted the other knights who were there, and they all gave him the same advice as I had given him. After hearing what they said, he asked me to let go his horse, which I was holding by the bridle; so I let him take it.

He went over to the Comte d'Anjou and begged him to come to the rescue of me and my people. A person of some importance who was with the count tried to dissuade him, but he said he would do as my knight had asked. So he turned his horse's head to come to our help, and a number of his sergeants set spurs to their horses as well. As soon as the Saracens saw them coming, they turned to leave us. Pierre d'Auberive, who was riding in front of the sergeants with his sword clenched in his fist, saw them leaving and charged right into the midst of the Saracens who were holding Raoul de Wanou, and rescued him, sorely wounded.

As I stood there on foot with my knights, wounded as I have told you, King Louis came up at the head of his battalions, with a great sound of shouting, trumpets, and kettledrums. He halted with his troops on a raised causeway. Never have I seen a finer or more handsome knight! He seemed to tower head and shoulders above all his people; on his head was a gilded helmet, and a sword of German steel was in his hand.

The moment he stopped, those good knights in his division whom I have already named to you, together with other valiant knights of his, flung themselves right at the Turks. It was, I can assure you, a truly noble passage of arms, for no one there drew either bow or crossbow; it was a battle of maces against swords between the Turks and our people, with both sides inextricably entangled.

One of my squires, who had fled away with my banner, but had rejoined me, brought up one of my Flemish horses, on which I mounted and rode to take up my place beside the king. While we were there together, the worthy knight Jean de Valery came up to the king and said he advised him to bear to the right towards the river, so as to have the support of the Duc de Bourgogne, and also to give his Majesty's sergeants a chance of something to drink, for by now the day had grown very hot.

The king ordered his sergeants to go and fetch the good knights of his council who were round about, indicating each of them by name. The sergeants went and summoned them from the thick of the fight, where the struggle between the Turks and our people was most intense. They came to the king, who asked them what they advised. They replied that they considered Jean de Valery's advice very sound. So the king ordered his standard-bearers to move with the great flag of Saint Denis to the right towards the river. As the royal army began to move there was once again a great sound of trumpets, kettledrums, and Saracen horns.

The king had scarcely advanced more than a few paces when he received several messages from the Comte de Poitiers, the Comte de Flandre, and other men in high command who were there with their troops, all begging him not to move, because they were so hard pressed by the Turks that they could not possibly follow him. The king summoned the worthy knights of his council once more, and they all advised him to wait. Shortly after, Jean de Valery came back, and reproached the king and his council for remaining stationary.

On this all the members of his council recommended the king to move towards the river as Jean de Valery advised.

At this moment the Constable Imbert de Beaujeu came to tell the king that his brother the Comte d'Artois was defending himself in a house in Mansourah, and begged his Majesty to go to his relief. 'You go on ahead of me, Constable,' said the king, 'and I will follow.' I told the constable I would accompany him as his knight, for which he thanked me heartily. So we both began to make our way towards Mansourah.

As we were going there, a sergeant armed with a mace came after the constable in a terrible state of fright, and told him that the king's advance was halted, and that the Turks had placed themselves between his Majesty and us. We turned round, and saw that there were more than a thousand of them between us and the king's army; and we were no more than six. So I said to the constable: 'My lord, we can't get back to the king through this mass of men, so let's go upstream, and place this gully you can see in front of you between the enemy and ourselves. In this way we may manage to get back to the king.' The constable took my advice; but I can assure you that if the Turks had paid any attention to us they would certainly have killed us all. However at the time they were giving no thought to anything except the king and the big battalions of men, and so assumed we were some of their own people.

While we were coming back down the bank of the river, between a brooklet and the main stream, we saw that the king had come up close to the river. The Turks were driving back his other battalions, slashing and striking at them with swords and maces, and gradually forcing them, together with the king's own battalion, back upon the river. The rout there was so complete that many of our people attempted to swim across to join the Duc de Bourgogne; but they were unable to do so, for their horses were weary, and the day had become very hot. So, as we were coming downstream towards them, we saw the river strewn with lances and shields, and full of men and horses drowning in the water.

As we came to a little bridge that spanned the brook I said to the constable: 'Let's stay here and defend this bridge, for if we abandon it the Turks will hurl themselves against the king from this side too, and if our people are attacked from two sides they may well be overpowered.' So we did as I advised. Later on we learnt that we should have all been lost that day if it had not been for the king. For, as Pierre de Courtenay and Jean de Saillenay told me, six Turks had seized the king's horse by the bridle and were leading him away captive, when he delivered himself without anyone's help by slashing at them with great strokes of his sword. When his men saw how the king was defending himself their courage revived, and many of them, giving up all thought of escaping across the river, rallied round to help him.

Riding straight towards us, as we were holding the little bridge, came the Comte Pierre de Bretagne, with a sword-cut across his face from which blood ran down into his mouth. He was mounted on a very handsome pony. He had thrown its reins over the pummel of his saddle, which he was gripping with both his hands, for fear his men, who were following him too close for comfort, might jostle him out of position as they crossed the narrow bridge. It would seem he had a very poor opinion of them; for as he spat the blood out of his mouth he kept ejaculating: 'Good Lord, did you ever see such scum!' Behind his men came the Comte de Soissons and Pierre de Neuville who was nicknamed 'Caier'; they had both received blows enough that day.

After these men had crossed the bridge, the Turks, seeing that we were guarding it with our faces turned towards them, stopped following the Comte Pierre and his party. I went up to the Comte de Soissons, who happened to be my wife's cousin, and said to him: 'I think it would be a good thing, sir, if you stayed to hold this bridge, for if we leave it unguarded the Turks over there will rush across it, and the king will be attacked both from the front and rear.' He asked me whether, if he stayed, I would remain there with him. 'I most certainly will,' I replied. On hearing this the constable told me not to move from the place till he returned, and said he would go in search of help for us.

I remained there, mounted on my sturdy cob, with the Comte de Soissons on my right hand, and Pierre de Neuville on my left. Suddenly a Turk came riding towards us from the direction of the king's troops, which were to our rear, and struck Pierre such a fierce blow from behind with his mace that he forced him down on to the neck of his horse; then, darting across the bridge, he rushed in amongst his own people.

When the Turks saw that we were not going to abandon the little bridge, they crossed the brook and placed themselves between it and the river, as we had done when we were going downstream. Thereupon we moved towards them so as to be ready to charge them if they attempted either to go in the direction of the king's troops or to cross our little bridge.

Just ahead of us were two of the king's sergeants – one called Guillaume of Boon and the other Jean of Gamaches. The Turks who had come between the brook and the river had brought along a large number of peasants on foot, who kept on pelting these two men with clods of earth, but were never able to force them back to where we stood. Finally the Turks brought up a low fellow who threw Greek fire at them three times in succession. Once Guillaume of Boon warded off a bucket-load of the stuff by catching it on his shield, for if the flames had caught any of his clothing he would certainly have been burnt alive.

We were all covered with the darts that failed to hit the sergeants. By some lucky chance I happened to find a Saracen's tunic, padded with tow. I turned the open side towards me and used the garment as a shield. It did me good service, for I was only wounded by the enemy's darts in five places, though my horse was wounded in fifteen. It also happened that a certain worthy fellow from Joinville brought me a pennon with my arms affixed to a lance head, and every time we saw the Turks pressing too hardly on the sergeants we charged them and sent them flying.

The good Comte de Soissons, hard put to it as we were at that moment, still made a joke of it and said to me gaily: 'Seneschal, let these dogs howl as they will. By God's bonnet' – that was his favourite oath – 'we shall talk of this day yet, you and I, sitting at home with our ladies!'

That evening, as the sun was setting, the constable came up with a company of the king's unmounted crossbowmen, who drew up in rank in front of us. As soon as the Saracens saw them setting foot to the stirrup of their crossbows, they left us and fled. Then the constable said to me: 'Seneschal, that's a good thing done. Now go to the king and don't leave his side till he's back again in his pavilion.' Just as I reached the king, Jean de Valery came up to him and said: 'Your Majesty, the Lord of Châtillon asks you to give him command of the rear-guard.' The king consented very willingly, and then rode on. As we were going, I made him take off his helmet, and lent him my steel cap so that he might have some air.

After the king had crossed the river Brother Henri de Ronnay, Provost of the Hospitallers, came up to him and kissed his mailed hand. The king asked him if he had any news of the Comte d'Artois, to which the provost replied that indeed he had news of him, for he was certain that his Majesty's brother was now in paradise. 'Ah, your Majesty,' added the provost, 'take comfort in the thought that no King of France has gained such honour as you have gained today. For, in order to fight your enemies, you swam across a river, to rout them utterly and drive them from the field. Besides this, you have captured their machines, and also their tents, in which you will be sleeping tonight.' 'May God be worshipped for all He has given me,' replied the king; and then big tears began to fall from his eyes.

When we reached the camp we found some of the unmounted Saracen troops pulling at the ropes of a tent they had just taken down, while some of our own troops were tugging away on the other side. The Master of the Temple and I charged in among them, so that the enemy fled and the tent remained in our hands.

In the course of that day's battle there had been many people, and of fine appearance too, who had come very shamefully flying over the little bridge you know of and had fled away so panic-stricken that all our attempts to make them stay with us had been in vain. I could tell you some of their names, but shall refrain from doing so, because they are now dead.

I shall not however fail to mention the name of Guy Mauvoisin, for he returned with honour from Mansourah. All the way the constable and I had followed up the river, he followed down. And just as the Turks had pressed hard on the Comte de Bretagne and his men, so they harassed Guy Mauvoisin and his; but Mauvoisin's men, as well as he, won great honour for their part in that day's fighting. Nor is it to be wondered at that they acquitted themselves so well, since – as I learnt from those who knew of the arrangement of his troops – his whole company, with very few exceptions, was composed of knights who were either members of his family or his own vassals.

After we had routed the Turks and driven them from their tents, and while our people had left their camp empty, the Bedouins rushed in to plunder it, for the Turks who had been quartered there were men of high rank and great possessions. The marauders left nothing at all behind them, but carried away everything the Turks had left. I did not, however, hear that the Bedouins, though they were subject to the Saracens, were any less well thought of for stealing and carrying off this booty – it being well known that the habit of these people is to regard the weaker side as their lawful prey.

As it is connected with my subject, I will now tell you what kind of people the Bedouins are. They do not follow Mahomet, but accept the teaching of Ali, who was Mahomet's uncle. (The Old Man of the Mountain, who maintains the Assassins, is of this persuasion too.) These people believe that when a man dies for his lord, or in any other good cause, his soul goes into another body, a better and a happier one than before. That is why the Assassins care little whether they are killed when carrying out their master's commands. However, I will say no more about the Old Man of the Mountain for the present, but speak only of the Bedouins.

These people do not live in villages, or cities, or castles, but sleep always out in the open fields. At night, or by day when the weather is bad, they house their servants, their wives, and their children in a sort of shelter they make with the hoops of barrels tied to poles, somewhat like ladies' litters. Over these hoops they throw sheepskins, cured with alum, which are known as Damascus hides.

The Bedouins themselves wear great hairy mantles that cover the whole of the body, including the legs and feet. When it rains in the evening, or the weather is bad by night, they wrap themselves up in these mantles, and taking the bits from their horses' mouths, leave them to browse on the grass near by. In the morning they spread out their mantles in the sun, then rub them and give them a new dressing of alum, after which there remains no trace of their ever having been wetted.

They believe that no one can die before the appointed day, and for this reason refuse to wear any sort of armour. Whenever they wish to curse their children they say to them: 'Be accursed like a Frank, who puts on armour for fear of death!' In battle they carry nothing but swords or spears.

Nearly all of them wear a long tunic like the surplice worn by priests. Their heads are all bound round with cloths that go underneath the chin, so that, what with these and the jet-black colour of their hair and their beards, they are an ugly people, and frightful to look at.

They live on the milk from their beasts, paying rent to the wealthy men who own the plains for the pasturage on which these animals subsist. No man can tell the number of these people; for they are to be found in the kingdom of Egypt, the kingdom of Jerusalem, and in all the other lands belonging to the Saracens and other heathen peoples, to whom they pay a large sum of money in tribute every year.

In our own country, since I returned from the land oversea, I have come across certain disloyal Christians who follow the Bedouin faith in holding that no man can die except on the appointed day. This belief is in effect a denial of our religion, since it amounts to saying that God has no power to help us. For those of us who serve God would indeed be fools if we did not think He has power to prolong our lives, and to preserve us from evil and misfortune. Most certainly we ought to put our faith in Him, seeing that He has power to do all things.

CHAPTER 8

Victory and its Aftermath
FEBRUARY–APRIL 1250

I WILL now go on to tell you that at nightfall the king and all the rest of us, after our return from the perilous battle I have already described, settled down in the very place from which we had dislodged our enemies. My men, who had remained in the camp from which we had first set out, brought me a tent which the Templars had given me and pitched it in front of the machines we had taken from the Saracens, and over which the king now set a guard.

When at last I had retired to my bed – where indeed I had good need of rest because of the wounds I had received during the day – no rest was allowed me. Before the day had fully dawned a cry rang through the camp: 'To arms! to arms!' I roused my chamberlain, who was sleeping at the foot of my bed, and told him to go and see what was up. He came back shaking with terror, and crying out: 'Get up, my lord, get up! the Saracens are here. They have come in a body, both on foot and mounted, and have routed the king's sergeants who were guarding the machines and driven them back on to the ropes of our pavilions.'

I got up, threw a quilted tunic over my back, clapped a steel cap on my head, and shouted out to our sergeants: 'By Saint Nicholas, they shall not stay here!' My knights gathered round me, all wounded as they were, and we drove the Saracen sergeants away from our own machines and back towards a great body of mounted Turks who had stationed themselves quite close to the ones we had taken from them. I sent to the king for help, for neither I nor my knights could put on our hauberks because of the wounds we had received. The king sent us Gautier de Châtillon, who took up his position in front of us, between the Turks and ourselves.

When our defenders had driven off the Saracen foot sergeants these had fallen back to rejoin a great body of mounted Turks who had drawn up in front of our camp so as to prevent our making a surprise attack on the main part of their army, which was encamped behind them. Eight of the leading officers of this body had dismounted, all fully armed, and had set up a sort of entrenchment with blocks of hewn stone so that our crossbowmen should not wound them. These eight men shot flight after flight of arrows into our camp, wounding several of our people and our horses.

After consulting together, my knights and I agreed that, as soon as it was dark, we would take away the stones behind which these men had entrenched themselves. A priest of mine, named Jean de Voysey, who was present at our discussion, was not content to wait so long. Leaving our camp all by himself, wearing a quilted tunic and a steel cap on his head, he advanced towards the Saracens, trailing his spear behind him under his arm, with the point towards the ground, so that the Saracens should not catch sight of it.

When he came near the Saracens, who scorned him because they saw he was all alone, he quickly drew his spear from under his arm and ran at them. Not a single one of the eight thought of defending himself, but all turned and fled. When the Saracens on horseback saw their lords flying towards them, they spurred forward to rescue them, while at the same time some fifty of our sergeants came rushing out of camp. The mounted Saracens continued to urge on their horses, but not daring to attack our footmen, they suddenly swerved aside.

After they had done this two or three times, one of our sergeants grasped his lance by the middle and hurled it at one of the Turks, so that it struck him between the ribs. The wounded man turned back, with the lance hanging by its head from his body. On seeing this the Turks no longer dared to advance, and retreated before us. Our sergeants immediately removed the stones. From that time onwards my priest was very well known throughout the army, and one man or another would point him out and say: 'Look, that's my Lord of Joinville's priest, who got the better of eight Saracens.'

The events I have just related took place on the first day in Lent. That same day a valiant Saracen – elected by the enemy as their leader in place of their old sheikh's son, Scecedin, whom they had lost in the battle on Shrove Tuesday – took the coat of arms that had belonged to the Comte d'Artois, who had been killed in that same battle, and displayed it in front of all his people, telling them that it was the royal coat of arms, and that the king himself was dead.

'I am showing you this trophy,' he said, 'because a body without a head is not to be feared, nor a people without a king. Therefore, if you are willing, we will attack them on Friday. You must, so it seems to me, agree to this, since we cannot fail to take them all, now that they have lost their leader.' Everyone agreed to launch an attack on us on the Friday.

Now the king's spies, who were in the Saracen camp, came to him with news of the projected attack. In consequence his Majesty ordered all the commanding officers of the several divisions to have their men armed by midnight and get them drawn up in the space between the tents and the surrounding palisade. (This enclosure had been made of long wooden stakes put up to prevent the Saracens from making sudden inroads into our camp, yet fixed in the ground in such a way that you could pass through them on foot.) The king's orders were carried out exactly as he had commanded.

Precisely at sunrise the Saracen whom I have already referred to as the enemy's chosen leader, brought against us a good four thousand mounted Turks, whom he ranged all round our camp and round his own person, in a formation extending from the river that comes from Cairo to the one that went from our camp towards a town called Rosetta.[1] After this they brought against us such an enormous body of Saracens on foot that they surrounded our camp in the same way as the mounted battalions. Besides these two bodies of troops I have just mentioned, all the forces of the Sultan of Cairo were standing by, ready to give the others support if any were needed.

As soon as this operation had been carried out, the Saracen leader came forward all alone, riding on a little cob, to inspect the disposition of our troops. Wherever he saw our forces were stronger in one place than another, he went back to fetch more men, to reinforce his battalions against us. After this he sent the Bedouins, of whom there were at least three thousand, over towards the camp held by the Duc de Bourgogne, which lay between the two rivers. He did this because he thought the king would send some of his men to help the duke against the Bedouins, and consequently weaken his own forces.

It took the Saracen till midday to make all these arrangements. Then he gave orders for the kettledrums to be beaten, and immediately all their troops, both horse and foot, charged at us in a body. I will tell you first about the King of Sicily (at that time Comte d'Anjou) because he was in the forefront of our army on the side towards Cairo. The enemy tackled him in the way that men play chess, for first of all they sent their footmen forward to attack him, and these

[1] Actually Ashmun-Thanna.

hurled Greek fire at his troops. Then all the Saracens, both mounted and unmounted, pressed so hard on our people that the King of Sicily, who was on foot amongst his knights, was quite overpowered.

Messengers came to King Louis to tell him of the great danger in which his brother stood. On hearing of this, his Majesty rode spurring into the midst of his brother's troops, and, sword in hand, dashed so far forward among the ranks of the Turks that they burnt his horse's crupper with Greek fire. But by making this charge our king rescued the King of Sicily and drove the Turks from the camp.

Next to the King of Sicily's troops came the battalion of the barons of Outremer, in command of Guy d'Ibelin and his brother Baudouin; next to it was the battalion under Gautier de Châtillon, containing a full complement of gallant men, all noted for their knightly deeds. These two battalions defended themselves so vigorously that the Turks were never able to pierce their ranks or oblige them to fall back.

The next to meet the enemy's onset was Brother Guillaume de Sennac, Master of the Temple, with the few members of his Order left to him after the battle on Shrove Tuesday. He had had a barricade erected in front of his men made up of the machines we had taken from the Saracens. When the enemy came to attack him they hurled Greek fire at the defences he had put up; these caught fire quickly, for the Templars had used a great quantity of deal planks in building them. The Turks, I may say, did not wait for the fire to burn itself out, but rushed in and attacked the Templars amid the flames. In this engagement the Master of the Temple lost an eye; he had lost the other on Shrove Tuesday. This accident resulted in his death – may God grant him mercy! Behind the Templars there was a tract of land, about as large as a labourer could till in a day, which was so thickly covered with the Saracens' darts that you could not see the ground beneath them.

Next to the Templars came the troops led by Guy Mauvoisin, and these the Turks were never able to overcome. None the less they managed to cover Guy Mauvoisin so completely with Greek fire that his men had the greatest difficulty in extinguishing it.

Starting from the place where Guy Mauvoisin was stationed, the palisade that enclosed our camp went down about a stone's throw towards the river.[1] From there it passed in front of the troops com-

[1] The Bagh-as Saghir.

manded by the Comte Guillaume de Flandre and stretched as far as the river that flowed towards the sea. Our own battalion faced the palisade on the same side as Guy Mauvoisin's; but since the Comte de Flandre's men were stationed directly opposite their army, the Turks never ventured to come and attack us. In this God treated us very graciously; for neither I nor my knights were wearing hauberks or carried shields, because of the wounds we had all received in the battle on Shrove Tuesday.

The Turks, both on foot and on horseback, made a vigorous and spirited attack on the Comte de Flandre. When I saw what was going on I ordered my crossbowmen to shoot at those who were mounted. As soon as these men saw that they were being wounded from our side, they promptly took to flight. On seeing them flee the count's men left the camp, and leaping over the barriers ran in among the unmounted Saracens and overpowered them. Many of the enemy were killed, and many of their shields were captured. Gautier de la Horgne, who carried the Lord of Apremont's banner, displayed great courage and vigour in this encounter.

The next battalion to engage the enemy was the one led by the king's brother, the Comte de Poitiers. These troops were on foot, and the count was the only man who was mounted. The Turks utterly routed them and led the Comte de Poitiers away captive. When the butchers and the other camp followers, including the women who sold provisions, saw this happen they raised a cry of alarm throughout the camp; and with God's help the count was rescued and the Turks were driven out of our quarters.

After the troops led by the Comte de Poitiers came those led by Josserand de Brancion, who had come to Egypt with the count, and was one of the best knights in the army. He had so arranged his men that all his knights were on foot, while he himself was mounted, as were his son Henri and the son of Josserand de Nanton, whom he had placed on horseback because of their extreme youth. Several times the Turks gained the upper hand, but each time he saw his people in distress he set spurs to his horse and attacked the enemy from behind. On several such occasions the Turks left off harassing his people to charge at him.

All the same this would not have availed to prevent the Turks from killing them all on the field of battle had it not been for Henri de Cône, a wise, valiant, and very sensible knight who was in the Duc de Bourgogne's battalion. Every time he saw the Turks pressing hard on the Lord of Brancion he got the king's crossbowmen to shoot at them from across the river. Thus Josserand de Brancion was saved from that day's peril; but not without the loss of twelve knights out of the twenty he had with him, apart from other men of lesser rank. He himself had been so badly handled that from that time he was never able to stand on his feet, and in the end died of those injuries received in the service of God.

I will now tell you something more about Josserand de Brancion. At the time of his death he had taken part in thirty-six battles and minor engagements, and had always borne away the prize for valour. I met him once when we were together on a military expedition led by his cousin, the Comte de Chalon. He came to me on a Good Friday and said to me and my brother: 'Come and help me, nephews, you and your people, for the Germans are destroying the church.' We went with him, and fell on the Germans with our swords drawn; with great difficulty and after a fierce struggle we drove them from the church.

At the close of that contest this worthy man fell on his knees before the altar, and prayed aloud to our Saviour. 'Lord,' said he, 'I pray Thee to have mercy on me, and take me out of these wars among Christians in which I have spent a great part of my life; and grant that I may die in Thy service, and so come to enjoy Thy kingdom in paradise.' I have told you these things because I believe our Lord heard his prayer, as you may gather from what I have said before.

After this battle, which took place on the first Friday in Lent, King Louis summoned all his barons before him, and said to them: 'We owe great thanks to our Saviour, since He has done us honour twice this week: on Shrove Tuesday, when we drove the enemy out of the camp in which we ourselves are now quartered, and on the following Friday, now just past, on which we defended ourselves against opponents on horseback, while we fought only on foot.' The king also said many kind and gracious things to his barons, to comfort them and inspire them with new courage.

Since in pursuing my story I find it necessary to touch on certain subsidiary matters, I think it well, at this point, to explain how the sultans kept their forces in good shape and condition. We know for certain that the leading men in their armies were for the most part foreigners, whom merchants had brought for sale from other lands, and whom the Saracens were glad to buy, even at a very high price. These people the merchants brought into Egypt were usually drawn from the East, because when one Eastern ruler defeated another, he took the poor wretches he had conquered and sold them to the merchants, who in their turn came and sold them again to the Egyptians.

If any of these were children the sultan would bring them up in his own house till their beards began to grow. He would see to it that they had bows proportioned to their strength and as it increased would have the weaker bows consigned to the arsenal and get the Master General of the Ordnance to supply them with bows as strong as they could bend.

These boys, who were known as *bahariz* (or people from the sea), were privileged to wear the same coat of arms – which was in gold – as the sultan himself. As soon as their beards began to grow he made them knights. They continued to wear his arms, but with a difference – that is to say, they added certain crimson devices, such as roses, stripes, or birds, or other designs, according to their choice.

They were now known as the *Halca* (or royal bodyguard) because they slept in the sultan's tents. When he was in camp they were given quarters near him, and set to guard his person. The sultan's door-keepers lived in a little tent at the entrance to his quarters, together with his minstrels, whose chief instruments were horns, drums, and a species of tambourine. They made such a din with these at sunrise and sunset that while those who were near could hardly hear one another speak, the sound of them was clearly heard throughout all the camp.

The minstrels would never have been rash enough to play their instruments during the day, except by command of the captain of the *Halca*. So if ever the sultan wished them to perform he would send for this officer and give the order through him. Then the captain of the *Halca* would command the minstrels to play, and all the army would assemble to hear them. Such were the captain's orders, and they were naturally obeyed.

When the sultan went to war those knights of the *Halca* who had distinguished themselves in battle were made emirs, and placed in command of two or three hundred knights. The more they proved their valour, the more knights would be set under them.

The special reward reserved for their distinguished service is this: When they become so famous and so powerful that no one dares to challenge them, and the sultan fears they might kill him or usurp his place, he has them arrested and put to death, and their wives deprived of everything they possess. That is how the sultan dealt with those who had captured the Comte de Montfort and the Comte de Bar, and that too is how Bundukdari acted towards those who had defeated the King of Armenia. For these latter, expecting to have some reward, dismounted and went to pay their respects to Bundukdari while he was hunting wild beasts. 'I have no greeting for you,' he replied, for they had interrupted his hunting; and he ordered them to be beheaded.

I will now resume my story and tell you how the late sultan had a son[1] who was wise, adroit and cunning. Fearing this young man would dispossess him, the sultan had given him a kingdom which he had in the East. After his father's death the emirs sent for the son, who, on his return to Egypt, immediately took away the golden rods of office from his father's seneschal, his constable, and his marshal, and gave them to men who had come with him from the East.

The three emirs, finding themselves thus deprived of office, were very angry, as were the other emirs of the late sultan's council, who all felt they had been greatly shamed by their new ruler. Convinced that the son would deal with them as the father had dealt with those who had captured the Comte de Bar and the Comte de Montfort, they entered into negotiations with the men of the *Halca*, whose duty, as I have told you, was to guard their master's person, and got them to promise that as soon as the emirs asked them to do so, they would kill the sultan.

Soon after the two battles I have described, the army entered on a period of great distress. At the end of nine days the bodies of our people killed by the Saracens came to the surface of the water, owing, so it was said, to the fact that the gall had putrified. These bodies came floating down to the bridge between our two camps, but could not pass under it because the water was up to the arches. There was such a number of them that all the river was full of corpses, from one bank to the other, and as far upstream as one could cast a small stone.

The king had hired a hundred rough fellows, who took a good week to clear the river. They flung the bodies of the Saracens, who

[1] Turanshah.

were circumcized, over the further side of the bridge, and let them
float down with the current; the Christians were buried in great
trenches, all together. I saw the Chamberlains of the Comte d'Artois,
and many other people, seeking for their friends among the dead;
but I never heard that any one of them was found there.

The only fish we had to eat in camp for the whole of Lent were
eels, which, being greedy creatures, feed on the dead. On account of
this evil circumstance, and because of the unhealthy climate – for not
a drop of rain ever falls in Egypt – a disease[1] spread through the army,
of such a sort that the flesh on our legs dried up, and the skin became
covered with black spots and turned a brown earthy colour like an
old boot. With those who had this disease the flesh on the gums
became gangrened; and no one who fell a victim to it could hope to
recover, but was sure to die. An infallible sign of death was bleeding
from the nose.

A fortnight later the Turks did something that came as a great shock
to our people. In order to starve us they took several of their galleys
lying upstream above our camp, and after dragging them overland
put them back into the river, a good league below the place where
our tents were pitched. These galleys caused a famine among us; for
because they were there no one dared to come up the river from
Damietta to bring us fresh supplies of food. We ourselves were
completely ignorant of all this until a little ship, belonging to the
Comte de Flandre, took advantage of the current to slip past the
blockade, and gave us news of the enemy's position, informing us
at the same time that the sultan's galleys had captured some eighty
of ours as they were coming up the river from Damietta, and
slaughtered every man aboard them.

In consequence there was a great scarcity of provisions in the camp;
so much so that by Easter an ox was valued at eighty *livres*, a sheep or
a pig at thirty *livres* each, while an egg cost twelve *deniers*, and you
had to pay ten *livres* for a barrel of wine.

When the king and the barons took stock of the situation they
agreed that he should shift his camp, which was on the side towards
Cairo, and move to the place where the Duc de Bourgogne was
encamped, alongside the river that flowed towards Damietta. In
order to collect his troops with greater safety the king had an outwork erected in front of the bridge between our two camps which

[1] Scurvy.

was constructed in such a way that no one could enter it from either side on horseback.

As soon as this outwork was ready, all the troops armed themselves. The Turks seized this moment to make an attack on our camp. However, neither the king nor his army moved forward till all the baggage had been taken across the river, after which he passed over at the head of his men. All his barons followed, with the exception of Gautier de Châtillon, who was in command of the rear-guard. As the troops were entering the outwork, Érard de Valery went to the rescue of his brother Jean, whom the Turks had seized and were about to carry off.

When the main part of the army had crossed over those who remained in the outwork were left in great danger, for its walls were not very high, so that the mounted Turks could shoot straight at them, while those on foot threw clods of earth right into their faces. They would all have been lost if it had not been for the Comte d'Anjou, who went to their rescue and brought them out safe and sound. Of all the men in the outwork Geoffroy de Mussambourc fought most valiantly, and won the greatest glory on that day.

I will now tell you of a curious incident that I had been witness of on the eve of Shrove Tuesday. That day they were burying Hugues de Landricourt, a knight-banneret who had been with me in the army. As he lay on a bier in my chapel, six of my knights were there, lolling against some sacks full of barley. Because they were speaking in a loud tone of voice in my chapel and disturbing the priest, I went up to them and told them to keep silent, and said it was most discourteous on the part of knights and gentlemen to talk while mass was being sung. They began to laugh and told me, with a chuckle, that they were arranging the remarriage of the dead man's wife. I spoke sharply to them, pointing out that talking of such things was neither right nor fitting, and that they seemed to have forgotten their companion over-soon. God took such vengeance on them that the very next day, in the great battle of Shrove Tuesday, they were all of them either killed outright or mortally wounded, so that the wives of all six were in a position to marry again.

Owing to the wounds I had received on Shrove Tuesday I fell a victim to the sickness that had stricken the army, and it affected my mouth and legs. I was also suffering from a double tertian fever, and so severe a cold in my head that the mucus streamed from my nostrils. On account of all these ailments I was forced in mid-Lent to take to my bed. So it happened that my priest came to sing mass for me at my bedside, in my pavilion. He was suffering from the same complaint as myself, and just at the moment of the consecration, he happened to turn faint. Seeing him about to fall, I leapt barefoot out of bed, clad only in my tunic, and taking him in my arms told him to go gently and proceed with the consecration at his leisure, for I should not let go of him till he had finished. He recovered himself and after completing the consecration, sang mass right through to the end. But he never sang it again.

A little later the king's councillors and the sultan's fixed a day on which to come to an agreement. The conditions proposed were these: we were to surrender Damietta to the sultan, and he in his turn was to hand over the kingdom of Jerusalem to our king. In addition, the sultan was to take charge of the sick in Damietta, keep the salt meat in store for us – since the Saracens did not eat pork – and hold the machines belonging to our army until such time as the king was able to send and take his property away.

The sultan's councillors inquired of ours what security would be given them for their master's recovery of Damietta. Our people offered to let them keep one of the king's brothers, either the Comte d'Anjou or the Comte de Poitiers, as a hostage until Damietta was placed in the sultan's hands. The Saracens said they would not treat with us unless the king himself were left with them in pledge. At this the good knight Geoffroy de Sargines exclaimed that he would rather the Saracens should kill them all or take them prisoner than bear the reproach of having left their king in pawn.

The sickness that had stricken the army now began to increase to such an alarming extent, and so many people suffered from mortification of the gums that the barber surgeons had to remove the gangrenous flesh before they could either chew their food or swallow it. It was pitiful to hear around the camp the cries of those whose dead flesh was being cut away; it was just like the cry of a woman in labour.

CHAPTER 9

The French in Captivity

WHEN at length the king realized that he and his people could only remain there to die he made up his mind to leave, and issued orders to the army to strike camp late at night on the Tuesday after the octave of Easter and return to Damietta. He sent to tell the men in charge of the galleys to collect the sick and take them to that city. He also commanded Josselin de Cornaut, with his brothers and the other engineers, to cut the ropes that held the bridge between us and the Saracens; however, they did nothing about it.

I and the two of my knights who were left with me, together with my servants, embarked on the Tuesday afternoon, after dinner. As night was beginning to fall, I told my sailors to weigh anchor and let us go downstream with the current; but they said they dared not, because the men in the sultan's galleys, which were between us and Damietta, would be certain to put us to death. Meanwhile the crews who manned our galleys had made great fires to attract the attention of the sick who had managed to drag themselves to the bank of the river. As I was urging my sailors to let us get away, the Saracens entered the camp, and I saw by the light of the fires that they were slaughtering the poor fellows on the bank.

While my crew were weighing anchor, the sailors whose duty it was to collect the sick cut the cables of their anchors and the ropes that tied their galleys, and coming alongside our little ship crowded so closely round us on one side and the other that they almost ran us down. After we had escaped that danger and were going down with the stream, the king, who was suffering from the sickness that had attacked the army, and from very bad dysentery as well, could easily have got away in the galleys, had he wished to do so; but he said, please God, he would never desert his people. That night he fainted several times, and because the dysentery from which he suffered continually obliged him to visit the privy, they had to cut away the lower part of his drawers.

The men on the bank cried out to us as we were beginning to go down the river, telling us to wait for the king; and when we would not wait they started shooting bolts at us from their crossbows. So we had to stop until they gave us leave to go on.

At this point I will break off, to tell you how the king was taken prisoner, as he himself related it to me. He told me that he had left his own battalion, and gone with Geoffroy de Sargines to attach himself to the one in charge of Gautier de Châtillon, who commanded the rear-guard. He said that he himself was mounted on a little cob with a housing of silk. He told me also that of all his knights and sergeants the only one who had remained with him was Geoffroy de Sargines, who had taken him to a little village, the one, in fact, in which he was eventually captured. In the account the king gave me of this incident, he told me that Geoffroy de Sargines had defended him from the Saracens as a dutiful servant defends his lord's drinking-cup from flies. For every time the Saracens approached, he had taken his spear, which he had placed between himself and his saddle-bow, and putting it to his shoulder had charged at them and driven them away from the king.

In this way he had brought the king in safely to the little village, where he had been carried into a house and laid, more dead than alive, in the lap of a woman who happened to be a native of Paris. It was thought, at the time, that he would not last till night. Philippe de Montfort had come there and told him that he had seen the emir with whom he had discussed the question of a truce, and, if his Majesty was willing, he would go back to this man and renew negotiations for a truce on terms that would satisfy the Saracens. The king had begged him to go, adding that he was very willing to have this done. So Philippe de Montfort had gone back to the Saracen, and the latter had taken his turban from off his head and removed the ring from his finger as a sign that he would faithfully abide by the terms of the truce.

In the meantime an unlucky accident had brought disaster to our people. A disloyal sergeant, named Marcel, had started to cry out to the army: 'Surrender, all you knights, for the king commands it, and do not let his Majesty be slain!' Everyone had thought that the king had really issued such orders, and had given up their swords to the Saracens. The emir, seeing the Saracens bringing in our people as prisoners, had told Philippe de Montfort that it was not in keeping for him to grant a truce to our army since it was plain to see that our men had already been captured.

As it happened, when all the other people were taken, Philippe de Montfort, being an envoy, did not suffer the same fate. There is, however, a bad custom among the Saracens that when a king sends envoys to a sultan, or a sultan to a king, if either of these monarchs happens to die before the envoys' return, then these emissaries, no matter from where they come, or whether Christians or Saracens, are arrested and made slaves.

At the same time as some of our people had suffered the misfortune of being taken captive on land, I and my men, as I shall shortly tell you, had met with similar disaster on the water. The wind had been blowing from the direction of Damietta, thus depriving us of any advantage the current might have afforded. Moreover, the knights whom the king had placed in the lighter vessels to defend the sick had fled. Thus our sailors, unable to steer a straight course with the current, had got into a creek, and we had been forced to turn back towards the Saracen lines.

While we were going downstream, we had arrived, a little before daybreak, at a stretch of the river where the sultan's galleys, that had prevented the coming of supplies from Damietta, were all drawn up. Here there was great confusion and tumult, for the Turks had aimed at us, and at our mounted men on the bank, so great a number of arrows tipped with Greek fire that it seemed as if the stars were falling from heaven.

After our sailors had brought us out of the creek into which they had taken us, we saw the small ships (which the king had given us to shelter our sick) flying towards Damietta. Then the wind had begun to blow so strongly from the north, that, in spite of the current, we could make no headway.

Alongside both banks of the river were a great number of small craft belonging to those of our people who had not been able to get down the stream, and had consequently been stopped and captured by the Saracens. These wretches were killing our men and flinging their bodies into the water, and dragging chests and baggage out of the boats they had taken. The mounted Saracens on the bank shot arrows at us because we refused to go over to them. My men had given me a jousting hauberk to put on, to prevent my being wounded by the shafts that kept on falling into our boat.

Suddenly my men, who were standing aft, cried out to me: 'My lord, my lord, your crew, alarmed by the Saracens' threats, are going to take you to the bank!' I got someone to lift me up by the arms, and, weak as I was, I drew my sword upon the crew, and told them I would kill them if they took me to land. They answered that I must make my choice; whether to be taken to the bank, or lie anchored in mid-stream till the wind had fallen. I told them I would rather they should anchor in mid-stream than take me to the bank, where the only prospect before us was certain death. So they anchored.

Very shortly after this we saw four of the sultan's galleys coming towards us, with a good thousand men aboard. So I called my knights and the rest of my men together and asked them which they would prefer – to surrender to the sultan's galleys or to the Saracens on shore. We all agreed that we would rather surrender to the sultan's galleys, because in that way we should remain together, than yield ourselves to the enemy on land, who would separate us, and sell us to the Bedouins.

Then one of my cellarers, who was born at Doulevant, said to me: 'My lord, I can't agree with this decision.' I asked him what he would agree to do, and he replied: 'What I advise is that we should all let ourselves be slain, for thus we shall go to paradise.' But we none of us heeded his advice.

Now that I realized we should have to let ourselves be taken I snatched up my casket and my jewels and threw them into the river, together with my relics. Then one of my crew said to me: 'My lord, unless you give us leave to say you're the king's cousin, they'll kill everyone of you, and us along with you.' So I told him I was quite willing for him to say what he liked.

As soon as the men on the foremost galley, which was coming towards us to ram us amidships, heard this man's announcement, they cast anchor alongside our boat. At this juncture God sent me a Saracen from the Emperor of Germany's land. He came swimming across the stream, clad in breeches of unbleached linen, and got aboard our ship. He clasped me round the waist and said to me: 'My lord, unless you act quickly and resolutely you are lost. What you must do is to leap from your ship on to the prow that overhangs the keel of this galley. If you do this, no one will notice you, for they're thinking only of the booty to be gained from your ship.' A rope was flung to me from the galley, and by God's will I leapt on to the projecting deck. I was, however, so unsteady on my feet, that if the Saracen had not leapt after me to hold me up I should have fallen back into the water.

I was drawn forward into the galley, where there were a good two hundred and eighty of the enemy, while the Saracen still kept his arms around me. Then they threw me to the ground and flung themselves on my body to cut my throat, for any man who killed me would have thought to win honour by it. But the Saracen still held me in his arms, and cried: 'He's the king's cousin!' All the same they twice bore me to the ground, and once forced me to my knees. It was then I felt the knife at my throat. But in this ordeal God saved me with the help of the Saracen, who led me to one of the castles on the ship where the Saracen knights were assembled.

As soon as I met them they took off my hauberk; then, out of pity for me, they threw over me a scarlet wrap of my own lined with miniver, which my dear mother had given me. One of them brought me a white leather belt. I strapped this round me over the wrap, after making a hole in the latter, in order to use it as a garment. Another man brought me a hood which I put over my head. Then, because of the fright I was in, and also on account of the sickness that troubled me, I was seized with a terrible fit of trembling. So I asked for a drink, and they brought me some water in a pitcher. But no sooner had I put the pitcher to my mouth than the water spurted out of my nostrils.

When I saw this happen, I sent for my men and told them I was a dying man, since I had a tumour in my throat. They asked me how I knew it, so I showed them. As soon as they saw the water spurting from my throat and nostrils, they began to weep. When the Saracen knights saw my people in tears, they asked the man who had rescued us why these men were weeping. He replied that he understood I had a tumour in my throat and so could not hope to recover. Then one of the Saracen knights told our rescuer to bid us take comfort, for he would give me something to drink that would cure me within two days. And this, I may say, he did.

Raoul de Wanou, who was one of my following, had been hamstrung in the great battle on Shrove Tuesday and could not stand on his feet. I should like you to know that an old Saracen knight who was in that galley, used to carry him pick-a-back to the privy whenever he so required.

The admiral in command of the galleys sent for me and asked me whether I really were the king's cousin. I answered 'No,' and told him how and why the sailor had said I was. The admiral told me I had acted wisely, for otherwise we should all have been put to death. He asked if by any chance I happened to be related to the Emperor Frederick of Germany. I replied that I had reason to believe that my lady mother was his first cousin; whereupon the admiral remarked that he loved me all the more for it.

While we were dining he summoned a citizen of Paris to appear before us. When the man arrived he said to me: 'My lord, what are you doing?' 'Why, what can I be doing?' said I. 'In God's name,' he replied, 'You're eating meat on a Friday.' As soon as I heard this I put my bowl behind me. The admiral asked my Saracen why I had acted thus, so he told him. The admiral replied that God would not hold what I had done against me, seeing that I had not realized I was doing wrong.

I may tell you that the same reply was given me by the legate after we were freed from captivity. None the less I did not cease to fast on bread and water every Friday in Lent from that time onwards. This made the legate very angry with me, since I was the only man of high standing who had remained with the king.

On the following Sunday, by the emir's orders, I and all the others taken prisoner on the water were landed on the river bank. While they were taking Jean, my good priest, out of the hold of the galley, he fainted. The Saracens killed him and threw his body into the river. His clerk, who also fainted, from weakness due to the army fever, had a mortar flung at his head. They killed him too, and cast his body into the stream.

While the rest of the sick were being landed from the galleys in which they had been held prisoner, there were Saracens standing by, with their swords ready drawn, to deal with all those who fell as they had dealt with my priest. I sent my Saracen to tell them that I thought this a very wrong thing to do, because it was contrary to the teaching of Saladin, who has said you should never kill a man once you had shared your bread and salt with him. The admiral replied that the men in question did not count, because the sickness from which they suffered had left them incapable of doing anything to help themselves.

He subsequently had all my crew brought before me, and told me that every one of them had renounced their faith. I warned him not to put any trust in them, for just as lightly as they had left our side so they would leave his, if they saw either time or opportunity to do so. The admiral replied that he agreed with me, for as Saladin used to say, one never saw a bad Christian become a good Saracen, nor a bad Saracen become a good Christian.

Shortly after this he mounted me on a palfrey and made me ride along beside him. We passed over a bridge of boats and went to Mansourah, where the king and his people were held prisoner. We came to the entrance of a big pavilion which housed the sultan's scribes. There they wrote down my name. At this point my Saracen said to me: 'My lord, I shall not be going any further with you, for I cannot. But let me beg you, my lord, to keep hold of the hand of the child who is with you, lest the Saracens should take him away.' The child he mentioned was called Barthélemy; he was the bastard son of the Lord of Montfaucon.

After my name had been written down the admiral took me to another pavilion, where the barons and more than ten thousand other people were gathered. As I entered, the barons gave vent to such loud expressions of joy that we could hardly hear each other speak. They gave thanks to our Lord for my safe-keeping, and said they thought they had lost me.

We had not been there very long before the Saracens ordered the chief men among us to rise, and took us away to another pavilion. Many of the knights and other people were kept inside a courtyard enclosed by mud walls. The custom of our enemies was to take them from this enclosure, one by one, and ask them: 'Are you willing to abjure your faith?' Those who refused to abjure were set on one side, and their heads were cut off; those who consented were kept on the other side.

At this point the sultan sent his council to speak with us. They asked to whom they should deliver their master's message, so we told them to address themselves to the good Comte Pierre de Bretagne. They had with them certain people known as dragomans, men, that is, who knew our language as well as theirs, and these translated the sultan's message from Saracen into French for the Comte Pierre's benefit.

What passed in this interview was as follows: 'My lord,' said the Saracens, 'the sultan has sent us to you to inquire if you wish to be set free?' The count replied in the affirmative. 'What would you give the sultan to obtain your freedom?' they asked next. 'Whatever we can,' replied the count, 'so long as it is within reason.' 'Would you give us,' said they, 'any of the castles belonging to the barons oversea?' The count replied that he had no power to hand over any of these castles, because they were held from the reigning Emperor of Germany. They then asked whether, to obtain our freedom, we would surrender any of the castles belonging to the Templars or the Hospitallers. The count replied that this could not be done; for the governors of these castles, when taking office, were made to swear on the Holy Gospels that they would never surrender any one of these castles to procure a man's release from captivity. At this the council remarked that it seemed to them we had no desire to be set free, and told us they would go and send us men who would make sport of us with their swords, as they had done with the others of our army. Then they went away.

As soon as they had gone a great crowd of young Saracens with swords at their sides rushed into our pavilion. They brought with them a man of very great age, with hair as white as snow, who asked us if we believed in a God who had been taken prisoner for our sake, wounded and put to death for us, and who on the third day had risen again? We answered that this was so. Then he told us we ought not to be disheartened if we had suffered these persecutions for His sake; 'For,' said he, 'you have not yet died for Him, as He died for you; and if He had power to come to life again you may rest assured that He will deliver you whenever it pleases Him to do so.'

Then he went away, and all the young Saracens with him. For my part I was extremely glad about this, for I had most certainly thought they had come to cut off our heads. It was not long after this that the sultan's people came to tell us that our king had made arrangements with their master for us to be set free.

This happened shortly after the departure of the old man who had spoken those words of comfort to us. The sultan's council returned to tell us that the king had procured our release, and that we must send four of our company to hear how he had done it. We sent the worthy Jean de Valery, Philippe de Montfort, Baudouin d'Ibelin,

Seneschal of Cyprus, and Guy d'Ibelin, Constable of that same island, one of the most accomplished knights I have ever known, and one who most loved the islanders in his care. These four brought us back an account of how the king had obtained our release from captivity.

CHAPTER 10

Negotiations with the Saracens
APRIL–MAY 1250

THE sultan's councillors had made the same tentative approaches to the king as they had done in our case, in order to find out whether he himself would promise to hand over to them any of the castles in possession of the Templars or the Hospitallers, or any of those belonging to the barons of the land. By God's will his Majesty's answer had been precisely the same as ours. In consequence the Saracens had threatened him, and said that if he would not do as they wished they would have him put in the *barnacle*, which is the most cruel form of torture that any man can suffer.

This instrument is made of two pliable pieces of wood, notched at the edges with interlocking teeth, and fastened together at both ends with stout strips of ox-hide. When the Saracens wish to subject any-one to this torture, they lay him down on his side and put his legs between the teeth. Then they get a man to sit down on top of the *barnacle*; and as a result not half a foot of bone remains uncrushed. Moreover – to do the very worst they can – at the end of three days, when the legs have become inflamed, they put the swollen limbs back into the *barnacle*, and crush the bones all over again. In reply to these threats the king had answered that he was their prisoner, and they could do with him as they pleased.

When the Saracens had seen that they could not prevail over our good king with threats, they had come back to him and asked him how much money he was prepared to pay the sultan, and whether he would also surrender Damietta. The king had replied that if the sultan was willing to accept a reasonable sum he would send and advise the queen to pay that amount for their ransom. 'How is it,' they had asked, 'that you won't tell us definitely whether you'll do this?' The king had answered that he did not know whether or not the queen would consent, since, as his consort, she was mistress of her actions.

So the councillors had gone to confer with the sultan, and had later returned to tell the king that if the queen was prepared to pay a million gold bezants – a sum amounting to five hundred thousand *livres* in our currency – their master would set him at liberty. Thereupon the king had asked them to swear that if the queen agreed to pay such a sum the sultan would, in fact, release him, and his people. The councillors had gone back once more to speak with the sultan, and on their return had solemnly sworn to the king that their master would release him on these conditions.

Now that the emirs had given him their sworn word, the king in his turn had assured them that he would willingly pay the five hundred thousand *livres* for the release of his people, and would surrender Damietta to ransom his own person, since it was not fitting for a man of his high rank to purchase his liberty with money. When all this was reported to the sultan he had exclaimed: 'By Allah! this Frank is a very generous-minded man not to have haggled over paying so great a sum! So go and tell him I'll let him off a hundred thousand *livres* of the ransom money.'

The sultan now gave orders for the chief men among us to be put aboard four galleys and taken towards Damietta. In the same galley as myself were the worthy Comte Pierre de Bretagne, the Comte Guillaume de Flandre, the good Comte Jean de Soissons, my lord Imbert de Beaujeu, High Constable of France, the good knight Baudouin d'Ibelin and his brother Guy.

Those who were taking us in this galley brought our vessel to land in front of a camp which the sultan had established by the riverside and laid out on the following plan: right in front stood a tower made of fir poles and completely encased in dyed canvas; this served as the main entrance to the camp. Behind this was a pavilion in which the emirs left their swords and other equipment when they went to speak with the sultan. Immediately beyond was another tower exactly like the first, giving access to a very large pavilion which served as the sultan's hall. Next came another tower of similar character to the others which led into the sultan's private quarters. Adjoining these was a courtyard in the middle of which stood a tower that was higher than any of the others and to which the sultan resorted whenever he wished to survey the country around the camp or see what was going on inside it. From this courtyard a passage ran down to the river, where the sultan had set up a large tent that stretched out over the water and was used as a bathing-place. The whole of this encampment was enclosed within a wall of wooden trellis-work, the outer side of which was covered in blue canvas – the same, in fact as had been used for the towers – so that those who were outside the camp should not be able to see in.

It was on a Thursday, exactly a week before Ascension Day, that we reached the place where this camp was pitched. The four galleys in which we were all confined together anchored in front of the sultan's quarters; the king was taken to a pavilion close by. The sultan had arranged that Damietta was to be surrendered to him on the Saturday before Ascension Day, and on the same date he was to release the king.

Those emirs whom the Sultan had dismissed from his council in order to appoint men he had brought with him from foreign parts, now decided to hold a meeting. A shrewd and cunning Saracen addressed them thus: 'My lords,' he said, 'you know how the sultan has shamed and dishonoured us by taking from us the high offices to which we were appointed by his father. On this account you may be sure that once he is established in the strong city of Damietta he will have us all arrested and sent to die in prison, as his grandfather did with the emirs who captured the Comte de Bar and the Comte de Montfort. Therefore, so it seems to me, it would be better to have him put to death before he escapes out of our hands.'

So the emirs approached the sultan's bodyguard (the *Halca*) and demanded of these men that they should kill the sultan immediately after a dinner to which they themselves had been invited. So it happened that when the meal was over and the sultan, having taken leave of his emirs, was about to retire to his pavilion, one of the knights of the bodyguard who was the sultan's sword-bearer, aimed a blow with that same sword at the middle of his master's hand, right between the four fingers, and split it open up to the arm. At this the sultan turned to the emirs, who had instigated the deed, and said: 'Save me, my lords, from my bodyguard. You can see they mean to kill me.' Thereupon the whole of his bodyguard shouted in chorus 'As you say we wish to kill you, it's better for us to do it than let ourselves be killed by you.'

Then the signal was given for the kettledrums to be beaten and the whole of the sultan's army assembled to know what his orders were. The emirs told them that Damietta was taken; the sultan was going there and had ordered them to follow. So the troops armed themselves and spurred towards Damietta. When we saw them going in the direction of that city, we were very sad at heart, for we thought that it had fallen to the enemy.

Meanwhile the sultan, who was young and agile, had fled with three of his *imams* who had been dining with him to the top of the high tower he had built, and which, as I have already told you, was just behind his private quarters. The members of his bodyguard, five hundred horsemen in number, wrecked his pavilions, crowded round the tower in which he and his *imams* had taken refuge, and shouted out to him to come down. He said he would do so, but only if they guaranteed his life would be safe. They told him they would force him to come down, and reminded him that he was not in Damietta. After this they launched Greek fire at him, and the tower, made, as you know, of pine planks and canvas, was set alight. It flared up quickly; never have I seen finer or straighter flames.

As soon as the sultan saw the fire taking hold, he rushed down from the tower and went flying towards the river, all along the passage I have mentioned to you before. His bodyguard had hacked and slashed to bits the whole of that covered way with their swords. As the sultan was hurrying to get down to the water, one of these men gave him a lance-thrust in the ribs. He continued his flight with the weapon trailing from the wound. His pursuers followed after, till they all had to take to swimming. So they came and killed him in the river, not far from the place where our galley lay. One of the knights, whose name was Faress-Eddin-Octay, cut him open with his sword and took the heart out of his body. Then, with his hand all dripping with blood, he came to our king and said: 'What will you give me now that I have killed your enemy. Had he lived, you can be sure he would have killed you.' But the king did not answer him a word.

A good thirty of the Saracens now boarded our ship, with drawn swords in their hands, and Danish axes hanging at their necks. I asked Baudouin d'Ibelin, who was well acquainted with their language, what these men were saying. He told me they were saying that they had come to cut off our heads. At once a great number of people crowded round to confess their sins to a monk of the Holy Trinity, named Jean, who was in the service of the Comte Guillaume de Flandre. I for my part, unable to recall any sins I had committed, spent the time thinking that the more I tried to defend myself, or to get out of this predicament, the worse it would be for me.

So I crossed myself, and as I knelt at the feet of one of the Saracens who was holding a Danish axe such as carpenters use, I said to myself 'thus Saint Agnès died.' Guy d'Ibelin, Constable of Cyprus, knelt down beside me, and confessed himself to me. 'I absolve you,' I said to him, 'with such power as God has granted me.' However, when I rose to my feet, I could not remember a word of what he had told me.

The Saracens made us all get up from where we were, and locked us up in the hold of the galley. Many of our people thought they had done this because they did not wish to attack us all together, but kill us one by one. We lay in the hold that evening, and all through the night, in great misery, and so closely packed together that my feet came up against the good Comte Pierre de Bretagne, and his were touching my face.

The next day the emirs gave orders for us to be taken from our prison in the hold, and sent messengers to tell us that we were to go and speak with them on the subject of renewing the treaty which the late sultan had made with us. These men also told us we might take it for certain that if the sultan had lived he would have had the king beheaded, and all of us as well. Those who were able to go went to see the emirs. The Comte de Bretagne, the constable, and I, who were seriously ill, remained where we were; but the Comte de Flandre, the Comte Jean de Soissons, the two Ibelin brothers, and all the rest who were in a fit state of health to go attended the conference.

Those of our side who were there came to an arrangement with the emirs to the effect that as soon as Damietta was handed over to the Saracens they would release the king and the other men of rank they were holding prisoner. As for the people of lesser importance, the sultan had already sent them to Cairo, with the exception, of course, of those whom he had put to death. He had done this contrary to the agreement he had made with the king, so that it seems very probable that if he had obtained possession of Damietta, he would immediately have had us put to death as well.

As a further stipulation the king was to swear to satisfy the Saracens' claims by paying them two hundred thousand *livres* before he left the river, and an equal amount on reaching Acre. The Saracens, on their side, according to the terms of this treaty, were to take charge of the sick in Damietta, and to keep the crossbows, the armour, the salted meat, and the machines in that city until such time as the king sent for them.

The oaths which the emirs were to swear to the king were set down in writing, and were to this effect: that if they did not observe their covenant with the king they should be held as dishonoured as a man who, in penance for a sin he has committed, goes on a pilgrimage to Mahomet at Mecca, with his head uncovered; or as worthy of shame as a man who, after repudiating his wife, takes her back again. (For in that case, according to the law of Mahomet, a man who thus abandons his wife can never have her back again, unless he previously finds her sleeping with another man.) Their third oath was as follows: that if they broke faith with the king, they were to incur the same disgrace as a Saracen who has eaten pork. The king was satisfied with these oaths I have just mentioned, because Nicole d'Acre, a priest who knew their language, assured him that according to their law they could have devised no oaths that were stronger or more binding.

After the emirs had sworn, they had the oath they wished the king to swear set down in writing. It was drawn up on the advice of certain renegade priests who had gone over to the side of the Saracens, and began as follows: that if the king did not observe the terms of his treaty with the emirs he should be as dishonoured as a Christian who denies our Lord and His mother, and becomes an outcast from the fellowship of His twelve apostles and all the saints. To this the king agreed very willingly. However the last point in the oath was to this effect: that if the king did not keep faith with the emirs he should be as dishonoured as a Christian who denies God and His law, and in contempt of Him, spits on the cross and tramples it underfoot. When this was read to the king he declared that, please God, he would never take such an oath.

Since Nicole d'Acre knew their language the emirs gave him a message to take to the king. 'Your Majesty,' he said, 'the emirs are taking it very ill that, while they have sworn what you required of them, you for your part, refuse to swear what they require of you. Rest assured that if you do not swear this oath, they will have your head cut off, and the heads of all your people as well.' The king replied that the emirs could do as they pleased in this matter; but as far as he himself was concerned, he would rather die a good Christian than live at enmity with our Lord and His mother.

The patriarch of Jerusalem, an old and reverend man of eighty years of age, had obtained a safe-conduct from the Saracens, and had come to help the king secure his release. Now it happens to be the custom between Christians and Saracens that whenever a king or a sultan dies those who are acting as envoys at the time, whether it be in a Christian or a pagan land, are held as prisoners and slaves. Since the sultan who had given the patriarch a safe-conduct was now dead, this reverend man was a prisoner just as we were. After the king had given his answer to the emirs, one of them declared that this had been done on the patriarch's advice and said to the other Saracens: 'If you'll trust me, I'll make the king swear, for I'll send the patriarch's head flying into his Majesty's lap.'

The other emirs would not listen to him; all the same they took the patriarch away from the king's side and tied him to the pole of the royal pavilion, with his hands so tightly bound behind his back that they swelled to the size of his head and the blood started to flow from his nails. He cried to the king: 'Your Majesty, swear without fear; for provided you truly intend to keep your oath, I will take on my own soul whatever sin there may be in what you are asked to swear.' I do not know how the matter was settled; but in the end the emirs were satisfied with the way in which the oath was sworn, both by the king and the other men of rank who were with him.

Very shortly after the sultan's death the insignia of his office had been placed before the king's tent, and he had been informed that the emirs, having met in council, had expressed a great desire to make him Sultan of Egypt. The king asked me if I thought he would have taken this kingdom if it had been offered to him. I told him that if he had done so he would have acted very foolishly, seeing that these emirs had killed their former lord. He told me, however, that in fact he would not have refused it.

I may say that, according to report, nothing further came of this, if only because the Saracens said the king was the most steadfast Christian that could be found. In proof of this they instanced that every time he left his tent he placed himself crosswise on the ground, and made the sign of the cross all over his body. They said that if Mahomet had allowed them to be so maltreated as the king had been they would never have kept their belief in him. Furthermore, they said that if the Saracens made the king their sultan, they would all have to become Christians, or else he would have them put to death.

After the treaty between the king and the emirs had been settled and confirmed by oath, it was agreed that the Saracens would release us on the day after Ascension Day, and that, as soon as Damietta had been surrendered to the emirs, they would release the king and all the important people with him. On the Thursday evening those who were in charge of our four galleys anchored them in the middle of the river, above the bridge of Damietta, and set up a pavilion by the bridge, at the place where the king was to land.

At sunrise Geoffroy de Sargines entered Damietta and took charge of its surrender to the emirs. The sultan's flags were hoisted on all the towers. The Saracen knights poured into the city and began to drink the wines, so that very soon all of them were drunk. One of these men boarded our galley, and drawing his sword all stained with blood, declared that for his part he had killed six of our people.

Before Damietta was surrendered, the queen had been received on board our ships, together with all our people who had been in the city, with the exception of the sick. These last the Saracens were bound by their oath to keep in safety; but they killed every one of them. The king's machines, which they were also bound to preserve, were hacked to pieces. As for the salt meat, which they ought to have kept for us, since they do not eat pork, that was destroyed. They heaped up the machines in one pile, the salt pork in another, the dead in a third, and set the whole lot alight. It was so great a fire that it lasted all Friday, Saturday, and Sunday.

The king, and all of us who were there, ought to have been set free at sunrise, but the Saracens kept us till sunset. All that time we had nothing to eat, nor the emirs either; and they spent the whole of that day disputing with each other. One of them, speaking for those who sided with him, said to the rest: 'My friends, if you'll listen to me and to those who think as I do, you'll kill the king and all the people of any importance who are with him. Then, for the next forty years we'll be in no danger, since their children are young, and we hold Damietta. So we can do this with the greater security.'

Another Saracen, named Sebreci, who was a native of Mauritania, opposed this suggestion: 'If we kill the king,' said he, 'after killing our sultan, everyone will say that the Egyptians are the wickedest and most treacherous people in the world.' Those who wished us to be killed rejoined: 'It's quite true we've acted very wickedly in getting rid of our sultan by putting him to death; for in doing so we've gone counter to the law of Mahomet, who commanded us to guard our lord as the apple of our eye. Here is the commandment written in this book. But just listen,' he added, 'to this other commandment that comes later.' With that he turned over a page of the book he was holding in his hand and showed them another commandment, which ran: 'To preserve the faith, slay the enemy of the law!' 'Now,' said he 'you can see how we've broken one of Mahomet's commandments by killing our lord; but we shall do still worse if we don't kill the king, since he is the most powerful enemy of our Moslem law.'

Our death was nearly agreed on; and so it happened that one of the emirs, who was against us, thinking we were all to be killed, came to the bank of the river and began to cry out in the Saracen tongue to the men in charge of the galleys, at the same time taking his turban off and waving it as a sign. The crews immediately weighed anchor, and took us back a full league upstream in the direction of Cairo. At this we gave ourselves up for lost, and many tears were shed.

But God, who does not forget His own, so willed that, round about sunset, it was agreed that we should be released. So we were brought back and our four galleys drawn up alongside the bank. We demanded to be allowed to go, but the Saracens said they would not let us leave until we had had a meal, for, said they, 'Our emirs would be shamed if you left our prisons fasting.' So we told them to bring us some food, and we would eat. The food they gave us consisted of cheese fritters, baked in the sun to keep them free from maggots, and hard-boiled eggs cooked three or four days before, the shells of which, in our honour, had been painted in various colours.

After they had landed us, we went to meet the king, who was being escorted to the river from the pavilion in which he had been detained. A good twenty thousand Saracens, with swords in their belts, followed after him on foot. On the river, right in front of the king, lay a Genoese galley, which seemed to have only one man on board. As soon as this fellow saw the king on the bank of the river he blew a whistle. At the sound of it eighty crossbowmen poured out of the hold of the galley, all fully equipped, with their crossbows wound up, and in a moment they had the bolts in their sockets. On seeing these men emerge the Saracens took to flight like so many sheep, and no more than two or three remained beside the king.

A plank was thrown from the galley to the bank to let his Majesty go on board. With him went his brother the Comte d'Anjou, Geoffroy de Sargines, Philippe de Nemours, Henri du Mez, Marshal of France, the Master of the Trinity, and myself. The Comte de Poitiers was kept a prisoner until such time as the king had paid the Saracens the two hundred thousand *livres* which he was to hand over as ransom money before he left the river.

On the Saturday after Ascension Day – that is to say the day after our release – the Comte de Flandre, the Comte de Soissons, and several other men of rank who had been held captive in the galleys came to take leave of the king. His Majesty told them that, in his opinion, they would do well to wait until his brother the Comte de Poitiers had been released. However, they said they could not wait, since their galleys were all ready for sea. So they embarked and set off for France, taking with them the good Comte Pierre de Bretagne, who was so ill that he only lived another three weeks, and died at sea.

Preparations for paying the ransom to the Saracens began on the Saturday morning. It took the whole of that day and the next day until night to count the money, which was reckoned by weight in the scales, each measure amounting in value to ten thousand *livres*. Round about six o'clock on Sunday evening the king's men who were weighing out the money sent to tell him they were still a good thirty thousand *livres* short of the sum required. At the time the king had with him only the Comte d'Anjou, the Marshal of France, the Master of the Trinity, and myself. All the rest were busy counting the ransom money.

I told the king it would be a good thing if he sent for the Commander and the Marshal of the Temple – the Master being dead – and asked them to lend him the thirty thousand *livres* still needed to obtain his brother's release. So the king sent to fetch the Templars, and instructed me to tell them what we wanted. After I had spoken to them brother Étienne d'Otricourt, the Commander of the Temple, gave me their reply. 'My lord of Joinville,' he said, 'this advice you have given the king is neither good nor reasonable. For you know that all money placed in our charge is left with us on condition of our swearing never to hand it over except to those who entrusted it to us.' On this many hard and insulting words passed between us.

While we were thus disputing brother Renaud de Vichiers, who was Marshal of the Temple, intervened to say: 'Your Majesty, let us call a halt to this quarrel between the Commander and my lord of Joinville. For indeed, as our Commander says, we could not advance any of this money without breaking our oath. But as to what your seneschal advises, namely to take the money if we will not lend it, I find nothing very surprising in such a suggestion and you must do as you think best. Anyhow, if you do take what is ours here in Egypt, we have so much of what is yours in Acre that you can easily give us adequate compensation.'

I told the king I would go and take the money if he was willing; and he ordered me to go. So I went to one of the galleys belonging to the Temple, the chief galley in fact, and as I was about to go down into the hold where the treasure was kept I asked the Commander of the Temple to come and see what I took; but he did not deign to do so. The Marshal, however, said that he would come, and be a witness of the violence I should do him.

As soon as I had got down to where the treasure was I asked the Treasurer of the Temple, who was there, to give me the keys of a chest which was just in front of me. But he, seeing me all haggard as I was and wasted by sickness, replied that he would not give me any of his keys. I caught sight of a hatchet lying there; I picked it up and told him I would make it serve as his Majesty's key. At this the Marshal seized hold of me by the wrist and said to me: 'Since you evidently intend to use force against us, we will let you have the keys.' So he ordered the treasurer to give them to me, which he did. When the Marshal told him who I was the man was quite dumbfounded.

On opening one of the chests I found it belonged to Nicolas de Choisi, a sergeant of the king. I threw out all the money I found inside; then I went back to the boat that had brought me and sat down in the bows. I got hold of the Marshal of France and left him, together with the Master of the Trinity, in charge of the money in the galley. There the Marshal handed it over to the Master, and he passed it over to me on the boat where I was sitting. As we came towards the king's galley I started to shout to him: 'My lord, my lord, see how well I am provided!' The saintly man was very glad to see me, and welcomed me with great joy. We handed over what I had brought to the men who were dealing with the ransom money.

After those of the king's councillors who were in charge of this transaction had completed their reckoning, they came to the king and told him that the Saracens would not consent to set his brother free until the money was actually in their possession. Certain members of his council held the opinion that the king should not hand over this money until he had his brother back again. The king replied that he would hand it over, since he had promised the Saracens to do so; as for them, if they wished to deal honestly, they would also keep their promise to him.

After payment had been made, Philippe de Nemours said to the king that they had been out in their reckoning of the money to the extent of ten thousand *livres* to the prejudice of the Saracens. At this the king became very angry, and said that as he had promised to pay the Saracens the whole two hundred thousand *livres* before he left the river, he insisted that the ten thousand *livres* should be restored to them. Just then I stamped on my lord Philippe's foot, and told the king not to believe him, since the Saracens were the shrewdest reckoners in the world. My lord Philippe admitted that what I said was true, and added that he had only been speaking in jest. The king told him that such jesting was uncalled for and in very bad taste. 'I command you,' he said to my lord Philippe, 'by the loyalty which you owe me as my vassal, that if by any chance you have not paid those ten thousand *livres* to the Saracens, you will have them paid without fail.'

Many of his people had advised the king to withdraw to his ship, which was waiting for him on the sea, so as to be out of the hands of the Saracens. But he had refused to listen to them, declaring that he would remain by the river, as he had promised the Saracens he would, until such time as he had paid the whole two hundred thousand *livres*. As soon, however, as the payment had been made he told us, without being urged to do so, that from that moment he held himself acquitted of his oath, and we were to leave the river and go to the ship that was on the sea.

Soon our galley began to move forward, but we had gone a full league and more before anyone said a word to his companions, so distressed were we at leaving the Comte de Poitiers still in captivity. Just then Philippe de Montfort came up to us in a galleon, and hailed the king. 'My lord, my lord,' he shouted, 'speak to your brother, the Comte de Poitiers, who is in this other ship!' At this the king called out: 'Light up! Light up!' This was quickly done. The joy we all felt at the moment was as great as any joy could be. The king went over to the count's ship, and so did we. A poor fisherman, who went to tell the Comtesse de Poitiers that he had seen her husband released, received from her twenty *livres parisis*.

Before I go further I must not forget to tell you of certain things that happened while we were still in Egypt. First I will speak of Gautier de Châtillon. One of our knights, whose name was Jean de Monson, told me he had seen him in a street of the village where the king was taken prisoner. This street ran straight through the village, so that you could see the open fields at either end; in it was Gautier de Châtillon, with a naked sword in his hand. On seeing the Turks come into the street he had rushed at them, sword in hand, and driven them out of the village; but as they fled, being able to shoot as easily backwards as forwards, they had covered him from head to foot with their darts. As soon as he had chased them from the village, he had pulled out the darts that were sticking in his armour, then replaced his coat of mail, and rising in his stirrups, with his sword-arm uplifted, had cried out: 'Châtillon, knight, Châtillon, where are my trusty men?' When he had turned round and seen that the Turks had entered the street at the other end, he had rushed at them again, sword in hand, and had chased them away. He had done this three times, and with the same result.

After the admiral of the galleys had taken me to join those of our companions who had been captured on land, I had asked for news of Gautier de Châtillon from men who had been associated with him. I could, however, find no one to tell me how he was captured; but I did hear from the good knight Jean Fouinon that when he himself was being taken as a prisoner to Mansourah he had seen a Turk mounted on Gautier de Châtillon's horse, and its crupper was all covered with blood. The good knight had asked the Turk what he had done to the man to whom that horse belonged, and he had replied that he had cut his throat while he was on that horse, as could easily be seen from the blood that covered its crupper.

There was another very valiant man in our army, the Bishop of Soissons, whose name was Jacques de Castel. When he saw our troops in retreat towards Damietta, he himself, whose great desire was to be with God, had felt no wish to return to the country where he was born. So he had made haste to be with God, by spurring on his horse and rushing to attack the Turks single-handed. These had cut him down with their swords, and thus sent him to be in God's company among the number of the martyrs.

While the king was waiting for payment to be made for the release of his brother, the Comte de Poitiers, a certain Saracen, who was very well-dressed and of very handsome appearance, had come to bring his Majesty a present of some jars containing milk, and flowers of different colours and kinds, on behalf of the children of Nasac, who had been Sultan of Cairo. As he offered these gifts he had spoken to the king in French.

When the king had asked him where he had learnt French the man had replied that he had once been a Christian. Thereupon the king had said to him: 'Go away! I don't wish to speak with you any further!' I had drawn the man aside and asked him to tell me his circumstances. He had told me that he was born in Provins, and had come to Egypt; he had married an Egyptian and was now a person of great importance. 'Don't you realize,' I had said to him, 'that if you die in this condition you will be damned and go to hell?' He had replied that he knew it, and was moreover certain that no religion was so good as the Christian religion. 'But,' he had added, 'I'm afraid to face the poverty and the shame I'd have to suffer if I returned to you. Every day someone or other would say to me: "Hullo, you rat!" So I prefer to live here rich and at ease than place myself in such a position as I can foresee.' I had pointed out to him that on the day of judgement, when his sin would be made plain to all, he would have to suffer greater shame than any he spoke of at that moment. I had given him much good Christian advice, but all to little effect. So he had left me, and I never saw him again.

Now you have already heard of the great suffering the king and all the rest of us endured. The queen (who was then in Damietta) did not, as I am about to tell you, escape from tribulations herself. Three days before she gave birth to a child news had come to her that the king was taken prisoner. This had frightened her so much that every time she slept in her bed it seemed to her that the room was full of Saracens, and she would cry out! 'Help! Help!' So that the child she was bearing should not die, she had made an old knight lie down beside her bed and hold her by the hand. Every time she cried out he would say to her: 'Don't be afraid, my lady, I am here.'

Just before the child was born she had ordered everyone except this knight to leave her room. Then she had knelt down before the old man and begged him to do her a service; he had consented and sworn to do as she asked. So she had said to him: 'I ask you, on the oath you have sworn to me, that if the Saracens take this city, you will cut off my head before they can also take me.' The knight had replied: 'Rest assured that I will do so without hesitation; for I already had it in mind to kill you before they took us all.'

The queen gave birth to a son who was named Jean. Her people called him Tristram, because of the great sorrow that had attended his birth. On the very day on which she was confined she was told that the men of Pisa, Genoa, and the other free cities were intending to flee from Damietta. The next day she had them all summoned to her bedside, so that the room was quite full, and had said to them: 'Gentlemen, for God's sake, do not leave this city; for it must be plain to you that if we lose it the king and all those who have been taken captive with him would be lost as well. If this plea does not move you, at least take pity on the poor weak creature lying here, and wait till I am recovered.'

They had answered: 'My lady, what can we do? We're dying of hunger in this city.' The queen had told them that they need not leave for fear of starvation. 'For,' said she, 'I will order all the food in this city to be bought in my name, and from now on will keep you all at the king's expense.' After talking the matter over among themselves they had come back to the queen and told her they would willingly remain. Then the queen – may God grant her grace! – had had all the food in the city bought in at a cost of more than three hundred and sixty thousand *livres*. But before due time she had had to leave her bed, because the city had to be surrendered to the Saracens. So she had gone to Acre to await the king's arrival.

While his Majesty was waiting for the release of the Comte de Poitiers he had sent brother Raoul, a predicant friar, to an emir called Faress-Eddin-Octay, who was one of the most honest Saracens I have ever seen. This friar had told him that the king was much amazed that he and the other emirs could have allowed the treaty to be so grossly violated; for they had killed the sick whom they were bound by oath to care for, had hacked his machines to pieces, and burnt the bodies of the sick, as well as the salt pork which they were equally bound to preserve.

In his reply to the friar Faress-Eddin-Octay had said: 'Go and tell your king that because of my law I can do nothing to make amends;

but I am very grieved about it. And warn his Majesty also from me not to show any sign that this matter distresses him so long as he remains in our hands – for that would mean his death.' The emir had also expressed the opinion that as soon as the king was safely in Acre he might take the matter up again.

CHAPTER II

The King in Acre

MAY 1250–MARCH 1251

ON his arrival on board his ship the king had found that his people had got nothing ready for him, neither bedding nor clothing. So until we reached Acre he had to lie on the mattresses given him by the sultan, and wear the clothes the sultan had had made for him. These were of black satin, lined with miniver and grey squirrel's fur and adorned with a vast quantity of buttons, all of pure gold.

Because of my weak state of health I spent the whole of the six days we were on the water sitting beside the king. During that time he told me how he had been captured, and how, by God's help, he had negotiated his own ransom and ours. He made me tell him in my turn how I had been taken prisoner on the water, and after listening to my story he told me I owed great thanks to our Lord for having delivered me from such serious peril. He grieved very much over the death of his brother, the Comte d'Artois, and said that, had he been alive, he would not have avoided his company as the Comte de Poitiers had done, but would certainly have come to see him on board his galley.

The king also complained to me of his other brother, the Comte d'Anjou, because, although they were both on board the same ship, the latter gave him little of his company. One day, having asked what the Comte d'Anjou was doing, the king was told that he was playing a game of chance with Gautier de Nemours. Weak as he was through illness, his Majesty tottered towards the players. He snatched up dice and boards, flung the whole lot into the sea, and scolded his brother very soundly for taking to gambling so soon. My lord Gautier, however, came off best, for he tipped all the money on the table – and there was plenty of it – into his lap and took it away with him.

I now propose to tell you something about the trials and troubles I experienced during my stay in Acre, and from which God, in Whom I trusted and still do trust, in the end delivered me. I am having these things written down so that those who hear of them may put their trust in God in their own time of trouble, and find Him ready to help them as He helped me.

Let me first relate how, when the king arrived at Acre, all the clergy and the people of that city came down to the sea-shore in procession, to meet him and welcome him with very great rejoicing. Someone brought me a palfrey, but as soon as I was mounted I felt faint, and asked the man who had brought it to hold me up, for fear I might fall. With great difficulty I was taken up the steps to the king's hall, where I went and sat by a window. A little boy about ten years old stood near me. He was Barthélemy, the bastard son of Ami de Montbéliard, Lord of Montfaucon.

I was sitting there, unnoticed by anyone, when a servant wearing a red tunic with two yellow stripes approached me. He bowed to me and asked me whether I knew him. I said I did not. Then he told me that he came from my uncle's castle at Oiselay. I asked him whose servant he was, and he said he was attached to no one, but would remain with me if I wished. So I told him I should be very glad to engage him. Thereupon he went and fetched me some white caps to cover my head, and combed my hair for me very neatly.

Shortly after this the king sent for me to dine with him. I went to him in the short tunic that had been made for me out of scraps from my coverlet while I was a prisoner. I had given the rest of the coverlet to little Barthélemy, together with four ells of mohair that had been given me, for the love of God, before the Saracens released me. My new man, Guillemin, came and carved my meat for me, and procured some food for the boy while we were eating.

Guillemin came to tell me that he had got rooms for me near the baths, where I might wash off the filth and the sweat I had brought with me from prison. When night came, and I was in my bath, I suddenly felt giddy and fainted. My man had great difficulty in taking me out of the bath and carrying me to my bed. The next day an old knight called Pierre de Bourbonne came to see me, and I kept him in my service. He stood surety for me in the city with regard to what I needed in the way of clothes and equipment.

As soon as I was suitably dressed, which was some four days after we reached Acre, I went to see the king. He reproached me and said I had not done well in delaying so long to come and see him. He commanded me, as I valued his love, to come and have meals with him every day, both morning and evening, until such time as he had decided what we ought to do – whether to go back to France or remain oversea.

I told the king that Pierre de Courtenay owed me four hundred *livres* of my pay, which he refused to give me. His Majesty replied that he himself would reimburse me out of the money he owed Pierre de Courtenay; and so he did. On Pierre de Bourbonne's advice we kept back forty *livres* for current expenses, and gave the rest into the keeping of the commander of the palace of the Templars. When I had spent all these forty *livres* I sent the father of Jean Caym of Sainte-Menehould, whom I had engaged in my service oversea, to fetch me a similar amount. The commander told him that he had no money of mine, and did not know me.

I therefore went to see Brother Renaud de Vichiers, whom the king, on account of the consideration the Templar had shown him when he was a prisoner, had helped to make Master of the Temple. I complained to him of his commander, who would not give me back the money I had entrusted to him. On hearing this the Master was much upset and said to me: 'My lord of Joinville, I have a great liking for you; but I must assure you that unless you cease to urge this claim I shall no longer look on you as a friend. For what you are trying to do is to make people believe that the members of our Order are thieves.' I told him, please God, I should not withdraw my claim.

For four whole days I suffered such anxiety as a man must feel when he has no money to meet expenses. At the end of that time the Master of the Temple came to me and told me with a smiling face that he had recovered my money. As to the way in which it was recovered, I can only say that he had transferred the commander of the palace to the village of Sephouri, and the man who was put in his place gave me back my money.

The Bishop of Acre, who was by the way a native of Provins, let me have the use of a house belonging to the priest of Saint Michael's. Jean Caym of Sainte-Menehould, who had served me well in the past two years, was one of those I retained in my service, together with several others.

There happened to be at the head of my bed a little ante-room through which one could go to enter the church. Now it chanced that a prolonged attack of fever took hold of me and my men, so that we were all confined to our beds. During the whole of this time there was not a day on which I had anyone to help me or lift me up. More-over I looked forward to nothing but death, on account of an ominous sound that constantly reached my ear, as not a day passed without their bringing twenty or more dead men into the church, and from my bed I could hear the chant: *'Libera me, Domine.'* Every time this happened I burst into tears, and gave thanks to God, as I addressed Him thus: 'Lord, I adore and praise Thee for this suffering Thou hast sent me; for I have given way to too much pride as I lay down to sleep or rose from my bed in the morning. And I pray Thee, Lord, to deliver me from this sickness.'

Soon after my recovery, I required Guillemin, my newly-made squire, to give me an account of the money he had spent. When he showed it to me I found he had cheated me to the extent of more than ten *livres tournois*. On my demanding restoration of this sum, he said he would refund the money as soon as he could. I dismissed him from my service, but told him I forgave him what he owed me, since he well deserved to keep it. I afterwards learnt from certain Burgun-dian knights recently released, who had brought the fellow with them to the land oversea, that he was the most well-mannered thief that ever existed; for whenever a knight was in need of a knife, a strap, gloves or spurs, or anything else, he would go and steal it, and then give it to his master.

While the king was in Acre his brothers indulged in playing at dice. The Comte de Poitiers was such a good-mannered player that on occasions when he won he would have the doors of his room thrown open and invite any gentlemen or ladies, if any, who were outside to come in. Then he would distribute money to them in handfuls, from his own pocket as well as what he had won in play. When he lost, he would buy, at a valuation, the money of those with whom he had been playing, whether it was his brother the Comte d'Anjou or anyone else, and would then give everything away, both his own money and what he had obtained from others.

One Sunday, during our stay in Acre, the king sent for both his brothers, together with the Comte de Flandre and other men of rank who were there. 'My lords,' he said to them, 'Her Royal Highness the Queen Mother has sent me a message begging me most urgently to return to France, because my kingdom is in great peril, since neither peace nor truce has been established between myself and the King of England. However, the people of these parts whom I have consulted tell me that if I go away this land will be lost, since all the men now in Acre will follow me, none daring to remain where the people are so few. I therefore beg you to give serious thought to the matter. Since it is so important I will allow you time to consider it, and you shall give me your answer, according as you think right, exactly a week from today.'

In the course of that week the legate came to me and said that he did not see how the king could possibly remain oversea. He begged me very earnestly to return to France with him in his ship. I told him I could not do this, for I had no money at all, having, as he knew well, lost everything I possessed when I was taken prisoner on the water. If I answered thus it was not because I would not have been very glad to go with him, but on account of something my cousin the Lord of Boulaincourt – God grant him mercy! – had said to me when I was about to go on crusade. 'You are going oversea,' said he, 'but take care how you come back; for no knight, whether rich or poor, can return without dishonour if he leaves our Lord's humbler servants, in whose company he set out, at the mercy of the Saracens.' The legate was much annoyed with me, and told me I ought not to have rejected his offer.

On the following Sunday we appeared again before the king. He asked his brothers, the Comte de Flandre, and the other barons whether they advised him to go or to stay. They all replied that they had charged Guy Mauvoisin to tell his Majesty what they wished to advise. So the king commanded him to carry out his commission, and he spoke as follows: 'Your Majesty,' he said, 'your brothers and the other nobles here present have considered your position, and have come to the conclusion that you cannot remain in this land without prejudice to your own honour and that of your realm. Out of all the knights that came in your company – two thousand eight hundred of whom you brought with you to Cyprus – there are now in this city hardly a hundred remaining. We therefore advise your Majesty to go back to France, and there procure men and money, and thus provided return with all speed to this land to take vengeance on the enemies of God who have held you in captivity.'

The king, however, was not content to go by what Guy Mauvoisin had said, but questioned the Comte d'Anjou, the Comte de Poitiers, the Comte de Flandre and several others of high rank who were sitting near them. They all agreed with Guy Mauvoisin. The legate asked the Comte de Jaffa, who was just behind him, what he thought. The count begged the company to excuse him from replying to this question. 'For,' said he, 'my castle lies on the frontier, and if I advised his Majesty to remain, people would think I did so for my own advantage.' The king pressed him as hard as he could to give his opinion. So the count replied that if his Majesty could manage to carry on the campaign for another year, he would do himself great honour by remaining. Thereupon the legate questioned those who were sitting beside the Comte de Jaffa, and they all agreed with Guy Mauvoisin.

I was in the row in front of the legate, about fourteen seats away. He asked me what I thought, so I replied that I agreed with the Comte de Jaffa. Then he asked me very angrily how I imagined the king could carry on a campaign with so few men as he had. Feeling very angry myself, because I thought he said this just to annoy me, I answered: 'I will tell you, sir, since you want to know. People say, though I don't know if it's true, that so far the king has not spent any of his own money, but only money from the revenues of the church. So let the king spend some of his own resources in getting knights from Morea and other parts oversea. When they hear that he is paying well and generously, knights will come flocking in from everywhere, so that, please God, he will be able to hold the field for a year. In the meantime, by remaining, he will be able to deliver those poor prisoners who have been taken captive in the service of God and of himself, and who will never be set free if he goes away.' There was no one in that place who had not some close friends in captivity; so no one reproved me, and all began to weep.

After I had answered the legate, he turned to the good knight Guillaume de Beaumont, who was then Marshal of France, and asked him for his opinion. He replied that he thought I had spoken very sensibly, 'and,' he added, 'I will tell you why I think so.' However, at that moment his uncle the worthy knight Jean de Beaumont, who was very anxious to return to France, started to address him in most insulting terms. 'You filthy rascal!' he cried, 'whatever d'you mean? Sit down and hold your tongue.' Thereupon the king said to Jean de Beaumont: 'Sir, that was very wrong of you. Let him say what he has to say.' 'Indeed, sir, I will not,' replied the knight. The marshal, however, felt obliged to keep silent, nor did anyone afterwards agree with me, except the lord of Chatenay. Finally the king said: 'My lords, I have taken due account of what you have said, and will tell you in a week's time what I intend to do.'

As soon as we had left the meeting people began to jeer at me from all sides. 'The king must indeed be crazy, my Lord of Joinville, if he doesn't listen to you in preference to the council of the whole realm of France!' After the tables had been laid the king made me sit beside him during dinner, as he always did when his brothers were not present. He said nothing to me during the whole of the meal, which was contrary to his usual custom, for he had always paid some attention to me while we were eating. I thought in fact that he must be annoyed with me, because I had said he had not as yet spent any of his own money, and ought to be spending it freely.

While the king was hearing grace I went over to a barred window in an embrasure at the head of his bed. I passed my arms through the bars of the window, and stood there thinking that if the king went back to France, I would go to the Prince of Antioch, who was a relative of mine, and had already asked me to come and join him. There I would remain until such time as another expedition came out to the land oversea, by means of which the prisoners might be delivered, as the Lord of Boulaincourt had advised.

While I was standing there the king came up to me, and leaning on my shoulders put both his hands on my head. I thought it was Philippe de Nemours, who had already plagued me too much that day because of the advice I had given. So I exclaimed: 'Stop bothering me, my good Philippe!' By chance, as I was turning my head, the king's hand slid down over my face, and I recognized who it was by the emerald ring on his finger. 'Keep quite quiet,' he said, 'for I want to ask you how a young man like yourself could be so bold as to advise me to stay here, against the advice of all the great and wise men of France who have advised me to go?'

'Your Majesty,' said I, 'even if such a bad idea had ever entered my mind, I'd never have advised you to go.' 'Do you mean to say,' he asked, 'that I'd be doing wrong if I went away?' 'Yes, sir, so God help me,' said I. Then he said: 'If I stay here, will you stay too?' 'Certainly, if I can,' I answered, 'either at my own expense or some-one else's.' 'You may rest easy on that score,' said he, 'for I'm very well pleased with you for the advice you've given me. But don't speak of this to anyone till the week is up.'

I felt much more at ease after hearing this, and defended myself all the more boldly against those who attacked me. Now it happens that the peasants of that region are known as 'colts'. Maître Pierre d'Avallon, who lived in Tyre, heard reports that I was being called a 'colt', because I had advised the king to remain in their country. So he sent to tell me this, and urged me to defend myself against those who so described me by saying that I would rather be a colt than an old broken-down nag like one of them.

The following Sunday we all came back again to see the king. As soon as he saw we were all assembled he made the sign of the cross on his mouth before addressing us. (This I imagine was by way of invoking the Holy Spirit; for as my dear mother once told me, every time I wished to say anything I should invoke the aid of the Holy Spirit, and cross my mouth.)

'My lords,' said the king, 'I sincerely thank all those who have advised me to return to France, as also those who have advised me to remain here. But I have come to the opinion that if I stay there will be no danger of losing my realm, since the Queen Mother has people enough to defend it. I have also considered that the barons resident in this country tell me that if I leave here the kingdom of Jerusalem will be lost, for no one will dare to remain after I have left. I have therefore decided that I will not on any account abandon the kingdom of Jerusalem, which I came here to re-conquer and defend. So I have finally determined to remain here for the present. Now I say to all of you, both to you, my nobles, who are here at this moment, and to all other knights who may wish to remain with me, to come and speak to me as boldly and frankly as you will; and I will offer you such generous terms that the fault will not be mine, but yours, if you do not choose to stay.' Many of those who heard these words were filled with amazement, and many there were who wept.

The king, it is said, ordered his brothers to return to France; but whether this was at their own request or by his wish I cannot really say. His Majesty's announcement of his intention to remain oversea was made on Saint John's Day. A month later, on Saint James's Day – I had gone on pilgrimage to his shrine and he had conferred great benefits on me – the king returned to his room after mass and summoned those of his council who had remained with him. These were his chamberlain Pierre, the most loyal and upright man I ever met in the royal household, the good and worthy knight Geoffroy de Sargines, and the equally estimable Gilles le Brun, whom the king had made Constable of France after the death of the good Imbert de Beaujeu.

The king spoke to them in a loud tone of voice and in a way that showed his displeasure. 'My lords,' he said, 'already a month has passed since it was known that I was staying here, and I have not yet heard that you have retained any knights in my service.' 'Your Majesty,' they replied, 'we have done all we can to get them; but all of them, since they really wish to go back to their own country, set such a high price on their services that we dare not give them what they ask.' 'And which of them,' said the king, 'could you get most cheaply?' 'Indeed, your Majesty,' they replied, 'it would be the Seneschal of Champagne; but we dare not give him as much as he demands.'

I happened to be in the king's room at the time, and heard what they were saying. 'Call the seneschal over here,' said the king. So I went up to him and knelt before him. He made me sit down and said to me: 'You know, seneschal, I've always been very fond of you; but my people tell me they find you hard to deal with. Why is that?' 'Your Majesty,' I replied, 'I cannot help it. As you know, when I was taken prisoner on the water, not one of my possessions was left to me; I lost all I had.' He asked what I demanded, and I told him I wanted two hundred thousand *livres* to last me till Easter, which would be two thirds of the year.

'Now tell me,' said he, 'have you tried to strike a bargain with any of the knights?' 'Yes,' said I, 'with Pierre de Pontmolain, one of three knights-banneret, who would each cost me four hundred *livres* till Easter.' The king reckoned on his fingers. 'Then your new knights,' said he, 'will cost you twelve hundred *livres*.' 'But sir,' said I, 'pray consider if it will not cost me a good eight hundred *livres* to procure a horse and armour for myself, as well as getting food for my knights; for you wouldn't, I suppose, wish us to eat with you.' So the king said to his councillors: 'I see nothing excessive in this.' Then turning to me he added: 'I retain you in my service.'

Shortly after this the king's brothers and the other nobles in Acre got their ships ready. Just as they were about to leave, the Comte de Poitiers borrowed some jewels from those who were returning to France and distributed them freely and liberally to those of us who were staying behind. Both the king's brothers begged me most earnestly to take good care of him, and told me there was no one among all those remaining with him on whom they placed such reliance. When the Comte d'Anjou saw that the time had come when he must embark, he showed such grief that everyone was amazed. All the same he went back to France.

Not long after the king's brothers had left Acre envoys arrived from the Emperor of Germany, bringing with them letters of credence to his Majesty, and assurances that their master had sent them to bring about our release. These men showed the king a letter which the Emperor had addressed to the late sultan – not knowing he was dead – telling him to give credence to what the envoys had to say with regard to freeing the king. Many people said it would not have been well for us if the envoys had found us still in captivity, since the Emperor, in their opinion, had rather sent them to embarrass us than to set us free. However, the envoys found us at liberty; so they went away.

While the king was at Acre the Sultan of Damascus sent envoys to see him and make bitter complaints against those Egyptian emirs who had killed his cousin. He promised the king that if he would help him, he for his part would hand over to him the kingdom of Jerusalem which was in his own possession at the time. The king decided to send the Sultan of Damascus an answer by envoys of his own. With them he sent Brother Yves le Breton, a friar of the Order of Predicants, who knew the Saracen tongue.

As they were on their way from their lodgings to the sultan's palace Brother Yves caught sight of an old woman going across the street, with a bowl full of flaming coals in her right hand and a flask filled with water in her left. 'What are you going to do with these?' he asked her. The old woman answered that with the fire she intended to burn up paradise and destroy it utterly, and with the water she would quench the fires of hell, so that it too would be gone for ever. 'Why do you want to do that?' asked Brother Yves. 'Because,' said she, 'I don't want anyone ever to do good in the hope of gaining paradise, or from fear of hell; but solely for the love of God, Who deserves so much from us, and Who will do us all the good He can.'

Round about the same time, John the Armenian, who was Master of Ordnance to the king, went to Damascus to buy horn and glue for making crossbows. While he was there he saw an extremely old man seated in the Bazaar. This old man called out to him and asked him if he was a Christian, and John replied that he was. Then the old man said to him: 'You Christians must be hating each other very much. For once, long ago, I saw King Baudouin of Jerusalem, who was a leper, defeating Saladin, though he had only three hundred men-at-arms, while Saladin had three thousand. But now, through your sins, you have been brought so low that we take you in the fields just as if you were cattle.'

Thereupon John told him that he would do well to keep quiet about the sins of the Christians, seeing that those committed by the Saracens were far greater ones. The Saracen replied that he had answered very foolishly; so John asked him why. The old man said he would tell him why; but first he would ask him a question. So he asked John if he had any children. 'Yes,' said John, 'I have a son.' The old man asked which would annoy him most – to receive a blow from him, the Saracen, or from his own son. John replied that he would be more annoyed with his son, if he did such a thing, than with the Saracen.

'I will now,' said the old man, 'give you my reply in this way. You Christians consider yourselves the sons of God, and take your title from the name of Christ. And God has shown you so much grace as to give you learned teachers, from whom you may know when you do right, or when you do wrong. That is why He is more displeased with you on account of some little sin you may commit than with us for committing a greater one, since we are completely ignorant, and so blind that just because Mahomet has told us we shall be saved by water at our death, we think we shall be cleansed of all our sins if we can wash ourselves with water before we die.'

Once, after we had returned from oversea, and I was on my way to Paris, John the Armenian was in my company. While we were having a meal in a great pavilion, a huge crowd of people who had come to beg alms of us for God's sake created a disturbance. One of our people who was present called out to a servant: 'Get up at once, and drive these fellows out.' 'Ah!' said John, 'it was very wrong of you to say that. If at this moment the King of France had sent his messengers with a hundred silver marks for each of us we should not have driven them out. Yet you are driving away these messengers who offer you the utmost that can be given. In other words, they ask you to give to them for God's sake, which means that you will give them some of what is yours, and they will give you God Himself.

For we have God's own word for it that those in want have power to make such a gift. The saints, moreover, tell us that the poor can help us to make our peace with God; for just as water quenches fire, so alms can blot out sin. See to it therefore,' said John, 'that you never again drive the poor away; but give to them, and God will give to you.'

CHAPTER 12

The Old Man of the Mountain

DURING the king's stay in Acre envoys from the Old Man of the Mountain arrived to see him. As soon as he had returned from hearing mass he had them brought before him. He ordered them to be seated in such a way that an emir, very handsomely dressed and well turned out, was in front, while behind him sat a young man of evidently good family, who was also very finely attired. In his clenched fist he held three knives, with blades that each fitted into the handle of another; these, if the emir's proposals were rejected, he was to present to the king in token of defiance. Behind this young man was another, who had a stout roll of linen wound round his arm, which he was to present to the king as a winding-sheet for his burial if he refused the Old Man of the Mountain's demands.

After the king had asked the emir to tell him why he had come, this noble presented his letters of credence and said: 'My lord has sent me to ask you if you know him.' The king replied that he did not know him, for he had never seen him; but he had often heard people speak of him. 'Since you have heard my lord spoken of,' said the emir, 'I am greatly surprised that you have not sent him such an amount of your money as would keep him as your friend – just as the Emperor of Germany, the King of Hungary, the Sultan of Cairo, and other rulers do year by year, because they know for certain that they can remain alive only so long as our master pleases. If it does not suit you to do this,' continued the emir, 'then you must arrange for him to be released from paying the tribute he owes to the Hospital and the Temple, and he will consider you have fulfilled your obligation.'

I may say that at that time the Old Man of the Mountain was paying tribute to both these Orders; for neither the Templars nor the Hospitallers had any fear of the Assassins, since their lord knew well that if he had either the Master of the Temple or of the Hospital killed, another, equally good, would be put in his place; therefore he had nothing to gain by their death. Consequently, he had no wish to sacrifice his Assassins on a project that would bring him no advantage.

The king told the emir he would see him again in the afternoon.

On his return the envoy found his Majesty seated so as to have the Master of the Hospital on one side of him and the Master of the Temple on the other. The king told the emir to repeat the message he had delivered that morning. The man replied that he had no intention of repeating what he had said except in the presence of those who had been with the king at the first interview. Thereupon both the Masters said to him: 'We command you to repeat your message.' The emir replied that as they had commanded it he would do so. After this the two Masters had orders given him, in the Saracen tongue, to come and speak with them at the Hospital on the following day.

When in obedience to their orders, the emir appeared the next day before the Masters they had him told (through an interpreter) that his lord had acted very rashly in daring to send such an insolent message to the king. They told him further that if the honour of the king, to whom he and his fellows had come as envoys, had not been involved they would have had them drowned in the filthy sea of Acre, in despite of the Old Man of the Mountain. 'We therefore command you,' said the Masters, 'to go back to your lord and return here within a fortnight, bringing with you, on your lord's behalf, such a letter and such jewels as may appease his Majesty and make him graciously pleased with you.'

Before the fortnight was up, the Old Man of the Mountain's envoys returned to Acre, and brought their lord's shirt with them to the king. They told him, on the Old Man's behalf, to take this as meaning that as the shirt is closer to the body than any other garment, so did their lord hold his Majesty as closer to himself in love than any other king. He also sent the king his own ring, which was of the finest gold, and had his name engraved on it; and with this the message that by this ring he joined himself in close alliance with the king, wishing from that time onward that they should be united, as if they were wedded to each other.

Among other costly gifts the Old Man sent the king he included a very well-made figure of an elephant, another of an animal called a giraffe, and apples of different kinds, all of which were of crystal; with these he sent gaming boards and sets of chessmen. All these objects were profusely decorated with little flowers made of amber, which were attached to the crystal by means of delicately fashioned clips of good fine gold. I might add that when the envoys opened the caskets containing these gifts, so sweet a scent arose from them that the whole room was filled with perfume.

The king sent the envoys back to the Old Man, and with them a great quantity of jewels, pieces of scarlet cloth, cups of gold, and horses' bits of silver. He also deputed Brother Yves le Breton, as an expert in the Saracen tongue, to go in their company. The friar found that the Old Man of the Mountain was not a follower of Mahomet, but subscribed to the laws of Ali, who was Mahomet's uncle.

Ali had raised Mahomet to the place of honour which he held; but once the latter had established himself as lord over the people he had begun to despise his uncle, and become alienated from him. On realizing this, Ali had gathered as many people around him as he could, and had taught them a different faith from that which Mahomet was teaching. Thus it still happens that all those who observe the laws laid down by Ali affirm that those who follow Mahomet are misbelievers, while those who accept the teaching of Mahomet maintain on their side that the followers of Ali are unsound in their faith.

One of the points laid down by Ali is that if a man is killed while obeying his lord's orders his soul goes into a more pleasing body than before. That is why the Assassins are not in any way averse to being killed as and when their lord orders, because they believe they will be happier after death than when they were alive.

Another belief of theirs is that no man can die before the day appointed for his death. This is a belief no man should hold, seeing that God has power to prolong our lives or to shorten them as He pleases. The Bedouins follow Ali on this point, and for that reason refuse to put on armour before going into battle, since by doing so they think they would be acting contrary to what their law commands. So when they curse their children they say to them: 'Be accursed like a Frank who puts on armour for fear of death.'

Brother Yves found a book by the head of the Old Man's bed in which were written many of the things our Lord had said to Saint Peter while He was on earth. 'Ah! my lord,' said the friar, 'For God's sake read this book very often, for these are very good words.' The Old Man replied that he did in fact read it very often, 'Because,' said he, 'Saint Peter is very dear to me. For at the beginning of the world the soul of Abel, after he was killed, entered the body of Noah; and after Noah's death it returned to enter Abraham's body; and when

Abraham died it passed from his body into Saint Peter's, at the time Our Lord came on earth.'

On hearing this Brother Yves pointed out to the Old Man that he was mistaken in this belief, and expounded much sound doctrine to him; but the Old Man would not listen. On his return to us the good friar reported all these things to the king.

Whenever the Old Man of the Mountain went out riding, a crier would go before him bearing a Danish axe with a long haft encased in silver, to which many knives were affixed. As he went the man would continually cry out: 'Turn out of the way of him who bears in his hands the death of kings!'

CHAPTER 13

The Tartars

I HAD forgotten to tell you of the reply King Louis made to the Sultan of Damascus. It was to the effect that he had no intention of joining forces with the sultan until he knew whether the Egyptian emirs would offer him amends for the treaty they had broken. He would therefore send to the emirs, and, if they refused him reparation, he would willingly help the sultan to avenge his cousin, the Sultan of Cairo, whom these men had slain.

The king sent Jean de Valenciennes from Acre into Egypt, with instructions to demand of the emirs that they should make reparation for the outrages they had committed against his Majesty. They replied that they would willingly do so, provided the king would enter into an alliance with them against the Sultan of Damascus. Jean de Valenciennes reproached them bitterly for the great wrong they had done the king. He also advised them that it would be well, if they wished to make his Majesty feel more kindly disposed towards them, to send him all the knights they still held captive. The emirs did as he advised, and in addition sent the king all the bones of the Comte de Brienne, so that these might be buried in consecrated ground.

After Jean de Valenciennes had come back to Acre, bringing with him two hundred knights released from captivity, besides many other men of lesser rank, Madame de Saida, who was the Comte Gautier's cousin, and the sister of Gautier de Reynel – whose daughter I married after my return from oversea – took the good count's remains and had them buried in the Church of the Hospitallers in Acre. She had the service conducted in such a way that each knight offered a wax candle and a silver *denier*, while the king offered a wax candle and a gold bezant – all of which was at her own expense. People were greatly surprised when the king agreed to this, for up till then he had never been known to offer any money but his own. However he did so on this occasion out of politeness to the lady.

Among the knights Jean de Valenciennes had brought back, I found a good forty belonging to the court of Champagne. I had tunics

and surcoats of green cloth made for them, and bringing them before
the king begged him to offer them such good terms that they would
remain in his service. The king listened to what they asked for, but
said nothing in reply.

One of the knights of his council told me I had not acted well in
making such proposals to the king, since he was already seven
thousand *livres* in debt. I told him I hoped he would be sorry he had
made that remark, and added that we, the men of Champagne, had
lost some thirty-five knights, all bannerets, from among those
belonging to our court. 'The king,' I went on to say, 'will not do well
if he listens to you, seeing what need he has of knights.' When I had
finished speaking I burst into tears. Thereupon the king told me
to keep quiet, and he would give these knights all I had asked.
So his Majesty engaged them as I wished, and posted them to my
battalion.

The king now gave his answer to the envoys from Egypt. He told
them he would make no treaty with the emirs unless, in the first
place, they sent him all the heads of Christians they had hung round
the walls of Cairo since the time when the Comte de Bar and the
Comte de Montfort were taken prisoner; secondly, unless they
handed over all the children who had been taken young and had
renounced their faith; and lastly, unless they let him off payment of
the two hundred thousand *livres* he still owed them. The king sent
the Egyptian envoys back to their country accompanied by that
wise and valiant man, Jean de Valenciennes.

At the beginning of Lent the king made ready, with all the forces
he had, to go and fortify Caesarea, a town some forty leagues from
Acre on the way to Jerusalem, which the Saracens had destroyed.
Raoul de Soissons, who had remained in Acre because he was ill,
accompanied his Majesty on that expedition. I cannot say how it
happened, unless it was by God's will, but the Saracens did no harm
to us during the whole of that year. While the king was busy fortifying Caesarea, the envoys he had sent to the country of the Tartars
returned. I will now tell you of the news they brought.

As I have already told you, while the king was staying in Cyprus,
envoys had come to him from the Tartars and had given him to
understand that they would help him to conquer the kingdom of
Jerusalem from the Saracens. When sending the envoys back the king
had sent with them, by his own envoys, a chapel made to his own

orders of scarlet cloth. Moreover, to attract the Tartars to our faith, he had ordered a set of figures to be placed in this chapel representing every point of our religion: the Annunciation of the Angel, the Nativity, the ceremony of our Lord's Baptism, all the stages of the Passion, the Ascension, and the coming of the Holy Ghost. With the chapel he had also sent cups, books, and everything necessary for the celebration of mass, and two predicant friars to chant the service before the Tartars.

The king's envoys had arrived at the port of Antioch; from there it had taken them a full year's travel, riding ten leagues a day, to reach the great King of the Tartars. They had found all the land they passed through subject to this monarch, and seen many cities the Tartars had destroyed, and great heaps of dead men's bones.

They had asked how the Tartars had come to acquire such authority, and had killed and ruined so many people. This, as the envoys told the king, was how they had managed to do it. The Tartars had originally come from a vast plain of sand, where no good thing would grow. At the farthest limit of this plain were certain huge and awe-inspiring rocks, right on the edge of the world, towards the East. No man, so the Tartars affirmed, had ever managed to get past them. They said that within these rocks are enclosed the giant race of Gog and Magog, who are to appear at the end of the world, when Antichrist will come to destroy all things.

The people of the Tartars lived on this plain, and were subject to Prester John[1] and to the Shah of Persia,[2] whose land came next to his, as well as to several other heathen kings, to whom they paid tribute and rendered service every year for the pasturage of their beasts; they had no other means of livelihood. Prester John, the Shah of Persia, and the other kings had such a contempt for the Tartars that when these people brought them their rent, they would never receive them face to face, but turned their backs on them.

There was a wise man among the Tartars, who travelled all over the plains and spoke to other wise men who lived there in many

[1] The name given in the Middle Ages to an alleged Christian prince supposed to reign in the extreme Orient, but whose existence has never been proved.

[2] Actually the King of the Khorasmins. See Glossary.

different places, pointing out to them the servitude they had to endure and exhorting them to consider how they could free themselves from such bondage. He worked so effectively that he gathered all the Tartars together at the far end of the plain, near the land of Prester John, and explained matters to them. They told him to say what he wanted and they would see it done. The wise man said they could not succeed unless they had a king to rule over them. Then he showed them how to set about electing a king, and they agreed to follow his advice.

The method they adopted was this: each out of the fifty-two tribes comprising their nation had to bring an arrow marked with its name; by general consent of the people it was agreed that all these arrows should be placed in front of a five-year-old child, and whatever arrow the child picked up first should mark the tribe from which the king would be chosen. After the child had picked up one of the arrows the wise men ordered all the other tribes to draw back. It was settled that the tribe from which the king was to be chosen should select among themselves fifty-two of their best and wisest men. When these had been chosen each one brought an arrow marked with his name. Then it was agreed that the man whose arrow the child picked up should be made king. The child took up one of the arrows, and it was the one belonging to the wise man who had instructed the Tartars. The people were all so glad at this that everyone gave free vent to his joy. The wise man told them all to be silent. 'Sirs,' said he, 'if you wish to have me as your king, swear to me by Him who made both earth and heaven that you will always do as I command you!' All the people swore to do so.

The laws the wise man gave them were framed to maintain peace among his people, and were to this effect: that no one should steal another man's goods, nor any man strike another, on pain of having his hand cut off; and that no one should have illicit relations with another man's wife or daughter, on pain of losing his hand, or even his life. He also made many other good laws for the maintenance of peace among his subjects.

After he had established law and order among the Tartars, the king said to them: 'Sirs, the most powerful enemy we have is Prester John. I therefore command you all to be ready to launch an attack on him tomorrow. If he happens to defeat us – which God forbid! – let each man fend for himself as best he can. If on the other hand we defeat him, I order that the slaying of his men shall last for three days and three nights, and that, during that time, no one shall be so rash as to lay a hand on the spoil, but everyone be bent on killing the enemy. After we have made our victory secure, I will distribute the booty so fairly and loyally that each of you will remain satisfied.' This proposal met with general agreement.

The next day the Tartars attacked their enemies, and, as God willed, defeated them. All those they found bearing arms and able to defend themselves they cut down and killed, but spared the lives of those whom they found in religious habit, priests and monks alike. The people from Prester John's land who had not taken part in the fighting placed themselves in subjection to the Tartars.

A prince from one of the tribes I have mentioned above disappeared for three months, and no one heard any news of him. On his return he felt neither thirsty nor hungry, and thought he had remained away no more than one night at the most. The news he brought back was that he had gone to the top of a very high mound where he had come across a very great number of people, the most beautiful beings he had ever seen, the most richly dressed and most finely adorned. At the far end of the mound he had seen a king, a much handsomer man than all the rest, in richer and more gorgeous attire. This king was seated on a golden throne; on his right sat six other kings, all wearing crowns and a dazzling array of precious stones; as many more kings were on his left. Near him, a little to the right, knelt a queen intent on imploring him to consider her people; to left of him knelt a man of exceeding beauty, with two wings that shone resplendent as the sun. Round the king stood a company of very handsome people, all of them with wings.

The king had called the prince to him and said: 'You have come from the army of the Tartars.' 'That is true, your Majesty,' the prince had replied. Then the king had said: 'You must go to your king and tell him how you have seen me, who am the Lord of heaven and earth. You are also to tell him to render thanks to me for the victory I have given him over Prester John and his people. And say to him, as from me, that I give him power to make the whole earth subject to him.' 'But your Majesty,' the prince had asked, 'How shall I make him believe me?' 'You will tell him to believe you by these signs: you shall go and fight against the Shah of Persia with three hundred men, and no more; and so that your great king may believe that I have power to do all things I will give him victory over this monarch, who will come against you with more than three thousand armed men. But before you go to fight the Shah you must ask your king to give into your charge all the priests and the monks he has taken in the recent battle, and you and your people must listen to them, and firmly believe what they teach you.' 'Your Majesty,' the prince had said, 'I cannot find my way back from here unless you give me a guide.'

The king had turned towards a great crowd of knights, all marvellously well-armed and equipped. He had called to one of them: 'George, come here!' The knight had come and knelt before him. Then the king had said to him: 'Rise, and lead this man back safe and sound to his tent.' This the knight had done one morning at break of day.

As soon as his people saw the prince both they and all the rest of the army showed such joy that no words can be found to express it. He asked the great king to let him have the priests. His request was granted, and both he and his people were so favourably impressed by the teaching of the priests that they were all baptized. After this the prince chose three hundred men-at-arms, ordered them to make their confession and prepare for battle, and then went and fought against the Shah of Persia. They defeated him and drove him from his kingdom, so that he went flying for refuge to the kingdom of Jerusalem. (This same Shah was the one who defeated our people and captured the Comte Gautier de Brienne, as I shall be telling you later.) The people under the rule of this Christian prince were so numerous that he had, as the king's envoys told us, as many as eight hundred chapels mounted on waggons in his camp.

The Tartars' way of living is such that they eat no bread, but exist on meat and milk alone. The best meat they have is horseflesh, which they steep in brine and afterwards leave it to dry until they can cut it as one would black bread. Their favourite drink, and the strongest too, is mare's milk, flavoured with herbs. On one occasion a horse, that had come with a load of flour from a distance of three months' journey away, was brought as a present to the great King of the Tartars; he gave the stuff away to the king's envoys.

Apart from the Christians I have already mentioned, as also men of another religion, there are among the Tartars a great number of people who adhere to the Greek Church. Whenever the Tartars wish to make war on the Saracens they send these Christians to fight against them, and on the other hand employ the Saracens in any war against Christians. Childless women of all classes go with the army on campaigns, and these are paid at the same rate as the men, according to their strength and vigour. The king's envoys told us that the men and women soldiers had their meals together in the quarters of the leader under whom they served. The men, in obedience to the law ordained by their first king, never ventured to have relations with the women.

These people eat the flesh of every beast that dies in their camp. The women who have children look after them and keep them from harm, and also prepare food for the men who are going into battle. The soldiers put uncooked meat between their saddles and the tails of their coats, and when the blood is well pressed out they eat it quite raw. What they cannot eat at the moment they throw into a leather bag, and when they are hungry they open their bags and always eat the oldest bits first. I myself once saw a Khorasmin, one of the Shah of Persia's men who kept guard over us during our imprisonment, open his bag, and as he did so we held our noses, unable to bear the horrible stench that came out of it.

Now let me go back to the matter in hand, and tell you how the great king of the Tartars, after receiving our king's envoys with his presents, summoned together, under safe-conduct, several rulers who had not as yet submitted to him. When they came he had his new chapel pitched for all to see and addressed them as follows: 'My lords, the king of France has sued for mercy and submitted himself to us. Here you can see the tribute he has sent us. If you do not submit yourselves to us, we will send for him to destroy you.' Many of them, out of fear of the French king, submitted to the King of the Tartars.

When his Majesty's envoys returned they were accompanied by others from the King of the Tartars who brought a letter to our king to this effect: 'Peace is a good thing; for when a land is at peace those that go on four feet graze in the fields undisturbed, while those who go on two can also till the earth – from which all good things come – in perfect tranquillity. This we tell you by way of warning, since you cannot have peace unless you are at peace with us. For Prester John rose up against us, and so did such and such kings' – here he named a great many – 'and we have put them all to the sword. We therefore advise you to send us a sufficient amount of your money in yearly contributions for us to remain your friends. If you refuse to do this we will destroy you as we have destroyed the kings already named.' His Majesty, I can assure you, bitterly regretted that he had ever sent his envoys to the great King of the Tartars.

CHAPTER 14

Life in Caesarea

I WILL now pick up the main thread of my story again, and tell you that, while the king was fortifying Caesarea, a certain Alenard, a nobleman from Senaingan, arrived at our camp. He told us that he had built his ship in the kingdom of Norway, which lies at the world's end, towards the west. During his voyage to see the king he had sailed all round the coast of Spain, and passed through the straits of Morocco, experiencing very great perils before he reached Caesarea. The king retained him in his service, together with nine of his knights. Alenard told us that, in the land of Norway, the nights are so short in summer that every evening you saw the light of the passing day merge into the dawn of a new one.

He and his men set out to hunt lions. They captured several at very great risk to themselves; for as they advanced to shoot these beasts they would spur on their horses as fast as they could; as soon as they loosed their arrows the lion would spring at them, and would have seized and devoured them if one of them had not let fall a piece of old cloth, which the lion leapt on, tore, and devoured, thinking he had got hold of a man. While the lion was tearing the cloth another hunter would go and shoot at him; the beast would leave off mauling the cloth to go after this new enemy. He in turn would let fall another piece of cloth, which the lion promptly leapt on. In this way they managed to kill the beast with their arrows.

While King Louis was still busy at Caesarea, Philippe de Toucy came to join him. The king called him cousin, because he was descended from a sister of King Philip of France who had married an Emperor of Constantinople. His Majesty retained him in his service for a year, together with nine of his knights. After that he left and went back to Constantinople, whence he had come.

He told the king that the Emperor of Constantinople and the nobles in that city had allied themselves with a people known as the Comans, so as to have their support against Vataces, Emperor of the Greeks. To make sure that each party would help the other loyally the Emperor of Constantinople and the nobles in his company had submitted to being bled, and their blood had been put into a great silver goblet. The King of the Comans and the nobles with him had done the same in their turn, and had mingled their blood with the blood of our people. After water and wine had been added, both parties had drunk from the goblet and had thereupon declared themselves blood-brothers. Then a dog had been made to run between our people and the Comans, and both sides had slashed at it and cut it to bits with their swords, at the same time vowing that whoever on either side failed the other in this alliance would be cut in pieces in the same way.

Philippe de Toucy also told us of a most amazing spectacle he had witnessed while in the Comans' camp. A knight of very high rank among them having died, they had dug a grave, very deep and wide, in the earth. In it they had placed the knight, very richly attired and seated in a chair; they had also lowered the best horse he had, and his best sergeant, into the grave alive. Before, however, the sergeant had been put into the grave he had taken leave of the King of the Comans and the other great lords. While he was bidding them farewell, each of these lords had put a great quantity of gold and silver into his scarf, saying to him: 'When I come into the other world you shall give me back what I now put into your care.' 'That I will most gladly do,' the sergeant had replied.

Next the great King of the Comans had given the sergeant a letter addressed to the first of their kings, telling him that this worthy man, having lived a good life and served his master well, deserved to be duly rewarded. After this the sergeant had been lowered into the grave with his lord, and with the live horse. Then the mouth of the grave had been covered by throwing closely fitting boards across it. Meanwhile all the men in the army had run to get stones and earth, and before going to sleep that night they had raised a great mound above the tomb in memory of those they had thus buried.

One day, while the king was in Caesarea, I went to see him in his quarters. He was talking to the legate, but as soon as he saw me enter his room he rose and drew me aside to speak to me. 'You know,' he said, 'I have only retained your services till Easter; so please tell me what I can give you to keep you with me for a year beyond that date.' I told him I did not want him to give me any more of his money than he had done already; but I wished to make another bargain with him.

'Since you get angry,' said I, 'whenever you are asked for anything, I want you to make an agreement with me that if I make any request to you during the whole of that year, you won't show any annoyance; while if you refuse what I ask, I on my side won't get angry either.' On hearing this the king burst out laughing, and said he would keep me in his service on those terms. Then he took me by the hand, and leading me towards the legate and his councillors told them of the bargain we had made. They were delighted to hear of it, because I was the man of highest rank and most influence in the army.

I will now tell you how I planned and arranged my life during the four years I remained oversea after the king's brothers had gone back to France. I had two chaplains who recited my Hours to me. One chanted mass for me as soon as dawn appeared, the other waited till my own knights and those attached to my battalion had risen. As soon as I had heard mass I went to see the king. If he wished to go out riding, I accompanied him. It sometimes happened that messengers arrived to see him, so that we had much business to settle during the morning.

My bed was placed in my pavilion in such a position that no one could enter without seeing me as I lay there. I did this to prevent anyone harbouring evil suspicions of me with regard to women. Every year, at the time of the Feast of Saint Remigius (1 October) I had pigs bought to fill my styes and sheep for my sheepfolds, as well as enough flour and wine to keep my quarters supplied for the whole winter. This I did because during the winter season, owing to the fact that transport by sea is more uncertain than in the summer, provisions became dearer.

I used to buy in a good hundred barrels of wine, and always had the best drunk first. I had wine mixed with water issued to my servants, and gave the same to my squires, but with a lesser proportion of water. At my own table a large flask of wine and a bottle containing water were placed before each of the knights, so that he might mix his drink as he wished.

The king had given me fifty knights for my battalion. At every meal I had ten of these at my table together with my own ten. According to the custom of the country they ate facing each other, seated on mats on the ground. Every time there was a call to arms I would answer the summons by sending fifty-four of my knights; these were known as *dizeniers*, because each of them commanded ten men. Whenever we rode out armed I would give these knights a meal in my quarters on their return. At all the annual festivals I used to invite the leading men in the army to dine with me, so that it sometimes happened that the king had to borrow some of my guests.

I will now tell you about what I saw of the way in which justice was administered and sentences were pronounced at Caesarea while the king was staying there. I will mention first of all the case of a knight arrested in a brothel, and to whom, according to the custom of the country, a certain choice was left. This was either to be led through the camp by the prostitute, in his shirt and shamefully bound by a rope, or to surrender his horse and arms and be dismissed from the army. The knight gave up his horse and arms to the king and left the camp. I went to his Majesty and asked him to give me the horse for a poor gentleman in the army. He replied that this was not a reasonable request, since the horse was still worth eighty *livres*. So I said to him: 'Now you've broken the agreement you made with me, for you're annoyed with me for making such a request.' He answered me, laughing heartily: 'Say what you like, I'm not annoyed with you.' All the same I did not get the horse for the poor gentleman.

The second judgement was this: as the knights of our battalion were hunting a wild animal called a gazelle (which is a kind of deer) certain Hospitallers leapt out upon them, hustled them, and drove them away. So I complained to the Master of the Hospital. He replied that he would make amends to me, according to the customs of the Holy Land, by ordering those Hospitallers who had committed the outrage to eat sitting on their mantles until such time as those they had offended should ask them to rise.

The Master dealt with them as he had promised. When we saw they had been eating for some time sitting on their mantles I went to the Master, whom I found at dinner, and begged him to tell these men to rise; the knights on whom the outrage had been committed also made the same request. The Master replied that he would do nothing of the kind, for he would not allow the members of his Order to misbehave towards those who came on pilgrimage to the Holy Land. When I heard this I sat down on the ground with the Hospitallers and began to eat with them, telling the Master I should not get up until they did. He told me I was forcing his hand, and granted my request. Then he invited me and the knights who were with me to dine at his table, while the Hospitallers went to join their companions at another.

The third sentence I saw enforced at Caesarea was this: one of the king's sergeants, called Le Goulu, had laid a hand on a knight in my battalion. I went and complained to the king, who told me he thought I might as well let the matter rest, since the sergeant had only given my knight a push. I told the king I would not withdraw my complaint, and if he did not do me justice I would leave his service, since his sergeants were allowed to push knights about.

So the king did me justice according to the custom of the land, in this manner: the sergeant came to my quarters barefoot, wearing only his shirt and drawers, and with a naked sword in his hand. He knelt before the knight he had offended, took hold of the sword by the point and offered the knight its pommel. 'My lord,' he said, 'I have come to make amends for having laid a hand on you, and have brought you this sword so that you may cut this hand off at the wrist, if it pleases you to do so.' I asked the knight to forgive him his offence, and he consented.

The fourth penalty inflicted was as follows: Brother Hugues de Jouy, who was Marshal of the Temple, was sent by the Master of his Order to the Sultan of Damascus to negotiate an agreement respecting a large tract of land which the Temple had been holding, but which the sultan wished to divide so that he should have one half and the Temple the other. The agreement was accordingly made, subject to the king's consent. Brother Hugues brought back with him an emir sent by the Sultan of Damascus, together with a document to prove that the contract had been duly executed.

However, when the Master of the Temple told the king what had been done, his Majesty was greatly surprised, and said to him that he had been over-bold in negotiating such an agreement without first consulting him. The king added that some reparation must be made. The form it took was this: the king had the flaps of three of his pavilions raised, and all the lower ranks of the army were given leave to come and see what was going on. The Master of the Temple and all his knights advanced barefoot, right through the camp, because their quarters were outside it. The king made the Master of the Temple and the sultan's envoy sit in front of him, and then addressed the former in a loud voice. 'Master,' he said, 'you will tell the sultan's envoy that you regret having made any treaty with his lord without first speaking to me. You will add that since you did not consult me you must hold the sultan released from the agreement he has made with you, and hand all relevant documents back to him.' Thereupon the Master of the Temple produced the written agreement and handed it to the emir, saying as he did so: 'I give you back the contract I have wrongly entered into, and express my regret for what I did.'

Then the king told the Master and the other Templars to rise, which they accordingly did. 'Now,' said his Majesty, 'kneel down, and make reparation to me for having thus approached the sultan against my will.' The Master knelt down, and holding out the hem of his mantle towards the king, surrendered to him everything his Order possessed, so that his Majesty might take from it whatever compensation he might determine. 'I declare in the first place,' said the king, 'that Brother Hugues, who made this agreement, shall be banished from the whole kingdom of Jerusalem.' Neither the Master (who with the king was godfather to the Comte d'Alençon, born at Châtel-Pélerin), nor even the queen, nor any other person, was able to do anything on behalf of Brother Hugues, or save him from being forced to leave the Holy Land and the kingdom of Jerusalem.

CHAPTER 15

Expedition to Jaffa

WHILE the king was fortifying the city of Caesarea his envoys returned from Egypt, bringing with them a treaty drawn up according to the terms his Majesty had already prescribed. The agreement between the king and the emirs was to the effect that on a certain day he was to go to Jaffa, while they bound themselves by oath to be at Gaza that same day to deliver the kingdom of Jerusalem into his hands. The king and all the leading men in the army swore to observe the terms of the treaty as it had been transmitted to them by the envoys; this meant that we were bound by our oaths to help the emirs against the Sultan of Damascus.

As soon as this sultan knew that we had allied ourselves with the Egyptians he sent a well-equipped force of four thousand Turks to Gaza, where the army from Egypt was to arrive. He did this because he was well aware that if these troops could join us it might be to his loss. None the less the king did not put off his plan of marching to Jaffa. On hearing that he was coming the Comte de Jaffa set to work to get his castle in such a condition that it would appear ready to withstand an attack. At each opening in the battlements – there were a good five hundred – he set a shield with his arms, and a pennon. This was a most beautiful sight to see, for his arms were *or*, with a cross of *gules patté*.

We encamped in the fields round the castle, which lies on the sea and runs on both sides down to the shore. The king immediately began to build new fortifications all round the old castle and stretching to left and right as far as the sea. I often saw his Majesty carrying a hod full of earth to the trenches so as to gain the promised indulgence.

The Egyptian emirs failed to keep their agreement to meet us; for they did not dare to come to Gaza because of the troops of the Sultan of Damascus that were there. All the same they honoured their covenant with us in so far as to send us all the heads of Christians hung on the walls of the castle of Cairo since the time when the Comte de Bar and the Comte de Montfort were captured. His

Majesty had them buried in consecrated ground. They also sent us the children who had been taken when the king was captured; but they did this with regret, for these youngsters had already renounced their faith. Along with these they sent the king an elephant, which his Majesty shipped to France.

While we were encamped at Jaffa an emir, who was on the side of the Sultan of Damascus, came to reap the corn at a village three leagues away from our camp. We agreed to go and attack him, but as soon as he saw us he took to flight. As he was fleeing, a young squire of good family started to chase after him. He bore two of the emir's knights to the ground without breaking his lance, and then struck at the emir himself so fiercely that the lance snapped in the Saracen's body.

Envoys from the Egyptian emirs now came to beg the king to appoint a day on which their lords might come to see him; they promised to come without fail. The king decided not to refuse their request, and fixed a day for them. They bound themselves by oath to be at Gaza on that date.

While we were waiting for the day appointed for the meeting with the Egyptian emirs to come round, the Comte d'Eu, who was at that time a squire, arrived at the camp. He brought with him the good knight Arnoul de Guines, his own two brothers, and seven other persons. He remained in the king's service and was knighted by his Majesty.

Round about the same time the Prince of Antioch returned to the camp with the princess his mother. The king paid him much honour, and dubbed him a knight with due pomp and ceremony. The prince was only sixteen, but I have never seen a lad of such intelligence. He asked the king to give him an audience in the presence of his mother, and when the king gave his consent spoke as follows: 'Your Majesty,' he said, 'it is no doubt true that my mother should be my legal guardian for four years more; all the same it is not right for her to allow my land to go to waste and be lost. I say this to you, sir, because the city of Antioch is being ruined in her hands. I therefore appeal to your Majesty to ask her to grant me money and men so that I may go to protect my people in that city and give them the help they need. Indeed, sir, it is only right that she should do so; for if I remain in Tripoli, great expense will necessarily be incurred, and all that expense will be for nothing.'

The king leant a willing ear to the lad's request, and did all in his power to persuade the mother to give her son as much as could be extracted from her. Immediately after leaving the king the prince went off to Antioch, where his coming was gladly welcomed. With the king's consent he quartered his arms, which were *gules*, with the arms of France, because the king had made him a knight.

Three minstrels from Great Armenia had come with the prince. They were brothers, and were going to Jerusalem on pilgrimage. They had three horns which were so constructed that the sound came out from the side of their faces. When they began to play them you would have said it was the voice of swans rising out of a pond; they made such sweet and delicate music that it was wonderful to hear. All three of these men also performed the most amazing leaps. When a mat was put under their feet they would execute a somersault from a standing position and finish with their feet back again on the mat. Two of them could make a somersault backwards. The eldest did this too, but whenever he was asked to make one head foremost, he would cross himself, for he was afraid of breaking his neck as he turned.

Now since it is a good thing that the memory of Gautier, Comte de Brienne, and also Comte de Jaffa, should not be forgotten, I will speak of him at this point. He had held Jaffa for many years, defending it by gallant and vigorous action, and living, for the most part, on what he gained from the Saracens and other enemies of the faith. Thus it once happened that he defeated a great band of Saracens who were transporting a huge quantity of silk and cloth of gold, and captured all their goods. Then, after bringing back his spoil to Jaffa, he had distributed everything among his knights, so that he had nothing left for himself. It was his habit, after taking leave of his knights, to go and shut himself up in his chapel and spend a long time praying there before going at night to sleep with his wife. She was a very wise and virtuous lady, and the sister of the King of Cyprus.

After the Shah of Persia, whose name was Barbaquan, had been, as I have told you, defeated by one of the Tartar princes, he had marched with all his army into the kingdom of Jerusalem. There he had taken the castle of Tabarie, which had been fortified by Eudes de Montbéliard, the constable, who was Lord of Tabarie through his wife. The Shah of Persia had inflicted great harm on our people, for he had laid waste all the land and destroyed everything he could find outside Châtel Pélerin, Acre, Safad, and also round about Jaffa. After doing all this damage, he had turned in the direction of Gaza to join forces with the Sultan of Cairo, who was coming there to do what mischief he could to our people.

The barons of the land, together with the patriarch of Jerusalem, had decided to go and attack the Shah before the Sultan of Cairo arrived. In order to have some support they had sent for the Sultan of Homs, one of the best knights among the Moslems, and had showed him such great honour in Acre that they had carpeted the streets through which he was to pass with cloth of gold and silk. Then they had all marched to Jaffa, taking the Sultan of Homs with them.

The patriarch had excommunicated the Comte Gautier because he would not give up a tower that he held in Jaffa which was known as the Patriarch's Tower. Our people had begged the count to go with them and fight against the Shah. He had replied that he would willingly do so, provided the patriarch would give him absolution till their return. The patriarch had refused to do anything about it; none the less the Comte Gautier had made ready and had gone with the army.

Our troops were in three divisions, one of which was under the Comte Gautier, another under the Sultan of Homs, while the patriarch and the people of the land formed the third. The Hospitallers were in the Comte Gautier's division. They had all ridden forward till they came within sight of the enemy. As soon as our people had seen them, they had halted; the opposing forces had also drawn up in three divisions. While the Khorasmins were marshalling their men, the Comte Gautier had turned to our people and cried: 'Sirs, for God's sake, let's go and attack them, for we're giving them time while we remain halted.' But no one would listen to him.

On realizing this, the count had gone up to the patriarch and asked for absolution on the terms already proposed. The patriarch, however, had utterly refused to grant it. Now there was in the Comte Gautier's division a certain valiant cleric who was Bishop of Ramleh and who had performed many exploits in the count's company. He had said to the count: 'Don't let your conscience worry you because the patriarch won't absolve you, for he's in the wrong, and you're in the right. I myself absolve you in the name of the Father, the Son, and the Holy Spirit. And now let's at them!'

So they had dug their spurs into their horses and attacked one of the

Shah of Persia's divisions, which formed the rear. A very great number of men had been killed on one side and the other. The Comte Gautier had been taken in the fight, for all our people had fled in such shameful disorder that many in their despair had drowned themselves in the sea. The reason for their thus losing hope was that one of the Shah of Persia's divisions had attacked the troops led by the Sultan of Homs, and he had lost so many men in defending his position that out of two thousand Turks he had led into battle only two hundred and eighty remained with him when he left the field.

Thinking that the sultan could not hold out very long after losing so many of his men, the Shah had decided to go and besiege him in his castle at Homs. When the sultan saw him coming he had gone to his people and told them that he intended to go out and confront the enemy, since if he allowed himself to be besieged, he would be lost. The plan of action he had adopted was to send all those of his men who were poorly armed out by a hidden valley. The moment they had heard the sultan's drums beating they had attacked the Shah's camp from the rear, and had started to kill the women and children.

The Shah, who had gone out on to the open plain to fight the sultan's troops which he saw arrayed before him, had no sooner heard the cry of his people from the camp than he had turned back towards it to rescue the women and children. The sultan's men had immediately hurled themselves at the Shah and his army, and attacked them so successfully that out of the twenty-five thousand Persians present not a single man or woman had remained alive; all were either killed in the fight or put to the sword.

Before the Shah had gone to besiege Homs, he had brought the Comte Gautier before the walls of Jaffa. The Persians had hung him by the arms to a forked pole, and told him that they would not take him down till the Castle of Jaffa was in their possession. While he was thus hanging he had called out to the men in the castle not to surrender because of any harm the enemy might do him, and had said that if they surrendered he would kill them with his own hands.

As soon as the Shah had known of this he had sent the Comte Gautier to Cairo as a present to the sultan of that city, together with the Master of the Temple and several others he had taken prisoner. Those who had brought the count to Egypt were about three hundred in number, and these had not been killed when the Shah had met his death before Homs. These three hundred men, who were Khorasmins, were among those who afterwards attacked us on the Friday, when we were on foot. They carried red banners, with indentations right up the shafts of their lances, at the tip of which they had fixed heads made out of hair, that looked like the heads of devils.

Several of the merchants in Cairo had appealed to the sultan to do them justice against the Comte Gautier for the great losses they had suffered at his hands. The sultan had given them permission to take their revenge on the count. So they had gone and killed him in prison, where he died for the faith. On this account we may believe for certain that he is now in heaven among the company of the martyrs.

Now to return to our main story. The Sultan of Damascus assembled his men that were at Gaza, and entered Egypt. The emirs came and fought against them. The division commanded by the sultan defeated the emirs with whom they had engaged, but the other Egyptian division defeated the sultan's rear-guard. After the fight the Sultan of Damascus went back to Gaza, wounded in the head and in the hand. Before he left that place the Egyptian emirs sent their envoys to make peace with him, and so failed to keep any of the agreements they had made with us. From that time onwards there was neither truce nor peace between us and the people of Damascus or the people of Cairo. During all this time, I may say, the greatest number of men-at-arms we had available never amounted to more than fourteen hundred.

While the king was before Jaffa, the Master of Saint Lazarus had spied out near Ramleh, a town some three good leagues away, a number of cattle and various other things from which he thought to collect some valuable booty. So being a man of no standing in the army, and who therefore did exactly as he pleased, he went off to that place without saying a word to the king. But after he had collected his spoils the Saracens attacked him, and so thoroughly defeated him that of all the men he had in his company no more than four escaped.

As soon as he returned to camp he raised a call to arms. I went and armed myself and begged the king to let me go to the place. He gave me leave, and ordered me to take the knights of the Temple and the Hospital with me. When we got there we found that certain Saracens from outlying districts had come down into the valley where the Master of Saint Lazarus had been defeated. While these men were looking at the dead the captain of the king's crossbowmen had suddenly attacked them, and before we arrived our people had routed them all and killed several.

One of the king's sergeants and one of the Saracens had thrown each other to the ground with one thrust of their lances. Another of the king's men, seeing this happen, had taken their two horses and started to lead them away to steal them. So that no one might see him, he had hidden himself inside the walls of the city of Ramleh. While he was leading the horses off an old cistern over which he was passing had given way beneath him. He and the three horses, so I was told, had fallen to the bottom. I went to look at the place, and saw that the cistern was still falling in on top of them, so that they were almost completely covered. So we returned to camp without loss, except for for what the Master of Saint Lazarus had suffered.

Immediately after making peace with the Egyptian emirs the Sultan of Damascus had sent to recall those of his men who were at Gaza. These troops passed at less than two leagues away from our camp, but never ventured to attack us, although their forces amounted to a good two thousand Saracens and ten thousand Bedouins as well. Before they came so close to us the master of the king's crossbowmen and his battalion had kept a close watch over their movements for three whole days and nights, to prevent their making a surprise attack on our camp.

On Saint John the Evangelist's Day, soon after Easter, the king went to hear a sermon. While the preacher was still talking, a sergeant belonging to the master crossbowman's company entered the king's chapel, fully armed, and told him that the Saracens had surrounded their leader. I asked the king for leave to go and help him. He granted my request and told me to take with me four or five hundred men-at-arms, naming those whom he wished me to take. As soon as we marched out of camp the Saracens, who had taken up a position between the master of the crossbowmen and the camp, moved off to join an emir who was on a hillock in front of the master crossbowman with a good thousand men-at-arms.

Then began a fight between the Saracens and the master of the crossbowmen's sergeants, of whom there were about a hundred and eighty in all. At one moment when the emir saw that his men were being hard pressed he sent them reinforcements, and in such numbers that they drove our sergeants back upon the master's troops. As soon, however, as the master saw that our men were being hard pressed in their turn, he sent to their help a hundred or a hundred and twenty men-at-arms, who drove their assailants back upon the emir's division.

While we were there, the legate and the barons of Outremer, who had remained with the king, told him that he had acted most unwisely in exposing me to such danger. On their advice the king sent to recall me, together with the master of the crossbowmen. However, at this point the Turks withdrew, and we all went back to the camp. Many people wondered why they did not come to attack us, and certain others said that if they had failed to do so it was because they and their horses had been starved at Gaza, where they had been staying for nearly a year.

After these Saracens had withdrawn from their camp outside Jaffa and had settled down before Acre they sent to tell the Lord of Arsuf, who was constable of the kingdom of Jerusalem, that they would destroy the gardens of the city unless he sent them fifty thousand bezants.* He sent back to tell them that he would not give them a single one. So they marshalled their troops and posted them all along the sands of Acre, so near to the city as to be well within the range of a swivel-crossbow. The Lord of Arsuf marched out of Acre and took up his position on Mount Saint John, where lies the cemetery of Saint Nicholas, so as to defend the gardens. Our foot sergeants also came out of the city, and started to harass the Saracens with bows and crossbows.

The Lord of Arsuf summoned a Genoese knight named Giannone, and ordered him to go and recall the unmounted troops that had come out of Acre, so that they should not run into danger. As he was leading them back, one of the enemy started to call out to him in the Saracen tongue that he would tilt with him if he was willing. Sir Giannone said he would gladly do so; but as he was going towards the Saracen he looked to his left and caught sight of a little band of Turks, about eight in number, who had halted to watch the encounter. Thereupon he turned away from the Saracen, and rode towards the Turks, who were standing quite still to get a good view of the tilting, and ran one of them through the body with his lance, laying him dead.

On seeing this the other Turks rushed at Sir Giannone as he was going back to join our men, and one of them struck him a great blow on his steel cap with a mace. As the Turk passed by him Sir Giannone slashed at him with his sword, struck the turban he wore round his head, and sent it flying across the field. (The Turks wear these turbans when they are going into battle, because they can withstand a heavy blow from a sword.) Another Turk came spurring towards the knight, intending to give him a thrust with his spear between the shoulders; but Giannone saw the spear coming, and swerved aside. Then, as the Saracen passed, he gave the man a backhanded blow with his sword across the arm, so that the spear flew off into the field. So Giannone returned, and brought his unmounted troops back to Acre. These three fine strokes of his were delivered in the sight of the Lord of Arsuf, and were also witnessed by the leading citizens in Acre and all the women who had gathered on the walls of the city to watch the fight.

As you know, the great host of Saracens assembled before Acre had not dared to fight against us nor against the men of Acre. When they heard the report (a true one) that the king had sent no more than a very small contingent of good men to fortify the city of Saida,[1] they marched in that direction. Simon de Montbéliard, who was master of the king's crossbowmen and in command of his Majesty's forces in that city, no sooner heard that the Saracens were advancing than he withdrew to the fortress of Saida, which is very strong and surrounded on all sides by the sea. He did this because he was well aware that he had no power to resist the enemy. He took shelter in the castle with as many people as he could, but these were only a few, for space there was extremely limited.

The Saracens poured into Saida and met with no resistance, for the town was not completely surrounded by walls. They killed more than two thousand of our people, and then went off to Damascus with the booty they had gained in the town. When news of this reached the king he was deeply vexed. (Ah! if only he could have repaired the loss!) The barons of the land, however, considered it a very fortunate occurrence, because the king had otherwise intended to go and fortify a piece of rising ground on the way from Jaffa to Jerusalem, on which an ancient fortress had stood since the days of the Maccabees.

The barons of Outremer did not think it advisable to have the walls of this old castle rebuilt, because it was five leagues from the sea so that no provisions could be sent there from the ports without the risk of their falling into the hands of the Saracens, who were stronger than we were. So when news of the destruction of Saida reached the

[1] Otherwise Sidon. See glossary.

camp, these men came to the king and told him that it would be more to his honour to re-fortify that town than to build a new fortress. The king agreed to follow their advice.

While his Majesty was at Jaffa he was told that the Sultan of Damascus would be willing for him to go to Jerusalem and would assure him safe-conduct. The king held a general council to consider the matter, as a result of which no one advised him to go, since, in the end, he would have to leave the Holy City in the hands of the Saracens.

By way of argument the king's councillors instanced what had happened on a previous occasion. When the great King Philip had left Acre to return to France he had allowed all his people to remain in the army under the Duc Hugues de Bourgogne, the grandfather of the duke lately deceased. While the duke was still at Acre, and King Richard of England with him, news had come to them that if they wished they could take Jerusalem the very next day, since all the forces of the Sultan of Damascus, including his knights, had left to join him elsewhere, on account of a war he was having with another sultan. The two kings had therefore assembled their troops; the King of England's men had formed the first division, while the Duc de Bourgogne, with all the King of France's men, had made up the second.

While they were on their way, with a good chance of taking the Holy City, a message had come from the duke's camp to the King of England, telling him to proceed no further, as the duke himself was retreating, and that for no other reason than because he did not wish it to be said that the English had taken Jerusalem. While King Richard and his people were talking of this, one of his knights had called out: 'My lord! My lord! Come over here, and I will show you Jerusalem!' On hearing this, the king had thrown his emblazoned tunic over his eyes, and, weeping bitterly, had cried to our Saviour: 'Dear Lord, I pray Thee to suffer me not to see Thy Holy City since I cannot deliver it from the hands of Thy enemies!'

The councillors quoted this instance to the king because they felt that if he, who was the greatest of all Christian monarchs, went on pilgrimage to Jerusalem without delivering the city from God's enemies, then all the other kings and pilgrims coming after him would rest content with doing no more than he had done, and would show no concern for the deliverance of that holy city.

King Richard became so noted for his daring exploits while oversea that when any horse belonging to a Saracen shied at a bush its master would say to it: 'D'you think that's King Richard of England?' And when the children of the Saracen women started to cry, their mothers would say to them: 'Stop it, do! Or I'll go and fetch King Richard, and he'll kill you!'

The Duc de Bourgogne, whom I have just mentioned, was a good knight as far as his lands were concerned, but he was never considered wise, either in his relations with God or in his conduct of worldly affairs, as may be easily understood from what I have told you about him. Because of this the great King Philip, on hearing that the Comte de Chalon had a son who had been named Hugues after the Duc de Bourgogne, had at once expressed the hope that God would make him as valiant a man as the duke. He was asked why he had not said as wise and worthy a man. 'Because,' said the king, 'there is a great difference between a valiant man and a wise and worthy one. For there are many valiant knights both in Christian lands and in the lands of the Saracens who have never believed in our Lord nor in His mother. So I say,' he added, 'that God grants a great gift, and a very special grace, to the Christian knight whom He endows with physical courage, and at the same time keeps him in His service by guarding him from mortal sin. The knight who thus governs himself is rightly called wise and worthy, since his ability to do noble deeds comes to him from God. Those I have mentioned above can only be called valiant, because although they have great physical courage they neither fear God nor are afraid of sin.'

I will not attempt to give you an accurate account of the huge sums the king spent in fortifying Jaffa, for they are too great to be reckoned. He fortified the town right down to the sea on both sides; there were twenty-four towers along the walls, and the moats were clear of mud both inside and outside. There were also three gates, one of which had been built at the legate's expense, together with a section of the wall.

To give you some idea of what the king spent on all this I will tell you that I asked the legate how much the gate and part of the wall had cost him. He asked me how much I thought, and I estimated that the gate must have cost a good five hundred *livres* and his part of the wall three hundred. He told me – as God was his witness – that wall and gate together had cost him full thirty thousand *livres*.

CHAPTER 16

Expedition to Saida

As soon as the fortifications of Jaffa were completed the king decided to go to Saida and rebuild its defences, which the Saracens had destroyed. He set out on the day of the feast of the Apostles Saint Peter and Saint Paul, and encamped for the night with his army outside the castle of Arsuf, which was strongly fortified. That evening he called his people together and told them that if they agreed he would go and take a city of the Saracens now called Nablus, but known as Samaria[1] in the Holy Scriptures.

The Templars, the Hospitallers, and the barons of Outremer all replied that they thought it a good plan to try and take that city; but they also thought that the king should not go there in person because, if anything happened to him, the whole land would be lost. The king said he would not let them go unless he himself went with them. The enterprise therefore remained in abeyance, because the barons would not consent to his accompanying them.

After marching for several days we arrived at the sands of Acre, where the king and his army encamped. While we were there a large band of people from Great Armenia came to see me. They were going on pilgrimage to Jerusalem, after paying a great sum as tribute to the Saracens, who were conducting them there. By means of an interpreter who knew their language and ours they begged me to show them the sainted king. I went to him and found him sitting in a pavilion, leaning against the central pole. He was seated on the bare sand, without a carpet or anything else underneath him. 'Sir,' said I, 'there's a huge troop of people from Great Armenia outside here who are going to Jerusalem. They've begged me to have our sainted king shown to them; but I've no desire as yet to kiss your bones.' The king burst out laughing and told me to go and bring them in; which I did. When they had seen him they commended him to God, and he returned their blessing.

On the following day the army spent the night at a place known

[1] Not Samaria but Shechem.

as the Colts Ford, where the water is very good; the people here use it to water the plants which produce sugar. While we were there, one of my knights came to me and said: 'My lord, I've found quarters for you in a much better spot than you were in yesterday.' Another knight, who had chosen my previous camping-ground, sprang at him in a furious temper, shouting: 'It's very rash of you to speak like that of anything I may have done.' Then he leapt at the other man and seized him by the hair. I sprang at him in turn, and hit him with my fist between the shoulders so that he let go. 'Quick, out of my quarters,' said I, 'for, so God help me, you shall never again be one of my men.'

The knight went away looking very sad and dejected, but soon returned in the company of Gilles le Brun, Constable of France, who because he saw the knight so truly sorry for his foolish action begged me as earnestly as he could to take him back into my quarters. I replied that I would not take him back unless the legate released me from my oath. They accordingly went to the legate and told him what had happened. He answered that he had no power to release me, because the oath was reasonable since the knight had well deserved his punishment. I am telling you of this incident so that you may refrain from taking any oath without reasonable justification. For, as the wise man says, 'Whoever swears too lightly, just as lightly breaks his oath.'

The next day the king encamped before Es Sur, which in the Bible is called Tyre. There he called together the chief men in the army and asked them whether it would be a good thing for him to go and take the city of Banyas before he went to Saida. We all thought it a good plan for the king to send his troops there; but no one considered it wise for him to go there himself, and after much difficulty he was persuaded to give up that idea. It was finally decided that the Comte d'Eu should go, in company with Philippe de Montfort, Gilles le Brun, Constable of France, the king's chamberlain Pierre, the Master of the Temple with the members of his Order, and the Master of the Hospital with his.

We armed ourselves at nightfall and arrived, a little before daybreak, at a plain outside the city which is now known as Banyas, but which the ancient Scriptures called Caesarea Philippi. In this city there rises a spring called Jor, and in the middle of the plain outside the city there rises another very beautiful spring called Dan. Now it so happens that when the streams from these two sources meet, they become the river which is called the Jordan, in whose waters our Lord was baptized.

By agreement between the Templars, the Comte d'Eu, the Hospitallers, and the barons of the land there present, it was decided that the king's division – in which division I was, because the king had taken into his service the forty knights who had been in mine – should take up their stand between the castle and the city, supported by the troops under the worthy knight Geoffroy de Sargines. The barons of the land, for their part, were to enter the city by the left, the Hospitallers by the right, while the Templars would ride straight on along the road by which we had come, to effect an entry that way.

We rode forward until we came quite near Banyas, only to find that the Saracens inside the walls had routed the king's sergeants and driven them out of the city. As soon as I knew of this I rode up to the officers in command of the Comte d'Eu's troops, and said to them: 'Gentlemen, unless you go where we have been ordered to go, between the city and the castle, the Saracens will kill all those who have already entered Banyas.' Getting there would be a very dangerous business, for the way by which we had to go was full of hazards. There were three double lines of dry walls that we had to cross, and the ground sloped so steeply that a horse could barely keep its footing, while the sides of the low hill we had to reach was crowded with mounted Turks.

While I was speaking to the Comte d'Eu and his knights I saw that our foot sergeants were breaking down the walls. As soon as I noticed it I said to those I was addressing that the king's division had been ordered to go to the place the Turks were holding, and since this had been ordered, I should go. As I and two of my knights turned in the direction of those who were pulling down the walls I caught sight of a mounted sergeant whose horse had fallen back on him as he was trying to get over the wall. On seeing this I dismounted, and took my horse by the bridle. However, as God willed, the moment the Turks saw us coming they abandoned the position we had to occupy. From there a rocky precipice went down sheer into the city.

When we got to the place which the Turks had left the Saracens inside Banyas gave up the fight, and abandoned the city to our people without offering any resistance. While I was on the hill the

Marshal of the Temple heard that I was in danger, and came climbing up the slope towards me. At the same time the Germans, who were in the Comte d'Eu's division, also came after me. When they saw the mounted Turks in full flight towards the castle they moved to go in pursuit of them. 'Sirs,' I called out, 'you're not doing right. We're in the position we were told to occupy, and you're exceeding your orders.'

The castle that stands above the city is called Subeibah. It is fully half a league up in the mountains of Lebanon, and the slope leading up to it is strewn with great rocks as big as chests. When the Germans realized that they were launched on a vain pursuit they turned back. The Saracens, seeing them turn, swung round and attacked them on foot, aiming at them great blows from the tops of the rocks with their maces, and dragging away the housings from their horses.

The sergeants who were with us, seeing the damage done to the Germans, began to lose heart. Thereupon I told them that if they went off I would have them dismissed from the king's service for ever. 'My lord,' said they, 'the stakes are not equal; for you're on horseback, and can easily escape, while we're on foot, and the Saracens will kill us.' 'As to that,' said I, 'I swear to you I'll never take to flight, but remain with you on foot.' So I dismounted and sent my horse back to the Templars, who were a full crossbow shot to the rear.

As the Germans were retreating, a quarrel* loosed by a Saracen struck one of my knights, named Jean de Bussey, in the throat; he fell dead at my feet. His uncle, Hugues d'Escot, who had borne himself very bravely in the Holy Land, said to me, 'Come and help us, my lord, to carry my nephew down the slope.' 'I wish the worst to anyone who helps you,' said I, 'for you went up there without my orders, and if you've met with misfortune, you've deserved it. Carry him down to the rubbish-heap yourself, for I'll not stir from here till I'm sent for.'

When Jean de Valenciennes heard of the danger in which we stood he went up to Olivier de Termes and the other leading men of Languedoc and said to them: 'My lords, I beg and command you, in the king's name, to help me rescue the seneschal.' While he was expressing his concern, Guillaume de Beaumont came to him and said: 'You're worrying yourself to no purpose; the seneschal's dead.' 'I don't care whether he's alive or dead,' replied my lord Jean. 'I'll go and get news of him for the king.' So he started off, and came to the place we had gone to on the mountain. As soon as he got near us he called out to me to come and speak to him; and so I did.

Olivier de Termes pointed out to me that we were in a very dangerous position. For if we went down by the way we had gone up we could not do so without great loss, since the slope was too steep and slippery, and the Saracens would come down on us from above. 'But if you'll listen to me,' he added, 'I'll help you to escape without loss.' I told him to explain what he wanted us to do, and I would see it done.

'I'll tell you,' said he, 'how we may escape. We'll go right along this slope, as if we were making for Damascus. The Saracens you see up there will think we're intending to attack them in the rear. As soon as we're down on the plains we'll set spurs to our horses and go round the city. We shall be across the stream before they can catch up with us; and in addition we shall do them great harm, for we'll set fire to the threshed corn lying over there in those fields.'

We followed his directions. He made us take some of those hollow canes such as are used for making flutes, stuff them with live coals, and thrust them in amongst the threshed corn. Thus, thanks to the wise advice of Olivier de Termes, God brought us back in safety. I must tell you, however, that when we came back to the camp where our people were, we found they had all put off their armour; for no one there had given a thought to us.

The next day we returned to Saida, where the king was staying. We found that he had personally supervised the burying of the bodies of all the Christians whom the Saracens had killed when they destroyed the city. He himself had carried some of the rotting, evil-smelling corpses to the trenches to be buried, and that without ever holding his nose, as others had done. He had sent for workmen from all the country round, and had started to re-fortify the city with high walls and towers. When we arrived at the camp we found that he himself had seen to measuring out the sites where our tents were to be set up. He had allotted me a place near to the Comte d'Eu, because he knew that this young knight was fond of my company.

I must tell you here of some amusing tricks the Comte d'Eu played on us. I had made a sort of house for myself in which my knights and I used to eat, sitting so as to get the light from the door, which, as it happened, faced the Comte d'Eu's quarters. The count, who was a very ingenious fellow, had rigged up a miniature ballistic machine with which he could throw stones into my tent. He would watch us as we were having our meal, adjust his machine to suit the length of our table, and then let fly at us, breaking our pots and glasses. On one occasion when I had bought a supply of fowls and capons, and some-one or other happened to have given the count a bear, he let the animal loose among my poultry, and it had killed a dozen of them before anyone could get there. The woman who looked after my fowls had beaten the bear with her distaff.

While the king was fortifying Saida certain merchants came to the camp and told us how the King of the Tartars had taken Bagdad, and captured the religious leader of the Saracens, who ruled over the city, and went by the title of Caliph of Bagdad. They told us how the capture of the city and its ruler had been effected, which was in this way: After laying siege to Bagdad the King of the Tartars had sent to the caliph to say he would be very willing to arrange a marriage between their children. The caliph's councillors had advised him to agree to this proposal. Thereupon the King of the Tartars had requested the caliph to send as many as forty members of his council to swear to the marriage; and the caliph had done so. After that the king had asked him to send him another forty men from amongst the richest and most distinguished people in his city; the caliph had done this too. The king had then sent a third time, asking the caliph for yet another forty of the best men of his court; again the caliph had complied. Now that he had all the principal men of the city in his power, the King of the Tartars had felt that the humbler citizens of Bagdad would not be able to defend themselves without leaders. So he had had the heads of all these six score men cut off; then he had ordered an assault on Bagdad, and had taken both the city and its caliph.

So as to cover up his treachery and throw the blame for the capture of the city on the caliph, the king had given orders for the latter to be taken and put into an iron cage, where he was kept as short of food as a man can be without actually dying of starvation. The king had then asked him if he was hungry; the caliph had said he was, which was not to be wondered at. So the king had had a great golden dish, loaded with jewels and precious stones, brought before his captive, and had asked him: 'Do you recognize these jewels?' The other had replied, 'Yes, they were mine.' The King of the Tartars had asked him if he prized them very much and the caliph had told him that he did. At this the king had said: 'Since you value them so highly take as much as you like of these jewels you see here, and eat.' The caliph had replied that he could not, since they were not food such as could be eaten. Thereupon the king had said to him: 'You may now see what might have been your means of defence; for if you had distributed your treasure – which at this moment is of no use to you – among your men-at-arms, you might, by spending it thus, have defended yourself successfully against us, whereas now it fails you in your hour of greatest need.'

One morning at daybreak, while the king was fortifying Saida, I went to see him and found him at mass. He asked me to wait for him, as he wished to go out riding; so I did. While we were out in the fields we passed in front of a little church and saw, as we rode by, a priest inside, chanting mass. The king told me that this church had been built in honour of the miracle performed by our Lord when he drove the Devil out of the body of the widow's daughter. He said to me that, if I was willing, he would stay to hear the mass the priest had just begun. I told him I thought it was a good thing to do.

When the time came for the *pax*[1] to be handed to us, I noticed that the clerk who was assisting at the service was a tall, dark, lean, and hairy fellow. I was afraid that he might be one of those wicked Assassins, and that when he offered the *pax* to the king he might kill him. So I got up and took the *pax*, and brought it to the king myself.

When mass was over, and we were once more on horseback, we came across the legate in the fields. The king rode up to him, and after calling me to come, said to him: 'I must complain to you of my seneschal, who brought me the *pax*, and would not let the poor clerk bring it.' I told the legate my reason for doing this, and he said I had acted rightly. 'No, indeed, he didn't!' said the king. This started a great argument between them; I, for my part, kept silent. I have told you this story as an illustration of the king's great humility.

As for the miracle our Lord performed on the widow's daughter, it is related in the Gospel, which says that at the time he performed it our Lord was *in parte Tyri et Sidonis*. For in those days the city I have called Es Sur was known as Tyre, and the city I have referred to in this book as Saida was called Sidon.

[1] A tablet with a representation of the Crucifix, kissed by the officiating priest and the congregation at mass.

While the king was still engaged in fortifying Saida envoys came to him from a great noble in the depths of Greece who styled himself the great Comnenus, Lord of Trebizond. These men brought the king a present of various jewels, and also, among other things, some bows made of cornel-wood. The notches for the shafts were screwed into the bows, and when these shafts were loosed you could see that they were very sharp and well-made.

These envoys asked the king to send one of the young unmarried ladies from his court as a wife for their lord. He replied that he had not brought any such ladies with him from oversea. However, he advised the envoys to go to Constantinople, and ask his cousin the Emperor to give them, as a wife for their lord, a lady who was related both to the Emperor and to himself. The king gave them this advice so that the Emperor of Constantinople might enter into alliance with this great and wealthy noble against Vataces, who was then Emperor of the Greeks.

The queen, who had but lately recovered from her confinement on giving birth to the Lady Blanche at Jaffa, now arrived at Saida, having come there by sea. As soon as I heard that she was there, I got up from where I was sitting beside the king and went to meet her, and escorted her back to the castle. When I returned to the king, whom I found in his chapel, he asked me whether his wife and children were well. On my telling him they were he remarked: 'When you got up and left me I knew very well that you were going to meet the queen, so I have asked them to postpone the sermon until your return.' I am telling you this because during all the five years I had been with the king he had never once spoken to me of his wife and children, nor, so far as I know, to anyone else. In my opinion it does not seem right and proper for a man to be so detached from his own family.

On All Saints' Day I invited all the chief men in the camp to my quarters, which were by the sea. While we were at dinner a poor knight and his wife, with their four children, arrived in a ship. I gave them a meal in my quarters. After we had finished eating I called together all my important guests and said to them: 'Let's perform a deed of charity and relieve this poor man of his children, each of you taking charge of one, while I take one myself.' They each agreed to take one, and quarrelled as to who should have which. On seeing this the poor knight and his wife began to weep for joy.

It so happened that as the Comte d'Eu was coming back from

dining with the king he stopped to look in on the men I had with me, and took away my child, who was about twelve years old. This lad served the count so well and faithfully that after we had returned to France his master arranged a marriage for him and made him a knight. Every time I happened to be in the same place as the count, this knight could scarcely keep away from me, and used to say to me repeatedly: 'May God reward you, my lord! for I owe all this honour I enjoy to you.' As for his three brothers, I do not know what became of them.

I asked the king to let me go on pilgrimage to our Lady of Tortosa. Her shrine was greatly resorted to by pilgrims, because it was there that the first altar was erected on earth in honour of the Mother of our Lord. Our Lady performed many great miracles there, of which the following is an example. There was a man who was quite out of his mind and possessed by the Devil. While his friends, who had brought him to this shrine, were praying to the Mother of our Lord to restore him to health, the Enemy, from inside his body, cried out to them: 'Our Lady is not here. She is in Egypt giving help to the King of France and the Christians, who will land this very day to fight on foot against the mounted forces of the heathen.' The date of this occurrence was written down and the document brought to the legate, who told me of it himself. I can assure you that our Lady did indeed help us that day, and would have helped us still more if, as I have already told you, we had not angered her and her Son.

The king gave me leave to go to Tortosa, and told me, on the advice of his council, to buy a hundred pieces of camlet in different colours for him to give to the Franciscans when we returned to France. This made me feel much more at ease, for it seemed to indicate that he would not be remaining much longer oversea.

When we came to Tripoli my knights asked me what I intended to do with all the pieces of camlet, and begged me to tell them. 'Perhaps,' said I, 'I've stolen them to sell them for my own advantage.' The Prince of Tripoli – may God grant him grace! – entertained us nobly and paid us all the honour he could. He would have given me and my knights most valuable presents, if we had been willing to accept them. But we refused to take anything except a few relics, some of which I took to the king, together with the camlet I had bought for him.

I also sent four pieces of camlet to her Majesty the queen. The knight who came to present them carried them wrapped up in a piece of white linen. When the queen saw him enter her room she knelt before him, while he in his turn knelt before her. The queen said to him: 'Rise up, my good knight, it is not fitting for you to kneel when you are the bearer of relics.' 'Madam,' replied the knight, 'these are not relics, but pieces of camlet sent to you by my lord.' On hearing this the queen and her ladies began to laugh. 'Tell your lord I wish him the worst of luck,' said the queen to my knight, 'since he has made me kneel before his camlet.'

During the king's stay at Saida someone brought him a stone that split into flakes. It was the most marvellous stone in the world, for when you lifted one of the flakes you found the form of a sea-fish between the two pieces of stone. This fish was entirely of stone, but there was nothing lacking in its shape, eyes, bones, or colour to make it seem otherwise than if it had been alive. The king gave me one of these stones. I found a tench inside; it was brown in colour, and in every detail exactly as you would expect a tench to be.

It was while he was in Saida that the king received news of his mother's death.[1] He was so prostrated with grief that for two whole days no one could speak to him. After that he sent one of the servants of his household to summon me. When I came into his presence and found him sitting all alone in his room, he stretched out his arms to me as soon as he saw me, and said: 'Ah, seneschal, I have lost my mother!' 'Sir,' said I, 'this news does not astonish me, since she had to die. But I'm surprised that you, who are a wise man, should show such grief at this event. For, as you know, a certain sage philosopher has said that whatever grief a man may feel in his heart, nothing of it should appear on his face, because by showing his grief he gives his enemies cause for joy and brings distress to his friends.' The king had many fine services held for the Queen Mother oversea; and subsequently sent to France a chest full of letters addressed to all the churches, asking them to pray for her soul.

Madame Marie de Vertus, a very good and pious lady, came to tell me that the queen was plunged in grief, and asked me to go to her and comfort her. When I arrived there, I found her in tears. So I said to her that the man who said one can never tell what a woman will do

[1] Queen Blanche died in November 1252. News of her death was very slow in coming if it did not reach King Louis till after June 1253. Possibly Joinville's memory is at fault.

spoke truly. 'For,' said I, 'the woman who hated you most is dead, and yet you are showing such sorrow.' She told me it was not for Queen Blanche that she was weeping, but because of the grief the king was showing in his mourning over the dead, and also because of her own daughter – later Queen of Navarre – who was now left in the sole guardianship of men.

Queen Blanche had treated Queen Marguerite so harshly that, in so far as she could help it, she had not allowed her son to be in his wife's company except when he went to sleep with her at night. The palace in which the young king and his wife had most liked to live was at Pontoise, because there the king's room was on an upper floor and the queen's room just below it. They had so arranged matters that they had managed to meet and talk together on a spiral staircase that led from one room to the other. They had also arranged that whenever the ushers saw Queen Blanche approaching her son's room they would knock on the door with their rods, and the king would run quickly up to his room so that his mother might find him there. Queen Marguerite's gentlemen of the bedchamber did the same when Queen Blanche was going to her daughter-in-law's room, so that she might find the young queen safely installed within.

The king was once by his wife's side, at a time when she was in great danger of dying on account of the injuries she had suffered in giving birth to a child. Queen Blanche had come to her room, and taking the king by the hand, had said to him: 'Come away; you're doing no good here.' Queen Marguerite seeing that the Queen Mother was taking the king away, had cried out: 'Alas! Whether I live or die, you will not let me see my husband!' Then she had fainted, and they had all thought she was dead. The king, convinced that she was dying, had turned back; and with great difficulty they had brought her round.

CHAPTER 17

Return to France

WITH the fortifications of Saida nearly completed, the king ordered several processions to be made throughout the camp. After each procession the legate exhorted the people to pray that God would so order the king's affairs according to His will, that he should do whatever was most pleasing in His sight, whether he returned to France or remained oversea.

After all the processions had been made, the king called me from where I was sitting with the nobles of Outremer and led me into a courtyard, where he made me stand with my back towards them. Then the legate said to me: 'The king is greatly pleased with your services, seneschal, and would gladly see that they bring you both profit and honour. Moreover, to set your heart at rest, he has asked me to tell you that he has settled to go back to France at this coming Easter.' 'God grant he may carry out his wish,' I replied.

The legate got up and told me to accompany him to his quarters; which I did. He led me into a private room, where no one else was with us, and shutting the door, took both my hands in his and began to weep very bitterly. As soon as he could speak he said to me: 'I'm extremely glad, seneschal, and give thanks to God that the king and you, and all the other pilgrims, have escaped from the great perils you've been exposed to over here. But I'm sad at heart at having to leave the company of such upright men as yourself and return to the court of Rome, among the treacherous people there. However, I'll tell you what I propose to do. I intend to make it possible for me to stay on here for a year after you've left, and spend all I have in fortifying the suburbs of Acre. In this way I'll be able to show those men in Rome that I certainly haven't brought any money back with me, and so, my hands being empty, they'll not come running after me.'

I once told the legate of two sins one of my priests had related to me. He said to me in reply: 'No one knows as well as I do of all the mean and treacherous sins committed in Acre. That is why God will have to exact such vengeance for them that Acre shall be washed clean in the blood of its inhabitants and other people come to live there in their place.' This good man's prophecy has been partly fulfilled; for the city has certainly been well washed in the blood of its inhabitants,[1] but those who are to live there have not come as yet. God grant that those He sends there will be good men, whose actions will be according to His will!

Some time later the king sent for me and ordered me to arm myself. On my asking him why he told me that it was to escort the queen and her children to Es Sur, some seven leagues away. I did not say a word in reply, though he was sending me on a very dangerous errand, for at the time there was neither peace nor truce between us and the Saracens of Egypt, or of Damascus. God be thanked, we got to Es Sur by nightfall, quite peacefully and without hindrance, though we had to dismount twice to make a fire for cooking our food, and to give the children something to eat, or let them be suckled.

Before the king left Saida – which he had fortified with high walls and towers, and wide moats cleared of mud within and without – the patriarch and the barons of the land came to him, and addressed him as follows: 'Your Majesty, you have fortified the city of Saida, the city of Caesarea, and the town of Jaffa, all of which is of very great advantage to the Holy Land. You have also greatly strengthened the defences of Acre by the walls and towers you have built around it. We have talked things over among ourselves and we do not see how it will profit the kingdom of Jerusalem for you to remain here any longer. We therefore strongly advise you to go to Acre in the coming Lent and and prepare for your voyage home, so that you may be able to return to France after Easter.' Following the advice of the patriarch and the barons the king left Saida and went to Es Sur, where the queen was staying. From there we went on to Acre, where we arrived at the beginning of Lent.

During the whole of Lent the king saw to getting his ships ready to return to France. There were thirteen in all, counting both sailing ships and galleys. All these vessels were got ready in time for the king and queen to embark on the eve of Saint Mark's Day, shortly after Easter. The wind was fair as we set sail. On Saint Mark's day the king told me that it was his birthday; I replied that he might in future say that on that day he had been re-born, for certainly he had entered on a new life when he escaped from that perilous land.

1 It was sacked by the Saracens in 1291.

By Saturday we came within sight of Cyprus and a mountain on that island which is called the Mountain of the Cross. That day a mist rose from the land and spread from there down on to the sea, so that our sailors, seeing only the top of the mountain above the mist, thought we were further away from Cyprus than we actually were. Therefore they sailed on boldly, and so it happened that our ship struck against a bank of sand below the water. If we had not chanced to come up against that little sandbank where we struck, we should have collided with a great mass of sunken rocks, where our ship would have been dashed to pieces, and all of us have been wrecked and drowned.

As soon as our ship struck, a great cry rose from those on board. Everyone was calling out in distress; the sailors and the rest wrung their hands because they were all in fear of being drowned. As soon as I heard the noise I rose from my bed, where I was lying, and went up on deck to join the sailors in the forecastle. As I got there, Brother Raymond, who was a Templar and in command of the crew, said to one of his men: 'Throw down the lead.' No sooner had he done so than he cried out: 'Mercy on us! we're aground!' On hearing this Brother Raymond ripped his clothes right down as far as his belt, and started to tear his beard, at the same time crying: 'We're lost! We're lost!'

At that moment one of my knights, called Jean de Monson – he was the father of Abbot Guillaume of Saint Michel – did me a great kindness by bringing me a lined surcoat of mine, and throwing it over my back without a word, because I had only put on my tunic. I shouted out to him: 'What use to me is this surcoat you've brought me, when we're drowning?' He answered: 'On my soul, sir, I'd rather see all of us drowned, than let you catch some illness from the cold, and get your death by it.'

Our sailors cried: 'Yo ho, galleys, come and take the king!' But out of the four galleys the king had there, not one came near us. In this they acted very wisely; for there were a good eight hundred aboard our ship, and these would have leapt into the galleys to save their lives, and so have made them sink.

The man who had the lead threw it down a second time, and then came back to Brother Raymond to tell him that the ship was no longer aground. Brother Raymond went to tell the king. He found him lying prostrate on the deck in front of the Body of Our Lord on the altar, his arms stretched out to form a cross, barefoot, in his tunic only and with his hair uncombed, like a man who fully expected to be drowned.

As soon as it was light we saw in front of us the rock on which we should have struck if our ship had not come up against the sandbank. During the morning the king summoned the master mariners of all the ships, and they sent four divers down to the bottom of the sea. After their return from diving the king and the master mariners heard them singly, one after the other, so that no diver knew what the others had said. However it was learnt from all four that, in scraping against the sand, over twenty feet of the keel on which our ship was built had been ripped off.

The king summoned the master mariners before us and asked them what they would advise in view of the damage done to the ship. After consulting together, they told the king that they advised him to leave his ship and go aboard another. 'We tell you to do this,' said they, 'because we believe for certain that all the timbers of your ship are out of joint, and so we're afraid that when she gets out on the high seas she'll not be able to stand up against the battering of the waves, and will go to pieces. For, as you know, when you were coming from France one of your ships struck in much the same way; when she met with rough water out at sea she could not stand up against the violence of the waves, and broke up. Everyone on board her perished except one woman and her child, who floated to safety on a piece of the ship.' (I myself can affirm that they were speaking the truth, for I saw the woman and her child in the Comte de Joigny's house, where he had given them shelter for the love of God.)

The king consulted his lord chamberlain Pierre, Gilles le Brun, Constable of France, Gervais d'Escraines, chief caterer to the royal household, the archdeacon of Nicosia, custodian of the royal seal – he was later made a cardinal – and last of all, myself. He asked us what we advised him to do in the matter. We replied that in all worldly concerns one ought to be guided by those who have the most expert knowledge. 'Therefore,' said we, 'we advise you, for our part, to do as these seamen tell you.'

The king turned to the master mariners and said: 'I ask you, on your word of honour, whether, if the ship were your own, and loaded with your own merchandise, you would abandon her?' They replied, all together, that they would not; for they would rather expose their bodies to the risk of drowning than buy a new ship at a cost of four thousand *livres* or more. 'Then why,' said the king, 'do you advise me to leave this ship?' 'Because,' they replied, 'the stakes are not equal. For neither the value of yourself, nor your wife, nor your children, who are with you on this ship can be reckoned in terms of gold or silver. That is why we advise you not to risk your life or theirs.'

'My good sirs,' said the king, 'I have heard your opinion, and the opinion of my own people. Now I tell you mine, which is this: If I leave this ship, there are five hundred people or more on board who will land on this island of Cyprus for fear of danger to themselves – for there's not one of them who doesn't love his life as much as I love mine – and these, perhaps, will never return to their own country. That is why I would rather place myself, my wife, and my children in God's hands, than do such harm to such a great number of people as are here.'

The great harm the king would have done to these people may be seen from what happened to Olivier de Termes, who was in his Majesty's ship. He was one of the boldest men I have ever seen, and had distinguished himself above all the rest of his fellows in the Holy Land. Yet he did not dare to stay with us for fear of drowning, and so remained in Cyprus. Here he found so many obstacles in his way that he did not manage to rejoin the king till a year and a half later; and that although he was a man of wealth and position who could easily have paid for his passage. Just think how people of lesser rank, with not enough money to pay for their journey home, would have fared, when such a man was so greatly hindered!

No sooner were we out of this danger, from which God had delivered us, than we ran into another. The wind, which had driven us on to the coast of Cyprus, where we might easily have drowned, now began to blow so hard and with such violence that it forced us back upon the island once more. The sailors threw out their anchors to counteract the wind, but could not manage to stop the ship till they had thrown out five. It became necessary to take down the sides of the king's cabin on the upper deck, and no one dared to remain up there for fear the wind might sweep him off into the sea. Just at that moment, as Gilles le Brun and I were lying down in the king's own room, the queen opened the door, thinking to find her husband inside. I asked her what she was looking for. She told me she had come to speak to the king, and ask him to make a vow to God, or to His saints, to go on some pilgrimage so that the Lord might deliver us from the peril in which we were; for the sailors had said we were all in danger of drowning. 'Madam,' I said to her, 'promise to make a journey to the shrine of Saint Nicholas at Varangeville, and I will stand surety for him that God will bring you back to France, together with the king and your children.' 'I would do so very willingly, seneschal,' she replied, 'but the king has such a curious temper that if he knew I had made that promise without his knowledge he would never let me go.'

'At all events,' said I, 'there is one thing you can do: you can promise that if God brings you back to France, you will offer a ship of silver, worth five marks, for the king, yourself, and your three children. Then I guarantee that God will bring you back to France; for I myself made a vow to Saint Nicholas that if he saved us from the peril we were in last night, I would go from Joinville, on foot and unshod, to visit his shrine at Varangeville.' The queen replied that, as for the silver ship worth five marks, she would promise it to Saint Nicholas, and I was to stand surety for him. I told her I would gladly do so. Then she went off, but did not stay away long. She soon came back and said to me: 'Saint Nicholas has saved us from our present peril, for the wind has fallen.'

When the queen – may God show her mercy! – had come back to France, she had the silver ship made for her in Paris. In it were figures of herself, the king, and their three children, all in silver. The same metal was used for the sailors, the mast, the rudder, and the rigging of the ship, while all the sails were sewn with silver thread. The queen told me it had cost a hundred *livres* to make. When it was ready she sent the ship to me at Joinville, so that I might have it taken to the chapel of Saint Nicholas; which I did. I saw it still there in his chapel when we were escorting the present king's sister to Haguenau for her marriage to the Emperor of Germany's son.

Now let us return to our main theme and continue the story. After we had escaped from these two perils, the king sat down on the bulwarks of the ship and, telling me to sit at his feet, said to me: 'You know, seneschal, God has manifested His great power quite plainly to us, in that one of His little winds – not any of the four major ones – has come near to drowning the king of France, his wife and children, and all his company. We are therefore bound to show our gratitude and give Him thanks for delivering us from such peril.

'The saints,' he added, 'tell us that when people are called upon to undergo such trials, or are struck down by some grave disease, or subjected to violent persecution, these are to be regarded as warnings, or threats, from our Lord and Saviour. For just as He says to those who have recovered from some serious illness: "See how I might have brought about your death, if such had been my will," even so He could now say to us: "You see how I might have drowned you, if I had willed you should die."

'Therefore,' the king went on, 'we ought to look within ourselves to see if there is anything in us which displeases our Lord, and on account of which He has so terrified us; and if we find anything in us to offend Him, we must instantly cast it out. For if we do otherwise after this warning He has given us, He will punish us with death, or with some other great calamity, which will harm us body and soul.

'Seneschal,' added the king, 'the saint says: "Lord God, why dost Thou threaten us? For if Thou destroyest us all, it will not make Thee any the poorer; nor wilt Thou be any the richer if Thou dost preserve us. From this we may see," says the saint, "that these warnings God sends us are not given either to increase His profit, nor to save Himself from loss; but He sends them solely out of His great love, to awaken us, so that we may have a clear sense of our shortcomings, and purge our hearts of all that is displeasing to Him." So let us do this,' said the king, 'and we shall be acting wisely.'

After taking in a supply of drinking water and such other things as we required, we left the island of Cyprus, and sailed to another island called Lampedusa, where we caught a great number of rabbits. We found there an old hermitage among the rocks, with a garden which the hermits who had lived there long ago had laid out. It was planted with olive trees, fig trees, and vines, and other trees and bushes of various kinds. A stream that rose from a spring ran through the garden. The king and all the rest of us went to the bottom of the garden, where we found, in the first cave we came to, an oratory with whitewashed walls that contained a terracotta cross. On entering the second cave we found two bodies of dead men from which the flesh had rotted. Their ribs still held together, and the bones of the hands were on their breasts. Their bodies had been laid towards the east, in the same way as those that are consigned to earth.

When we got back to our ship we found that one of our sailors was missing; our captain thought he must have remained on the island to be a hermit. So Nicolas de Soisi, who was the king's chief sergeant, left three bags of biscuits so that the man might find them and have something to sustain him.

After we had left Lampedusa we came in sight of a great island in the middle of the sea. It was called Pantalaria, and was inhabited by Saracens who were subject to the King of Sicily and the King of Tunis. The queen begged the king to send three galleys there to get fruit for her children. The king consented, and ordered the captains of the galleys to go there, and be ready to rejoin him as soon as his ship passed before the island. The galleys made their way there and entered a little harbour; but it so happened that when the king's ship passed in front of the haven there was no sign of them.

The sailors began to murmur among themselves. Thereupon the king had all the crews summoned before him, and asked them what they thought had happened. They said it seemed to them that the Saracens had captured the king's people and their galleys. 'But,' said they, 'we strongly advise your Majesty not to wait for them. For you are now between the kingdoms of Sicily and Tunis, neither of which have any love for you. But if you'll let us sail on, we'll get you out of danger before morning; for by that time we shall have passed through this strait.'

'Indeed,' said the king, 'I've no intention of taking your advice, and leaving my people in the hands of the Saracens without at least doing all in my power to rescue them. So I order you to turn your sails round so that we may attack the enemy.' When the queen heard of this, she began to show great distress, and said: 'Alas! this is all my doing!'

As they were setting the sails of the king's ship and of all the others to catch the shoreward wind, we saw the galleys leaving the island. As soon as they came near the king, he asked the crews why they had stayed so long. They replied that they could not help themselves; the fault lay with certain sons of Paris burghers, six in number, who had lingered in the gardens, eating fruit. It had been impossible to get them off, and they had not wanted to leave them behind. The king ordered the six culprits to be put in the long-boat. At this they began to cry and howl. 'For God's sake, your Majesty,' said they, 'take all we have as ransom, but don't put us where murderers and thieves are stowed, or we'll be for ever disgraced.'

The queen and all of us did what we could to make the king change his mind; but he would not listen to any of us. So all the six were put into the long-boat, and remained there until we came to land. They were in such danger and discomfort that when the sea rose high the waves flew over their heads, and they had to remain sitting all the time for fear the wind might sweep them off into the water. And it served them right; for the harm their greediness had caused us was such that our voyage lasted a whole week longer than it should have done, because the king had made the ships reverse their course.

Before we finally came to land we had another adventure at sea. One of the lay sisters in attendance on the queen was so careless that, after putting her mistress to bed, she took the kerchief the queen had been wearing round her head, and threw it down near the iron stove on which the queen's candle was burning. After this good soul had gone to bed in the cabin where the women slept, below the queen's bedroom, the candle went on burning till its flame was low enough to set the kerchief alight, and from there the fire passed to the cloths that covered the queen's clothing.

The queen woke to find her cabin all in flames. She jumped out of bed quite naked, picked up the kerchief, and threw it all burning into the sea, and then extinguished the fire on the cloths. The men in the long-boat behind the ship cried softly: 'Fire! Fire!' I raised my head and saw the kerchief still burning brightly on the calm sea. I put on my tunic as quickly as I could, then went and sat with the sailors.

While I was there my squire, who had been sleeping at the foot of my bed, came and told me that the king was awake, and had asked where I was. 'I told him,' said he, 'that you were in your cabin; and the king said to me; "You're lying."' As we were speaking, the king's clerk, Maître Geoffroy, suddenly came up to us. 'Don't be afraid,' he said to me, 'everything's all right.' 'Maître Geoffroy,' said I, 'go and tell the queen the king is awake, and ask her to go to him to set his mind at rest.'

Next day, the Constable of France, the king's chamberlain, Pierre, and Gervais, master of the royal pantry, said to the king: 'What happened in the night that we heard talk of fire?' I for my part kept silent, but the king replied: 'It was some sort of accident about which the seneschal is apparently more reticent than myself. However, I will tell you how it chanced that we all narrowly escaped from being burnt last night.' So he told them what had happened, and then said to me: 'Seneschal, I order you from now on not to go to bed till you have seen to putting out all fires, except the main fire in the ship's hold. And take note that I shall not go to bed either till you come back to tell me this has been done.' I performed this duty as long as we were at sea; and the king never went to bed till I had gone back to him.

Yet another incident occurred in the course of our voyage. My Lord Dragonet, a gentleman of Provence, was asleep one morning in his ship, which was a good league in advance of ours. On waking up he called to one of his squires and said to him: 'Get something to cover that porthole, for the sun's striking on my face.' The squire, finding that he could not cover the porthole except from the outside, got over the side of the ship. While he was busy putting up a covering, his foot slipped and he fell into the water. As the ship was only a small one it had no long-boat in tow, and had very soon left the squire a long way behind. Those of us who were in the king's ship saw him, but since the man in the water was making no effort to help himself, we took him for some kind of bundle or barrel.

One of the king's galleys fished him out and brought him to our ship, where he told us how the accident had happened. I asked him why he had not tried to help himself, either by swimming or in any other way. He answered that there had been no need or urgency for him to think of doing so because, as soon as he began to fall, he had commended himself to our Lady of Vauvert, and she had held him up by the shoulders from the time he fell until the king's galley had picked him up. In honour of this miracle, I have had it depicted on the walls of my chapel at Joinville, as also in the stained glass windows at Blécourt.

After we had been ten weeks at sea we came to a port some two leagues distant from the castle of Hyères, which belonged to the Comte de Provence, who later became King of Sicily. The queen and all the council agreed that the king ought to disembark there, because the land belonged to his brother. The king however replied that he would not leave his ship till we came to Aigues-Mortes, which was in his own territory. On this point he held out against us on the

Wednesday and the Thursday, nor could we force him to change his mind.

All the ships built at Marseilles have two rudders each attached to a tiller in such a marvellous way that you can turn these vessels to the right hand or to the left as easily as you can turn a horse when ploughing. On the Friday, as the king was sitting on one of these tillers, he called me to him and said: 'What is your opinion, seneschal, about this matter?' 'Sir,' said I, 'you would only deserve it if you met with the same fate as Madame de Bourbon, who would not land at this port, but set off again for Aigues-Mortes, and remained at sea for six whole weeks.'

The king called his council together, and after telling them what I had said asked them what they advised. They were all of the opinion that he ought to land there and then, since it would not be wise on his part if, now that they were out of danger, he exposed himself, his wife, and his children to further perils on the sea. The king accepted the advice we gave him, and this decision greatly delighted the queen.

The king and his family consequently disembarked near the castle of Hyères. While he was waiting there to get horses for his journey back to the Île de France the Abbot of Cluny – who later became Bishop of Olive – presented him with two palfreys which would be well worth five hundred *livres* today, one for the king himself and the other for the queen. After presenting them the abbot said to the king: 'I will come again tomorrow, your Majesty, to speak to you about my personal affairs.' The next day the abbot returned. The king listened at length and very attentively to what he had to say. When he had gone I went to the king and said to him: 'I should like to ask you, if you will allow me, whether you gave a more favourable hearing to the Abbot of Cluny because of the two palfreys he gave you yesterday?' The king thought a long time, and then said: 'To tell you the truth, I did.'

'Your Majesty,' said I, 'do you know why I asked you this question?' 'Why did you?' said he. 'Because,' I replied, 'I earnestly advise your Majesty, when you are back in your own kingdom, to forbid all those of your councillors sworn to administer justice to accept anything from those who have any matter to bring before you. For you may be certain that, if they accept any present, they will listen more willingly and with greater attention to those who have given them something; just as you yourself have done in the case of

the Abbot of Cluny.' The king immediately called his council together and told them what I had said; they answered that the advice
I had given him was good.

The king heard reports of a certain Franciscan named Brother
Hugues, and because of this friar's great reputation he summoned
him so that he might see him and hear him preach. On the day Brother
Hugues came to Hyères we looked along the road by which he was
coming and saw a great crowd of men and women following him on
foot. The king asked him to preach. He began his sermon with
comments on those in monastic orders. 'My lords,' he said, 'I see too
many monks in the king's court, and in his company. In the first place,'
he added, 'I myself am one too many here; and I say this because the
monks here are in no condition to be saved – unless the Holy Scriptures lie to us, which is impossible. For these sacred writings tell us
that a monk cannot live out of his cloister, any more than a fish can
live out of water. If then those monks who are with the king maintain
that the court is a cloister, I can only say to them that it is the largest
cloister I have ever seen, for it extends from this sea-coast to the other;
and if they declare that in such a cloister they can lead a hard life for
the salvation of their souls, I do not believe them. For I tell you that
while I have been with them here I have eaten an abundance of many
kinds of meat, and drunk many strong and sparkling wines of
excellent quality. From this I can confidently affirm that if they had
been in their cloisters, they would not have lived in such ease and
comfort as they now do with the king.'

In the course of his sermon the friar told the king how he should
govern for the good of his people. He ended his address by saying
that he had read the Bible and many works that help to explain it,
but he had never seen, either in Christian or non-Christian writings,
that any kingdom or other dominion was lost, or transferred from
one ruler to another, unless the claims of right and justice had
previously been ignored. 'Therefore,' said he, 'let the king, who is
now returning to his kingdom, take heed so to rule his people in
justice and equity that he may ever be worthy of God's love, and that
God may not take his kingdom from him so long as he lives.'

I said to the king that he ought to keep Brother Hugues in his company as long as ever he could. He told me he had already begged the
friar to stay with him, but for all this he had refused to remain. Then
the king took me by the hand and said: 'Let us both go and plead

with him.' We went to see him, and I said to him: 'Pray do what my lord asks you, sir, and stay with him as long as we are in Provence.' He answered me very angrily: 'Indeed, sir, I shall do no such thing. I shall go where God will love me better than if I were in the king's company.' He stayed one day with us, and left the following morning. I have since heard that he lies buried in the city of Marseilles, and there works many fine miracles.

On the day the king left Hyères he went down from the castle on foot because the hill was too steep. He walked on so far that, not being able to get back to his palfrey, he had to mount on mine. When his own palfrey came up he turned very angrily on Ponce, his squire. After he had given the fellow a good scolding I said to the king: 'Your Majesty, you ought to forgive much to Ponce, your squire; for he has served your grandfather, your father, and yourself.' 'Seneschal,' he replied, 'he has not served us, but we have served him, by allowing him to remain with us in spite of his bad qualities. For King Philip, my grandfather, once told me that we ought to reward our servants, some more, some less, according to the way they have carried out their duties. He also used to say that no one can govern a country well unless he knows how to refuse as boldly and firmly as he knows how to give. I'm telling you these things,' he added, 'because the world is so greedy in its demands that very few people take thought for the salvation of their souls, or the claims of personal honour, provided they can get possession of other people's goods, whether rightfully or wrongfully.'

On his way through the county of Provence the king passed through a city in those parts called Aix, where the body of Mary Magdalene was said to lie buried. We went to look at a very lofty cave in a rock where the saint was reported to have lived as an anchoress for seventeen years. When the king reached Beaucaire, and I saw him on his own land and in his own dominions, I took leave of him, and went off to visit my niece the Dauphine de Vienne, my uncle the Comte de Chalon, and the Comte de Bourgogne, his son.

After staying for a time at Joinville, where I attended to my private affairs, I went to rejoin the king, whom I found at Soissons. He welcomed me with such joy that all who were with him marvelled at it. I found the Comte Jean de Bretagne there, with his wife, the daughter of King Thibaut I of Navarre. She had come to do homage to the king for all such rights as she might have in Champagne.

However, the king adjourned the matter, and referred her, as also King Thibaut II, to a conference being held in Paris, where they might be heard, and justice done to the interested parties.

The King of Navarre and his council came to this conference, as did the Comte de Bretagne. During the proceedings King Thibaut asked for the hand of the king's daughter, the Lady Isabelle, in marriage. Notwithstanding all the things our people of Champagne were saying behind my back, because of the love they had seen the king show me at Soissons, I was not deterred from going to the king to speak to him about this alliance. 'Go and get the Comte de Bretagne to agree,' said the king, 'and then we'll conclude our marriage.' I told him not to let such a consideration make him give up the idea. He replied that he would not on any account have the marriage take place until an agreement had been reached; for no one should ever say that in marrying his children he had deprived his barons of their heritage.

I reported this conversation to Queen Marguerite of Navarre, as also to her son, King Thibaut, and to their council. As soon as they heard what King Louis had said they hastened to come to an agreement. When all the parties concerned had come to terms, the King of France gave his daughter to King Thibaut. The marriage was celebrated at Melun, with full pomp and ceremony. Afterwards King Thibaut went with his bride to Provins, where their entry was welcomed by a great concourse of barons.

CHAPTER 18

The King's Administration of his Realm

AFTER the king's return from oversea he lived with such a disregard
for worldly vanities that he never wore ermine or squirrel fur, nor
scarlet cloth, nor were his stirrups or his spurs gilded. His clothes
were made of camlet or grey woollen cloth; the fur on these and on
the coverings of his bed was either deerskin, hare-skin, or lambskin.
He had such sober tastes in food that he never ordered any special
dish for himself, but took what his cook prepared, and ate whatever
was put before him. He had water mixed with his wine and drank it
from a glass goblet, with more or less water according to the strength
of the wine; he would hold the goblet in his hand while his servants
were preparing the wine behind his table. He always took care to
see that his poor were fed and, after they had eaten, sent money to
be distributed among them.

When minstrels in some nobleman's service arrived with their
viols to entertain him after dinner, the king would always wait till
they had finished singing before he would let grace be said. Then he
would rise, and the priests would stand before him to say grace. On
occasions when we paid him an informal visit, he would sit at the foot
of his bed. If some predicant friar or Franciscan in the company
happened to speak of a book he might like to hear read the king
would say: 'Don't read it to me. There's no book so good after meals
as free and friendly conversation, when everybody says just what it
pleases him to say.' Whenever strangers of some importance came to
dine with the king, they always found him the best of company.

I will now speak to you of his wisdom. There were times indeed
when men were heard to declare that no one on his council was so
wise as the king himself. That this was so was apparent from the fact
that when anyone consulted him on a certain matter he would not
say: 'I will take advice on this question'; but if he saw the right
solution clearly and plainly he would answer without reference to
his council, and at once. That, so I have heard, is how he answered all
the prelates of his realm in the case of a petition they once presented
to him.

On this occasion the Bishop of Auxerre addressed him on behalf of all his fellow prelates. 'Your Majesty,' he said, 'the archbishops and bishops here present have charged me to tell you that the honour of Christendom is declining in your hands. It will decline still further unless you give some thought to it, because no man stands in fear of excommunication at this present time. We therefore require your Majesty to command your bailiffs and your other officers of the law to compel all persons who have been under sentence of excommunication for a year and a day to make their peace with the Church.' The king replied, without taking any advice, that he would willingly command his bailiffs and other officers to constrain such persons in the manner desired, provided he were given full knowledge of the sentence in each case, so that he might judge whether it was just or not.

After consulting together the prelates informed the king that they would not give him such knowledge, since this was solely a matter for the ecclesiastical courts. The king replied that he in his turn would not give them knowledge of such matters as fell within his jurisdiction, nor order his officers to compel all excommunicated persons to obtain absolution, irrespective of whether sentence of excommunication had been rightly or wrongly pronounced. 'For if I did so,' he added, 'I should be acting contrary to God's laws and the principles of justice. I will give you as an instance the following case: the bishops in his province held the Comte de Bretagne under sentence of excommunication for seven years, at the end of which he obtained absolution from the court of Rome. Now if I had used constraint on him at the end of the first year, I should have been doing him wrong.'

It happened, after we had returned from oversea, that the monks of Saint Urbain elected two abbots. Bishop Pierre de Châlons – may God have mercy on his soul! – drove them both out, and gave the abbot's crozier with his blessing to Jean de Mymeri, whom he appointed to that post. I would not acknowledge this man as abbot, because he had wronged the Abbot Geoffroy, who had appealed against him, and taken his case to the court of Rome. I held the abbey so long in my hands that Geoffroy won the crozier, and the man on whom the bishop had bestowed it did not get it after all; but while the dispute lasted the bishop kept me under a ban of excommunication. That is why, at a conference held in Paris, Bishop Pierre de Châlons and I quarrelled violently with each other, as did the Comtesse Marguerite de Flandre with the Archbishop of Rheims, whom she accused of not telling the truth.

At a conference which followed shortly after, all the prelates begged the king to come and speak with them in private. On his return from his interview with these dignitaries his Majesty came to us, who were waiting for him in the judgement-hall, and told us, laughing heartily, of the trouble he had had with the prelates. First of all, the Archbishop of Rheims had said to him: 'Your Majesty, what are you going to give me in exchange for the wardship of Saint Remi of Rheims, which you are taking from me? For by the relics here before us I swear I would not, for all the kingdom of France, have such a sin on my conscience as you have on yours.' 'By the relics here before us,' the king had replied, 'I swear that with your covetous character you would do as much for Compiègne alone. So now one of us two is forsworn!'

'Next,' said the king, 'the Bishop of Chartres demanded of me that I should give him back whatever of his I had in my possession. I told him I should not do so until such time as he had paid me my dues. I further pointed out that although he had done me homage with his hands in mine, yet he was not dealing either well or loyally with me in trying to deprive me of rights I had inherited.

'The Bishop of Châlons,' continued the king, 'now said to me: "What does your Majesty propose to do for me concerning my Lord of Joinville and that poor monk from whom he is withholding the Abbey of Saint Urbain?"' 'My lord bishop,' the king had replied, 'you and your fellow prelates have settled it among you that no excommunicated person is to be heard in a lay court. I have gathered from a letter, sealed with thirty-two seals, that you yourself are under such a ban. Therefore I will not listen to you until you have got yourself absolved.' I am telling you all this so that you may see quite clearly how the king could handle any business he had to settle by himself, and with no other aid than his own good sense.

After I had arranged matters for the Abbot Geoffroy of Saint Urbain he returned me evil for good by lodging an appeal against me. He gave our saintly king to understand that his abbey was under royal jurisdiction. I asked the king to investigate the matter, so as to establish without doubt whether it was in his custody or in mine. 'Your Majesty,' said the abbot, 'please God you shall do no such thing; but rather arrange that the point at issue between us shall be submitted to arbitration in a court of law; for those of us to whom the abbey belongs by inheritance would rather have it in your jurisdiction than in his.' The king said to me: 'Are they telling the truth when they say that the abbey is in my custody?' 'Certainly not, your Majesty,' said I, 'it is in mine.'

Then the king said to the abbot: 'It may be that the abbey is yours by inheritance, but that does not mean you have a right to claim it is under your sole control. Indeed, from what you say yourself and from what the seneschal tells me, the question of custody is a matter between him and me alone. Therefore, in spite of anything you may have said, I shall not refrain from taking steps to arrive at the truth of the matter myself. For if I compelled my Lord of Joinville to plead at law, I should be doing wrong to him, who is my vassal, since I should place his right at the mercy of the common court, whereas he now offers me, as his lord, full opportunity of arriving at the truth.' So the king himself instituted an inquiry, and as soon as the truth was known, he gave me full custody of the abbey, with sealed documents establishing my right.

Our saintly king worked so long and so effectively that he persuaded the King of England to come to France with his wife and children to negotiate a peace between their two countries. The members of our king's council were strongly opposed to making such a peace, and said to him: 'We are greatly surprised to find your Majesty ready to give the King of England so large a part of the territory which you and your predecessors have won from him, and which he has forfeited by his own misconduct. Now it seems to us that if you believe you have no right to this land, you are not making full restitution unless you restore all that you and your predecessors have conquered. If on the other hand you believe you have a right to it, then it seems to us that whatever you restore is so much loss to yourself.'

To this the saintly king replied: 'My Lords, I am convinced that the King of England's predecessors were justly dispossessed of all the land I now hold by right of conquest. But as for the land I am giving him, I do not regard it as something I am bound to surrender either to himself or his heirs, but rather as a means of establishing a bond of love between my children and his, who are first cousins. Moreover, it seems to me that what I give him is to good purpose, since he has not hitherto been my vassal, but will now do me homage as his lord.'

CHAPTER 19

A Fatal Crusade
1267–70

ONE Lent, some time after the incidents I have been speaking of, King Louis happened to summon all his barons to Paris. I excused myself from going on account of a quartan fever from which I was suffering at the time, and begged his Majesty to let me off this journey. However, he sent me word that he insisted on my coming, because there were good physicians in Paris who well knew how to cure such ailments.

So I went to Paris. But when I arrived there on the eve of Lady Day in March, I found no one, neither the queen nor any other, who could tell me why I had been summoned by the king. Now it happened, as God willed, that I fell asleep during matins; and it seemed to me, while I slept, that I saw the king on his knees before an altar. It also seemed to me that several prelates, robed as for a service, were vesting him with a red chasuble of Rheims serge.

After seeing this vision I sent for Guillaume, my priest, who was very wise, and told him what I had dreamt. 'My lord,' he said to me, 'you will see that the king will take the cross tomorrow.' I asked him why he thought so, and he told me it was because of the dream I had had; for the chasuble of red serge signified the Cross, which was red from the blood our Lord had shed from His side, His feet, and His hands. 'And because the chasuble is of Rheims serge,' he added, 'it means that the Crusade will be of little profit, as you will see if God grants you to live so long.'

After hearing mass at the Madeleine in Paris I went to the king's chapel, and found him there. He had gone up to the platform where the relics were kept and was having the fragment of the true Cross taken down. As he was coming down again, two knights, who were members of his council, started to speak to each other. 'Never believe me again,' said one, 'if the king doesn't take the cross here in this chapel.' 'If he does,' replied the other, 'it will be one of the saddest days France has ever seen. For if we don't take the cross ourselves, we shall lose the king's favour; and if we do, we shall be out of favour with God, because we shall not be taking it for His sake, but for fear of displeasing the king.'

Now it so happened that on the following day the king took the cross, and his three sons with him. And afterwards the Crusade turned out to be of little profit, just as my priest had foretold.

The King of France and the King of Navarre both pressed me very earnestly to take the cross. To this I replied that while I was in the service of God and of the king oversea, and since I had returned home, his Majesty's serjeants and the King of Navarre's had so ruined and impoverished my people that there would never be a time when they and I could possibly be worse off. I told them that if I wished to do what was pleasing to God I should remain here to help and defend the people on my estates. For if, while seeing quite clearly that it would be to their detriment, I put my life in danger by venturing on this pilgrimage of the Cross, I should anger our Lord, who gave His own life to save His people.

I considered that all those who had advised the king to go on this expedition committed mortal sin. For at that time the state of the country was such that there was perfect peace throughout the kingdom, and between France and her neighbours, while ever since King Louis went away the state of the kingdom has done nothing but go from bad to worse.

It was besides a great sin on the part of those who advised the king to go, seeing that he was physically so weak that he could neither bear to be drawn in a coach, nor to ride – so weak, in fact, that he let me carry him in my arms from the Comte d'Auxerre's house, where I went to take leave of him, to the abbey of the Franciscans. And yet, weak as he was, if he had remained in France he might have lived for some time longer, and have done much good, and carried out many fine projects.

I will not attempt to describe the king's journey to Tunis, nor tell you of anything that happened, because – thank God! – I did not take part in it, and have no wish to put in my book anything of which I am not absolutely certain. So I will speak only of our saintly king, and tell you how, after he had landed at Tunis, in front of the castle of Carthage, he fell a victim to enteric fever, and his eldest son Philippe was laid low by a quartan ague, aggravated by the same complaint as his father. The king took to his bed, and felt that he must shortly pass out of this world into the next.

He sent for his son the Prince Philippe and commanded him, as if he were making his will, to observe all the instructions he was leaving him. These you can now find set down in French,[1] as they were written, so it is said, with the king's own saintly hand:

My dear son, the first thing I would teach you is to set your heart to love God; for without that no one can be saved. Keep yourself from doing anything that is displeasing to God, that is to say, from mortal sin. Rather than commit such a terrible offence you must on the contrary be ready to suffer every kind of torment.

If God sends you adversity, accept it patiently, and give thanks for it to our Saviour; consider that you have deserved it, and hope that He will make it turn to your advantage. If, on the other hand, God sends you prosperity, then thank Him humbly, so that you do not become worse from pride, or any other cause, when such a blessing should make you better. For we ought not to use God's gifts to fight against Him.

Go often to confession, and choose for confessor a wise and upright man who knows how to teach you what you ought, and what you ought not, to do. Always behave yourself in such a way that your confessor and your friends will not be afraid of reproving you when you have done wrong. Listen to the services of Holy Church reverently and devoutly, and without chattering. Pray to God with your heart as well as your lips, and most of all during mass at the moment of the consecration. Let your heart be tender and full of pity towards the poor, the unhappy, and the afflicted; and comfort and help them to the utmost of your power.

Maintain the good customs of your realm and abolish the bad ones. Do not be greedy in your demands on your people, or impose heavy taxes on them except in a case of emergency.

If anything lies heavy on your heart speak of it to your confessor or to some wise and discerning man who has not too glib a tongue. In this way your trouble will be easier to bear.

Take care to have around you people, whether clerics or laymen, who are wise, upright, and loyal, and free from covetousness. Talk with them often, but shun and fly from association with the wicked. Listen willingly to the Word of God, and keep it in your heart; be eager to obtain prayers and indulgences. Love all that is good and beneficial; hate all that is evil wherever you find it.

Let no one be so bold as to say in your presence anything that may entice and move men to sin, nor do anything so presumptuous as to speak evil of another behind his back in order to belittle him. Nor must you allow anything in disparagement of God and His saints to be said before you. Render thanks to God continually for all the good things

[1] Joinville probably refers to the *Vie de Saint Louis* by Guillau me de Nangis.

he has given you, so that you may be considered worthy to receive further benefits.

In order to deal justly and equitably with your subjects, be straight-forward and firm, turning neither to the right hand nor to the left, but always following what is just, and upholding the cause of the poor till the truth be made clear. If anyone brings a suit against you, make full inquiry until you know all the truth; for then your counsellors, having the facts before them, will be able to give sentence more confidently, whether for or against you.

If through your own act, or the act of your predecessors, you hold anything which should belong to another, and his right to it is proved beyond question, restore it to him without delay. If on the other hand there is some doubt about the matter, have it investigated, promptly and thoroughly, by wise and knowledgeable men.

You must give your attention to ensuring that your subjects live peaceably and uprightly under your rule. Above all maintain the good cities and communes of your realm in the same condition and with the same privileges as they enjoyed under your predecessors. If there is any-thing in them that needs reform, do what is necessary to set it right; and keep them ever in your favour and your love. For because of the wealth and power of your great cities not only your own subjects, and especially your great lords and barons, but also the people of other countries will fear to undertake anything against you.

Love and honour all persons in the service of Holy Church, and see that no one takes away or diminishes the gifts and donations made to them by your predecessors. It is related of King Philip, my grandfather, that one of his councillors once said to him that the servants of Holy Church were doing him much wrong and injury, in that they deprived him of his rights and trespassed on his authority, and that it was a great marvel that he allowed it to be so. The good king answered that this might well be true, but after considering the benefits God had bestowed on him and His many gracious acts of kindness, he thought it better to forego some of his rights than embark on any dispute with the people of Holy Church.

Honour and respect your father and mother, and obey their com-mands. Bestow the benefices of Holy Church on persons of upright character and a clean life; and do this on the advice of good and honourable men.

Beware of undertaking a war against any Christian prince without careful deliberation; if it has to be undertaken see that you do no harm to Holy Church, or to persons who have done you no injury. In the case of wars and dissensions arising among your subjects, make peace between the disputants as soon as ever you can.

Take special care to have good bailiffs and provosts, and often inquire of them, as also of people attached to your household, how they conduct themselves, and whether any of them are addicted to the vice of excessive covetousness, or untruthfulness, or shifty behaviour. Endeavour to drive out of your land all hateful and unrighteous practices, and in particular do all in your power to root out evil swearing and heresy. Take care to keep the expenses of your household within reasonable limits.

Finally, my very dear son, have masses sung for my soul and prayers said for me throughout your kingdom; and give me a full and special share in all the good you do. My own dear child, I give you all the blessings a good father can give to his son. May the blessed Trinity and all the saints keep and defend you from all evils; and may God grant you grace to do His will always, so that He may be honoured through you, and that you and I, after this mortal life is ended, may both be with Him together, and join in praising Him to all eternity. Amen.

When the good king had given these instructions to his son, the illness from which he suffered began to take stronger hold on him. He asked for the sacraments of Holy Church, and received them with a clear mind and in full possession of his faculties, as was evident from the fact that while the priests were anointing him and reciting the seven special psalms he repeated each verse after them in turn.

I have heard his son, the Comte d'Alençon, say that when the king was near to death he called on the saints to help and protect him, and specially on Saint James, reciting, as he invoked him, the prayer of this apostle which begins: '*Esto Domine*, etc.' – that is to say, 'O Lord be the sanctifier and guardian of Thy people.' Then he called to his aid Saint Denis, patron saint of France, reciting his prayer, which is to this effect: 'Lord God, grant that we may so despise the prosperity of this world that we stand in no fear of adversity.'

I also heard the Comte d'Alençon – on whom God have mercy – relate how after this his father called on Saint Genevieve. Next, the saintly king asked to be laid on a bed covered with ashes, where he crossed his hands on his breast, and looking towards heaven, rendered up his spirit to our Creator. This was at the same hour of the day that the Son of God died on the cross for the world's salvation.

It is a pious duty, and a fitting one, to weep for the death of this saintly prince, who ruled his kingdom and kept guard over it so righteously and loyally, who was so generous in giving alms there, and who established there so many noble foundations. And as the scribe who, when producing a manuscript, illuminates it with gold and azure, so did our king illuminate his realm with the many fine abbeys he built there, the great number of hospitals, and the houses for Predicants, Franciscans, and other religious orders, of which I have already told you.

On the day after the feast of Saint Bartholomew the Apostle, in the year of our Lord 1270, the good King Louis passed out of this world. His bones were put in a casket and taken to France, where they were laid to rest at Saint Denis, the place he had chosen for his burial. At this tomb in which he was buried God has since then performed many fine miracles in his honour, and by his merit.

CHAPTER 20

Canonization of Saint Louis
1282–98

SOME years after the death of King Louis, at the urgent request of the reigning King of France, and by command of the Pope, the Archbishop of Rouen and Brother Jean de Samois – who has since become a bishop – came to the church of Saint Denis in the Île de France, and remained there for some considerable time to make inquisition into the life, the works, and miracles of this saintly king. I was summoned to meet them, and they kept me there two days. After they had questioned me and certain others their findings were set down and sent to the Court of Rome. The Pope and the Cardinals carefully scrutinized the evidence they had received and on the grounds of what they saw there they gave the king his rightful due by placing him among the number of the confessors.

At this there was joy, and rightly so, throughout the whole kingdom of France. It has brought, moreover, great honour to those of the good king's line who are like him in doing well, and equal dishonour to those descendants of his who will not follow him in good works. Great dishonour, I repeat, to those of his line who choose to do evil; for men will point a finger at them and say that the saintly king, from whom they have sprung, would have shrunk from acting so ill.

After the good news had come from Rome, the King of France decreed that on the day after the Feast of Saint Bartholomew (25 August 1298) the holy body should be lifted from its grave. After this had been done the first to bear it were the then Archbishop of Rheims – on whom God have mercy – together with my nephew, at the time Archbishop of Lyons. Afterwards it was borne by many others, archbishops as well as bishops, more than I can name, and finally lifted on to a platform that had been specially erected.

At the ceremony Brother Jean de Samois preached the sermon. Among other noble deeds our saintly king had performed he recalled one of the fine actions to which I had testified on oath, and of which I had been witness. 'So that you may see,' said he, 'that the king was the most loyal and upright man of his time, I will tell you that he was such a man of his word that he honoured an agreement he had made with the Saracens, even though he had made it by word of mouth only, and if he had failed to keep his promise, would have saved himself ten thousand *livres* or more.' He told them the whole story as I have told it in an earlier part of this book. After relating it he added: 'Do not think I am lying to you, for I see before me the very man who bore witness to this act, and did so on oath.'

After the sermon was ended the king and his brothers bore the saint's body back to the church, with the help of others of their family to whom such an honour was due. And indeed a great honour has been done them, if only they prove themselves worthy of it, as I have said above. Let us pray to the sainted king to ask God to give us what is needful for our souls and bodies. Amen!

I will tell you of certain other things that are to the honour of our saintly king, as for instance of what I once saw as I lay asleep in bed. It seemed to me, in my dream, that I saw the king standing in front of my chapel at Joinville. He was, so I thought, marvellously joyful and glad at heart, and I myself was very glad to see him in my castle. 'My lord,' I said to him, 'when you go away from here I will make a place for you in a house I own in a village of mine called Chevillon.' 'My lord of Joinville,' he answered laughing, 'I have no wish to go from here so soon.'

When I awoke I started to think. It seemed to me that it would be pleasing both to God and to the king if I lodged him in my chapel. This I did, for I built him an altar, to the honour of God and in his own honour, and there masses shall be sung in reverent memory of him for ever. I have created a perpetual endowment so that this may be done. I have told all this to my lord King Louis (of Navarre), who has inherited his name. It seems to me he would do what is agreeable both to God and to our sainted King Louis, if he procured some genuine relics of the holy body, and sent them to the above-named chapel of Saint Laurent at Joinville, so that those who in the future come to the sainted king's altar, may worship there with still greater devotion.

I wish to make known to all that I myself actually saw and heard a great part of what I have told you here concerning the saintly king. Another considerable portion of it is based on what I found in a certain book, written in French, and which I have incorporated in this chronicle. I am drawing your attention to this so that those who hear this book read may have full confidence in the truth of what it says I saw and heard. As for the other things recorded here, I offer no guarantee of their truth, because I did not witness them myself.

This work was completed in the month of October, in the year of our Lord 1309.

Notes on the Translation

THIS version of the chronicles is based on the text as given in (a) Villehardouin, *La Conquête de Constantinople*, edited by Edmond Faral (2 vols., Paris, 1938-9), and (b) Joinville, *Histoire de Saint Louis*, edited by Natalis de Wailly (Paris, 1874). In both these editions a translation closely modelled on the Old French text is printed side by side with the original.

As they appear in manuscript, both chronicles run continuously without any headings. The editors mentioned above give each little episode a heading, though M. Faral also groups his sections under a more general title. My own division of these works into chapters with headings to indicate the main course of the story is, I venture to think, sufficient to give the reader an idea of the contents.

In dealing with names and titles, I have departed from the common – though not always consistent – practice of historians to anglicize those that have a possible (if sometimes archaic) English equivalent, and, with only a few exceptions, have given them their native form. Not only does this seem to me more in line with modern usage (e.g. Henri de Régnier, King Baudouin, the Comte de Paris, etc.), but there are also certain indications in the chronicles – as in the case of Joinville's two uncles, Villehardouin and his nephew, the three Ibelin brothers, etc. – that the place of origin with the particle 'de' was already in use as a family name.

For the general background of this period I have found Sir Steven Runciman's encyclopedic *History of the Crusades* particularly useful. Details about the two chroniclers have been mainly gathered (a) from M. Faral's informative introduction to his edition of the earlier work, supplemented by reference to such works as M. Longnon's *Recherches sur la vie de Geoffroy de Villehardouin*, and (b) from M. Delaborde's *Jean de Joinville et les Sieurs de Joinville* and M. Didot's *Études sur la vie et les travaux de Jean, Sieur de Joinville*.

Glossary

1. Naval and military terms

CASTLE: a wooden tower erected on the deck of a ship. Medieval
warships had two of these, one fore, one aft, to protect the men and
command a better view of the enemy's deck. The term survives, with
a different meaning, in *forecastle*.

CAT-HOUSE: a movable pent-house on wheels, flanked by wooden
towers.

MANGONEL: a military machine constructed on the principle of the
catapult, for casting stones, etc., by means of a gigantic sling.
Gunpowder as a propelling agent was not in use at the time of the
Crusades.

PETRARY: a machine of much the same type and purpose as a mangonel.

QUARREL: a short, heavy, square-headed bolt or arrow.

SERGEANT: a tenant on a nobleman's estate below the rank of a knight
who owed military service to his lord by reason of the land he held
from him. Such men, with the knights, made up the main body of
the troops. The term *soldier*, i.e. a man who serves in the army for pay,
would not be a proper equivalent.

TURCOPLES: Syrians of mixed parentage (Turco-Greek) employed as
auxiliaries in the Christian army.

2. Official titles

ADVOCATE: the chief magistrate of a city or district (e.g. of Béthune).

BAILIFF: an official with administrative authority under the Sheriff. His
district was called a *bailiwick*.

CHAMBERLAIN: steward to a king or a great lord.

CHANCELLOR: official secretary to the king or a great lord.

CHÂTELAIN: governor or constable of a castle. The Châtelain de
Coucy had also some reputation as a poet.

CLERK: according to the context: a scholar, an aspirant to the priest-
hood, or a cleric.

CONSTABLE: chief officer of the royal household, with special military
functions, or warden of a royal fortress or castle.

IMAM: the officiating priest of a Mohammedan mosque.

MAÎTRE: form of address used in reference to theologians (e.g. Maître
Robert de Sorbon). In France today applied to lawyers, especially
barristers.

357

MARSHAL: see Introduction, p. 10.

PROVOST: chief magistrate and administrator of law and order in a town (as once in Scotland).

SENESCHAL: see Introduction, p. 19. for seneschal of a province. The seneschal of a town was in charge of civil affairs as the constable was responsible for the military side.

SERJEANT: an official of the Crown whose main duty was to arrest offenders against the law.

VIDAME: an official who held lands from a bishop, and acted as his representative and defender in temporal matters.

3. Towns and localities

The correct form of places mentioned in the chronicles has been checked by reference to Faral, Wailly, and other authorities. Most of these places are marked on the maps at the end of this book. A few comments are necessary.

ES SUR and SAIDA: Arabic names of cities more commonly referred to by historians as Tyre and Sidon. In view, however, of Joinville's explicit statement that Tyre and Sidon were names given in the Bible to places known in his day as Sur and Sayette, the Arabic form is given in this translation.

HOMS: Arabic name of a town known to the Romans as Emessa. Although Joinville gives his own version of the Latin name, the local one has been adopted as more usual in histories of the Crusades.

ÎLE DE FRANCE: a territory in the centre of Northern France which formed the most important part of the royal domains. Paris was its chief city and the seat of government. In distinguishing it from other provinces over which the king had no direct control the chroniclers call this territory France, but apply this name to the whole country when the 'barons of France' are united by a common purpose.

KIBOTOS: a town in Asia Minor called Civetot by English Crusaders and Chivetot by the French.

MOREA: a peninsula at the southern extremity of Greece, also called the Peloponnesus.

NEGROPONT: also called the I. of Euboea. No town of the same name is marked on ancient or modern maps of Greece. It was most probably its principal port Chalcis, which lies on the western shores of the island.

NILE: while Joinville gives the two main branches of the Nile correctly, he makes a mistake in placing the scene of operations between the Rosetta, or western arm of the river, and the one that flows far east of it to Damietta. Fighting actually took place on the island between the Damietta branch and the Bagh-as Saghir, a smaller stream that left

the main river just below Mansourah and ran past Ashmun-Tannah
to Lake Manzaleh, east of Damietta. Joinville's ignorance of the
source of the Nile is natural enough, since this was only discovered
in the last century.

STRAITS OF SAINT GEORGE: name given at this time to the whole
stretch of water from the Aegean Sea up to the Black Sea, including
the Dardanelles, the Sea of Marmora, and the Bosporus.

UNIDENTIFIED PLACES: these all occur in Villehardouin's work, and
are perforce left as he gives them. They include two castles: *La
Blanche*, near Philippi, and *Moniac*, in the valley of the Arda; and four
towns: *Fraim* and *Rodestuic*, both on the Arda, *Blisme*, on the northern
borders of the Empire, a day's journey from Beroë, and *Eului* in
Wallachia.

WALLACHIA: a country in Eastern Europe, north of the Empire of
Constantinople, inhabited by a Latin-speaking race, called Wallachians or Vlachs by the Greeks, but styling themselves *Roumans*,
and claiming descent from Roman colonists. The name Roumania,
given at a much later date to the kingdom formed by the fusion of
Wallachia with the neighbouring principality of Moldavia, would
keep alive this connexion with Rome. In 1186 the Wallachians, led
by Johanitza and his two brothers, repudiated their already loose
allegiance to the Byzantine Emperor Isaac, and allying themselves
with the Bulgarians established a Bulgaro-Wallachian kingdom.

ZARA: On the eastern shores of the Adriatic. The capital city of
Dalmatia, which at that time was combined with Croatia and
Slavonia. Its possession had been a constant source of dispute between
the Venetians and the Hungarians, and it had changed hands frequently since it first sought protection from the Venetians in 1000.
Since its conquest in 1202 by the Venetians, who finally bought it
from Hungary in 1409, it has been subject to many changes of
ownership.

4. *Peoples and communities*

ASSASSINS: the followers of the Old Man of the Mountain, were
so-called because they were addicted to the drug 'hashish', which
kept them in the requisite state of intoxication to perform their
atrocious deeds. The modern meaning of the word is derived from
their habit of committing violent murders.

BÉGUINES: members of certain lay sisterhoods originating in the Low
Countries in the twelfth century. They led a religious life, but took
no vows, and were free to leave the order and marry.

COMANS (or CUMANS): a Turkish people established in Moldavia, to
the east of Wallachia.

FRANKS: originally the name of the Germanic people who conquered Gaul in the sixth century, it was later applied by Levantines and Moslems to all peoples of Western Europe. Villehardouin uses it to distinguish the French and German Crusaders from the Italians of Venice, but in separate reference to his own people speaks of them as the French.

HOSPITALLERS (the Knights of the Order of Saint John of Jerusalem): an order of military monks, founded in 1048. Originally keepers of a hospital for the benefit of poor pilgrims to the Holy Land, the Hospitallers expanded to form a military organization for the defence of Christendom in the East.

KHORASMINS (or KHWARISMIAN TURKS): natives of the Persian province of Khorassan. In the first quarter of the thirteenth century one of their kings, Mohammed-Shah, had made himself master of an empire that stretched from Kurdistan to the Aral Sea. According to Wailly, the 'Emperor of Persia' mentioned by Joinville in his report on the Tartars was either this king or his son, Jelal ad-Din, both of whom were defeated (1220–1) by the Mongol emperor, the great Jenghiz-Khan. In 1244 another Khorasmian king, whom Joinville calls the Emperor Barbaquan (a possible distortion of his real name) led his army into Syria, and after ravaging the land and sacking Jerusalem advanced, in company with the Egyptian forces, to attack Gaza. Joinville's description of the disastrous battle that followed is fairly in accordance with the facts, except that he makes it take place before Jaffa. In his account of the subsequent defeat and annihilation of the Khorasmian army all that can be verified is that the Sultan of Homs was one of the leaders on the opposing side.

LATINS: name applied (in opposition to Greeks) to European peoples speaking a language derived from Latin, and more particularly, in Villehardouin's chronicle, to Spaniards, Portuguese, and Italians settled in Eastern Europe or Asia Minor.

TARTARS: a people inhabiting the north-east corner of what we now call China, and some of whose descendants may still be found among the Russian Tartars. Joinville's report of the mission to their 'great King' is often inaccurate. The French envoys, instead of starting from Cyprus in 1248, left Acre in 1253, shortly before King Louis returned to France. Nor in fact did they approach the Tartars, a people who for half a century had been in subjection to their Mongol conquerors, and were consequently not important enough to be sought as allies. What appears to have actually happened was that they first visited the great grandson of Jenghiz-Khan, a Mongol prince who was said to have been converted to Christianity. Not finding him powerful enough to conclude an alliance with their king, the envoys travelled on across Asia to the court of the Great Khan Batu, supreme ruler of the Mongol Empire, and the prince's father. This being understood, it should be said, in fairness to Joinville, that although the mixed horde of tribesmen which swept across Asia and invaded Eastern Europe also included Turks and Mongols, to the men of his day all such Asiatics were known as Tartars.

TEMPLARS: a military and religious order, founded about 1118 for the protection of the Holy Sepulchre and pilgrims to the Holy Land. As may be gathered from Joinville's chronicle, it became very rich and powerful. In the end, whether through envy or some better motive, accusations of heresy and evil practices were laid against its members, and after many confessions of guilt had been extracted by torture or other means, the order was suppressed by command of the Pope in 1312.

5. Costumes

HAUBERK: a long military tunic, usually of ring or chain mail, with a hood of mail attached to protect the head and neck. No one below the rank of knight was privileged to wear it. Thus, in reporting events at Saumur in 1241, Joinville uses the expression 'I had never worn a hauberk' to indicate that he had not at that time been knighted.

MINIVER and VAIR: two kinds of fur much in use in the Middle Ages for lining and trimming ceremonial costumes. There appears to be some doubt as to the animals from which these furs were taken, but it is more generally supposed that miniver was the skin of a species of grey squirrel, while vair was the skin of a squirrel with a grey back and a white belly.

SURCOAT: a long outer coat or garment, with or without sleeves, which was commonly of rich material and was worn by people of both sexes. A *tabard* was a short surcoat worn by a knight over his armour and emblazoned with his armorial bearings.

6. Coinage

The value of money depends so much on its purchasing power that it is impossible to give more than a rough estimate of medieval currency, even if one reckons by the gold standard.

BEZANT: a coin first struck at Byzantium (in other words Constantinople). There were gold bezants, varying in value between a sovereign and a half-sovereign, and silver ones worth from a florin to a shilling.

DENIER: a French coin of very small value, roughly equivalent to a penny.

LIVRE: The *livre tournois* was more or less the equivalent of a sovereign, the *livre parisis* worth about five shillings more.

MARK: not a coin, but a denomination in weight of gold or silver usually regarded as equal to 8 oz. Wailly estimates the marks payable to the Venetians for providing a fleet as equal in value to 885,000 francs, i.e. about £44,000 at the rate of exchange current in 1874 (the date of Wailly's edition of Villehardouin). Such a sum, large as it may have seemed to the Crusaders, illustrates the difficulty of comparing medieval and modern money values.

Maps

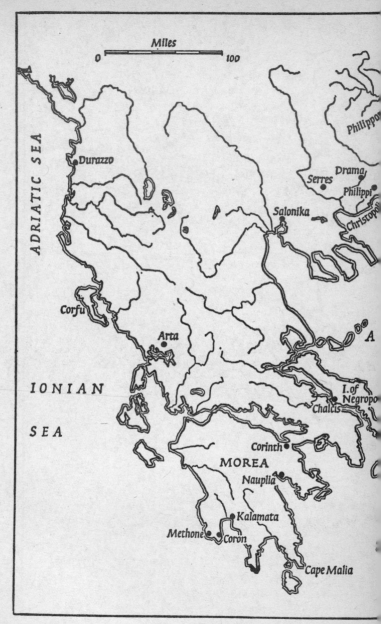

Sketch-map to illustrate Villehardou

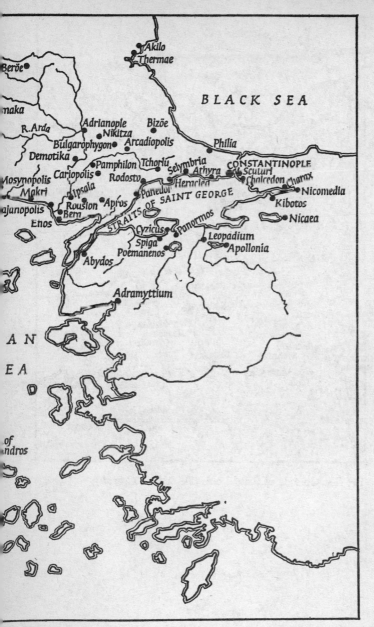

Beröe

Akilo
Thermae

BLACK SEA

maka

R.Arda   Adrianople   Bizöe
          Nikitza
Bulgarophygon Arcadiopolis   Philia
Demotika
           Pamphilon   Tchorlú   Selymbria   CONSTANTINOPLE
Mosynopolis Cariopolis   Rodosto   Athyra   Scutiri
Makri   Ipsala   Heraclea   Chalcedon Charax
                          Panedor   Nicomedia
ajunopolis   Rousion Apros   STRAITS OF SAINT GEORGE   Kibotos
Enos   Bera   Nicaea
                        Cyzicus   Panormos
                     Spiga   Leopadium
                 Poemanenos   Apollonia
          Abydos

A N

E A
                Adramyttium

of
ndros

quest of Constantinople

The first Crusade of Saint Louis (*the Seventh Crusade*)

READ MORE IN PENGUIN

In every corner of the world, on every subject under the sun, Penguin represents quality and variety – the very best in publishing today.

For complete information about books available from Penguin – including Puffins, Penguin Classics and Arkana – and how to order them, write to us at the appropriate address below. Please note that for copyright reasons the selection of books varies from country to country.

In the United Kingdom: Please write to *Dept. JC, Penguin Books Ltd, FREEPOST, West Drayton, Middlesex UB7 OBR*

If you have any difficulty in obtaining a title, please send your order with the correct money, plus ten per cent for postage and packaging, to *PO Box No. 11, West Drayton, Middlesex UB7 OBR*

In the United States: Please write to *Penguin USA Inc., 375 Hudson Street, New York, NY 10014*

In Canada: Please write to *Penguin Books Canada Ltd, 10 Alcorn Avenue, Suite 300, Toronto, Ontario M4V 3B2*

In Australia: Please write to *Penguin Books Australia Ltd, 487 Maroondah Highway, Ringwood, Victoria 3134*

In New Zealand: Please write to *Penguin Books (NZ) Ltd, 182–190 Wairau Road, Private Bag, Takapuna, Auckland 9*

In India: Please write to *Penguin Books India Pvt Ltd, 706 Eros Apartments, 56 Nehru Place, New Delhi 110 019*

In the Netherlands: Please write to *Penguin Books Netherlands B.V., Keizersgracht 231 NL–1016 DV Amsterdam*

In Germany: Please write to *Penguin Books Deutschland GmbH, Friedrichstrasse 10–12, W–6000 Frankfurt/Main 1*

In Spain: Please write to *Penguin Books S. A., C. San Bernardo 117–6° E–28015 Madrid*

In Italy: Please write to *Penguin Italia s.r.l., Via Felice Casati 20, I–20124 Milano*

In France: Please write to *Penguin France S. A., 17 rue Lejeune, F–31000 Toulouse*

In Japan: Please write to *Penguin Books Japan, Ishikiribashi Building, 2–5–4, Suido, Tokyo 112*

In Greece: Please write to *Penguin Hellas Ltd, Dimocritou 3, GR–106 71 Athens*

In South Africa: Please write to *Longman Penguin Southern Africa (Pty) Ltd, Private Bag X08, Bertsham 2013*